50% OFF Online AFOQT Prep

Dear Customer,

We consider it an honor and a privilege that you chose our AFOQT Study Guide. As a way of showing our appreciation and to help us better serve you, we have partnered with Mometrix Test Preparation to offer you **50% off their online AFOQT Prep Course**. Many AFOQT courses are needlessly expensive and don't deliver enough value. With their course, you get access to the best AFOQT prep material, and **you only pay half price**.

Mometrix has structured their online course to perfectly complement your printed study guide. The AFOQT Prep Course contains **in-depth lessons** that cover all the most important topics, **60+ video reviews** that explain difficult concepts, over **1,900 practice questions** to ensure you feel prepared.

Online AFOQT Prep Course

Topics Included:
- Verbal Analogies
- Arithmetic Reasoning and Math Knowledge
- Word Knowledge
- Reading Comprehension
- Situational Judgment
- Physical Science
- Table Reading
- Instrumental Comprehension
- Block Counting
- Aviation Information

Course Features:
- AFOQT Study Guide
  - Get content that complements our best-selling study guide.
- Full-Length Practice Tests
  - With over 1,900 practice questions, you can test yourself again and again.
- Mobile Friendly
  - If you need to study on the go, the course is easily accessible from your mobile device.

To receive this discount, visit them at mometrix.com/university/afoqt or simply scan this QR code with your smartphone. At the checkout page, enter the discount code: **TPBAFOQT50**

If you have any questions or concerns, please contact them at support@mometrix.com.

 in partnership with

FREE Test Taking Tips Video/DVD Offer

To better serve you, we created videos covering test taking tips that we want to give you for FREE. **These videos cover world-class tips that will help you succeed on your test.**

We just ask that you send us feedback about this product. Please let us know what you thought about it—whether good, bad, or indifferent.

To get your **FREE videos**, you can use the QR code below or email freevideos@studyguideteam.com with "Free Videos" in the subject line and the following information in the body of the email:

> a. The title of your product
>
> b. Your product rating on a scale of 1-5, with 5 being the highest
>
> c. Your feedback about the product

If you have any questions or concerns, please don't hesitate to contact us at info@studyguideteam.com.

Thank you!

AFOQT Study Guide 2023-2024

1,000+ Practice Questions and Prep Book for the Air Force Officer Qualifying Test [10th Edition]

Joshua Rueda

Interested in buying more than 10 copies of our product? Contact us about bulk discounts:
bulkorders@studyguideteam.com

ISBN 13: 9781637756867
ISBN 10: 1637756860

Table of Contents

Welcome

Dear Reader,

Welcome to your new Test Prep Books study guide! We are pleased that you chose us to help you prepare for your exam. There are many study options to choose from, and we appreciate you choosing us. Studying can be a daunting task, but we have designed a smart, effective study guide to help prepare you for what lies ahead.

Whether you're a parent helping your child learn and grow, a high school student working hard to get into your dream college, or a nursing student studying for a complex exam, we want to help give you the tools you need to succeed. We hope this study guide gives you the skills and the confidence to thrive, and we can't thank you enough for allowing us to be part of your journey.

In an effort to continue to improve our products, we welcome feedback from our customers. We look forward to hearing from you. Suggestions, success stories, and criticisms can all be communicated by emailing us at info@studyguideteam.com.

Sincerely,
Test Prep Books Team

FREE Videos/DVD OFFER

Doing well on your exam requires both knowing the test content and understanding how to use that knowledge to do well on the test. We offer completely FREE test taking tip videos. **These videos cover world-class tips that you can use to succeed on your test.**

To get your **FREE videos**, you can use the QR code below or email freevideos@studyguideteam.com with "Free Videos" in the subject line and the following information in the body of the email:

   a. The title of your product
   b. Your product rating on a scale of 1-5, with 5 being the highest
   c. Your feedback about the product

If you have any questions or concerns, please don't hesitate to contact us at info@studyguideteam.com.

SCAN HERE

Quick Overview

As you draw closer to taking your exam, effective preparation becomes more and more important. Thankfully, you have this study guide to help you get ready. Use this guide to help keep your studying on track and refer to it often.

This study guide contains several key sections that will help you be successful on your exam. The guide contains tips for what you should do the night before and the day of the test. Also included are test-taking tips. Knowing the right information is not always enough. Many well-prepared test takers struggle with exams. These tips will help equip you to accurately read, assess, and answer test questions.

A large part of the guide is devoted to showing you what content to expect on the exam and to helping you better understand that content. In this guide are practice test questions so that you can see how well you have grasped the content. Then, answer explanations are provided so that you can understand why you missed certain questions.

Don't try to cram the night before you take your exam. This is not a wise strategy for a few reasons. First, your retention of the information will be low. Your time would be better used by reviewing information you already know rather than trying to learn a lot of new information. Second, you will likely become stressed as you try to gain a large amount of knowledge in a short amount of time. Third, you will be depriving yourself of sleep. So be sure to go to bed at a reasonable time the night before. Being well-rested helps you focus and remain calm.

Be sure to eat a substantial breakfast the morning of the exam. If you are taking the exam in the afternoon, be sure to have a good lunch as well. Being hungry is distracting and can make it difficult to focus. You have hopefully spent lots of time preparing for the exam. Don't let an empty stomach get in the way of success!

When travelling to the testing center, leave earlier than needed. That way, you have a buffer in case you experience any delays. This will help you remain calm and will keep you from missing your appointment time at the testing center.

Be sure to pace yourself during the exam. Don't try to rush through the exam. There is no need to risk performing poorly on the exam just so you can leave the testing center early. Allow yourself to use all of the allotted time if needed.

Remain positive while taking the exam even if you feel like you are performing poorly. Thinking about the content you should have mastered will not help you perform better on the exam.

Once the exam is complete, take some time to relax. Even if you feel that you need to take the exam again, you will be well served by some down time before you begin studying again. It's often easier to convince yourself to study if you know that it will come with a reward!

Test-Taking Strategies

1. Predicting the Answer

When you feel confident in your preparation for a multiple-choice test, try predicting the answer before reading the answer choices. This is especially useful on questions that test objective factual knowledge. By predicting the answer before reading the available choices, you eliminate the possibility that you will be distracted or led astray by an incorrect answer choice. You will feel more confident in your selection if you read the question, predict the answer, and then find your prediction among the answer choices. After using this strategy, be sure to still read all of the answer choices carefully and completely. If you feel unprepared, you should not attempt to predict the answers. This would be a waste of time and an opportunity for your mind to wander in the wrong direction.

2. Reading the Whole Question

Too often, test takers scan a multiple-choice question, recognize a few familiar words, and immediately jump to the answer choices. Test authors are aware of this common impatience, and they will sometimes prey upon it. For instance, a test author might subtly turn the question into a negative, or he or she might redirect the focus of the question right at the end. The only way to avoid falling into these traps is to read the entirety of the question carefully before reading the answer choices.

3. Looking for Wrong Answers

Long and complicated multiple-choice questions can be intimidating. One way to simplify a difficult multiple-choice question is to eliminate all of the answer choices that are clearly wrong. In most sets of answers, there will be at least one selection that can be dismissed right away. If the test is administered on paper, the test taker could draw a line through it to indicate that it may be ignored; otherwise, the test taker will have to perform this operation mentally or on scratch paper. In either case, once the obviously incorrect answers have been eliminated, the remaining choices may be considered. Sometimes identifying the clearly wrong answers will give the test taker some information about the correct answer. For instance, if one of the remaining answer choices is a direct opposite of one of the eliminated answer choices, it may well be the correct answer. The opposite of obviously wrong is obviously right! Of course, this is not always the case. Some answers are obviously incorrect simply because they are irrelevant to the question being asked. Still, identifying and eliminating some incorrect answer choices is a good way to simplify a multiple-choice question.

4. Don't Overanalyze

Anxious test takers often overanalyze questions. When you are nervous, your brain will often run wild, causing you to make associations and discover clues that don't actually exist. If you feel that this may be a problem for you, do whatever you can to slow down during the test. Try taking a deep breath or counting to ten. As you read and consider the question, restrict yourself to the particular words used by the author. Avoid thought tangents about what the author *really* meant, or what he or she was *trying* to say. The only things that matter on a multiple-choice test are the words that are actually in the question. You must avoid reading too much into a multiple-choice question, or supposing that the writer meant something other than what he or she wrote.

3

5. No Need for Panic

It is wise to learn as many strategies as possible before taking a multiple-choice test, but it is likely that you will come across a few questions for which you simply don't know the answer. In this situation, avoid panicking. Because most multiple-choice tests include dozens of questions, the relative value of a single wrong answer is small. As much as possible, you should compartmentalize each question on a multiple-choice test. In other words, you should not allow your feelings about one question to affect your success on the others. When you find a question that you either don't understand or don't know how to answer, just take a deep breath and do your best. Read the entire question slowly and carefully. Try rephrasing the question a couple of different ways. Then, read all of the answer choices carefully. After eliminating obviously wrong answers, make a selection and move on to the next question.

6. Confusing Answer Choices

When working on a difficult multiple-choice question, there may be a tendency to focus on the answer choices that are the easiest to understand. Many people, whether consciously or not, gravitate to the answer choices that require the least concentration, knowledge, and memory. This is a mistake. When you come across an answer choice that is confusing, you should give it extra attention. A question might be confusing because you do not know the subject matter to which it refers. If this is the case, don't eliminate the answer before you have affirmatively settled on another. When you come across an answer choice of this type, set it aside as you look at the remaining choices. If you can confidently assert that one of the other choices is correct, you can leave the confusing answer aside. Otherwise, you will need to take a moment to try to better understand the confusing answer choice. Rephrasing is one way to tease out the sense of a confusing answer choice.

7. Your First Instinct

Many people struggle with multiple-choice tests because they overthink the questions. If you have studied sufficiently for the test, you should be prepared to trust your first instinct once you have carefully and completely read the question and all of the answer choices. There is a great deal of research suggesting that the mind can come to the correct conclusion very quickly once it has obtained all of the relevant information. At times, it may seem to you as if your intuition is working faster even than your reasoning mind. This may in fact be true. The knowledge you obtain while studying may be retrieved from your subconscious before you have a chance to work out the associations that support it. Verify your instinct by working out the reasons that it should be trusted.

8. Key Words

Many test takers struggle with multiple-choice questions because they have poor reading comprehension skills. Quickly reading and understanding a multiple-choice question requires a mixture of skill and experience. To help with this, try jotting down a few key words and phrases on a piece of scrap paper. Doing this concentrates the process of reading and forces the mind to weigh the relative importance of the question's parts. In selecting words and phrases to write down, the test taker thinks about the question more deeply and carefully. This is especially true for multiple-choice questions that are preceded by a long prompt.

4

9. Subtle Negatives

One of the oldest tricks in the multiple-choice test writer's book is to subtly reverse the meaning of a question with a word like *not* or *except*. If you are not paying attention to each word in the question, you can easily be led astray by this trick. For instance, a common question format is, "Which of the following is...?" Obviously, if the question instead is, "Which of the following is not...?," then the answer will be quite different. Even worse, the test makers are aware of the potential for this mistake and will include one answer choice that would be correct if the question were not negated or reversed. A test taker who misses the reversal will find what he or she believes to be a correct answer and will be so confident that he or she will fail to reread the question and discover the original error. The only way to avoid this is to practice a wide variety of multiple-choice questions and to pay close attention to each and every word.

10. Reading Every Answer Choice

It may seem obvious, but you should always read every one of the answer choices! Too many test takers fall into the habit of scanning the question and assuming that they understand the question because they recognize a few key words. From there, they pick the first answer choice that answers the question they believe they have read. Test takers who read all of the answer choices might discover that one of the latter answer choices is actually *more* correct. Moreover, reading all of the answer choices can remind you of facts related to the question that can help you arrive at the correct answer. Sometimes, a misstatement or incorrect detail in one of the latter answer choices will trigger your memory of the subject and will enable you to find the right answer. Failing to read all of the answer choices is like not reading all of the items on a restaurant menu: you might miss out on the perfect choice.

11. Spot the Hedges

One of the keys to success on multiple-choice tests is paying close attention to every word. This is never truer than with words like *almost*, *most*, *some*, and *sometimes*. These words are called "hedges" because they indicate that a statement is not totally true or not true in every place and time. An absolute statement will contain no hedges, but in many subjects, the answers are not always straightforward or absolute. There are always exceptions to the rules in these subjects. For this reason, you should favor those multiple-choice questions that contain hedging language. The presence of qualifying words indicates that the author is taking special care with his or her words, which is certainly important when composing the right answer. After all, there are many ways to be wrong, but there is only one way to be right! For this reason, it is wise to avoid answers that are absolute when taking a multiple-choice test. An absolute answer is one that says things are either all one way or all another. They often include words like *every*, *always*, *best*, and *never*. If you are taking a multiple-choice test in a subject that doesn't lend itself to absolute answers, be on your guard if you see any of these words.

12. Long Answers

In many subject areas, the answers are not simple. As already mentioned, the right answer often requires hedges. Another common feature of the answers to a complex or subjective question are qualifying clauses, which are groups of words that subtly modify the meaning of the sentence. If the question or answer choice describes a rule to which there are exceptions or the subject matter is complicated, ambiguous, or confusing, the correct answer will require many words in order to be expressed clearly and accurately. In essence, you should not be deterred by answer choices that seem

5

excessively long. Oftentimes, the author of the text will not be able to write the correct answer without offering some qualifications and modifications. Your job is to read the answer choices thoroughly and completely and to select the one that most accurately and precisely answers the question.

13. Restating to Understand

Sometimes, a question on a multiple-choice test is difficult not because of what it asks but because of how it is written. If this is the case, restate the question or answer choice in different words. This process serves a couple of important purposes. First, it forces you to concentrate on the core of the question. In order to rephrase the question accurately, you have to understand it well. Rephrasing the question will concentrate your mind on the key words and ideas. Second, it will present the information to your mind in a fresh way. This process may trigger your memory and render some useful scrap of information picked up while studying.

14. True Statements

Sometimes an answer choice will be true in itself, but it does not answer the question. This is one of the main reasons why it is essential to read the question carefully and completely before proceeding to the answer choices. Too often, test takers skip ahead to the answer choices and look for true statements. Having found one of these, they are content to select it without reference to the question above. Obviously, this provides an easy way for test makers to play tricks. The savvy test taker will always read the entire question before turning to the answer choices. Then, having settled on a correct answer choice, he or she will refer to the original question and ensure that the selected answer is relevant. The mistake of choosing a correct-but-irrelevant answer choice is especially common on questions related to specific pieces of objective knowledge. A prepared test taker will have a wealth of factual knowledge at his or her disposal, and should not be careless in its application.

15. No Patterns

One of the more dangerous ideas that circulates about multiple-choice tests is that the correct answers tend to fall into patterns. These erroneous ideas range from a belief that B and C are the most common right answers, to the idea that an unprepared test-taker should answer "A-B-A-C-A-D-A-B-A." It cannot be emphasized enough that pattern-seeking of this type is exactly the WRONG way to approach a multiple-choice test. To begin with, it is highly unlikely that the test maker will plot the correct answers according to some predetermined pattern. The questions are scrambled and delivered in a random order. Furthermore, even if the test maker was following a pattern in the assignation of correct answers, there is no reason why the test taker would know which pattern he or she was using. Any attempt to discern a pattern in the answer choices is a waste of time and a distraction from the real work of taking the test. A test taker would be much better served by extra preparation before the test than by reliance on a pattern in the answers.

Bonus Content

We host multiple bonus items online, including all three practice tests in digital format. Scan the QR code or go to this link to access this content:

testprepbooks.com/bonus/afoqt

The first time you access the page, you will need to register as a "new user" and verify your email address.

If you have any issues, please email support@testprepbooks.com.

Introduction to the AFOQT

Function of the Test

The Air Force Officer Qualifying Test (AFOQT) is a standardized test given by the United States Air Force. The exam evaluates a test taker's verbal and mathematical proficiency as well as their aptitude in certain areas specific to those necessary for potential Air Force career paths. The test is used as part of the admissions process to officer training programs, such as Officer Training School ROTC. Within the Air Force, it is used to qualify candidates for Pilot, Combat Systems Officer (CSO), and Air Battle Manager (ABM) training and is part of the Pilot Candidate Selection Method (PCSM) score. The AFOQT is required for all students receiving a scholarship as well as those in the Professional Officer Course (POC).

The test is taken nationwide by current and potential members of the United States Air Force. In the Air Force ROTC program, it is taken by sophomores prior to field training in the summer after their sophomore year.

Test Administration

The AFOQT is offered through Air Force ROTC programs on college campuses and through military recruiters at Military Entrance Processing facilities. There is no cost to take the AFOQT; instead, individuals wishing to take the test must make arrangements through their ROTC program, recruiter, or commanding officer, as appropriate. Rules for retesting depend on the purpose or program for which the test taker is seeking to use the results, but some ROTC programs permit one retest, with the most recent score counting.

Test Format

The test lasts almost five hours, including three hours and 36.5 minutes of testing time and a little over an hour in breaks and test administration time. It is taken with a pencil and scored by machine. It consists of twelve subtests: verbal analogies, arithmetic reasoning, word knowledge, math knowledge, reading comprehension, situational judgment, self-description inventory, physical science, table reading, instrument comprehension, block counting, and aviation information. All of the subtests have multiple-choice questions with four or five possible answers.

Scoring

Scores are based only on the number of correct answers. There is no penalty for guessing incorrectly, aside from the missed opportunity to achieve points from a greater number of correct answers. Scores from the various subtests are used to calculate composite scores, which are reported to the test taker and the Air Force. For example, the "Pilot" composite score is based on the results from the arithmetic reasoning, math knowledge, instrument comprehension, table reading, and aviation information subtests. Other composite scores include Academic Aptitude, Verbal, Quantitative, Combat Systems Officer, Air Battle Manager, and Situational Judgment. Test takers receive a percentile score from 1 to 99 in each of the five composite categories.

There is no set passing score. Instead, the scores needed vary widely depending on the intended job or program for which a test taker is seeking entry. For instance, a candidate seeking to become an officer may be able to do so with a relatively low percentile score (in other words, by only outperforming a

small number of other test takers), while an officer seeking to become a pilot may need much higher scores overall, particularly in the Pilot composite category.

Recent/Future Developments

The AFOQT is revised from time to time, based on feedback from the general needs of the Air Force and its officer training programs. The current subtests and content therein are in AFOQT Form T, which took effect on August 1, 2014.

A summary of the number of items on and the time allowed (not including administration time or breaks) for each subtest is as follows:

Subtest	Items	Time (min.)
Verbal Analogies	25	8
Arithmetic Reasoning	25	29
Word Knowledge	25	5
Math Knowledge	25	22
Reading Comprehension	25	38
Situational Judgment	50	35
Self-Description Inventory	240	45
Physical Science	20	10
Table Reading	40	7
Instrument Comprehension	25	5
Block Counting	30	4.5
Aviation Information	20	8
TOTAL	**550**	**3 hours, 36.5 minutes**

Study Prep Plan for the AFOQT Exam

1 **Schedule -** Use one of our study schedules below or come up with one of your own.

2 **Relax -** Test anxiety can hurt even the best students. There are many ways to reduce stress. Find the one that works best for you.

3 **Execute -** Once you have a good plan in place, be sure to stick to it.

One Week Study Schedule

Day 1	Verbal Analogies
Day 2	Math Knowledge
Day 3	Physical Science
Day 4	Table Reading
Day 5	Practice Tests #1 & #2
Day 6	Practice Test #3
Day 7	Take Your Exam!

Two Week Study Schedule

Day 1	Verbal Analogies	Day 8	Practice Test #1
Day 2	Word Knowledge	Day 9	Answer Explanations #1
Day 3	Reading Comprehension	Day 10	Practice Test #2
Day 4	Physical Science	Day 11	Answer Explanations #2
Day 5	Physics	Day 12	Practice Test #3
Day 6	Table Reading	Day 13	Answer Explanations #3
Day 7	Aviation Information	Day 14	Take Your Exam!

One Month Study Schedule							
Day 1	Verbal Analogies	Day 11	Situational Judgment	Day 21	Flight Envelope
Day 2	Arithmetic Reasoning	Day 12	Physical Science	Day 22	Flight Maneuvers
Day 3	Ratios and Proportions	Day 13	Chemistry	Day 23	Airport Information
Day 4	Data Analysis	Day 14	Chemical Reactions	Day 24	Practice Test #1
Day 5	Word Knowledge	Day 15	Physics	Day 25	Answer Explanations #1
Day 6	Math Knowledge	Day 16	Optics and Waves	Day 26	Practice Test #2
Day 7	Polynomials	Day 17	Table Reading	Day 27	Answer Explanations #2
Day 8	Systems of Equations	Day 18	Instrument Comprehension	Day 28	Practice Test #3
Day 9	Reading Comprehension	Day 19	Block Counting	Day 29	Answer Explanations #3
Day 10	Cause and Effect	Day 20	Aviation Information	Day 30	Take Your Exam!

Build your own prep plan by visiting:
testprepbooks.com/prep

Verbal Analogies

Verbal Analogies

The verbal analogies test portion of the AFOQT tests the candidate's ability to analyze words carefully and find connections in definition and/or context. The test-taker must compare a selected set of words with answer choices and select the ideal word to complete the sequence. While these exercises draw upon knowledge of vocabulary, this is also a test of critical thinking and reasoning abilities. Naturally, such skills are critical for building a career. Mastering verbal analogies will help people think objectively, discern critical details, and communicate more efficiently.

Question Layout

Verbal analogy sections are on other standardized tests such as the SAT. The format on the AFOQT remains basically the same. First, two words are paired together that provide a frame for the analogy, and then there is a third word that must be found as a match in kind. It may help to think of it like this: A is to B as C is to D. Examine the breakdown below:

Apple (A) is to fruit (B) as carrot (C) is to vegetable (D).

As shown above, there are four words: the first three are given and the fourth word is the answer that must be found. The first two words are given to set up the kind of analogy that is to be replicated for the next pair. We see that apple is paired with fruit. In the first pair, a specific food item, apple, is paired to the food group category it corresponds with, which is fruit. When presented with the third word in the verbal analogy, carrot, a word must be found that best matches carrot in the way that fruit matched with apple. Again, carrot is a specific food item, so a match should be found with the appropriate food group: vegetable! Here's a sample prompt:

Morbid is to dead as jovial is to
    a. Hate.
    b. Fear.
    c. Disgust.
    d. Happiness.
    e. Desperation.

As with the apple and carrot example, here is an analogy frame in the first two words: morbid and dead. Again, this will dictate how the next two words will correlate with one another. The word morbid can be defined as an abnormal or unhealthy interest in death or other disturbing topics. In other words, morbid can mean ghastly or death-like, which is why the word dead is paired with it. Dead relates to morbid because it describes morbid. With this in mind, jovial becomes the focus. Jovial means joyful, so out of all the choices given, the closest answer describing jovial is happiness (D).

Prompts on the exam will be structured just like the one above. "A is to B as C is to ?" will be given, where the answer completes the second pair. Or sometimes, "A is to B as ? is to ?" is given, where the second pair of words must be found that replicate the relationship between the first pair. The only things that will change are the words and the relationships between the words provided.

Discerning the Correct Answer

While it wouldn't hurt in test preparation to expand vocabulary, verbal analogies are all about delving into the words themselves and finding the right connection, the right word that will fit an analogy. People preparing for the test shouldn't think of themselves as human dictionaries, but rather as detectives. Remember, how the first two words are connected dictates the second pair. From there, picking the correct answer or simply eliminating the ones that aren't correct is the best strategy.

Just like a detective, a test-taker needs to carefully examine the first two words of the analogy for clues. It's good to get in the habit of asking the questions: What do the two words have in common? What makes them related or unrelated? How can a similar relationship be replicated with the word I'm given and the answer choices? Here's another example:

Pillage is to steal as meander is to
- a. Stroll.
- b. Burgle.
- c. Cascade.
- d. Accelerate.
- e. Pinnacle.

Why is pillage paired with steal? In this example, pillage and steal are synonymous: they both refer to the act of stealing. This means that the answer is a word that means the same as meander, which is stroll. In this case, the defining relationship in the whole analogy was a similar definition.

What if test-takers don't know what stroll or meander mean, though? Using logic helps to eliminate choices and pick the correct answer. Looking closer into the contexts of the words pillage and steal, here are a few facts: these are things that humans do; and while they are actions, these are not necessarily types of movement. Again, pick a word that will not only match the given word, but best completes the relationship. It wouldn't make sense that burgle (B) would be the correct choice because meander doesn't have anything to do with stealing, so that eliminates burgle.

Pinnacle (E) also can be eliminated because this is not an action at all but a position or point of reference. Cascade (C) refers to pouring or falling, usually in the context of a waterfall and not in reference to people, which means we can eliminate cascade as well. While people do accelerate when they move, they usually do so under additional circumstances: they accelerate while running or driving a car. All three of the words we see in the analogy are actions that can be done independently of other factors. Therefore, accelerate (D) can be eliminated, and stroll (A) should be chosen. Stroll and meander both refer to walking or wandering, so this fits perfectly.

The **process of elimination** will help rule out wrong answers. However, the best way to find the correct answer is simply to differentiate the correct answer from the other choices. For this, test-takers should go back to asking questions, starting with the chief question: What's the connection? There are actually many ways that connections can be found between words. The trick is to look for the answer that is consistent with the relationship between the words given. What is the prevailing connection? Here are a few different ways verbal analogies can be formed.

Finding Connections in Word Analogies

Connections in Categories
One of the easiest ways to choose the correct answer in word analogies is simply to group words together. Ask if the words can be compartmentalized into *distinct categories*. Here are some examples:

Terrier is to dog as mystery is to
    a. Thriller.
    b. Murder.
    c. Detective.
    d. Novel.
    e. Investigation.

This one might have been a little confusing, but when looking at the first two words in the analogy, this is clearly one in which a category is the prevailing theme. Think about it: a terrier is a type of dog. While there are several breeds of dogs that can be categorized as a terrier, in the end, all terriers are still dogs. Therefore, mystery needs to be grouped into a category. Murders, detectives, and investigations can all be involved in a mystery plot, but a murder (B), a detective (C), or an investigation (E) is not necessarily a mystery. A thriller (A) is a purely fictional concept, a kind of story or film, just like a mystery. A thriller can describe a mystery, but the same issue appears as the other choices. What about novel (D)? For one thing, it's distinct from all the other terms. A novel isn't a component of a mystery, but a mystery can be a type of novel. The relationship fits: a terrier is a type of dog, just like a mystery is a type of novel.

Synonym/Antonym
Some analogies are based on words meaning the same thing or expressing the same idea. Sometimes it's the complete opposite!

Marauder is to brigand as
    a. King is to peasant.
    b. Juice is to orange.
    c. Soldier is to warrior.
    d. Engine is to engineer.
    e. Paper is to photocopier.

Here, soldier is to warrior (C) is the correct answer. Marauders and brigands are both thieves. They are synonyms. The only pair of words that fits this analogy is soldier and warrior because both terms describe combatants who fight.

Cap is to shoe as jacket is to
    a. Ring.
    b. T-shirt.
    c. Vest.
    d. Glasses.
    e. Pants.

Opposites are at play here because a cap is worn on the head/top of the person, while a shoe is worn on the foot/bottom. A jacket is worn on top of the body too, so the opposite of jacket would be pants (E) because these are worn on the bottom of the body. Often the prompts on the test provide a synonym or antonym relationship. Just consider if the sets in the prompt reflect similarity or stark difference.

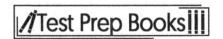

Parts of a Whole

Another thing to consider when first looking at an analogy prompt is whether the words presented come together in some way. Do they express parts of the same item? Does one word complete the other? Are they connected by process or function?

Tire is to car as
a. Wing is to bird.
b. Oar is to boat.
c. Box is to shelf.
d. Hat is to head.
e. Knife is to sheath.

We know that the tire fits onto the car's wheels and this is what enables the car to drive on roads. The tire is part of the car. This is the same relationship as oar is to boat (B). The oars are attached onto a boat and enable a person to move and navigate the boat on water. At first glance, wing is to bird (A) seems to fit too, since a wing is a part of a bird that enables it to move through the air. However, since a tire and car are not alive and transport people, oar and boat fit better because they are also not alive, and they transport people. Subtle differences between answer choices should be found.

Other Relationships

There are a number of other relationships to look for when solving verbal analogies. Some relationships focus on one word being a *characteristic/NOT a characteristic* of the other word. Sometimes the first word is *the source/comprised of* the second word. Still, other words are related by their *location*. Some analogies have **sequential relationships**, and some are **cause/effect relationships**. There are analogies that show **creator/provider relationships** with the *creation/provision*. Another relationship might compare an *object* with its *function* or a *user* with their *tool*. An analogy may focus on a *change of grammar* or a *translation of language*. Finally, one word of an analogy may have a relationship to the other word in its *intensity*. The type of relationship between the first two words of the analogy should be determined before continuing to analyze the second set of words.

One effective method of determining a relationship between two words is to form a comprehensible sentence using both words and then to plug the answer choices into the same sentence. For example, consider the following analogy: *Bicycle is to handlebars as car is to steering wheel.* A sentence could be formed that says: A bicycle navigates using its handlebars; therefore, a car navigates using its steering wheel. If the second sentence makes sense, then the correct relationship has likely been found. A sentence may be more complex depending on the relationship between the first two words in the analogy. An example of this may be: *food is to dishwasher as dirt is to carwash.* The formed sentence may be: A dishwasher cleans food off of dishes in the same way that a carwash cleans dirt off of a car.

Dealing with Multiple Connections

There are many other ways to draw connections between word sets. Several word choices might form an analogy that would fit the word set in your prompt. When this occurs, the analogy must be explored from multiple angles as, on occasion, multiple answer choices may appear to be correct. When this occurs, ask yourself: which one is an even closer match than the others? The framing word pair is another important point to consider. Can one or both words be interpreted as actions or ideas, or are they purely objects? Here's a question where words could have alternate meanings:

Hammer is to nail as saw is to
    a. Electric.
    b. Hack.
    c. Cut.
    d. Machete.
    e. Groove.

Looking at the question above, it becomes clear that the topic of the analogy involves construction tools. Hammers and nails are used in concert since the hammer is used to pound the nail. The logical first thing to do is to look for an object that a saw would be used on. Seeing that there is no such object among the answer choices, a test-taker might begin to worry. After all, that seems to be the choice that would complete the analogy—but that doesn't mean it's the only choice that may fit. Encountering questions like this test one's ability to see multiple connections between words—don't get stuck thinking that words can only be connected in a single way. The first two words given can be verbs instead of just objects. To hammer means to hit or beat; oftentimes it refers to beating something into place. This is also what nail means when it is used as a verb. Here are the word choices that reveal the answer.

First, it's known that a saw, well, saws. It uses a steady motion to cut an object, and indeed to saw means to cut! Cut (C) is one of our answer choices, but the other options should be reviewed. While some tools are electric (a), the use of power in the tools listed in the analogy isn't a factor. Again, it's been established that these word choices are not tools in this context. Therefore, machete (D) is also ruled out because machete is also not a verb. Another important thing to consider is that while a machete is a tool that accomplishes a similar purpose as a saw, the machete is used in a slicing motion rather than a sawing/cutting motion. The verb that describes machete is hack (B), another choice that can be ruled out. A machete is used to hack at foliage. However, a saw does not hack. Groove (E) is just a term that has nothing to do with the other words, so this choice can be eliminated easily. This leaves cut (C), which confirms that this is the word needed to complete the analogy.

Practice Quiz

1. **Cow** is to **milk** as:
   a. Horse is to cow.
   b. Egg is to chicken.
   c. Chicken is to egg.
   d. Glass is to milk.
   e. Milk is to glass.

2. **Web** is to **spider** as **den** is to:
   a. Living room.
   b. Eagle.
   c. Fox.
   d. Dog.
   e. Turtle.

3. **Sad** is to **blue** as **happy** is to:
   a. Glad.
   b. Yellow.
   c. Smiling.
   d. Laugh.
   e. Calm.

4. **Door** is to **store** as **deal** is to:
   a. Money.
   b. Purchase.
   c. Sell.
   d. Wheel.
   e. Market.

5. **Dog** is to **veterinarian** as **baby** is to:
   a. Daycare.
   b. Mother.
   c. Puppy.
   d. Babysitter.
   e. Pediatrician.

See answers on next page

Answer Explanations

1. C: Cows produce milk so the question is looking for another pair that has a producer and their product. Horses don't produce cows, Choice *A*, glasses don't produce milk, Choice *D*, and milk doesn't produce a glass, Choice *E*. The correct choice is *C*: chicken is to egg. The tricky one here is Choice *B*, egg is to chicken, because it has the correct words but the wrong order, and therefore it reverses the relationship. Eggs don't produce chickens, so it doesn't work with the first part of the analogy: cow is to milk.

2. C: The first part of the analogy—web is to spider—describes the home (web) and who lives in it (spider), so the question is looking for what animal lives in a den. The best choice is *C*, fox. Living room is another word or a synonym for a den.

3. A: *Sad* and *blue* are synonyms because they are both describing the same type of mood. The word *blue* in this case is not referring to the color; therefore, although yellow is sometimes considered a "happy" color, the question isn't referring to blue as a color (or any color for that matter) and *yellow* and *happy* are not synonyms. Someone who is happy may laugh or smile, but these words are not synonyms for happy. Lastly, someone who is happy may be calm, although he or she could also be excited, and calm and happy are not synonyms. The best choice is *glad*.

4. D: The key to answering this question correctly is to recognize that the relationship between *door* and *store* is that the words rhyme. One may at first consider the fact that stores have doors, but after reviewing the other word choices and the given word *deal*, he or she should notice that none of the other words have this relationship. Instead, the answer choice should be one that rhymes with *deal*. *Wheel* and *deal*, although spelled differently, are rhyming words, and therefore the correct answer is *D*.

5. E: This question relies on the test takers knowledge of occupations. Dogs are taken care of by veterinarians so the solution is looking for who takes care of babies. However, this level of detail is not yet specific enough because mothers and babysitters can also take care of babies. Veterinarians take care of sick dogs and act as a medical doctor for pets. Therefore, with this higher level of specificity and detail, test takers should select *pediatrician*, because pediatricians are doctors for babies and children.

Arithmetic Reasoning

The Scope of the Arithmetic Reasoning Section

Problems in the Arithmetic Reasoning section of the AFOQT are generally word problems, which will require the use of reasoning and mathematics to find a solution. The problems normally present some everyday situations, along with a list of choices for answers. Some of the things to know include rates, speeds, percentages, averages, fractions, and ratios. The practice problems given later will cover the different types of questions in this section, although every word problem is slightly different.

How to Prepare

These problems involve basic arithmetic skills as well as the ability to break down a word problem to see where to apply these skills in order to get the correct answer. The basics of arithmetic and the approach to solving word problems are discussed here.

Note that math requires practice in order to become proficient. Make sure to not just read through the material here, but also try out the practice questions, as well as check the answers provided. Just reading through examples does not necessarily mean that a student can do the problems themselves. Note that sometimes there can be multiple approaches to getting a solution when doing the problems. What matters is getting the correct answer, so it is okay if the approach to a problem is different than the solution method provided.

Basic Operations of Arithmetic

There are four different basic operations used with numbers: addition, subtraction, multiplication, and division.

- **Addition** takes two numbers and combines them into a total called the sum. The sum is the total when combining two collections into one. If there are 5 things in one collection and 3 in another, then after combining them, there is a total of:

$$5 + 3 = 8$$

Note the order does not matter when adding numbers. For example,

$$3 + 5 = 8$$

- **Subtraction** is the opposite (or "inverse") operation to addition. Whereas addition combines two quantities together, subtraction takes one quantity away from another. For example, if there are 20 gallons of fuel and 5 are removed, that gives $20 - 5 = 15$ gallons remaining. Note that for subtraction, the order does matter because it makes a difference which quantity is being removed from which.

- **Multiplication** is repeated addition. 3×4 can be thought of as putting together 3 sets of items, each set containing 4 items. The total is 12 items. Another way to think of this is to think of each number as the length of one side of a rectangle. If a rectangle is covered in tiles with 3 columns of 4 tiles each, then there are 12 tiles in total. From this, one can see that the answer is the same if the rectangle has 4 rows of 3 tiles each:

$$4 \times 3 = 12$$

  By expanding this reasoning, the order the numbers are multiplied does not matter.

- **Division** is the opposite of multiplication. It means taking one quantity and dividing it into sets the size of the second quantity. If there are 16 sandwiches to be distributed to 4 people, then each person gets $16 \div 4 = 4$ sandwiches. As with subtraction, the order in which the numbers appear does matter for division.

Addition

Addition is the combination of two numbers so their quantities are added together cumulatively. The sign for an addition operation is the + symbol. For example,

$$9 + 6 = 15$$

The 9 and 6 combine to achieve a cumulative value, called a **sum**.

Addition holds the commutative property, which means that the order of the numbers in an addition equation can be switched without altering the result. The formula for the commutative property is $a + b = b + a$. Let's look at a few examples to see how the commutative property works:

$$7 = 3 + 4 = 4 + 3 = 7$$

$$20 = 12 + 8 = 8 + 12 = 20$$

Addition also holds the associative property, which means that the grouping of numbers doesn't matter in an addition problem. In other words, the presence or absence of parentheses is irrelevant. The formula for the associative property is:

$$(a + b) + c = a + (b + c)$$

Here are some examples of the associative property at work:

$$30 = (6 + 14) + 10 = 6 + (14 + 10) = 30$$

$$35 = 8 + (2 + 25) = (8 + 2) + 25 = 35$$

Subtraction

Subtraction is taking away one number from another, so their quantities are reduced. The sign designating a subtraction operation is the – symbol, and the result is called the difference. For example,

$$9 - 6 = 3$$

The number *6* detracts from the number *9* to reach the difference *3*.

Unlike addition, subtraction follows neither the commutative nor associative properties. The order and grouping in subtraction impact the result.

$$15 = 22 - 7 \neq 7 - 22 = -15$$

$$3 = (10 - 5) - 2 \neq 10 - (5 - 2) = 7$$

When working through subtraction problems involving larger numbers, it's necessary to regroup the numbers. Let's work through a practice problem using regrouping:

$$\begin{array}{r} 3\ 2\ 5 \\ -\ 7\ 7 \\ \hline \end{array}$$

Here, it is clear that the ones and tens columns for 77 are greater than the ones and tens columns for 325. To subtract this number, borrow from the tens and hundreds columns. When borrowing from a column, subtracting 1 from the lender column will add 10 to the borrower column:

$$\begin{array}{c} 3\text{-}1 \quad 10+2\text{-}1 \quad 10+5 \\ -\qquad 7 \qquad\ 7 \end{array} = \begin{array}{r} 2\ \ 11\ \ 15 \\ -\qquad 7\ \ 7 \\ \hline 2\ \ 4\ \ 8 \end{array}$$

After ensuring that each digit in the top row is greater than the digit in the corresponding bottom row, subtraction can proceed as normal, and the answer is found to be 248.

Multiplication

Multiplication involves adding together multiple copies of a number. It is indicated by an $\times$ symbol or a number immediately outside of a parenthesis. For example:

$$5(8 - 2)$$

The two numbers being multiplied together are called factors, and their result is called a product. For example,

$$9 \times 6 = 54$$

This can be shown alternatively by expansion of either the 9 or the 6:

$$9 \times 6 = 9 + 9 + 9 + 9 + 9 + 9 = 54$$

$$9 \times 6 = 6 + 6 + 6 + 6 + 6 + 6 + 6 + 6 + 6 = 54$$

Like addition, multiplication holds the commutative and associative properties:

$$115 = 23 \times 5 = 5 \times 23 = 115$$

$$84 = 3 \times (7 \times 4) = (3 \times 7) \times 4 = 84$$

Multiplication also follows the distributive property, which allows the multiplication to be distributed through parentheses. The formula for distribution is:

$$a \times (b + c) = ab + ac$$

21

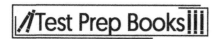

This is clear after the examples:

$$45 = 5 \times 9 = 5(3 + 6) = (5 \times 3) + (5 \times 6) = 15 + 30 = 45$$

$$20 = 4 \times 5 = 4(10 - 5) = (4 \times 10) - (4 \times 5) = 40 - 20 = 20$$

Multiplication becomes slightly more complicated when multiplying numbers with decimals. The easiest way to answer these problems is to ignore the decimals and multiply as if they were whole numbers. After multiplying the factors, place a decimal in the product. The placement of the decimal is determined by taking the cumulative number of decimal places in the factors.

For example:

$$
\begin{array}{ccc}
0.7 & 2.6 & 1.5 \\
\underline{\times 3} & \underline{\times 4.2} & \underline{\times 6.4} \\
2.1 & 10.92 & 9.60
\end{array}
$$

Let's tackle the first example. First, ignore the decimal and multiply the numbers as though they were whole numbers to arrive at a product: 21. Second, count the number of digits that follow a decimal (one). Finally, move the decimal place that many positions to the left, as the factors have only one decimal place. The second example works the same way, except that there are two total decimal places in the factors, so the product's decimal is moved two places over. In the third example, the decimal should be moved over two digits, but the digit zero is no longer needed, so it is erased, and the final answer is 9.6.

Division

Division and multiplication are inverses of each other in the same way that addition and subtraction are opposites. The signs designating a division operation are the ÷ and / symbols. In division, the second number divides into the first.

The number before the division sign is called the dividend or, if expressed as a fraction, the numerator. For example, in $a \div b$, a is the dividend, while in $\frac{a}{b}$, a is the numerator.

The number after the division sign is called the divisor or, if expressed as a fraction, the denominator. For example, in $a \div b$, b is the divisor, while in $\frac{a}{b}$, b is the denominator.

Like subtraction, division doesn't follow the commutative property, as it matters which number comes before the division sign, and division doesn't follow the associative or distributive properties for the same reason. For example:

$$\frac{3}{2} = 9 \div 6 \neq 6 \div 9 = \frac{2}{3}$$

$$2 = 10 \div 5 = (30 \div 3) \div 5 \neq 30 \div (3 \div 5) = 30 \div \frac{3}{5} = 50$$

$$25 = 20 + 5 = (40 \div 2) + (40 \div 8) \neq 40 \div (2 + 8) = 40 \div 10 = 4$$

If a divisor doesn't divide into a dividend evenly, whatever is left over is termed the remainder. The remainder can be further divided out into decimal form by using long division; however, this doesn't

22

always give a quotient with a finite number of decimal places, so the remainder can also be expressed as a fraction over the original divisor.

Division with decimals is similar to multiplication with decimals in that when dividing a decimal by a whole number, ignore the decimal and divide as if it were a whole number.

Upon finding the answer, or quotient, place the decimal at the decimal place equal to that in the dividend.

$$15.75 \div 3 = 5.25$$

When the divisor is a decimal number, multiply both the divisor and dividend by 10. Repeat this until the divisor is a whole number, then complete the division operation as described above.

$$17.5 \div 2.5 = 175 \div 25 = 7$$

Fractions

A **fraction** is a number used to express a ratio. It is written as a number x over a line with another number y underneath: $\frac{x}{y}$, and can be thought of as x out of y equal parts. The number on top (x) is called the **numerator**, and the number on the bottom is called the **denominator** (y). It is important to remember the only restriction is that the denominator is not allowed to be 0.

Imagine that an apple pie has been baked for a holiday party, and the full pie has eight slices. After the party, there are five slices left. How could the amount of the pie that remains be expressed as a fraction? The numerator is 5 since there are 5 pieces left, and the denominator is 8 since there were eight total slices in the whole pie. Thus, expressed as a fraction, the leftover pie totals $\frac{5}{8}$ of the original amount.

Another way of thinking about fractions is like this: $\frac{x}{y} = x \div y$

Two fractions can sometimes equal the same number even when they look different. The value of a fraction will remain equal when multiplying both the numerator and the denominator by the same number. The value of the fraction does not change when dividing both the numerator and the denominator by the same number. For example,

$$\frac{4}{8} = \frac{2}{4} = \frac{1}{2}$$

If two fractions look different, but are actually the same number, these are **equivalent fractions**.

A number that can divide evenly into a second number is called a **divisor** or **factor** of that second number; 3 is a divisor of 6, for example. If the numerator and denominator in a fraction have no common factors other than 1, the fraction is said to be **simplified**. $\frac{2}{4}$ is not simplified (since the numerator and denominator have a factor of 2 in common), but $\frac{1}{2}$ is simplified. Often, when solving a problem, the final answer generally requires us to simplify the fraction.

It is often useful when working with fractions to rewrite them so they have the same denominator. This process is called finding a **common denominator**. The common denominator of two fractions needs to

23

be a number that is a multiple of both denominators. For example, given $\frac{1}{6}$ and $\frac{5}{8}$, a common denominator is:

$$6 \times 8 = 48$$

However, there are often smaller choices for the common denominator. The smallest number that is a multiple of two numbers is called the **least common multiple** of those numbers. For this example, use the numbers 6 and 8. The multiples of 6 are 6, 12, 18, 24... and the multiples of 8 are 8, 16, 24..., so the least common multiple is 24. The two fractions are rewritten as $\frac{4}{24}, \frac{15}{24}$.

If two fractions have a common denominator, then the numerators can be added or subtracted. For example,

$$\frac{4}{5} - \frac{3}{5} = \frac{4-3}{5} = \frac{1}{5}$$

If the fractions are not given with the same denominator, a common denominator needs to be found before adding or subtracting them.

It is always possible to find a common denominator by multiplying the denominators by each other. However, when the denominators are large numbers, this method is unwieldy, especially if the answer must be provided in its simplest form. Thus, it's beneficial to find the least common denominator of the fractions—the least common denominator is incidentally also the least common multiple.

Once equivalent fractions have been found with common denominators, simply add or subtract the numerators to arrive at the answer:

1) $\frac{1}{2} + \frac{3}{4} = \frac{2}{4} + \frac{3}{4} = \frac{5}{4}$

2) $\frac{3}{12} + \frac{11}{20} = \frac{15}{60} + \frac{33}{60} = \frac{48}{60} = \frac{4}{5}$

3) $\frac{7}{9} - \frac{4}{15} = \frac{35}{45} - \frac{12}{45} = \frac{23}{45}$

4) $\frac{5}{6} - \frac{7}{18} = \frac{15}{18} - \frac{7}{18} = \frac{8}{18} = \frac{4}{9}$

One of the most fundamental concepts of fractions is their ability to be manipulated by multiplication or division. This is possible since $\frac{n}{n} = 1$ for any non-zero integer. As a result, multiplying or dividing by $\frac{n}{n}$ will not alter the original fraction since any number multiplied or divided by 1 doesn't change the value of that number. Fractions of the same value are known as equivalent fractions. For example, $\frac{2}{4}, \frac{4}{8}, \frac{50}{100}$, and $\frac{75}{150}$ are equivalent, as they all equal $\frac{1}{2}$.

To multiply two fractions, multiply the numerators to get the new numerator as well as multiply the denominators to get the new denominator. For example:

$$\frac{3}{5} \times \frac{2}{7} = \frac{3 \times 2}{5 \times 7} = \frac{6}{35}$$

Switching the numerator and denominator is called taking the **reciprocal** of a fraction. So, the reciprocal of $\frac{4}{5}$ is $\frac{5}{4}$.

To divide one fraction by another, multiply the first fraction by the reciprocal of the second. So:

$$\frac{3}{4} \div \frac{2}{5} = \frac{3}{4} \times \frac{5}{2} = \frac{15}{8}$$

If the numerator is smaller than the denominator, the fraction is a **proper fraction**. Otherwise, the fraction is said to be an **improper fraction**.

A **mixed number** is a number that is an integer plus some proper fraction and is written with the integer first and the proper fraction to the right of it. Any mixed number can be written as an improper fraction by multiplying the integer by the denominator, adding the product to the value of the numerator, and dividing the sum by the original denominator. For example:

$$3\frac{1}{2} = \frac{3 \times 2 + 1}{2} = \frac{7}{2}$$

Whole numbers can also be converted into fractions by placing the whole number as the numerator and making the denominator 1. For example, $3 = \frac{3}{1}$.

Percentages

Think of percentages as fractions with a denominator of 100. In fact, percentage means "per hundred." Problems often require converting numbers from percentages, fractions, and decimals. The following explains how to work through those conversions.

Converting Fractions to Percentages: Convert the fraction by using an equivalent fraction with a denominator of 100. For example:

$$\frac{3}{4} = \frac{3}{4} \times \frac{25}{25} = \frac{75}{100} = 75\%$$

Converting Percentages to Fractions: Percentages can be converted to fractions by turning the percentage into a fraction with a denominator of 100. Be wary of questions asking the converted fraction to be written in the simplest form. For example,

$$35\% = \frac{35}{100}$$

This, although correctly written, has a numerator and denominator with a greatest common factor of 5 and can be simplified to $\frac{7}{20}$.

Converting Percentages to Decimals: As a percentage is based on "per hundred," decimals and percentages can be converted by multiplying or dividing by 100. Practically speaking, this always amounts to moving the decimal point two places to the right or left, depending on the conversion. To convert a percentage to a decimal, move the decimal point two places to the left and remove the % sign. To convert a decimal to a percentage, move the decimal point two places to the right and add a % sign.

Here are some examples:

$$65\% = 0.65$$
$$0.33 = 33\%$$
$$0.215 = 21.5\%$$
$$99.99\% = 0.9999$$
$$500\% = 5.00$$
$$7.55 = 755\%$$

Questions dealing with percentages can be difficult when they are phrased as word problems. These word problems almost always come in three varieties. The first type will ask to find what percentage of some number will equal another number. The second asks to determine what number is some percentage of another given number. The third will ask what number another number is a given percentage of.

One of the most important parts of correctly answering percentage word problems is to identify the numerator and the denominator. This fraction can then be converted into a percentage, as described above.

The following word problem shows how to make this conversion:

A department store carries several different types of footwear. The store is currently selling 8 athletic shoes, 7 dress shoes, and 5 sandals. What percentage of the store's footwear are sandals?

First, calculate what serves as the "whole," as this will be the denominator. How many total pieces of footwear does the store sell? The store sells 20 different types (8 athletic + 7 dress + 5 sandals).

Second, what footwear type is the question specifically asking about? Sandals. Thus, 5 is the numerator.

Third, the resultant fraction must be expressed as a percentage. The first two steps indicate that $\frac{5}{20}$ of the footwear pieces are sandals. This fraction must now be converted into a percentage:

$$\frac{5}{20} \times \frac{5}{5} = \frac{25}{100} = 25\%$$

Ratios and Proportions

Ratios are used to show the relationship between two quantities. The ratio of oranges to apples in the grocery store may be 3 to 2. That means that for every 3 oranges, there are 2 apples. This comparison can be expanded to represent the actual number of oranges and apples, such as 36 oranges to 24 apples. Another example may be the number of boys to girls in a math class. If the ratio of boys to girls is given as 2 to 5, that means there are 2 boys to every 5 girls in the class. Ratios can also be compared if the units in each ratio are the same. The ratio of boys to girls in the math class can be compared to the ratio of boys to girls in a science class by stating which ratio is higher and which is lower.

Rates are used to compare two quantities with different units. **Unit rates** are the simplest form of rate. With unit rates, the denominator in the comparison of two units is one. For example, if someone can type at a rate of 1,000 words in 5 minutes, then their unit rate for typing is $\frac{1,000}{5} = 200$ words in one minute or 200 words per minute. Any rate can be converted into a unit rate by dividing to make the

denominator one. 1,000 words in 5 minutes has been converted into the unit rate of 200 words per minute.

Ratios and rates can be used together to convert rates into different units. For example, if someone is driving 50 kilometers per hour, that rate can be converted into miles per hour by using a ratio known as the **conversion factor**. Since the given value contains kilometers and the final answer needs to be in miles, the ratio relating miles to kilometers needs to be used. There are 0.62 miles in 1 kilometer. This, written as a ratio and in fraction form, is:

$$\frac{0.62 \text{ miles}}{1 \text{ km}}$$

To convert 50km/hour into miles per hour, the following conversion needs to be set up:

$$\frac{50 \text{ km}}{\text{hour}} \times \frac{0.62 \text{ miles}}{1 \text{ km}} = 31 \text{ miles per hour}$$

The ratio between two similar geometric figures is called the **scale factor**. For example, a problem may depict two similar triangles, A and B. The scale factor from the smaller triangle A to the larger triangle B is given as 2 because the length of the corresponding side of the larger triangle, 16, is twice the corresponding side on the smaller triangle, 8. This scale factor can also be used to find the value of a missing side, x, in triangle A. Since the scale factor from the smaller triangle (A) to larger one (B) is 2, the larger corresponding side in triangle B (given as 25) can be divided by 2 to find the missing side in A ($x = 12.5$). The scale factor can also be represented in the equation $2A = B$ because two times the lengths of A gives the corresponding lengths of B. This is the idea behind similar triangles.

Much like a scale factor can be written using an equation like $2A = B$, a *relationship* is represented by the equation $Y = kX$. X and Y are proportional because as values of X increase, the values of Y also increase. A relationship that is inversely proportional can be represented by the equation $Y = \frac{k}{X}$, where the value of Y decreases as the value of x increases and vice versa.

Proportional reasoning can be used to solve problems involving ratios, percentages, and averages. Ratios can be used in setting up proportions and solving them to find unknowns. For example, if a student completes an average of 10 pages of math homework in 3 nights, how long would it take the student to complete 22 pages? Both ratios can be written as fractions. The second ratio would contain the unknown.

The following proportion represents this problem, where x is the unknown number of nights:

$$\frac{10 \text{ pages}}{3 \text{ nights}} = \frac{22 \text{ pages}}{x \text{ nights}}$$

Solving this proportion entails cross-multiplying and results in the following equation:

$$10x = 22 \times 3$$

Simplifying and solving for x results in the exact solution: $x = 6.6$ nights. The result would be rounded up to 7 because the homework would actually be completed on the 7th night.

The following problem uses ratios involving percentages:

If 20% of the class is girls and 30 students are in the class, how many girls are in the class?

27

To set up this problem, it is helpful to use the common proportion:

$$\frac{\%}{100} = \frac{is}{of}$$

Within the proportion, % is the percentage of girls, 100 is the total percentage of the class, *is* is the number of girls, and *of* is the total number of students in the class. Most percentage problems can be written using this language. To solve this problem, the proportion should be set up as:

$$\frac{20}{100} = \frac{x}{30}$$

Then, solve for x. Cross-multiplying results in the equation:

$$20 \times 30 = 100x$$

This results in the solution $x = 6$. There are 6 girls in the class.

Ratios can be used to solve problems that concern length, volume, and other units. A problem may ask for the volume of a cone that has a radius, $r = 7$ m and a height, $h = 16$ m. Referring to the formulas provided on the test, the volume of a cone is given as:

$$V = \pi r^2 \frac{h}{3}$$

r is the radius and h is the height. Plugging $r = 7$ and $h = 16$ into the formula, the following is obtained:

$$V = \pi (7^2) \frac{16}{3}$$

Therefore, the volume of the cone is found to be approximately 821m³. Sometimes, answers in different units are sought. If this problem wanted the answer in liters, 821m³ would need to be converted.

Using the equivalence statement $1\text{m}^3 = 1,000\text{L}$, the following ratio would be used to solve for liters:

$$821 \text{ m}^3 \times \frac{1,000 \text{ L}}{1 \text{ m}^3}$$

Cubic meters in the numerator and denominator cancel each other out, and the answer is converted to 821,000 liters, or 8.21×10^5 L.

Other conversions can also be made between different given and final units. If the temperature in a pool is 30°C, what is the temperature of the pool in degrees Fahrenheit? To convert these units, an equation is used relating Celsius to Fahrenheit. The following equation is used:

$$T_{\text{°F}} = (1.8 \times T_{\text{°C}}) + 32$$

Plugging in the given temperature and solving the equation for T yields the result:

$$T_{\text{°F}} = (1.8 \times 30\text{°C}) + 32 = 86\text{°F}$$

Units in both the metric system and U.S. customary system are widely used.

28

Basic Geometry Relationships

The basic unit of geometry is a point. A point represents an exact location on a plane, or flat surface. The position of a point is indicated with a dot and usually named with a single uppercase letter, such as point *A* or point *T*. A point is a place, not a thing, and therefore has no dimensions or size. A set of points that lies on the same line is called collinear. A set of points that lies on the same plane is called coplanar.

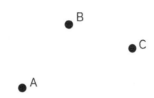

The image above displays point *A*, point *B*, and point *C*.

A line is as series of points that extends in both directions without ending. It consists of an infinite number of points and is drawn with arrows on both ends to indicate it extends infinitely. Lines can be named by two points on the line or with a single, cursive, lower case letter. The two lines below could be named line *AB* or line *BA* or $AB^{\leftrightarrow}$ or $BA^{\leftrightarrow}$; and line *m*.

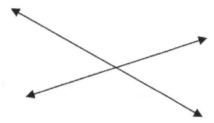

Two lines are considered parallel to each other if, while extending infinitely, they will never intersect (or meet). Parallel lines point in the same direction and are always the same distance apart. Two lines are

considered perpendicular if they intersect to form right angles. Right angles are 90°. Typically, a small box is drawn at the intersection point to indicate the right angle.

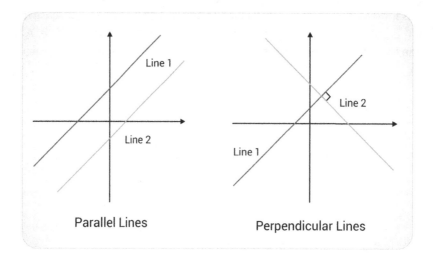

Line 1 is parallel to line 2 in the left image and is written as line 1 || line 2. Line 1 is perpendicular to line 2 in the right image and is written as line 1 ⊥ line 2.

A ray has a specific starting point and extends in one direction without ending. The endpoint of a ray is its starting point. Rays are named using the endpoint first, and any other point on the ray. The following ray can be named ray *AB* and written $\overrightarrow{AB}$.

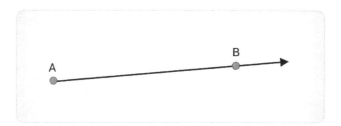

A line segment has specific starting and ending points. A line segment consists of two endpoints and all the points in between. Line segments are named by the two endpoints. The example below is named segment *KL* or segment *LK*, written $\underline{KL}$ or $\underline{LK}$.

Classification of Angles

An angle consists of two rays that have a common endpoint. This common endpoint is called the vertex of the angle. The two rays can be called sides of the angle. The angle below has a vertex at point *B* and the sides consist of ray *BA* and ray *BC*. An angle can be named in three ways:

1. Using the vertex and a point from each side, with the vertex letter in the middle.
2. Using only the vertex. This can only be used if it is the only angle with that vertex.
3. Using a number that is written inside the angle.

The angle below can be written ∠ABC (read angle ABC), ∠CBA, ∠B, or ∠1.

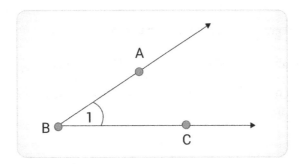

An angle divides a plane, or flat surface, into three parts: the angle itself, the interior (inside) of the angle, and the exterior (outside) of the angle. The figure below shows point M on the interior of the angle and point N on the exterior of the angle.

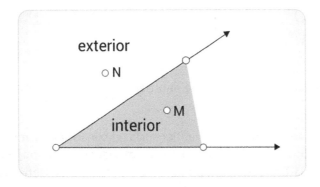

Angles can be measured in units called degrees, with the symbol °. The degree measure of an angle is between 0° and 180° and can be obtained by using a protractor.

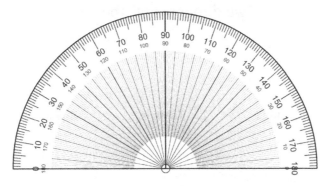

A straight angle (or simply a line) measures exactly 180°. A right angle's sides meet at the vertex to create a square corner. A right-angle measures exactly 90° and is typically indicated by a box drawn in the interior of the angle. An acute angle has an interior that is narrower than a right angle. The measure of an acute angle is any value less than 90° and greater than 0°. For example, 89.9°, 47°, 12°, and 1°. An obtuse angle has an interior that is wider than a right angle. The measure of an obtuse angle is any value greater than 90° but less than 180°. For example, 90.1°, 110°, 150°, and 179.9°.

- Acute angles: Less than 90°
- Obtuse angles: Greater than 90°

31

- Right angles: 90°
- Straight angles: 180°

If two angles add together to give 90°, the angles are **complementary**.

If two angles add together to give 180°, the angles are **supplementary**.

When two lines intersect, the pairs of angles they form are always supplementary. The two angles marked here are supplementary:

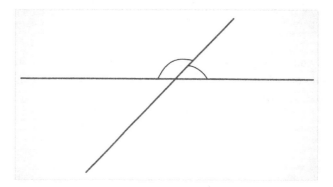

When two supplementary angles are next to one another or "adjacent" in this way, they always give rise to a straight line.

A polygon is a closed geometric figure in a plane (flat surface) consisting of at least 3 sides formed by line segments. These are often defined as two-dimensional shapes. Common two-dimensional shapes include circles, triangles, squares, rectangles, pentagons, and hexagons. Note that a circle is a two-dimensional shape without sides.

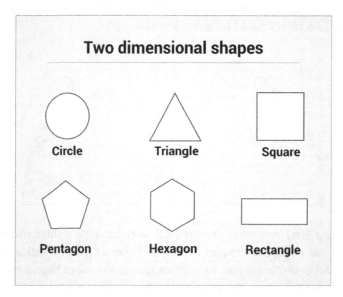

Two dimensional shapes

Circle   Triangle   Square

Pentagon   Hexagon   Rectangle

Polygons can be classified by the number of sides (also equal to the number of angles) they have. The following are the names of polygons with a given number of sides or angles:

# of Sides	Name of Polygon
3	Triangle
4	Quadrilateral
5	Pentagon
6	Hexagon
7	Septagon (or heptagon)
8	Octagon
9	Nonagon
10	Decagon

Triangles can be further classified by their sides and angles. A triangle with its largest angle measuring 90° is a right triangle. A triangle with the largest angle less than 90° is an acute triangle. A triangle with the largest angle greater than 90° is an obtuse triangle. Below is an example of a right triangle.

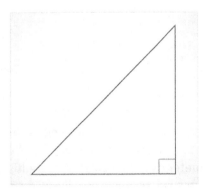

A triangle consisting of two equal sides and two equal angles is an isosceles triangle. A triangle with three equal sides and three equal angles is an equilateral triangle. A triangle with no equal sides or angles is a scalene triangle.

The three angles inside the triangle are called **interior angles** and add up to 180°.

For any triangle, the **Triangle Inequality Theorem** says that the following holds true:

$$A + B > C, A + C > B, B + C > A$$

In addition, the sum of two angles must be less than 180°.

If two triangles have angles that agree with one another, that is, the angles of the first triangle are equal to the angles of the second triangle, then the triangles are called **similar**. Similar triangles look the same, but one can be a "magnification" of the other.

Two triangles with sides that are the same length must also be similar triangles. In this case, such triangles are called **congruent**. Congruent triangles have the same angles and lengths, even if they are rotated from one another.

Quadrilaterals can be further classified according to their sides and angles. A quadrilateral with exactly one pair of parallel sides is called a trapezoid. A quadrilateral that shows both pairs of opposite sides parallel is a parallelogram. Parallelograms include rhombuses, rectangles, and squares. A rhombus has four equal sides. A rectangle has four equal angles (90° each). A square has four 90° angles and four equal sides. Therefore, a square is both a rhombus and a rectangle.

A solid figure, or simple solid, is a figure that encloses a part of space. Some solids consist of flat surfaces only while others include curved surfaces. Solid figures are often defined as three-dimensional shapes. Common three-dimensional shapes include spheres, prisms, cubes, pyramids, cylinders, and cones.

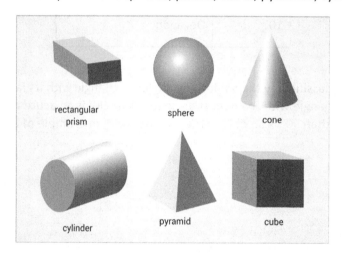

Perimeter is the measurement of a distance around something. It can be thought of as the length of the boundary, like a fence. It is found by adding together the lengths of all of the sides of a figure. Since a square has four equal sides, its perimeter can be calculated by multiplying the length of one side by 4. Thus, the formula is $P = 4 \times s$, where s equals one side. Like a square, a rectangle's perimeter is measured by adding together all of the sides. But as the sides are unequal, the formula is different. A rectangle has equal values for its lengths (long sides) and equal values for its widths (short sides), so the perimeter formula for a rectangle is:

$$P = l + l + w + w = 2l + 2w$$

l is length and w is width. Perimeter is measured in simple units such as inches, feet, yards, centimeters, meters, miles, etc.

In contrast to perimeter, area is the space occupied by a defined enclosure, like a field enclosed by a fence. It is measured in square units such as square feet or square miles. Here are some formulas for the areas of basic planar shapes:

1. The area of a rectangle is $l \times w$, where w is the width and l is the length
2. The area of a square is s^2, where s is the length of one side (this follows from the formula for rectangles)
3. The area of a triangle with base b and height h is $\frac{1}{2}bh$
4. The area of a circle with radius r is πr^2

Volume is the measurement of how much space an object occupies, like how much space is in the cube. Volume questions will typically ask how much of something is needed to completely fill the object. It is measured in cubic units, such as cubic inches. Here are some formulas for the volumes of basic three-dimensional geometric figures:

1. For a regular prism whose sides are all rectangles, the volume is $l \times w \times h$, where w is the width, l is the length, and h is the height of the prism.

2. For a cube, which is a prism whose faces are all squares of the same size, the volume is s^3.

3. The volume of a sphere of radius r is given by $\frac{4}{3}\pi r^3$.

4. The volume of a cylinder whose base has a radius of r and which has a height of h is given by $\pi r^2 h$.

Word Problems

Word problems can appear daunting, but don't let the verbiage psych you out. No matter the scenario or specifics, the key to answering them is to translate the words into a math problem. Always keep in mind what the question is asking and what operations could lead to that answer.

Translating Words into Math
To translate a word problem into an expression, look for a series of key words indicating addition, subtraction, multiplication, or division:

Addition: add, altogether, together, plus, increased by, more than, in all, sum, and total

Subtraction: minus, less than, difference, decreased by, fewer than, remain, and take away

Multiplication: *times*, *twice*, *of*, *double*, and *triple*

Division: divided by, cut up, half, quotient of, split, and shared equally

Identifying and utilizing the proper units for the scenario requires knowing how to apply the conversion rates for money, length, volume, and mass. For example, given a scenario that requires subtracting 8 inches from $2\frac{1}{2}$ feet, both values should first be expressed in the same unit (they could be expressed $\frac{2}{3}$ ft & $2\frac{1}{2}$ ft, or 8 in and 30 in). The desired unit for the answer may also require converting back to another unit.

Consider the following scenario: A parking area along the river is only wide enough to fit one row of cars and is $\frac{1}{2}$ kilometers long. The average space needed per car is 5 meters. How many cars can be parked along the river? First, all measurements should be converted to similar units: $\frac{1}{2}$ km $= 500$ m. The operation(s) needed should be identified. Because the problem asks for the number of cars, the total space should be divided by the space per car. 500 meters divided by 5 meters per car yields a total of 100 cars. Written as an expression, the meters unit cancels and the cars unit are left:

$$\frac{500 \text{ m}}{\left(\frac{5 \text{ m}}{1 \text{ car}}\right)} = 500 \text{ m} \times \frac{1 \text{ car}}{5 \text{ m}} = 500 \times \frac{1}{5} = 100 \text{ cars}$$

When dealing with problems involving elapsed time, breaking the problem down into workable parts is helpful. For example, suppose the length of time between 1:15pm and 3:45pm must be determined. From 1:15pm to 2:00pm is 45 minutes (knowing there are 60 minutes in an hour). From 2:00pm to 3:00pm is 1 hour. From 3:00pm to 3:45pm is 45 minutes. The total elapsed time is 45 minutes plus 1 hour plus 45 minutes. This sum produces 1 hour and 90 minutes. 90 minutes is over an hour, so this is converted to 1 hour (60 minutes) and 30 minutes. The total elapsed time can now be expressed as 2 hours and 30 minutes.

Example 1
Alexandra made $96 during the first 3 hours of her shift as a temporary worker at a law office. She will continue to earn money at this rate until she finishes in 5 more hours. How much does Alexandra make per hour? How much will Alexandra have made at the end of the day?

The hourly rate can be figured by dividing $96 by 3 hours to get $32 per hour. Now her total pay can be figured by multiplying $32 per hour by 8 hours, which comes out to $256.

Example 2

Bob had $20 and Tom had $4. After selling 4 ice cream cones to Bob, Tom has as much money as Bob. The cost of an ice cream cone is an unknown quantity and can be represented by a variable x. The amount of money Bob has after his purchase is four times the cost of an ice cream cone subtracted from his original.

$$\$20 \rightarrow 20 - 4x$$

The amount of money Tom has after his sale is four times the cost of an ice cream cone added to his original.

$$\$4 \rightarrow 4x + 4$$

After the sale, the amount of money that Bob and Tom have is equal.

$$\rightarrow 20 - 4x = 4x + 4$$

Solving for x yields $x = 2$.

Data Analysis

Representing Data

Most statistics involve collecting a large amount of data, analyzing it, and then making decisions based on previously known information. These decisions also can be measured through additional data collection and then analyzed. Therefore, the cycle can repeat itself over and over. Representing the data visually is a large part of the process, and many plots on the real number line exist that allow this to be done. For example, a **dot plot** uses dots to represent data points above the number line. Also, a **histogram** represents a data set as a collection of rectangles, which illustrate the frequency distribution of the data. Finally, a **box plot** (also known as a **box and whisker plot**) plots a data set on the number line by segmenting the distribution into four quartiles that are divided equally in half by the median.

Here's an example of a box plot, a histogram, and a dot plot for the same data set:

Box Plot

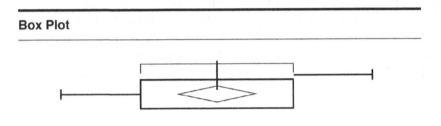

Histogram

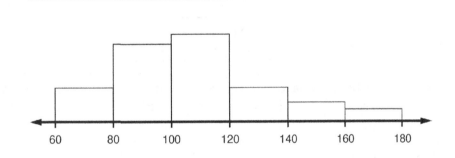

Dot Plot

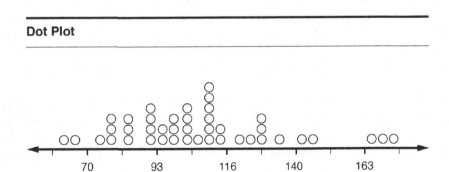

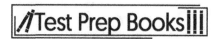

Comparing Data

Comparing data sets within statistics can mean many things. The first way to compare data sets is by looking at the center and spread of each set. The **center** of a data set can mean two things: median or mean. The **median** is the value that's halfway into each data set, and it splits the data into two intervals. The **mean** is the average value of the data within a set. It's calculated by adding up all of the data in the set and dividing the total by the number of data points. **Outliers** can significantly impact the mean. Additionally, two completely different data sets can have the same mean. For example, a data set with values ranging from 0 to 100 and a data set with values ranging from 44 to 56 can both have means of 50. The first data set has a much wider range, which is known as the **spread** of the data. This measures how varied the data is within each set. Spread can be defined further as either interquartile range or standard deviation.

The **interquartile range (IQR)** is the range of the middle 50 percent of the data set. This range can be seen in the large rectangle on a box plot. The **standard deviation** (s or σ) quantifies the amount of variation with respect to the mean. A lower standard deviation shows that the data set doesn't differ greatly from the mean. A larger standard deviation shows that the data set is spread out farther from the mean. The formula used for standard deviation depends on whether it's being used for a population or a sample (a subset of a population). The formula for sample standard deviation is:

$$s = \sqrt{\frac{\Sigma(x_i - \underline{x})^2}{n - 1}}$$

In this formula, s represents the standard deviation value, x is each value in the data set, $\underline{x}$ is the sample mean, and n is the total number of data points in the set. Note that sample standard deviations use *one less than the total* in the denominator. The population standard deviation formula is similar:

$$\sigma \doteq \sqrt{\frac{\Sigma(x_i - \mu)^2}{N}}$$

For population standard deviations, sigma (σ) represents the standard deviation, x represents each value in the data set, mu (μ) is the population mean, and N is the total number of data points for the population.

Interpreting Data

The shape of a data set is another way to compare two or more sets of data. If a data set isn't symmetric around its mean, it's said to be **skewed**. If the tail to the left of the mean is longer, it's said to be *skewed to the left*. In this case, the mean is less than the median. Conversely, if the tail to the right of the mean is longer, it's said to be *skewed to the right* and the mean is greater than the median. When classifying a data set according to its shape, its overall *skewness* is being discussed. If the mean and median are equal, the data set isn't *skewed*; it is **symmetric**, and is considered normally distributed.

An **outlier** is a data point that lies a great distance away from the majority of the data set. It also can be labeled as an **extreme value**. Technically, an outlier is any value that falls 1.5 times the IQR above the upper quartile or 1.5 times the IQR below the lower quartile. The effect of outliers in the data set is seen visually because they affect the mean. If there's a large difference between the mean and mode, outliers are the cause. The mean shows bias towards the outlying values. However, the median won't be affected as greatly by outliers.

Normal Distribution

A **normal distribution** of data follows the shape of a bell curve and the data set's median, mean, and mode are equal. Therefore, 50 percent of its values are less than the mean and 50 percent are greater than the mean. Data sets that follow this shape can be generalized using normal distributions. Normal distributions are described as **frequency distributions** in which the data set is plotted as percentages rather than true data points. A **relative frequency distribution** is one where the y-axis is between zero and 1, which is the same as 0% to 100%. Within a standard deviation, 68 percent of the values are within 1 standard deviation of the mean, 95 percent of the values are within 2 standard deviations of the mean, and 99.7 percent of the values are within 3 standard deviations of the mean. The number of standard deviations that a data point falls from the mean is called the **z-score.** The formula for the z-score is:

$$Z = \frac{x - \mu}{\sigma}$$

μ is the mean, σ is the standard deviation, and x is the data point. This formula is used to fit any data set that resembles a normal distribution to a standard normal distribution in a process known as **standardizing**.

Here is a normal distribution with labeled z-scores:

Normal Distribution with Labelled Z-Scores

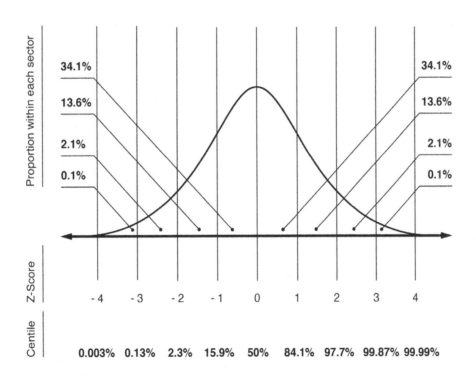

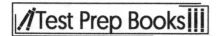

Population percentages can be estimated using normal distributions. For example, the probability that a data point will be less than the mean, or that the z-score will be less than 0, is 50%. Similarly, the probability that a data point will be within 1 standard deviation of the mean, or that the z-score will be between -1 and 1, is about 68.2%. When using a z-table, the left column states how many standard deviations (to one decimal place) away from the mean the point is, and the row heading states the second decimal place. The entries in the table corresponding to each column and row give the probability, which is equal to the area.

Areas Under the Curve

The area under the curve of a standard normal distribution is equal to 1. Areas under the curve can be estimated using the z-score and a table. The area is equal to the probability that a data point lies in that region in decimal form. For example, the area under the curve from $z = -1$ to $z = 1$ is 0.682.

Practice Quiz

1. Solve the following:

$$4 \times 7 + (25 - 21)^2 \div 2$$

    a. 512
    b. 36
    c. 60.5
    d. 22
    e. 46

2. What is $\frac{660}{100}$ rounded to the nearest integer?

    a. 67
    b. 66
    c. 60
    d. 6
    e. 7

3. Divide and reduce $\frac{5}{13} \div \frac{25}{169}$.

    a. $\frac{13}{5}$

    b. $\frac{65}{25}$

    c. $\frac{25}{65}$

    d. $\frac{5}{13}$

    e. $\frac{125}{2197}$

4. $5.88 \times 3.2 =$

    a. 18.816
    b. 16.44
    c. 20.352
    d. 17
    e. 1.8816

5. Solve the following:

$$(\sqrt{36} \times \sqrt{16}) - 3^2$$

    a. 30
    b. 21
    c. 15
    d. 13
    e. 2

See answers on next page

Answer Explanations

1. B: To solve this correctly, keep in mind the order of operations with the mnemonic PEMDAS (Please Excuse My Dear Aunt Sally). This stands for Parentheses, Exponents, Multiplication & Division, Addition & Subtraction. Taking it step by step, solve inside the parentheses first:

$$4 \times 7 + (4)^2 \div 2$$

Then, apply the exponent:

$$4 \times 7 + 16 \div 2$$

Multiplication and division are both performed next:

$$28 + 8$$

And then finally, addition to get $28 + 8 = 36$.

2. E: Dividing by 100 means shifting the decimal point of the numerator to the left by 2. The result is 6.6 and rounds to 7.

3. A: First, set up the division problem.

$$\frac{5}{13} \div \frac{25}{169}$$

Flip the second fraction and multiply.

$$\frac{5}{13} \times \frac{169}{25}$$

Simplify and reduce with cross multiplication.

$$\frac{1}{1} \times \frac{13}{5}$$

Multiply across the top and across the bottom to solve.

$$\frac{1 \times 13}{1 \times 5} = \frac{13}{5}$$

4. A: This problem can be multiplied as 588×32, except at the end, the decimal point needs to be moved three places to the left. Performing the multiplication will give 18,816, and moving the decimal place over three places results in 18.816.

5. C: Follow the order of operations in order to solve this problem. Solve the parentheses first, following the order of operations inside the parentheses as well. First, simplify the square roots.

$$(6 \times 4) - 9$$

Then, simplify the multiplication inside the parentheses.

$$24 - 9$$

Finally, subtract to get 5, Choice *C*.

Word Knowledge

Word Knowledge

Word knowledge is exactly what it sounds like: this portion of the exam is specifically constructed to test vocabulary skills and the ability to discern the best answer that matches the provided word. Unlike verbal analogies, which will test communication skills and problem-solving abilities along with vocabulary, word knowledge questions chiefly test vocabulary knowledge. While logic and reasoning come into play in this section, they are not as heavily emphasized as with the analogies. A prior knowledge of what the words mean is helpful in order to answer correctly. If the meaning of the words is unknown, that's fine, too; strategies should be used to rule out false answers and choose the correct ones. Here are some study strategies for an optimum performance.

Question Format

In contrast to the verbal analogies, word knowledge questions are very simple in construction. Instead of a comparison of words with an underlying connection, the prompt is just a single word. There are no special directions, alternate meanings, or analogies to work with. The objective is to analyze the given word and then choose the answer that means the same thing <u>or is closest in meaning</u> to the given word. Note the example below:

Blustery
 a. Hard
 b. Windy
 c. Mythical
 d. Stony
 e. Corresponding

All of the questions on the AFOQT word knowledge portion will appear exactly like the above sample. This is generally the standard layout throughout other exams, so some test-takers may already be familiar with the structure. The principle remains the same: at the top of the section, clear directions will be given to choose the answer that most precisely defines the given word. In this case, the answer is windy (B), since windy and blustery are synonymous.

Preparation

In truth, there is no set way to prepare for this portion of the exam that will guarantee a perfect score. This is simply because the words used on the test are unpredictable. There is no set list provided to study from. The definition of the provided word needs to be determined on the spot. This sounds challenging, but there are still ways to prepare mentally for this portion of the test. It may help to expand your vocabulary a little each day. Several resources are available, in books and online, that collect words and definitions that tend to show up frequently on standardized tests. Knowledge of words can increase the strength of your vocabulary.

Mindset is key. The meanings of challenging words can often be found by relying on the past experiences of the test-taker to help deduce the correct answer. How? Well, test-takers have been talking their entire lives—knowing words and how words work. It helps to have a positive mindset from the start. It's unlikely that all definitions of words will be known immediately, but the answer can still be

found. There are aspects of words that are recognizable to help discern the correct answers and eliminate the incorrect ones. Below are some of the factors that contribute to word meanings.

Word Origins and Roots

Studying a foreign language in school, particularly Latin or any of the romance languages (Latin-influenced), is advantageous. English is a language highly influenced by Latin and Greek words. The roots of much of the English vocabulary have Latin origins; these roots can bind many words together and often allude to a shared definition. Here's an example:

Fervent
    a. Lame
    b. Joyful
    c. Thorough
    d. Boiling
    e. Cunning

Fervent descends from the Latin word, *fervere*, which means "to boil or glow" and figuratively means "impassioned." The Latin root present in the word is *ferv*, which is what gives fervent the definition: showing great warmth and spirit or spirited, hot, glowing. This provides a link to boiling (D) just by root word association, but there's more to analyze. Among the other choices, none relate to fervent. The word lame (A) means crippled, disabled, weak, or inadequate. None of these match with fervent. While being fervent can reflect joy, joyful (B) directly describes "a great state of happiness," while fervent is simply expressing the idea of having very strong feelings—not necessarily joy.

Thorough (C) means complete, perfect, painstaking, or with mastery; while something can be done thoroughly and fervently, none of these words match fervent as closely as boiling does. Cunning (E) means crafty, deceiving or with ingenuity or dexterity. Doing something fervently does not necessarily mean it is done with dexterity. Not only does boiling connect in a linguistic way, but also in the way it is used in our language. While boiling can express being physically hot and undergoing a change, boiling is also used to reflect emotional states. People say they are "boiling over" when in heightened emotional states; "boiling mad" is another expression. Boiling, like fervent, also embodies a sense of heightened intensity. This makes boiling the best choice!

The Latin root *ferv* is seen in other words such as fervor, fervid, and even ferment. All of them are connected to and can be described by boil or glow, whether it is in a physical sense or in a metaphorical one. Such patterns can be seen in other word sets as well. Here's another example:

Gracious
    a. Fruitful
    b. Angry
    c. Grateful
    d. Understood
    e. Overheard

This one's a little easier; the answer is grateful (*C*) because both words mean thankful! Even if the meanings of both words are known, there's a connection found by looking at the beginnings of both words: *gra/grat*. Once again, these words are built on a root that stretches back to classical language. Both terms come from the Latin, *gratis*, which literally means "thanks."

Understanding root words can help identify the meaning in a lot of word choices, and help the test-taker grasp the nature of the given word. Many dictionaries, both in book form and online, offer information on the origins of words, which highlight these roots. When studying for the test, it helps to look up an unfamiliar word for its definition and then check to see if it has a root that can be connected to any other terms.

Pay Attention to Prefixes

The prefix of a word can actually reveal a lot about its definition. Many prefixes are actually Greco-Roman roots as well—but these are more familiar and a lot easier to recognize! When encountering any unfamiliar words, try looking at prefixes to discern the definition and then compare that with the choices. The prefix should be determined to help find the word's meaning. Here's an example question:

Premeditate
  a. Sporadic
  b. Calculated
  c. Interfere
  d. Determined
  e. Noble

With premeditate, there's the common prefix *pre*. This helps draw connections to other words like prepare or preassemble. *Pre* refers to "before, already being, or having already." Meditate means to think or plan. Premeditate means to think or plan beforehand with intent. Therefore, a term that deals with thinking or planning should be found, but also something done in preparation. Among the word choices, noble (E) and determined (D) are both adjectives with no hint of being related to something done before or in preparation. These choices are wrong. Sporadic (A) refers to events happening in irregular patterns, so this is quite the opposite of premeditated. Interfere (C) also has nothing to do with premeditate; it goes counter to premeditate in a way similar to sporadic. Calculated (B), however, fits! A route and the cost of starting a plan can be calculated. Calculated refers to acting with a full awareness of consequences, so inherently planning is involved. In fact, calculated is synonymous with premeditated, thus making it the correct choice. Just by paying attention to a prefix, the doors to a meaning can open to help easily figure out which word would be the best choice. Here's another example.

Regain
  a. Erupt
  b. Ponder
  c. Seek
  d. Recoup
  e. Enamor

Recoup (D) is the right answer. The prefix *re* often appears in front of words to give them the meaning of occurring again. Regain means to repossess something that was lost. Recoup, which also has the *re* prefix, literally means to regain. In this example, both the given word and the answer share the *re* prefix, which makes the pair easy to connect. However, don't rely *only* on prefixes to choose an answer. Make sure to analyze all of the options before marking an answer. Going through the other words in this sample, none of them come close to meaning regain except recoup. After checking to make sure that recoup is the best matching word, then mark it.

45

Positive Versus Negative Sounding Words

Another tool for the mental toolbox is simply distinguishing whether a word has a positive or negative connotation. Like electrical wires, words carry energy; they are crafted to draw certain attention and to have certain strength to them. Words can be described as positive and uplifting (a stronger word) or they can be negative and scathing (a stronger word). Sometimes they are neutral—having no particular connotation. Distinguishing how a word is supposed to be interpreted will not only help learn its definition, but also draw parallels with word choices. While it's true that words must usually be taken in the context of how they are used, word definitions have inherent meanings as well, meaning that they have a distinct vibe to pick up on. Here is an example.

Excellent
    a. Fair
    b. Optimum
    c. Reasonable
    d. Negative
    e. Agitation

As you know, excellent is a very positive word. It refers to something being better than good, or above average. In this sample, negative (D) and agitation (E) can easily be eliminated because these are both words with negative connotations. Reasonable (C) is more or less a neutral word: it's not bad but it doesn't communicate the higher quality that excellent represents. It's just, well, reasonable. This leaves the possible choices of fair (A) and optimum (B). Or does it? Fair *is* a positive word; it's used to describe things that are good, even beautiful. But in the modern context, fair is defined as good, but somewhat average or just decent: "You did a fairly good job" or, "That was fair." On the other hand, optimum is positive and a stronger word. Optimum describes the most favorable outcome. This makes optimum the best word choice that matches excellent in both strength and connotation. Not only are the two words positive, but they also express the same level of positivity! Here's another sample.

Repulse
    a. Draw
    b. Encumber
    c. Force
    d. Disgust
    e. Magnify

Repulse just sounds negative when said aloud. It is commonly used in the context of something being repulsive, disgusting, or that which is distasteful. It's also defined as an attack that drives people away. This tells us that we need a word that also carries a negative meaning. Magnify (E) is positive, while draw (A) and force (C) are both neutral. Encumber (B) and disgust (D) are negative. Disgust is a stronger negative than encumber. Of all the words given, only disgust directly defines a feeling of distaste and aversion that is synonymous with repulse and matches in both negativity and strength.

Parts of Speech

It is often very helpful to determine the part of speech of a word. Is it an adjective, adverb, noun, or verb, etc.? Often the correct answer will also be the same part of speech as the given word. Isolate the part of speech and what it describes and look for an answer choice that also describes the same part of

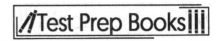

speech. For example: if the given word is an adverb describing an action word, then look for another adverb describing an action word.

Swiftly
    a. Fast
    b. Quietly
    c. Angry
    d. Sudden
    e. Quickly

Swiftly is an adverb that describes the speed of an action. Angry (C), fast (A), and sudden (D) can be eliminated because they are not adverbs, and quietly (B) can be eliminated because it does not describe speed. This leaves quickly (E), which is the correct answer. Fast and sudden may throw off some test-takers because they both describe speed, but quickly matches more closely because it is an adverb, and swiftly is also an adverb.

Placing the Word in a Sentence

Often it is easier to discern the meaning of a word if it is used in a sentence. If the given word can be used in a sentence, then try replacing it with some of the answer choices to see which words seem to make sense in the same sentence. Here's an example.

Remarkable
    a. Often
    b. Capable
    c. Outstanding
    d. Shining
    e. Excluding

A sentence can be formed with the word remarkable. "My grade point average is remarkable." None of the examples make sense when replacing the word remarkable in the sentence other than the word outstanding (C), so outstanding is the obvious answer. Shining (D) is also a word with a positive connotation, but outstanding fits better in the sentence.

Looking for Relationships

Remember that all except one of the answer choices are wrong. If a close relationship between three or four of the answer choices can be found and not the fourth or fifth, then some of the choices can be eliminated. Sometimes all of the words are related except one; the one that is not related will often be the correct answer. Here is an example.

Outraged
    a. Angry
    b. Empty
    c. Forlorn
    d. Vacated
    e. Lonely

Notice that all of the answer choices have a negative connotation, but four of them are related to being alone or in low numbers. While two answer choices involve emotions—angry (A) and lonely (E), lonely is related to the other wrong answers, so angry is the best choice to match outraged.

Picking the Closest Answer

As the answer choices are reviewed, two scenarios might stand out. An exact definition match might not be found for the given word among the choices, or there are several word choices that can be considered synonymous to the given word. This is intentionally done to test the ability to draw parallels between the words in order to produce an answer that best fits the prompt word. Again, the closest fitting word will be the answer. Even when facing these two circumstances, finding the one word that fits best is the proper strategy. Here's an example:

Insubordination
    a. Cooperative
    b. Disciplined
    c. Rebel
    d. Contagious
    e. Wild

Insubordination refers to a defiance or utter refusal of authority. Looking over the choices, none of these terms provide definite matches to insubordination like insolence, mutiny, or misconduct would. This is fine; the answer doesn't have to be a perfect synonym. The choices don't reflect insubordination in any way, except rebel (C). After all, when rebel is used as a verb, it means to act against authority. It's also used as a noun: someone who goes against authority. Therefore, rebel is the best choice.

As with the verbal analogies section, playing the role of "detective" is the way to go as you may encounter two or even three answer choices that could be considered correct. However, the answer that best fits the prompt word's meaning is the best answer. Choices should be narrowed one word at a time. The least-connected word should be eliminated first and then proceed until one word is left that is the closest synonym.

Sequence
    a. List
    b. Range
    c. Series
    d. Replicate
    e. Iconic

A sequence reflects a particular order in which events or objects follow. The two closest options are list (A) and series (C). Both involve grouping things together, but which fits better? Consider each word more carefully. A list is composed of items that fit in the same category, but that's really it. A list doesn't have to follow any particular order; it's just a list. On the other hand, a series is defined by events happening in a set order. A series relies on sequence, and a sequence can be described as a series. Thus, series is the correct answer.

Practice Quiz

1. WEARY
   a. Tired
   b. Clothing
   c. Happy
   d. Hot
   e. Whiny

2. VAST
   a. Rapid
   b. Expansive
   c. Small
   d. Ocean
   e. Uniform

3. DEMONSTRATE
   a. Tell
   b. Show
   c. Build
   d. Complete
   e. Make

4. ORCHARD
   a. Flower
   b. Fruit
   c. Grove
   d. Peach
   e. Farm

5. TEXTILE
   a. Fabric
   b. Document
   c. Mural
   d. Ornament
   e. Knit

See answers on next page

Answer Explanations

1. A: *Weary* most closely means *tired*. Someone who is weary and tired may be whiny, but they do not necessarily mean the same thing.

2. B: Something that is *vast* is far-reaching and *expansive*. Choice *D, ocean*, may be described as vast but the word alone doesn't mean vast. The heavens or skies may also be described as vast. Someone's imagination or vocabulary can also be vast.

3. B: To demonstrate something means to show it. The word *demonstration* comes from demonstrate and a demonstration is a modeling or show-and-tell type of example that is usually visual.

4. C: An *orchard* is most like a *grove* because both are areas like plantations that grow different kinds of fruit. *Peach* is a type of fruit that may be grown in an orchard but it is not a synonym for *orchard*. Many citrus fruits are grown in groves but either word can be used to describe many fruit-bearing trees in one area. Choice *E, farm*, may have an orchard or grove on the property, but they are not the same thing and many farms do not grow fruit trees.

5. A: A *textile* is another word for a fabric. The most confusing alternative choice in this case is *knit*, because some textiles are knit but *textile* and *knit* are not synonyms and plenty of textiles are not knit.

Math Knowledge

The Scope of the Math Knowledge Section

The Math Knowledge section of the test involves everything included in the Arithmetic Reasoning section, as well as some additional mathematical operations and techniques. It is, however, much less focused on word problems.

How to Prepare

Although this section of the test will be less focused on word problems, it is still very important to practice the types of problems in this section. As mentioned before, to really learn mathematics, it is important to practice and not just read through instructions. Approach this section the same as the Arithmetic Reasoning: first, read through the study guide here, then try the practice problems, and lastly, compare your answers with the solutions given below. You may utilize a slightly different method for solving a problem since there are sometimes multiple approaches that will work.

Exponents

An exponent is an operation used as shorthand for a number multiplied or divided by itself for a defined number of times.

$$3^7 = 3 \times 3 \times 3 \times 3 \times 3 \times 3 \times 3$$

In this example, the 3 is called the base, and the 7 is called the exponent. The exponent is typically expressed as a superscript number near the upper right side of the base but can also be identified as the number following a caret symbol (^). This operation would be verbally expressed as "3 to the 7th power" or "3 raised to the power of 7." Common exponents are 2 and 3. A base raised to the power of 2 is referred to as having been "squared," while a base raised to the power of 3 is referred to as having been "cubed."

Several special rules apply to exponents. First, the Zero Power Rule finds that any number raised to the zero power equals 1. For example, 100^0, 2^0, $(-3)^0$ and 0^0 all equal 1 because the bases are raised to the zero power.

Second, exponents can be negative. With negative exponents, the equation is expressed as a fraction, as in the following example:

$$3^{-7} = \frac{1}{3^7} = \frac{1}{3 \times 3 \times 3 \times 3 \times 3 \times 3 \times 3}$$

Third, the Power Rule concerns exponents being raised by another exponent. When this occurs, the exponents are multiplied by each other:

$$(x^2)^3 = x^6 = (x^3)^2$$

Fourth, when multiplying two exponents with the same base, the Product Rule requires that the base remains the same, and the exponents are added. For example,

$$a^x \times a^y = a^{x+y}$$

52

Since addition and multiplication are commutative, the two terms being multiplied can be in any order.

$$x^3 x^5 = x^{3+5} = x^8 = x^{5+3} = x^5 x^3$$

Fifth, when dividing two exponents with the same base, the Quotient Rule requires that the base remains the same, but the exponents are subtracted. So, $a^x \div a^y = a^{x-y}$. Since subtraction and division are not commutative, the two terms must remain in order.

$$x^5 x^{-3} = x^{5-3} = x^2 = x^5 \div x^3 = \frac{x^5}{x^3}$$

Additionally, 1 raised to any power is still equal to 1, and any number raised to the power of 1 is equal to itself. In other words, $a^1 = a$ and $14^1 = 14$.

Exponents play an important role in scientific notation to present extremely large or small numbers as follows: $a \times 10^b$. To write the number in scientific notation, the decimal is moved until there is only one digit on the left side of the decimal point, indicating that the number a has a value between 1 and 10. The number of times the decimal moves indicates the exponent to which 10 is raised, here represented by b. If the decimal moves to the left, then b is positive, but if the decimal moves to the right, then b is negative. See the following examples:

$$3,050 = 3.05 \times 10^3$$

$$-777 = -7.77 \times 10^2$$

$$0.000123 = 1.23 \times 10^{-4}$$

$$-0.0525 = -5.25 \times 10^{-2}$$

Roots

The square root symbol is expressed as $\sqrt{}$ and is commonly known as the radical. Taking the root of a number is the inverse operation of multiplying that number by itself some amount of times. For example, squaring the number 7 is equal to 7×7, or 49. Finding the square root is the opposite of finding an exponent, as the operation seeks a number that when multiplied by itself equals the number in the square root symbol.

For example, $\sqrt{36}$ is equal to 6 because 6 multiplied by 6 equals 36. Note, the square root of 36 is also -6 since:

$$-6 \times -6 = 36$$

This can be indicated using a plus/minus symbol like this: ± 6. However, square roots are often just expressed as a positive number for simplicity with it being understood that the true value can be either positive or negative.

Perfect squares are squares of whole numbers. The list of perfect squares begins with 0, 1, 4, 9, 16, 25, 36, 49, 64, 81, and 100.

Determining the square root of imperfect squares requires a calculator to reach an exact figure. It's possible, however, to approximate the answer by finding the two perfect squares that the number fits

between. For example, the square root of 40 is between 6 and 7 since the squares of those numbers are 36 and 49, respectively.

Square roots are the most common root operation. If the radical doesn't have a number to the upper left of the symbol $\sqrt{\ }$, then it's a square root. Sometimes a radical includes a number in the upper left, like $\sqrt[3]{27}$, as in the other common root type—the cube root. Complicated roots like the cube root often require a calculator.

Parentheses

Parentheses separate different parts of an equation, and operations within them should be thought of as taking place before the outside operations take place. Practically, this means that the distinction between what is inside and outside of the parentheses decides the order of operations that the equation follows. Failing to solve operations inside the parentheses before addressing the part of the equation outside of the parentheses will lead to incorrect results.

For example, let's analyze:

$$5 - (3 + 25)$$

The addition operation within the parentheses must be solved first. So $3 + 25 = 28$, leaving:

$$5 - (28) = -23$$

If this was solved in the incorrect order of operations, the solution might be found to be:

$$5 - 3 + 25 = 2 + 25 = 27$$

This would be wrong.

Equations often feature multiple layers of parentheses. To differentiate them, square brackets [ ] and braces { } are used in addition to parentheses. The innermost parentheses must be solved before working outward to larger brackets. For example, in $\{2 \div [5 - (3 + 1)]\}$, solving the innermost parentheses $(3 + 1)$ leaves:

$$\{2 \div [5 - (4)]\}$$

$[5 - (4)]$ is now the next smallest, which leaves $\{2 \div [1]\}$ in the final step, and 2 as the answer.

Order of Operations

When solving equations with multiple operations, special rules apply. These rules are known as the Order of Operations. The order is as follows: Parentheses, Exponents, Multiplication and Division from left to right, and Addition and Subtraction from left to right. A popular mnemonic device to help remember the order is Please Excuse My Dear Aunt Sally (PEMDAS). Evaluate the following two problems to understand the Order of Operations:

1) $4 + (3 \times 2)^2 \div 4$

> First, solve the operation within the parentheses: $4 + 6^2 \div 4$.
> Second, solve the exponent: $4 + 36 \div 4$.

Third, solve the division operation: $4 + 9$.
Fourth, finish the operation with addition for the answer, 13.

2) $2 \times (6 + 3) \div (2 + 1)^2$

$2 \times 9 \div (3)^2$
$2 \times 9 \div 9$
$18 \div 9$
2

Positive and Negative Numbers

Signs
Aside from 0, numbers can be either positive or negative. The sign for a positive number is the plus sign or the + symbol, while the sign for a negative number is the minus sign or the − symbol. If a number has no designation, then it's assumed to be positive.

Absolute Values
Both positive and negative numbers are valued according to their distance from 0. Look at this number line for +3 and -3:

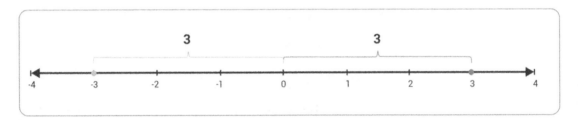

Both 3 and -3 are three spaces from 0. The distance from 0 is called its absolute value. Thus, both -3 and 3 have an absolute value of 3 since they're both three spaces away from 0.

An absolute number is written by placing | | around the number. So, |3| and |−3| both equal 3, as that's their common absolute value.

Implications for Addition and Subtraction

For addition, if all numbers are either positive or negative, simply add them together. For example,

$$4 + 4 = 8 \text{ and } -4 + -4 = -8$$

However, things get tricky when some of the numbers are negative, and some are positive.

Take $6 + (-4)$ as an example. First, take the absolute values of the numbers, which are 6 and 4. Second, subtract the smaller value from the larger. The equation becomes $6 - 4 = 2$. Third, place the sign of the original larger number on the sum. Here, 6 is the larger number, and it's positive, so the sum is 2.

Here's an example where the negative number has a larger absolute value: $(-6) + 4$. The first two steps are the same as the example above. However, on the third step, the negative sign must be placed on the sum, as the absolute value of (-6) is greater than 4. Thus,

$$-6 + 4 = -2$$

The absolute value of numbers implies that subtraction can be thought of as flipping the sign of the number following the subtraction sign and simply adding the two numbers. This means that subtracting a negative number will in fact be adding the positive absolute value of the negative number. Here are some examples:

$$-6 - 4 = -6 + -4 = -10$$

$$3 - -6 = 3 + 6 = 9$$

$$-3 - 2 = -3 + -2 = -5$$

Implications for Multiplication and Division

For multiplication and division, if both numbers are positive, then the product or quotient is always positive. If both numbers are negative, then the product or quotient is also positive. However, if the numbers have opposite signs, the product or quotient is always negative.

Simply put, the product in multiplication and quotient in division is always positive, unless the numbers have opposing signs, in which case it's negative.

Here are some examples:

$$(-6) \times (-5) = 30$$

$$(-50) \div 10 = -5$$

$$8 \times |-7| = 56$$

$$(-48) \div (-6) = 8$$

If there are more than two numbers in a multiplication problem, then whether the product is positive or negative depends on the number of negative numbers in the problem. If there is an odd number of negatives, then the product is negative. If there is an even number of negative numbers, then the result is positive.

Here are some examples:

$$(-6) \times 5 \times (-2) \times (-4) = -240$$

$$(-6) \times 5 \times 2 \times (-4) = 240$$

Polynomials

An expression of the form ax^n, where n is a non-negative integer, is called a **monomial** because it contains one term. A sum of monomials is called a **polynomial**. For example, $-4x^3 + x$ is a polynomial, while $5x^7$ is a monomial. A function equal to a polynomial is called a **polynomial function**.

The monomials in a polynomial are also called the **terms of the polynomial**.

The constants that precede the variables are called **coefficients**.

The highest value of the exponent of x in a polynomial is called the **degree** of the polynomial. So, $-4x^3 + x$ has a degree of 3, while $-2x^5 + x^3 + 4x + 1$ has a degree of 5. When multiplying polynomials, the degree of the result will be the sum of the degrees of the two polynomials being multiplied.

Addition and subtraction operations can be performed on polynomials with like terms. **Like terms** refers to terms that have the same variable and exponent. The two following polynomials can be added together by collecting like terms:

$$(x^2 + 3x - 4) + (4x^2 - 7x + 8)$$

The x^2 terms can be added as:

$$x^2 + 4x^2 = 5x^2$$

The x terms can be added as $3x + -7x = -4x$, and the constants can be added as:

$$-4 + 8 = 4$$

The following expression is the result of the addition:

$$5x^2 - 4x + 4$$

When subtracting polynomials, the same steps are followed, only subtracting like terms together.

To multiply two polynomials, each term of the first polynomial is multiplied by each term of the second polynomial and then the results are added.

For example:

$$(4x^2 + x)(-x^3 + x)$$

$$4x^2(-x^3) + 4x^2(x) + x(-x^3) + x(x)$$

$$-4x^5 + 4x^3 - x^4 + x^2$$

In the case where each polynomial has two terms, like in this example, some students find it helpful to use the FOIL method. FOIL is a technique for generating polynomials through the multiplication of binomials. A polynomial is an expression of multiple variables (for example, x, y, z) in at least three terms involving only the four basic operations and exponents. FOIL is an acronym for First, Outer, Inner, and Last. **First** represents the multiplication of the terms appearing first in the binomials. **Outer** means multiplying the outermost terms. **Inner** means multiplying the terms inside. **Last** means multiplying the last terms of each binomial.

1) Simplify $(x + 10)(x + 4) = (x \times x) + (x \times 4) + (10 \times x) + (10 \times 4)$
$\qquad\qquad\qquad\qquad\qquad\quad$ First $\qquad$ Outer $\qquad$ Inner $\qquad$ Last

After multiplying these binomials, it's time to solve the operations and combine like terms. Thus, the expression becomes:

$$x^2 + 4x + 10x + 40 = x^2 + 14x + 40$$

The process of **factoring** a polynomial means to write the polynomial as a product of other (generally simpler) polynomials. Here is an example:

$$x^2 - 4x + 3 = (x - 1)(x - 3)$$

Factors for polynomials are similar to factors for integers—they are numbers, variables, or polynomials that, when multiplied together, give a product equal to the polynomial in question. One polynomial is a factor of a second polynomial if the second polynomial can be obtained from the first by multiplying by a third polynomial.

$6x^6 + 13x^4 + 6x^2$ can be obtained by multiplying together:

$$(3x^4 + 2x^2)(2x^2 + 3)$$

This means $2x^2 + 3$ and $3x^4 + 2x^2$ are factors of:

$$6x^6 + 13x^4 + 6x^2$$

In general, finding the factors of a polynomial can be tricky. However, there are a few types of polynomials that can be factored in a straightforward way.

If a certain monomial is in each term of a polynomial, it can be factored out. There are several common forms polynomials take, which if you recognize, you can solve. The first example is a perfect square trinomial. To factor this polynomial, first expand the middle term of the expression:

$$x^2 + 2xy + y^2$$

$$x^2 + xy + xy + y^2$$

Factor out a common term in each half of the expression (in this case x from the left and y from the right):

$$x(x + y) + y(x + y)$$

Then the same can be done again, treating $(x + y)$ as the common factor:

$$(x + y)(x + y) = (x + y)^2$$

Therefore, the formula for this polynomial is:

$$x^2 + 2xy + y^2 = (x + y)^2$$

Next is another example of a perfect square trinomial. The process is the similar, but notice the difference in sign:

$$x^2 - 2xy + y^2$$

$$x^2 - xy - xy + y^2$$

Factor out the common term on each side:

$$x(x - y) - y(x - y)$$

Factoring out the common term again:

$$(x - y)(x - y) = (x - y)^2$$

$$\text{Thus: } x^2 - 2xy + y^2 = (x - y)^2$$

The next is known as a difference of squares. This process is effectively the reverse of binomial multiplication:

$$x^2 - y^2$$

$$x^2 - xy + xy - y^2$$

$$x(x - y) + y(x - y)$$

$$(x + y)(x - y)$$

Therefore:

$$x^2 - y^2 = (x + y)(x - y)$$

The following two polynomials are known as the sum or difference of cubes. These are special polynomials that take the form of $x^3 + y^3$ or $x^3 - y^3$. The following formula factors the sum of cubes:

$$x^3 + y^3 = (x + y)(x^2 - xy + y^2)$$

Next is the difference of cubes, but note the change in sign. The formulas for both are similar, but the order of signs for factoring the sum or difference of cubes can be remembered by using the acronym SOAP, which stands for "same, opposite, always positive." The first sign is the same as the sign in the first expression, the second is opposite, and the third is always positive. The next formula factors the difference of cubes:

$$x^3 - y^3 = (x - y)(x^2 + xy + y^2)$$

The following two examples are expansions of cubed binomials. Similarly, these polynomials always follow a pattern:

$$x^3 + 3x^2y + 3xy^2 + y^3 = (x + y)^3$$

$$x^3 - 3x^2y + 3xy^2 - y^3 = (x - y)^3$$

These rules can be used in many combinations with one another. For example, the expression $3x^3 - 24$ has a common factor of 3, which becomes:

$$3(x^3 - 8)$$

A difference of cubes still remains which can then be factored out:

$$3(x - 2)(x^2 + 2x + 4)$$

59

There are no other terms to be pulled out, so this expression is completely factored.

When factoring polynomials, a good strategy is to multiply the factors to check the result. Let's try another example:

$$4x^3 + 16x^2$$

Both sides of the expression can be divided by 4, and both contain x^2, because $4x^3$ can be thought of as $4x^2(x)$, so the common term can simply be factored out:

$$4x^2(x + 4)$$

It sometimes can be necessary to rewrite the polynomial in some clever way before applying the above rules. Consider the problem of factoring $x^4 - 1$. This does not immediately look like any of the previous polynomials. However, it's possible to think of this polynomial as $x^4 - 1 = (x^2)^2 - (1^2)^2$, and now it can be treated as a difference of squares to simplify this:

$$(x^2)^2 - (1^2)^2$$

$$(x^2)^2 - x^2 1^2 + x^2 1^2 - (1^2)^2$$

$$x^2(x^2 - 1^2) + 1^2(x^2 - 1^2)$$

$$(x^2 + 1^2)(x^2 - 1^2)$$

$$(x^2 + 1)(x^2 - 1)$$

Rational Expressions

A fraction, or ratio, wherein each part is a polynomial, defines **rational expressions**. Some examples include $\frac{2x+6}{x}$, $\frac{1}{x^2-4x+8}$, and $\frac{z^2}{x+5}$. Exponents on the variables are restricted to whole numbers, which means roots and negative exponents are not included in rational expressions.

Rational expressions can be transformed by factoring. For example, the expression $\frac{x^2-5x+6}{(x-3)}$ can be rewritten by factoring the numerator to obtain:

$$\frac{(x - 3)(x - 2)}{(x - 3)}$$

Therefore, the common binomial $(x - 3)$ can cancel so that the simplified expression is:

$$\frac{(x - 2)}{1} = (x - 2)$$

Additionally, other rational expressions can be rewritten to take on different forms. Some may be factorable in themselves, while others can be transformed through arithmetic operations. Rational expressions are closed under addition, subtraction, multiplication, and division by a nonzero expression. **Closed** means that if any one of these operations is performed on a rational expression, the result will still be a rational expression. The set of all real numbers is another example of a set closed under all four operations.

Adding and subtracting rational expressions is based on the same concepts as adding and subtracting simple fractions. For both concepts, the denominators must be the same for the operation to take place. For example, here are two rational expressions:

$$\frac{x^3 - 4}{(x - 3)} + \frac{x + 8}{(x - 3)}$$

Since the denominators are both $(x - 3)$, the numerators can be combined by collecting like terms to form:

$$\frac{x^3 + x + 4}{(x - 3)}$$

If the denominators are different, they need to be made common (the same) by using the Least Common Denominator (LCD). Each denominator needs to be factored, and the LCD contains each factor that appears in any one denominator the greatest number of times it appears in any denominator. The original expressions need to be multiplied times a form of 1, which will turn each denominator into the LCD. This process is like adding fractions with unlike denominators. It is also important when working with rational expressions to define what value of the variable makes the denominator zero. For this particular value, the expression is undefined.

Multiplication of rational expressions is performed like multiplication of fractions. The numerators are multiplied; then, the denominators are multiplied. The final fraction is then simplified. The expressions are simplified by factoring and canceling out common terms. In the following example, the numerator of the second expression can be factored first to simplify the expression before multiplying:

$$\frac{x^2}{(x - 4)} \times \frac{x^2 - x - 12}{2}$$

$$\frac{x^2}{(x - 4)} \times \frac{(x - 4)(x + 3)}{2}$$

The $(x - 4)$ on the top and bottom cancel out:

$$\frac{x^2}{1} \times \frac{(x + 3)}{2}$$

Then multiplication is performed, resulting in:

$$\frac{x^3 + 3x^2}{2}$$

Dividing rational expressions is similar to the division of fractions, where division turns into multiplying by a reciprocal. So, the following expression can be rewritten as a multiplication problem:

$$\frac{x^2 - 3x + 7}{x - 4} \div \frac{x^2 - 5x + 3}{x - 4}$$

$$\frac{x^2 - 3x + 7}{x - 4} \times \frac{x - 4}{x^2 - 5x + 3}$$

The $x - 4$ cancels out, leaving:

$$\frac{x^2 - 3x + 7}{x^2 - 5x + 3}$$

The final answers should always be completely simplified. If a function is composed of a rational expression, the zeros of the graph can be found from setting the polynomial in the numerator as equal to zero and solving. The values that make the denominator equal to zero will either exist on the graph as a hole or a vertical asymptote.

Linear Equations and Inequalities

Linear relationships describe the way two quantities change with respect to each other. The relationship is defined as linear because a line is produced if all the sets of corresponding values are graphed on a coordinate grid. When expressing the linear relationship as an equation, the equation is often written in the form $y = mx + b$ (slope-intercept form) where m and b are numerical values and x and y are variables:

$$y = 5x + 10$$

Given a linear equation and the value of either variable (x or y), the value of the other variable can be determined.

When graphing a linear equation, note that the ratio of the change of the y-coordinate to the change in the x-coordinate is constant between any two points on the resulting line, no matter which two points are chosen. In other words, in a pair of points on a line, (x_1, y_1) and (x_2, y_2), with $x_1 \neq x_2$ so that the two points are distinct, then the ratio $\frac{y_2 - y_1}{x_2 - x_1}$ will be the same, regardless of which particular pair of points are chosen. This ratio, $\frac{y_2 - y_1}{x_2 - x_1}$, is called the **slope** of the line and is frequently denoted with the letter m. If slope m is positive, then the line goes upward when moving to the right, while if slope m is negative, then the line goes downward when moving to the right. If the slope is 0, then the line is called **horizontal**, and the y-coordinate is constant along the entire line. In lines where the x-coordinate is constant along the entire line, y is not actually a function of x. For such lines, the slope is not defined. These lines are called **vertical** lines.

Linear functions may take forms other than $y = ax + b$. The most common forms of linear equations are explained below:

1. Standard Form: $Ax + By = C$, in which the slope is given by $m = \frac{-A}{B}$, and the y-intercept is given by $\frac{C}{B}$.

2. Slope-Intercept Form: $y = mx + b$, where the slope is m and the y intercept is b.

3. Point-Slope Form: $y - y_1 = m(x - x_1)$, where the slope is m and (x_1, y_1) is any point on the chosen line.

4. Two-Point Form:

$$\frac{y - y_1}{x - x_1} = \frac{y_2 - y_1}{x_2 - x_1}$$

(x_1, y_1) and (x_2, y_2) are any two distinct points on the chosen line. Note that the slope is given by:

$$m = \frac{y_2 - y_1}{x_2 - x_1}$$

5. Intercept Form:

$$\frac{x}{x_1} + \frac{y}{y_1} = 1$$

x_1 is the x-intercept and y_1 is the y-intercept.

These five ways to write linear equations are all useful in different circumstances. Depending on the given information, it may be easier to write one of the forms over another.

If $y = mx$, y is directly proportional to x. In this case, changing x by a factor changes y by that same factor. If $y = \frac{m}{x}$, y is inversely proportional to x. For example, if x is increased by a factor of 3, then y will be decreased by the same factor, 3.

The first steps to solving linear equations are distributing, if necessary, and combining any like terms on the same side of the equation. Sides of an equation are separated by an *equal* sign. Next, the equation is manipulated to show the variable on one side. Whatever is done to one side of the equation must be done to the other side of the equation to remain equal. Inverse operations are then used to isolate the variable and undo the order of operations backwards. Addition and subtraction are undone, then multiplication and division are undone.

For example, solve $4(t - 2) + 2t - 4 = 2(9 - 2t)$

Distributing: $4t - 8 + 2t - 4 = 18 - 4t$

Combining like terms: $6t - 12 = 18 - 4t$

Adding $4t$ to each side to move the variable: $10t - 12 = 18$

Adding 12 to each side to isolate the variable: $10t = 30$

Dividing each side by 10 to isolate the variable: $t = 3$

The answer can be checked by substituting the value for the variable into the original equation, ensuring that both sides calculate to be equal.

Linear inequalities express the relationship between unequal values. More specifically, they describe in what way the values are unequal. A value can be greater than (>), less than (<), greater than or equal to (≥), or less than or equal to (≤) another value. $5x + 40 > 65$ is read as *five times a number added to forty is greater than sixty-five.*

When solving a linear inequality, the solution is the set of all numbers that make the statement true. The inequality $x + 2 \geq 6$ has a solution set of 4 and every number greater than 4 (4.01; 5; 12; 107; etc.). Adding 2 to 4 or any number greater than 4 results in a value that is greater than or equal to 6. Therefore, $x \geq 4$ is the solution set.

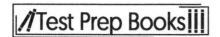

To algebraically solve a linear inequality, follow the same steps as those for solving a linear equation. The inequality symbol stays the same for all operations *except* when multiplying or dividing by a negative number. If multiplying or dividing by a negative number while solving an inequality, the relationship reverses (the sign flips). In other words, > switches to < and vice versa. Multiplying or dividing by a positive number does not change the relationship, so the sign stays the same. An example is shown below.

Solve $-2x - 8 \leq 22$ for the value of x.

Add 8 to both sides to isolate the variable:

$$-2x \leq 30$$

Divide both sides by -2 to solve for x:

$$x \geq -15$$

Solutions of a linear equation or a linear inequality are the values of the variable that make a statement true. In the case of a linear equation, the solution set (list of all possible solutions) typically consists of a single numerical value. To find the solution, the equation is solved by isolating the variable. For example, solving the equation $3x - 7 = -13$ produces the solution $x = -2$. The only value for x which produces a true statement is -2. This can be checked by substituting -2 into the original equation to check that both sides are equal. In this case, -2 is a solution:

$$3(-2) - 7 = -13 \rightarrow -13 = -13$$

Although linear equations generally have one solution, this is not always the case. If there is no value for the variable that makes the statement true, there is no solution to the equation. Consider the equation:

$$x + 3 = x - 1$$

There is no value for *x* in which adding 3 to the value produces the same result as subtracting one from the value. Conversely, if any value for the variable makes a true statement, the equation has an infinite number of solutions. Consider the equation:

$$3x + 6 = 3(x + 2)$$

Any number substituted for *x* will result in a true statement (both sides of the equation are equal).

By manipulating equations like the two above, the variable of the equation will cancel out completely. If the remaining constants express a true statement (ex. $6 = 6$), then all real numbers are solutions to the equation. If the constants left express a false statement (ex. $3 = -1$), then no solution exists for the equation.

Solving a linear inequality requires all values that make the statement true to be determined. For example, solving $3x - 7 \geq -13$ produces the solution $x \geq -2$. This means that -2 and any number greater than -2 produces a true statement. Solution sets for linear inequalities will often be displayed using a number line. If a value is included in the set ($\geq$ or $\leq$), a shaded dot is placed on that value and an arrow extends in the direction of the solution. For a variable > or $\geq$ a number, the arrow will point right on a number line, the direction where the numbers increase. If a variable is < or $\leq$ a number, the arrow will point left on a number line, which is the direction where the numbers decrease. If the value is not

64

included in the set (> or <), an open (unshaded) circle on that value is used with an arrow in the appropriate direction.

It looks like this:

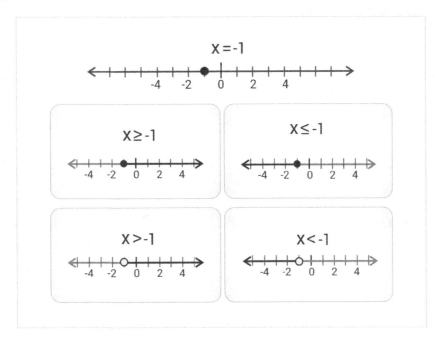

Similar to linear equations, a linear inequality may have a solution set consisting of all real numbers, or can contain no solution. When solved algebraically, a linear inequality in which the variable cancels out and results in a true statement (ex. $7 \geq 2$) has a solution set of all real numbers. A linear inequality in which the variable cancels out and results in a false statement (ex. $7 \leq 2$) has no solution.

Systems of Equations

To start, a review of linear equations is needed. When given a linear equation, the equation will show two expressions containing a variable that must be equal. Thus, one example would be:

$$3x + 1 = 16$$

To solve such an equation, remember two things. First, the final solution must equal x. Second, if two quantities are equal, one can add, subtract, multiply, or divide the same thing on both sides and end up with a true equation. In this case, subtract 1 from both sides, which would be a new equation, $3x = 15$. Then, divide both sides by 3 to get $x = 5$.

A system of equations can be solved by the same kinds of considerations, except that in this case, there are multiple equations that all have to be true at the same time. This means there are some new choices for finding solutions. First, if there are two equations, add the left side and the right side to get a new equation (the left side of the new equation is the sum of the left sides, and the right side of the new equation will be the sum of the right sides). Second, if one equation is solved in terms of one of the variables, the expression can be substituted into the other equation. Otherwise, the approach to solving these systems will be similar to solving a single equation.

A system of equations with at least one solution is called a **consistent system**. If a system has no solution, it is called an **inconsistent system**.

A **linear system** of equations with two variables and two equations is a system with variables x and y (or any other pair of variables) and equations that can be simplified to yield:

$$ax + by = c, dx + ey = f$$

There are two ways to solve such a system. The first is to solve for one variable in terms of the other and substitute it into the other equation. For example, from the first equation, $by = c - ax$, that means:

$$y = \frac{c - ax}{b}$$

$\frac{c-ax}{b}$ can be substituted for y in the second equation. This approach is called solving by **substitution**.

The other possibility is to multiply one of the equations on both sides by some constant, and then add the result to the other equation so that it eliminates one variable. For example, given the pair $ax + by = c, dx + ey = f$, multiply the first equation by $-\frac{d}{a}$. Then the first equation would become:

$$-dx - \frac{db}{a}y = -\frac{cd}{a}$$

Adding the equations results in the x terms canceling, and an equation that only involves the variable y. This approach is called solving by **elimination**.

To illustrate the two approaches, use the system of equations:

$$2x + 4y = 6, x + y = 2$$

This system will be solved using both methods.

By substitution: starting with the second equation, subtract y from both sides. The result of this step is:

$$x = 2 - y$$

Substitute $2 - y$ for x in the first equation, with a result of:

$$2(2 - y) + 4y = 6$$

This simplifies to:

$$4 - 2y + 4y = 6, 2y = 2, y = 1$$

Then, substitute 1 for y into $x = 2 - y$ to find the value for x: $x = 2 - 1 = 1$ or $x = 1$. So, $x = 1$ and $y = 1$.

To solve by elimination, start with:

$$2x + 4y = 6, x + y = 2$$

66

To cancel the $2x$ in the first equation, place $a - 2x$ in the second equation on the left. The second equation is then multiplied by -2 on both sides, which gives:

$$-2x - 2y = -4$$

The equations are added together:

$$2x + 4y + (-2x - 2y) = 6 - 4$$

The x terms cancel, and the result is $2y = 2$ or $y = 1$. Substituting this back into either of the original equations has a result of $x = 1$. So $x = 1, y = 1$.

Solving for X in Proportions

Proportions are commonly used to solve word problems to find unknown values such as x that are some percent or fraction of a known number. Proportions are solved by cross-multiplying and then dividing to arrive at x. The following examples show how this is done:

1) $\dfrac{75\%}{90\%} = \dfrac{25\%}{x}$

To solve for x, the fractions must be cross multiplied:

$$(75\% \times x = 90\% \times 25\%)$$

To make things easier, let's convert the percentages to decimals:

$$(0.9 \times 0.25 = 0.225 = 0.75x)$$

To get rid of x's coefficient, each side must be divided by that same coefficient to get the answer $x = 0.3$. The question could ask for the answer as a percentage or fraction in lowest terms, which are 30% and $\dfrac{3}{10}$, respectively.

2) $\dfrac{x}{12} = \dfrac{30}{96}$

Cross-multiply: $96x = 30 \times 12$
Multiply: $96x = 360$
Divide: $x = 360 \div 96$
Answer: $x = 3.75$

3) $\dfrac{0.5}{3} = \dfrac{x}{6}$

Cross-multiply: $3x = 0.5 \times 6$
Multiply: $3x = 3$
Divide: $x = 3 \div 3$
Answer: $x = 1$

You may have noticed there's a faster way to arrive at the answer. If there is an obvious operation being performed on the proportion, the same operation can be used on the other side of the proportion to solve for x. For example, in the first practice problem, 75% became 25% when divided by 3, and upon doing the same to 90%, the correct answer of 30% would have been found with much less legwork.

However, these questions aren't always so intuitive, so it's a good idea to work through the steps, even if the answer seems apparent from the outset.

Word Problems and Applications

In word problems, multiple quantities are often provided with a request to find some kind of relation between them. This often will mean that one variable (the dependent variable whose value needs to be found) can be written as a function of another variable (the independent variable whose value can be figured from the given information). The usual procedure for solving these problems is to start by giving each quantity in the problem a variable, and then figuring the relationship between these variables.

For example, suppose a car gets 25 miles per gallon. How far will the car travel if it uses 2.4 gallons of fuel? In this case, y would be the distance the car has traveled in miles, and x would be the amount of fuel burned in gallons (2.4). Then the relationship between these variables can be written as an algebraic equation, $y = 25x$. In this case, the equation is $y = 25 \times 2.4 = 60$, so the car has traveled 60 miles.

Some word problems require more than just one simple equation to be written and solved. Consider the following situations and the linear equations used to model them.

Suppose Margaret is 2 miles to the east of John at noon. Margaret walks to the east at 3 miles per hour. How far apart will they be at 3 p.m.? To solve this, x would represent the time in hours past noon, and y would represent the distance between Margaret and John. Now, noon corresponds to the equation where x is 0, so the y-intercept is going to be 2. It's also known that the slope will be the rate at which the distance is changing, which is 3 miles per hour. This means that the slope will be 3 (be careful at this point: if units were used, other than miles and hours, for x and y variables, a conversion of the given information to the appropriate units would be required first). The simplest way to write an equation given the y-intercept, and the slope is the Slope-Intercept form, which is $y = mx + b$. Recall that m here is the slope, and b is the y-intercept. So, $m = 3$ and $b = 2$. Therefore, the equation will be:

$$y = 3x + 2$$

The word problem asks how far to the east Margaret will be from John at 3 p.m., which means when x is 3. So, substitute $x = 3$ into this equation to obtain:

$$y = 3 \times 3 + 2 = 9 + 2 = 11$$

Therefore, she will be 11 miles to the east of him at 3 p.m.

For another example, suppose that a box with 4 cans in it weighs 6 lbs., while a box with 8 cans in it weighs 12 lbs. Find out how much a single can weighs. To do this, let x denote the number of cans in the box, and y denote the weight of the box with the cans in lbs. This line touches two pairs: $(4, 6)$ and $(8, 12)$. A formula for this relation could be written using the two-point form, with:

$$x_1 = 4, y_1 = 6$$

$$x_2 = 8, y_2 = 12$$

This would yield $\frac{y-6}{x-4} = \frac{12-6}{8-4}$, or:

$$\frac{y-6}{x-4} = \frac{6}{4} = \frac{3}{2}$$

However, only the slope is needed to solve this problem, since the slope will be the weight of a single can. From the computation, the slope is $\frac{3}{2}$. Therefore, each can weighs $\frac{3}{2}$ lb.

Practice Quiz

1. What is the length of the hypotenuse of a right triangle with one leg equal to 3 centimeters and the other leg equal to 4 centimeters?
    a. 7 cm
    b. 5 cm
    c. 25 cm
    d. 12 cm
    e. 49 cm

2. Solve this equation:
$$9x + x - 7 = 16 + 2x$$

    a. $x = -4$
    b. $x = 3$
    c. $x = \frac{9}{8}$
    d. $x = \frac{23}{8}$
    e. $x = \frac{3}{4}$

3. Which of the following statements is true about the two lines below?

    a. The two lines are parallel but not perpendicular.
    b. The two lines are perpendicular but not parallel.
    c. The two lines are both parallel and perpendicular.
    d. The two lines are neither parallel nor perpendicular.
    e. The two lines are vertical.

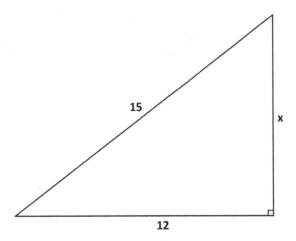
4. What is the value of x in the following triangle?

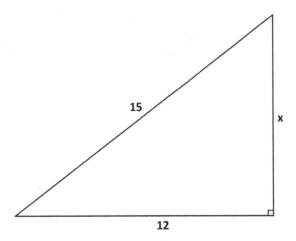

a. 19.2
b. 9
c. 3
d. 7.5
e. 81

5. If the sides of a cube are 5 centimeters long, what is its volume?
a. 10 cm^3
b. 15 cm^3
c. 50 cm^3
d. 125 cm^3
e. 25 cm^3

See answers on next page

Answer Explanations

1. B: This answer is correct because $3^2 + 4^2$ is $9 + 16$, which is 25. Taking the square root of 25 is 5. Choice A is not the correct answer because that is $3 + 4$. Choice C is not the correct answer because that is stopping at $3^2 + 4^2$ is $9 + 16$, which is 25. Choice D is not the correct answer because that is 3×4. Choice E is not correct because that is $(3 + 4)^2$.

2. D:

$$9x + x - 7 = 16 + 2x \qquad \text{Combine } 9x \text{ and } x.$$

$$10x - 7 = 16 + 2x$$

$$10x - 7 + 7 = 16 + 2x + 7 \qquad \text{Add 7 to both sides to remove the } -7.$$

$$10x = 23 + 2x$$

$$10x - 2x = 23 + 2x - 2x \qquad \begin{array}{l} \text{Subtract } 2x \text{ from both sides to move it to the other side} \\ \text{of the equation.} \end{array}$$

$$8x = 23$$

$$\frac{8x}{8} = \frac{23}{8} \qquad \text{Divide by 8 to get } x \text{ by itself.}$$

$$x = \frac{23}{8}$$

3. D: Parallel lines will never intersect. Therefore, the lines are not parallel. Perpendicular lines intersect to form a right angle (90°). Although the lines intersect, they do not form a right angle, which is usually indicated with a box at the intersection point. Therefore, the lines are not perpendicular. The lines are also not vertical lines.

4. B: This problem can be solved using the Pythagorean Theorem. The triangle has a hypotenuse of 15 and one leg of 12. These values can be substituted into the Pythagorean formula to yield:

$$12^2 + b^2 = 15^2$$

$$144 + b^2 = 225$$

$$81 = b^2$$

$$b = 9$$

In this problem, b is represented by x so $x = 9$ is the correct answer.

5. D: The volume of a cube with sides of length s is $V = s^3$. Here, $s = 5$, so $V = 5^3 = 125$.

Reading Comprehension

Good reading comprehension skills are vital for successful standardized test taking in the military. Reading comprehension is tested to determine whether prospective applicants are able to parse out critical and accurate information quickly and efficiently. The topics addressed in this section will help in this pursuit.

Topics and Main Ideas

One of the principle skills for effective reading comprehension is the ability to accurately and quickly identify an author's points and intentions. When presented with blocks of written information, it's easy for test takers to feel overwhelmed. One of the best ways to get a handle on a text is to visually divide the writing into manageable chunks.

First, test takers should begin by looking for the author's topic(s) and main idea(s), as there is a difference between them.

A **topic** is the subject of a written selection; it supports an overall theme, idea, or purpose of a passage. Here's where reading comprehension can get tricky. An author can choose to have more than one topic in a written passage, with each building on the previous one to support an overall conclusion or thesis.

The **main idea** is information that expands upon and supports a topic. Main ideas can be thought of as the supporting frame that makes up a building. As a whole, the structure—the building itself—is made up of various sections. Each section is positioned to support other sections and each section contributes to the whole structure. A writing passage offers a topic (the building) that's supported by the main ideas (an internal structure).

Another way to view topics and their main ideas is to consider these three words: *what, how,* and *why*. A written passage has a purpose—a *what*. The topic of a written passage is the *what*. The main ideas expand on *how* and *why*.

It's important to separate topics and main ideas from the rest of the text. In most cases, simply skimming a text selection is effective. Generally speaking, an author will use titles or important first paragraph sentences (called **topic sentences**) to indicate what the passage is about and what each main idea will address.

Review the passage below. In this case, words and phrases that indicate the *topic* appear in **bold**. Words and phrases that indicate *main ideas* appear in *italics*.

> **Forces acting on an aircraft are called the aerodynamics of flight.** *There are four: thrust, drag, lift, and weight.* It's essential for pilots to understand these forces (or aerodynamics) in order to control them during flight. *Thrust* is a forward-moving force caused by power. In the case of aircraft, this power is provided by propellers, rotors, and engines. Thrust works against the force of drag, which is a rear-moving force. *Drag* is caused by air disturbance created by the plane itself in terms of its wings or other protrusions. *Weight* is a downward force caused by gravity and includes factors such as the combined weight of the aircraft and crew. *Lift* is diametrically opposed to weight, acting in a perpendicular motion to the flight path. It's also produced by air effects.

The topic of the passage is the aerodynamics of flight—specifically, the forces acting on an aircraft. The topic is supported by the building blocks—its main ideas—that explain what and how aerodynamic forces affect aircraft. These main ideas include thrust, drag, lift, and weight. The passage continues to explain what each force is by definition and how it acts on an aircraft. By quickly separating the topic and main ideas, it becomes clear what the passage is about and where the author is going. In this case, additional words and phrases have been italicized, as they indicate main ideas. But boiled down, the first sentence and four words (thrust, drag, lift, and weight) indicate the author's topic and main ideas.

Supporting Details

There are many different construction materials in a single building. Supporting details are like those materials. Like steel, bricks, wood, and concrete, the supporting details support the larger structure (the main idea or ideas) and, in turn, the entire building itself (the topic).

Supporting details usually (but don't always) appear after the first sentence in a paragraph. Supporting details always give the specifics to develop and support the main idea. They may describe, explain, catalog items, identify, or expand with specifics. Understanding supporting details requires careful attention. The following paragraph has its main supporting details highlighted in **bold**. Notice that even the supporting detail of wing curvature is supported with examples.

> Lift is one of the four forces that affect flight and aerodynamics. These forces cause an object to move up, down, faster, or slower. **Lift is affected by the shape of a plane's wings and their curvature.** When air pressure is diminished over the top of the wings, an aircraft will follow an upward movement. **Changing the curvature of an object's wings is a way to manipulate lift. Even everyday objects are affected by potential lift in flight.** A kite, for example, is able to lift due to its curved shape.

Another way to identify supporting details is looking for words such as *first*, *second*, *next*, and *last*, and phrases such as *for example* and *for instance*. These words can indicate that supporting details follow. The paragraph below makes use of these words and phrases:

> Thrust, drag, weight, and lift are four forces that act in aerodynamics. *First*, thrust, or the forward force produced by power, overcomes drag. *Second*, drag is the force that disrupts aircraft in some manner. It's a rearward force that disrupts airflow around distended objects. *Next*, weight is the downward force caused by gravity. *For example*, the combined weight of any crew, baggage, and the craft itself will affect downward pull. *Lastly*, lift is the force that opposes weight, acting perpendicularly to the aircraft's flight path. All forces combined are referred to as the aerodynamics of flight.

In these examples, the first sentence of the paragraph indicates the topic (the four forces of aerodynamics). The subsequent sentences contain supporting details that expand on the topic.

Topic and Summary Sentences

Notice the last sentence in the last example: "All forces combined are referred to as the aerodynamics of flight." This summarizes the main topic and concludes the paragraph. It also re-emphasizes the topic sentence. Topic and summary sentences are another quick way to skim for the topic(s) the author intended and glean information about supporting detail.

Often, a paragraph will not be so neatly structured. Not all passages contain topic and summary sentences. In fact, larger passages of text will only contain transition ideas between supporting details or other topics. Writing structure is frequently complicated and not always conveniently organized within single paragraphs. In these instances, it's necessary to read more in order to identify a topic.

Test takers can think of topic and summary sentences as clear identifiers with consistent characteristics. Both are usually free of new terminology and avoid introducing new ideas. Ideally, a topic sentence appears first and a summary sentence appears last. Supporting details usually appear between them. The previous passage appears again below, now with the topic and summary sentences in **bold**.

> **Thrust, drag, weight, and lift are four forces that act in aerodynamics.** First, thrust, or the forward force produced by power, overcomes drag. Second, drag is the force that disrupts aircraft in some manner. It's a rearward force that disrupts airflow around distended objects. Next, weight is the downward force caused by gravity. For example, the combined weight of any crew, baggage, and the craft itself will affect downward pull. Lastly, lift is the force that opposes weight, acting perpendicularly to the aircraft's flight path. **All forces combined are referred to as the aerodynamics of flight.**

That was a fairly straightforward illustration, but what if a passage isn't so clearly constructed? Consider this example:

> Crew, baggage, and the aircraft itself all affect the force of weight. Lift becomes important in counteracting weight, acting perpendicularly to an aircraft's flight path. A thrusting force is produced by power and counteracts drag. Drag is the force that disrupts a craft's airflow. All these forces combined act within aerodynamics.

In the above passage, there's no "first" topic sentence. Simply assuming the last sentence is the summary sentence doesn't give all the information. At best, the last sentence indicates the paragraph is about combined forces acting within aerodynamics. Therefore, it's necessary to read the entire paragraph. Parsing out words and information becomes critical. By looking at the first words of each sentence, including potentially unfamiliar words, and at words separated by punctuation like commas, the main topic becomes easier to identify:

> *Crew*, *baggage*, and the *aircraft* itself all affect the *weight* of *force*. *Lift* becomes important in counteracting weight, acting perpendicularly to an aircraft's flight path. A *thrusting force* is produced by power and counteracts drag. *Drag* is the force that disrupts a craft's airflow. All these forces combined act within aerodynamics.

Paragraphs without concise topic and summary sentences can usually be understood with more detailed attention to reading.

Predictions Based on Prior Knowledge

Guessing what will happen next in a written passage is based on prior knowledge. This is called a **prediction**. Prior knowledge is the information a reader already possesses. This skill is important in

reading comprehension, as it allows the reader to logically predict what's ahead based on previous reading and experience. Predict what happens next in the below passage:

> The aircraft began rocking and rolling without warning. The plane rolled to the right, then to the left. There was a definite change in pressure. A loud metallic sound screeched throughout the cabin. Things were definitely not going according to plan any longer.

Based on the passage, the reader knows the aircraft is in some sort of distress. Furthermore, based on prior knowledge, the reader may predict one of two things: the aircraft will land safely or it won't. Notice that predicting the outcome while reading can be very tricky. Predictions are not always accurate (one way or another); but in the passage above, only two predictions are possible. These predictions are based on a reader's prior knowledge of flight experience and common sense. Determining the root cause of the aircraft's issue and final outcome would require further information. Therefore, a reader must be willing to readjust predictions as new details become available.

Making Inferences

An **inference** is a conclusion based on evidence and reason. Making inferences involves determining information that is implied rather than stated outright. A reader cannot usually infer conclusions merely by reading the first and last sentences of a passage. Making inferences requires attention to detail. It's important not to go beyond the written information in a passage and come to conclusions that are not inferred by the author. This can be tricky, but practice will help. Consider the following sentence:

> The pilot was relieved as the airstrip suddenly appeared below.

From this sentence, the reader can infer that the pilot was having difficulty during the flight. But one cannot infer that bad weather or an incorrect flight path was the cause of the problem. The reader also cannot infer that the complication was even resolved or that the flight ended safely. The reader can only infer that something unexpected occurred during the flight and, as a result, the pilot was relieved to make visual contact with the landing area. Consider more information below:

> The pilot was relieved as the airstrip suddenly appeared below. It had been a long journey. His head pounded and sweat poured down his back. His breathing was labored, and his chest felt heavy. He was burning up.

At this point, the reader can make new inferences based on the additional information. One is that the pilot felt ill. Another is that a problem caused excessive heat in the aircraft. Still, the reader cannot come to a final conclusion based on the passage. Although the sentences above provide detail about the pilot's condition, the reader can only make an educated guess as to the actual problem. Finally, read the passage that follows:

> The pilot was relieved as the airstrip suddenly appeared below. It had been a long journey. His head pounded and sweat poured down his back. His breathing was labored and his chest felt heavy. He was burning up. His nerves were frayed, and he was at wits' end. He never thought the flight simulation would be so difficult to navigate, but he'd done it, and he was about to bring it home.

At this point, the reader has enough detail to infer that the pilot was in training and simply glad to be on his way to finishing a difficult flight simulation. Keep in mind that making an inference involves drawing a conclusion based on evidence and reason. The evidence is the pilot's demeanor, physical symptoms,

and, most importantly, the words *flight simulation*. Reason dictates that this is most likely a training situation. Inference here, however, doesn't indicate that the pilot successfully completed the simulation in good health.

Drawing Conclusions

Using inference techniques and their own life experience, readers should be able to draw conclusions from the information they read. Words such as *may*, *can*, and *often* indicate calls for a conclusion. Again, readers must be careful to draw conclusions based only on the information contained in a particular passage. They should not embellish or fill in the blanks with their imagination. Making faulty assumptions can lead to incorrect conclusions and the wrong test answers.

In a reading comprehension passage, test takers should look for key words indicating that drawing a conclusion is appropriate, then they should check the corresponding test answers. It is generally recommended to avoid answers that use all-or-nothing indicators. Words and phrases such as *always* and *never* can usually be eliminated.

Sequence

The order within text is called **sequence**. Test takers should look for identifying words such as *initially*, *then*, and *last,* as well as words that indicate steps such as *first*, *second*, and *next*. Reading a passage for details that aren't in the correct order will lead to incorrect test answers, especially if the text covers specific how-to information.

Sequence may also be implied. Read the sentence below:

> The pilot prepared the flight plan, double-checked her gear, and then boarded the plane.

Clearly, the pilot boarded the plane last. She didn't double check her gear first, then prepare the flight plan. While the sentence doesn't state the pilot's actions in numerical steps, the sequence is implied by the position of the phrases and logical inference.

Sequence doesn't always occur first to last. Sometimes, an author may reverse sequence or imply sequence in a way that may require readers to keep track. In this instance, making a brief outline can be helpful.

Let's practice the sequence. Read the following paragraph:

> Obtaining a reliable weather report before taking off is an essential part of flight. First, have the flight route clearly mapped. Next, prepare any information that may be required by organizations that provide weather information (for example, pilot qualifications and the type of flight planned). Then, check any and all sources available to ensure the information is consistent and accurate.

In the above passage, sequence is clearly implied by the use of the words *first*, *next*, and *then*. The steps follow in order. A pilot must determine a flight route before checking weather reports. Additionally, deciding if the flight will follow visual flight rules or instrument flight rules (the type of flight) ahead of time will affect the weather information the pilot needs to consider. Conducting these steps out of sequence simply makes no sense and could lead to a risky flight.

Comparison and Contrast

A reader must be able to compare and contrast information within a text in order to comprehend an author's meaning. **Comparison** involves relating two or more concepts or objects by finding commonalities. **Contrasting** is finding dissimilar characteristics between concepts or objects. Think of the construction materials referred to earlier: bricks, mortar, wood, concrete. Comparing these materials involves determining what they have in common. All are materials used in construction. All are available for builders to use according to a construction plan, and all of these materials are used widely throughout the industry. Contrasting them involves determining how they are different. Brick is certainly made differently from concrete and uses different materials. Wood is organic. Mortar is the material that holds brick together. Being able to compare and contrast allows the reader to link ideas and to differentiate between concepts.

Cause and Effect

Text may be structured to show cause and effect. **Cause** is an event that results in an occurrence. **Effect** is the direct result or results of the cause. In order to identify cause and effect relationships, readers should look for words such as *because*, *since*, *due to*, or *as a result*. Text that begins with *consequently* or *therefore* also indicates cause and effect.

Cause and effect might not be directly stated. In the sentence, *"The pilot neglected to consult all available weather information, and the flight didn't go as planned,"* a direct cause and effect relationship is implied. Because the pilot didn't consult all available weather information (the cause), the flight didn't go as planned (the effect). In this example, no direct words indicate cause and effect; however, cause and effect are directly related.

Identifying an Author's Position

Many times, standard reading comprehension assessments will require the reader to be able to identify an **author's position**. This is the stance or belief the writer states or implies. When considering a writer's overall message, it's important for readers to be on the lookout for their position. Even factual texts can take on bias. An author's position can be clearly stated, such as in a passage that argues an opinion, or it can be implied, such as a text that uses emotional language without a definitive statement of belief.

Identifying an Author's Purpose

An author's purpose is closely aligned with an author's position; however, the two are different. An **author's purpose** is the reason for the text itself. The purpose of the text may be to entertain or inform. An author may try to convince the reader through a firm statement and subsequent data to back up an argument. A persuasive purpose should be approached with caution, as the author clearly has an agenda and wishes to persuade the reader into agreement.

Authors may approach purpose in a variety of ways. The stronger the emotional language and the more information an author presents to argue a particular position, the more persuasive the intent. When a passage doesn't take a particular stance, but instead, is primarily telling a story, its purpose is more likely to entertain.

Readers should be vigilant for text that makes claims. Such text is persuasive. Text that gives information without making claims is likely informative in nature. The purpose may be to instruct the reader or to help the reader reach factual conclusions.

Word Meaning from Context

Stumbling over unfamiliar vocabulary is common; therefore, a reader must be able to identify word definitions from context. Determining *word meaning from context* involves using the words around an unfamiliar term to determine its meaning. Read the sentence below and pay attention to the word in italics:

> The pilot had been *apprised* of the weather well in advance; however, all the information she'd been provided still didn't quiet her fears.

In this instance, the reader may be unfamiliar with the word *apprised*. By looking at the word within its context, it's likely that *apprised* means informed. The first phrase indicates the pilot has been given weather information in advance. The second phrase actually states she'd been provided with that information before the flight.

Sometimes, a definition may not be so clearly identifiable. Read the sentence below and pay attention to the word in italics:

> A *horde* rushed towards *The Spirit of St Louis* that day, but off to the side, all alone on the Le Bourget field, stood a small boy who dreamed of one day becoming a pilot like Charles Lindbergh.

This sentence requires the reader to infer the meaning of the word *horde* using comparison and contrast. Because the passage contrasts people rushing to the plane with a lone boy standing off to the side, the reader must infer that *horde* means a large group.

Identifying a Logical Conclusion

Being able to identify a logical conclusion is an essential skill in reading comprehension. **Identifying a logical conclusion** is being able to form an opinion after reading a textual passage. This can help readers determine if they agree or disagree with an author. Clarifying a logical conclusion requires a reader to keep track of all pertinent points in a written passage. It also requires the reader to ask questions while reading and searching for answers that an author may provide. It's possible to draw several conclusions from a particular passage. An author may not provide a clearly stated conclusion, so readers should be careful. Logical conclusions should be directly supported by text. Readers should avoid "reading into" a passage and inventing supported text that doesn't exist in order to come to a conclusion.

Practice Quiz

The next five questions are based on the following passage:

George Washington emerged out of the American Revolution as an unlikely champion of liberty. On June 14, 1775, the Second Continental Congress created the Continental Army, and John Adams, serving in the Congress, nominated Washington to be its first commander. Washington had fought under the British during the French and Indian War, and his experience and prestige proved instrumental to the American war effort. Washington provided invaluable leadership, training, and strategy during the Revolutionary War. He emerged from the war as the embodiment of liberty and freedom from tyranny.

After vanquishing the heavily favored British forces, Washington could have pronounced himself the autocratic leader of the former colonies without any opposition, but he famously refused and returned to his Mount Vernon plantation. His restraint proved his commitment to the fledgling state's republicanism. Washington was later unanimously elected as the first American president. But it is Washington's farewell address that cemented his legacy as a visionary worthy of study.

In 1796, President Washington issued his farewell address by public letter. Washington enlisted his good friend, Alexander Hamilton, in drafting his most famous address. The letter expressed Washington's faith in the Constitution and rule of law. He encouraged his fellow Americans to put aside partisan differences and establish a national union. Washington warned Americans against meddling in foreign affairs and entering military alliances. Additionally, he stated his opposition to national political parties, which he considered partisan and counterproductive.

Americans would be wise to remember Washington's farewell, especially during presidential elections, when politics hit a fever pitch. They might want to question the political institutions that were not planned by the Founding Fathers, such as the nomination process and political parties themselves.

1. Which of the following statements is based on the information in the passage above?
   a. George Washington's background as a wealthy landholder directly led to his faith in equality, liberty, and democracy.
   b. George Washington would have opposed America's involvement in the Second World War.
   c. George Washington would not have been able to write such a great farewell address without the assistance of Alexander Hamilton.
   d. George Washington would probably not approve of modern political parties.
   e. George Washington would likely befriend former President Barack Obama.

2. What is the purpose of this passage?
   a. To caution American voters about being too political during election times because George Washington would not have agreed with holding elections
   b. To introduce George Washington to readers as a historical figure worthy of study
   c. To note that George Washington was more than a famous military hero
   d. To convince readers that George Washington is a hero of republicanism and liberty
   e. To inform American voters about a Founding Father's sage advice on a contemporary issue and explain its applicability to modern times

80

3. What is the tone of the passage?
   a. Informative
   b. Excited
   c. Bitter
   d. Comic
   e. Somber

4. What does the word *meddling* mean in paragraph 3?
   a. Supporting
   b. Speaking against
   c. Interfering
   d. Gathering
   e. Avoiding

5. According to the passage, what did George Washington do when he was offered a role as leader of the former colonies?
   a. He refused the offer.
   b. He accepted the offer.
   c. He became angry at the offer.
   d. He accepted the offer then regretted it later.
   e. He ignored the offer.

6. Osteoporosis is a medical condition that occurs when the body loses bone or makes too little bone tissue. This can lead to brittle, fragile bones that easily break. Bones are already porous, and when osteoporosis sets in, the spaces in bones become much larger, causing them to weaken. Both men and women can develop osteoporosis, though it is most common in women over age 50. Loss of bone can be silent and progressive, so it is important to be proactive in prevention of the disease.

The main purpose of this passage is to:
   a. Discuss some of the ways people contract osteoporosis
   b. Describe different treatment options for those with osteoporosis
   c. Explain how to prevent osteoporosis
   d. Define osteoporosis

7. Vacationers looking for a perfect experience should opt out of Disney parks and try a trip on Disney Cruise Lines. While a park offers rides, characters, and show experiences, it also includes long lines, often very hot weather, and enormous crowds. A Disney Cruise, on the other hand, is a relaxing, luxurious vacation that includes many of the same experiences as the parks, minus the crowds and lines. The cruise has top-notch food, maid service, water slides, multiple pools, Broadway-quality shows, and daily character experiences for kids. There are also many activities, such as bingo, trivia contests, and dance parties that can entertain guests of all ages. The cruise even stops at Disney's private island for a beach barbecue with characters, waterslides, and water sports. Those looking for the Disney experience without the hassle should book a Disney cruise.

The main purpose of this passage is to:
   a. Explain how to book a Disney cruise
   b. Show what Disney parks have to offer
   c. Show why Disney parks are expensive
   d. Compare Disney parks to the Disney cruise

8. Coaches of kids' sports teams are increasingly concerned about the behavior of parents at games. Parents are screaming and cursing at coaches, officials, players, and other parents. Physical fights have even broken out at games. Parents need to be reminded that coaches are volunteers, giving up their time and energy to help kids develop in their chosen sport. The goal of kids' sports teams is to learn and develop skills, but it's also to have fun. When parents are out of control at games and practices, it takes the fun out of the sport.

From this passage, it can be concluded that:
   a.   Coaches are modeling good behavior for kids.
   b.   Organized sports are not good for kids.
   c.   Parents' behavior at their kids' games needs to change.
   d.   Parents and coaches need to work together.

9. As summer approaches, drowning incidents will increase. Drowning happens very quickly and silently. Most people assume that drowning is easy to spot, but a person who is drowning doesn't make noise or wave his arms. Instead, he will have his head back and his mouth open, with just his face out of the water. A person who is truly in danger of drowning is not able to wave his arms in the air or move much at all. Recognizing these signs of drowning can prevent tragedy.

The main purpose of this passage is to:
   a.   Explain the dangers of swimming.
   b.   Show how to identify the signs of drowning.
   c.   Explain how to be a lifeguard.
   d.   Compare the signs of drowning.

10. Technology has been invading cars for the last several years, but there are some new high-tech trends that are pretty amazing. It is now standard in many car models to have a rear-view camera, hands-free phone and text, and a touch screen digital display. Music can be streamed from a paired cell phone, and some displays can even be programmed with a personal photo. Sensors beep to indicate there is something in the driver's path when reversing and changing lanes. Rain-sensing windshield wipers and lights are automatic, leaving the driver with little to do but watch the road and enjoy the ride. The next wave of technology will include cars that automatically parallel park, and a self-driving car is on the horizon. These technological advances make it a good time to be a driver.

It can be concluded from this paragraph that:
   a.   Technology will continue to influence how cars are made.
   b.   Windshield wipers and lights are always automatic.
   c.   It is standard to have a rear-view camera in all cars.
   d.   Technology has reached its peak in cars.

See answers on next page

Answer Explanations

1. D: Although Washington was from a wealthy background, the passage does not say that his wealth led to his republican ideals, so Choice A is not supported. Choice B also does not follow from the passage. Washington's warning against meddling in foreign affairs does not mean that he would oppose wars of every kind, so Choice B is incorrect. Choice C is also unjustified since the author does not indicate that Alexander Hamilton's assistance was absolutely necessary. Choice E is incorrect because we don't know which particular presidents Washington would befriend. Choice D is correct because the passage states that Washington's farewell address clearly opposes political parties and partisanship. The author then notes that presidential elections often hit a fever pitch of partisanship. Thus, it follows that George Washington would probably not approve of modern political parties and their involvement in presidential elections.

2. E: The author finishes the passage by applying Washington's farewell address to modern politics, so the purpose probably includes this application. Choice B is incorrect because George Washington is already a well-established historical figure; furthermore, the passage does not seek to introduce him. Choice C is incorrect because the author is not fighting a common perception that Washington was merely a military hero. Choice D is incorrect because the author is not convincing readers. Persuasion does not correspond to the passage. Choice E states the primary purpose.

3. A: The tone in this passage is informative. Choice B, excited, is incorrect, because there are not many word choices used that would indicate excitement from the author. Choice C, bitter, is incorrect. Although the author does make a suggestion in the last paragraph to Americans, the statement is not necessarily bitter, but based on the preceding information. Choice D, comic, is incorrect, as the author does not try to make the audience laugh, nor do they make light of the situation in any way. Choice E, somber, is incorrect since the passage isn't sad or mournful.

4. C: Interfering. Meddling means to interfere in something. Choice A is incorrect. One helpful thing would be to use the word in the sentence: "Washington warned Americans against 'supporting' in foreign affairs" does not make that much sense, so we can mark it off. Choice B, *speaking against*, is incorrect. This phrase would make sense in the sentence, but it goes against the meaning that is intended. George Washington warned against interference in foreign affairs, not speaking *against* foreign affairs. Choice D is also incorrect, because "gathering in foreign affairs" does not sound quite right. Choice E, *avoiding*, is incorrect because it is nearly the opposite of meddling. Choice C, *interfering*, is therefore the best choice for this question.

5. A: When Washington was offered a role as leader of the former colonies, he refused the offer. This is explained in the first sentence of the second paragraph. He did not simply ignore the offer, as he "famously" refused it. All of the other answer choices are incorrect and not mentioned in the passage.

6. D: The main point of this passage is to define osteoporosis. Choice A is incorrect because the passage does not list ways that people contract osteoporosis. Choice B is incorrect because the passage does not mention any treatment options. While the passage does briefly mention prevention, it does not explain how, so Choice C is incorrect.

7. D: The passage compares Disney cruises with Disney parks. It does not discuss how to book a cruise, so Choice A is incorrect. Choice B is incorrect because though the passage does mention some of the

83

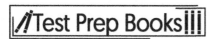

park attractions, it is not the main point. The passage does not mention the cost of either option, so Choice C is also incorrect.

8. C: The main point of this paragraph is that parents need to change their poor behavior at their kids' sporting events. Choice A is incorrect because the coaches' behavior is not mentioned in the paragraph. Choice B suggests that sports are bad for kids, when the paragraph is about parents' behavior, so it is incorrect. While Choice D may be true, it offers a specific solution to the problem, which the paragraph does not discuss.

9. B: The point of this passage is to show what drowning looks like. Choice A is incorrect because while drowning is a danger of swimming, the passage doesn't include any other dangers. The passage is not intended for lifeguards specifically, but for a general audience, so Choice C is incorrect. There are a few signs of drowning, but the passage does not compare them; thus, Choice D is incorrect.

10. A: The passage discusses recent technological advances in cars and suggests that this trend will continue in the future with self-driving cars. Choice B and C are not true, so these are both incorrect. Choice D is also incorrect because the passage suggests continuing growth in technology, not a peak.

Situational Judgment

This section of the test measures your judgment when responding to interpersonal situations that are similar to those that you will face as an officer. Your response will be scored relative to a consensus judgment across experienced U.S. Air Force officers.

For each situation, you must pick the MOST EFFECTIVE and the LEAST EFFECTIVE way to respond to the situation.

The best approach to these questions is an analytical one. Try to take emotion out of the picture and judge what is the best logical approach to each situation. Choose the answer that will resolve the issue at hand as easily and quickly as possible. Your choice should also be one that will not lead to any further or new issues in the future. Although everyone will not view each situation exactly the same, the census response will help make up for this. This helps ensure that the truly most effective answer is chosen.

Practice Quiz

Situation 1

A group of airmen in your squadron are bullying a female pilot on social media. They are not sexually harassing her, but they are intimidating her, and you think it is affecting her confidence. You also know that reporting bullying can make things worse for the victim, especially for women in the military.

Possible Actions:

A. Approach the men who are bullying the pilot but do not inform the pilot first. Let the men know you will report them if they do not stop the behavior.

B. Approach the pilot and offer your support. Let her know that the men need to be reported, and you will report them if she doesn't.

C. Approach the pilot and offer your support. Offer to talk to the bullies and/or their superiors on her behalf, but do not take action without her consent.

D. Report your concerns to your superior officer and ask him to decide how to respond.

E. Do nothing. It's none of your business.

> **1. Select the MOST EFFECTIVE action (A-E) in response to the situation.**
> **2. Select the LEAST EFFECTIVE action (A-E) in response to the situation.**

Situation 2

You are a team leader in charge of three junior airmen. One of your team members expresses the hope that they will be assigned a certain task. You had intended to assign that task to another airman, who you believe would be more capable in the role.

Possible Actions:

A. Give the job to the airman who wants the role the most.

B. Give the job to the airman who is most suited to the role.

C. Assign the role at random or rotate it among all three airmen.

D. Perform the task yourself to avoid causing conflict.

E. Ask the third team member how they would assign the role.

> **3. Select the MOST EFFECTIVE action (A-E) in response to the situation.**
> **4. Select the LEAST EFFECTIVE action (A-E) in response to the situation.**

See answers on next page

Answer Explanations

1. C: (Most effective) It is most effective to offer support to your team members so that they know they can rely on you.

2. E: (Least effective) It would be least effective to not step in and at the very least offer your support.

3. B: (Most effective) It is most effective to assign the role to the most qualified airman.

4. E: (Least effective) It is least effective to involve the opinions of the airmen up for the role.

Self-Description Inventory

The self-description inventory is a personality test provided in the AFOQT. The self-description inventory is not included in the final score, so no one answer is better than another. Since these questions are helpful in assessing your personal characteristics, answer them as best you can and don't spend much time analyzing them. The purpose is to find an appropriate career match by comparing your answers to others who hold Air Force positions.

Physical Science

Structure of Matter

Elements, Compounds, and Mixtures

Everything that takes up space and has mass is composed of **matter**. Understanding the basic characteristics and properties of matter helps with classification and identification.

An **element** is a substance that cannot be chemically decomposed to a simpler substance, while still retaining the properties of the element.

Compounds are composed of two or more elements that are chemically combined. The constituent elements in the compound are in constant proportions by mass.

When a material can be separated by physical means (such as sifting it through a colander), it is called a **mixture**. Mixtures are categorized into two types: **heterogeneous** and **homogeneous**. Heterogeneous mixtures have physically distinct parts, which retain their different properties. A mix of salt and sugar is an example of a heterogeneous mixture. With heterogeneous mixtures, it is possible that different samples from the same parent mixture may have different proportions of each component in the mixture. For example, in the sugar and salt mixture, there may be uneven mixing of the two, causing one random tablespoon sample to be mostly salt, while a different tablespoon sample may be mostly sugar.

A homogeneous mixture, also called a **solution,** has uniform properties throughout a given sample. An example of a homogeneous solution is salt fully dissolved in warm water. In this case, any number of samples taken from the parent solution would be identical.

Atoms, Molecules, and Ions

The basic building blocks of matter are **atoms,** which are extremely small particles that retain their identity during chemical reactions. Atoms can be singular or grouped to form elements. Elements are composed of one type of atom with the same properties.

Molecules are a group of atoms—either the same or different types—that are chemically bonded together by attractive forces. For example, hydrogen and oxygen are both atoms but, when bonded together, form water.

Ions are electrically-charged particles that are formed from an atom or a group of atoms via the loss or gain of electrons.

Basic Properties of Solids, Liquids, and Gasses

Matter exists in certain **states**, or physical forms, under different conditions. These states are called **solid**, **liquid**, or **gas**.

A solid has a rigid, or set, form and occupies a fixed shape and volume. Solids generally maintain their shape when exposed to outside forces.

Liquids and gasses are considered fluids, which have no set shape. Liquids are fluid, yet are distinguished from gasses by their incompressibility (incapable of being compressed) and set volume. Liquids can be transferred from one container to another, but cannot be forced to fill containers of different volumes via compression without causing damage to the container. For example, if one attempts to force a given volume or number of particles of a liquid, such as water, into a fixed container, such as a small water bottle, the container would likely explode from the extra water.

A gas can easily be compressed into a confined space, such as a tire or an air mattress. Gasses have no fixed shape or volume. They can also be subjected to outside forces, and the number of gas molecules that can fill a certain volume vary with changes in temperature and pressure.

Basic Structure of an Atom

Atomic Models

Theories of the atomic model have developed over the centuries. The most commonly referenced model of an atom was proposed by Niels Bohr. Bohr studied the models of J.J. Thomson and Ernest Rutherford and adapted his own theories from these existing models. Bohr compared the structure of the atom to that of the Solar System, where there is a center, or nucleus, with various sized orbitals circulating around this nucleus. This is a simplified version of what scientists have discovered about atoms, including the structures and placements of any orbitals. Modern science has made further adaptations to the model, including the fact that orbitals are actually made of electron "clouds."

Atomic Structure: Nucleus, Electrons, Protons, and Neutrons

Following the Bohr model of the atom, the nucleus, or core, is made up of positively charged **protons** and neutrally charged **neutrons**. The neutrons are theorized to be in the nucleus with the protons to provide greater "balance" at the center of the atom. The nucleus of the atom makes up the majority (more than 99%) of the mass of an atom, while the orbitals surrounding the nucleus contain negatively charged **electrons**. The entire structure of an atom is incredibly small.

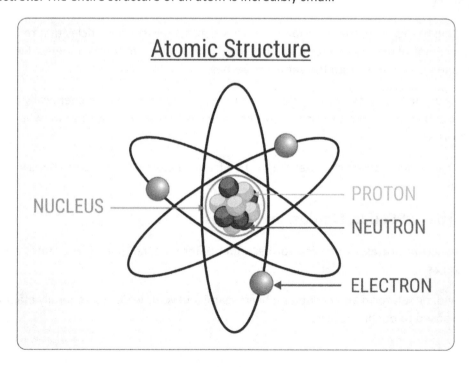

Atomic Number, Atomic Mass, and Isotopes

The **atomic number** of an atom is determined by the number of protons within the nucleus. When a substance is composed of atoms that all have the same atomic number, it is called an *element*. Elements are arranged by atomic number and grouped by properties in the **periodic table**.

An atom's **mass number** is determined by the sum of the total number of protons and neutrons in the atom. Most nuclei have a net neutral charge, and all atoms of one type have the same atomic number. However, there are some atoms of the same type that have a different mass number, due to an imbalance of neutrons. These are called **isotopes**. In isotopes, the atomic number, which is determined by the number of protons, is the same, but the mass number, which is determined by adding the protons and neutrons, is different due to the irregular number of neutrons.

Electron Arrangements

Electrons are most easily organized into distributions of subshells called **electron configurations**. Subshells fill from the inside (closest to the nucleus) to the outside. Therefore, once a subshell is filled, the next shell farther from the nucleus begins to fill, and so on. Atoms with electrons on the outside of a noble gas core (an atom with an electron inner shell that corresponds to the configuration of one of the noble gasses, such as Neon) and pseudo-noble gas core (an atom with an electron inner shell that is similar to that of a noble gas core along with (n -1) d^{10} electrons), are called **valence** electrons. Valence electrons are primarily the electrons involved in chemical reactions. The similarities in their configurations account for similarities in properties of groups of elements. Essentially, the groups (vertical columns) on the periodic table all have similar characteristics, such as solubility and reactivity, due to their similar electron configurations.

Basic Characteristics of Radioactive Materials

Radioisotopes

As mentioned, an isotope is a variation of an element with a different number of neutrons in the nucleus, causing the nucleus to be unstable. When an element is unstable, it will go through decay or disintegration. All man made elements are unstable and will break down. The length of time for an unstable element to break down is called the **half-life**. As an element breaks down, it forms other elements, known as daughters. Once a stable daughter is formed, the radioactive decay stops.

Characteristics of Alpha Particles, Beta Particles, and Gamma Radiation

As radioactive decay is occurring, the unstable element emits **alpha**, **beta**, and **gamma** radiation. Alpha and beta radiation are not as far-reaching or as powerful as gamma radiation. Alpha radiation is caused by the emission of two protons and two neutrons, while beta radiation is caused by the emission of either an electron or a positron. In contrast, gamma radiation is the release of photons of energy, not particles. This makes it the farthest-reaching and the most dangerous of these emissions.

Fission and Fusion

The splitting of an atom is referred to as fission, whereas the combination of two atoms into one is called fusion. To achieve fission and break apart an isotope, the unstable isotope is bombarded with high-speed particles. This process releases a large amount of energy and is what provides the energy in a nuclear power plant. Fusion occurs when two nuclei are merged to form a larger nucleus. The action of fusion also creates a tremendous amount of energy. To put the difference in the levels of energy between fission and fusion into perspective, the level of energy from fusion is what provides energy to the Earth's sun.

Basic Concepts and Relationships Involving Energy and Matter

The study of energy and matter, including heat and temperature, is called **thermodynamics**. There are four fundamental laws of thermodynamics, but the first two are the most commonly discussed.

First Law of Thermodynamics

The first law of thermodynamics is also known as the **conservation of energy**. This law states that energy cannot be created or destroyed, but is just transferred or converted into another form through a thermodynamic process. For example, if a liquid is boiled and then removed from the heat source, the liquid will eventually cool. This change in temperature is not because of a loss of energy or heat, but from a transfer of energy or heat to the surroundings. This can include the heating of nearby air molecules, or the transfer of heat from the liquid to the container or to the surface where the container is resting.

This law also applies to the idea of perpetual motion. A self-powered perpetual motion machine cannot exist. This is because the motion of the machine would inevitably lose some heat or energy to friction, whether from materials or from the air.

Second Law of Thermodynamics

The second law of thermodynamics is also known as the **law of entropy**. Entropy means chaos or disorder. In simple terms, this law means that all systems tend toward chaos. When one or more systems interact with another, the total entropy is the sum of the interacting systems, and this overall sum also tends toward entropy.

Conservation of Matter in Chemical Systems

The conservation of energy is seen in the conservation of matter in chemical systems. This is helpful when attempting to understand chemical processes, since these processes must balance out. This means that extra matter cannot be created or destroyed, it must all be accounted for through a chemical process.

Kinetic and Potential Energy

The conservation of energy also applies to the study of energy in physics. This is clearly demonstrated through the kinetic and potential energy involved in a system.

The energy of motion is called **kinetic energy**. If an object has height, or is raised above the ground, it has **potential energy**. The total energy of any given system is the sum of the potential energy and the kinetic energy of the subject (object) in the system.

Potential energy is expressed by the equation:

$$PE = mgh$$

Where m equals the object's mass, g equals acceleration caused by the gravitational force acting on the object, and h equals the height of the object above the ground.

Kinetic energy is expressed by the following equation:

$$KE = \frac{1}{2}\, mv^2$$

Where m is the mass of the object and v is the velocity of the object.

92

Conservation of energy allows the total energy for any situation to be calculated by the following equation:

$$KE + PE$$

For example, a roller coaster poised at the top of a hill has all potential energy, and when it reaches the bottom of that hill, as it is speeding through its lowest point, it has all kinetic energy. Halfway down the hill, the total energy of the roller coaster is about half potential energy and half kinetic energy. Therefore, the total energy is found by calculating both the potential energy and the kinetic energy and then adding them together.

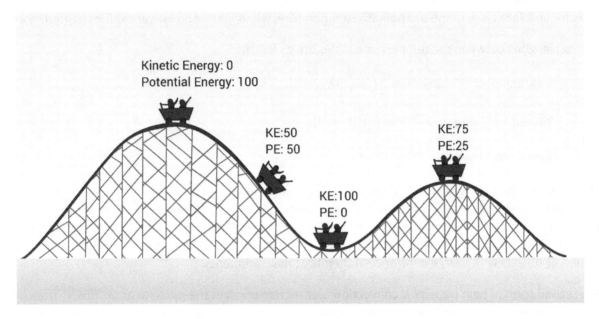

Transformations Between Different Forms of Energy

As stated by the conservation of energy, energy cannot be created or destroyed. If a system gains or loses energy, it is transformed within a single system from one type of energy to another or transferred from one system to another. For example, if the roller coaster system has potential energy that transfers to kinetic energy, the kinetic energy can then be transferred into thermal energy or heat released through braking as the coaster descends the hill. Energy can also transform from the chemical energy inside of a battery into the electrical energy that lights a train set. The energy released through nuclear fusion (when atoms are joined together, they release heat) is what supplies power plants with the energy for electricity. All energy is transferred from one form to another through different reactions. It can also be transferred through the simple action of atoms bumping into each other, causing a transfer of heat.

Differences Between Chemical and Physical Properties/Changes

A change in the physical form of matter, but not in its chemical identity, is known as a **physical change**. An example of a physical change is tearing a piece of paper in half. This changes the shape of the matter, but it is still paper.

Conversely, a **chemical change** alters the chemical composition or identity of matter. An example of a chemical change is burning a piece of paper. The heat necessary to burn the paper alters the chemical

93

composition of the paper. This chemical change cannot be easily undone, since it has created at least one form of matter different from the original matter.

Temperature Scales

There are three main temperature scales used in science. The scale most often used in the United States is the **Fahrenheit** scale. This scale is based on the measurement of water freezing at 32° F and water boiling at 212° F. The Celsius scale uses 0° C as the temperature for water freezing and 100° C for water boiling. The Celsius scale is the most widely used in the scientific community. The accepted measurement by the International System of Units (from the French Système international d'unités), or SI, for temperature is the Kelvin scale. This is the scale employed in thermodynamics, since its zero is the basis for absolute zero, or the unattainable temperature, when matter no longer exhibits degradation.

The conversions between the temperature scales are as follows:

$$°\text{Fahrenheit to } °\text{Celsius: } °C = \frac{5}{9}(°F - 32)$$

$$°\text{Celsius to } °\text{Fahrenheit: } °°F = \frac{9}{5}(°C) + 32$$

$$°\text{Celsius to Kelvin: } K = °C + 273.15$$

Transfer of Thermal Energy and Its Basic Measurement

There are three basic ways in which energy is transferred. The first is through **radiation**. Radiation is transmitted through electromagnetic waves and it does not need a medium to travel (it can travel in a vacuum). This is how the sun warms the Earth, and typically applies to large objects with great amounts of heat or objects with a large difference in their heat measurements.

The second form of heat transfer is **convection**. Convection involves the movement of "fluids" from one place to another. (The term **fluid** does not necessarily apply to a liquid, but any substance in which the molecules can slide past each other, such as gasses.) It is this movement that transfers the heat to or from an area. Generally, convective heat transfer occurs through diffusion, which is when heat moves from areas of higher concentrations of particles to those of lower concentrations of particles and less heat. This process of flowing heat can be assisted or amplified through the use of fans and other methods of forcing the molecules to move.

The final process is called **conduction**. Conduction involves transferring heat through the touching of molecules. Molecules can either bump into each other to transfer heat, or they may already be touching each other and transfer the heat through this connection. For example, imagine a circular burner on an electric stove top. The coil begins to glow orange near the base of the burner that is connected to the stove because it heats up first. Since the burner is one continuous piece of metal, the molecules are touching each other. As they pass heat along the coil, it begins to glow all the way to the end.

To determine the amount of heat required to warm the coil in the above example, the type of material from which the coil is made must be known. The quantity of heat required to raise one gram of a substance one degree Celsius (or Kelvin) at a constant pressure is called **specific heat**. This measurement can be calculated for masses of varying substances by using the following equation:

$$Q = C_p \times m \times \varDelta T$$

Where Q is the specific heat, C_p is the specific heat capacity of the material being used, m is the mass of the substance being used, and ΔT is the change in temperature.

A calorimeter is used to measure the heat of a reaction (either expelled or absorbed) and the temperature changes in a controlled system. A simple calorimeter can be made by using an insulated coffee cup with a thermometer inside. For this example, a lid of some sort would be preferred to prevent any escaping heat that could be lost by evaporation or convection.

Applications of Energy and Matter Relationships

When considering the cycling of matter in ecosystems, the flow of energy and atoms is from one organism to another. The **trophic level** of an organism refers to its position in a food chain. The level shows the relationship between it and other organisms on the same level and how they use and transfer energy to other levels in the food chain. This includes consumption and decomposition for the transfer of energy among organisms and matter. The sun provides energy through radiation to the Earth, and plants convert this light energy into chemical energy, which is then released to fuel the organism's activities.

Naturally occurring elements deep within the Earth's mantle release heat during their radioactive decay. This release of heat drives convection currents in the Earth's magma, which then drives plate tectonics. The transfer of heat from these actions causes the plates to move and create convection currents in the oceans. This type of cycling can also be seen in transformations of rocks. Sedimentary rocks can undergo significant amounts of heat and pressure to become metamorphic rocks. These rocks can melt back into magma, which then becomes igneous rock or, with extensive weathering and erosion, can revert to sediment and form sedimentary rocks over time. Under the right conditions (weathering and erosion), igneous rocks can also become sediment, which eventually compresses into sedimentary rock. Erosion helps the process by redepositing rocks into sediment on the seafloor.

All of these cycles are examples of the transfer of energy from one type into another, along with the conservation of mass from one level to the next.

Chemistry

Periodicity and States of Matter

Periodic Table of the Elements
Using the periodic table, elements are arranged by atomic number, similar characteristics, and electron configurations in a tabular format. The columns, called **groups**, are sorted by similar chemical properties and characteristics such as appearance and reactivity. This can be seen in the shiny texture of metals, the high melting points of alkali Earth metals, and the softness of post-transition metals. The rows are arranged by electron valence configurations and are called **periods**.

Periodic Table of the Elements

1A																	8A
1 H hydrogen 1.008	2A											3A	4A	5A	6A	7A	2 He helium 4.003
3 Li lithium 6.94	4 Be beryllium 9.012											5 B boron 10.81	6 C carbon 12.01	7 N nitrogen 14.01	8 O oxygen 16.00	9 F fluorine 19.00	10 Ne neon 20.18
11 Na sodium 22.99	12 Mg magnesium 24.31	3B	4B	5B	6B	7B	8B	8B	8B	11B	12B	13 Al aluminum 26.98	14 Si silicon 28.09	15 P phosphorus 30.97	16 S sulfur 32.06	17 Cl chlorine 35.45	18 Ar argon 39.95
19 K potassium 39.10	20 Ca calcium 40.08	21 Sc scandium 44.96	22 Ti titanium 47.88	23 V vanadium 50.94	24 Cr chromium 52.00	25 Mn manganese 54.94	26 Fe iron 55.85	27 Co cobalt 58.93	28 Ni nickel 58.69	29 Cu copper 63.55	30 Zn zinc 65.39	31 Ga gallium 69.72	32 Ge germanium 72.64	33 As arsenic 74.92	34 Se selenium 78.96	35 Br bromine 79.90	36 Kr krypton 83.79
37 Rb rubidium 85.47	38 Sr strontium 87.62	39 Y yttrium 88.91	40 Zr zirconium 91.22	41 Nb niobium 92.91	42 Mo molybdenum 95.96	43 Tc technetium (98)	44 Ru ruthenium 101.1	45 Rh rhodium 102.9	46 Pd palladium 106.4	47 Ag silver 107.9	48 Cd cadmium 112.4	49 In indium 114.8	50 Sn tin 118.7	51 Sb antimony 121.8	52 Te tellurium 127.6	53 I iodine 126.9	54 Xe xenon 131.3
55 Cs cesium 132.9	56 Ba barium 137.3	57-71	72 Hf hafnium 178.5	73 Ta tantalum 180.9	74 W tungsten 183.9	75 Re rhenium 186.2	76 Os osmium 190.2	77 Ir iridium 192.2	78 Pt platinum 195.1	79 Au gold 197.0	80 Hg mercury 200.5	81 Tl thallium 204.4	82 Pb lead 207.2	83 Bi bismuth 209.0	84 Po polonium (209)	85 At astatine (210)	86 Rn radon (222)
87 Fr francium (223)	88 Ra radium (226)	89-103	104 Rf rutherfordium (265)	105 Db dubnium (268)	106 Sg seaborgium (271)	107 Bh bohrium (270)	108 Hs hassium (277)	109 Mt meitnerium (276)	110 Ds darmstadtium (281)	111 Rg roentgenium (280)	112 Cn copernicium (285)	113 Uut ununtrium (284)	114 Fl flerovium (289)	115 Uup ununpentium (288)	116 Lv livermorium (293)	117 Uus ununseptium (294)	118 Uuo ununoctium (294)

Lanthanide Series

57 La lanthanum 138.9	58 Ce cerium 140.1	59 Pr praseodymium 140.9	60 Nd neodymium 144.2	61 Pm promethium (145)	62 Sm samarium 150.4	63 Eu europium 152.0	64 Gd gadolinium 157.2	65 Tb terbium 158.9	66 Dy dysprosium 162.5	67 Ho holmium 164.9	68 Er erbium 167.3	69 Tm thulium 168.9	70 Yb ytterbium 173.0	71 Lu lutetium 175.0

Actinide Series

89 Ac actinium (227)	90 Th thorium 232	91 Pa protactinium 231	92 U uranium 238	93 Np neptunium (237)	94 Pu plutonium (244)	95 Am americium (243)	96 Cm curium (247)	97 Bk berkelium (247)	98 Cf californium (251)	99 Es einsteinium (252)	100 Fm fermium (257)	101 Md mendelevium (258)	102 No nobelium (259)	103 Lr lawrencium (262)

Legend:
- Alkaline Metal
- Alkaline Earth
- Transition Metal
- Basic Metal
- Semimetal
- Nonmetal
- Halogen
- Noble Gas
- Lanthanide
- Actinide

96

The elements are set in ascending order from left to right by atomic number. As mentioned, the atomic number is the number of protons contained within the nucleus of the atom. For example, the element helium has an atomic number of 2 because it has two protons in its nucleus.

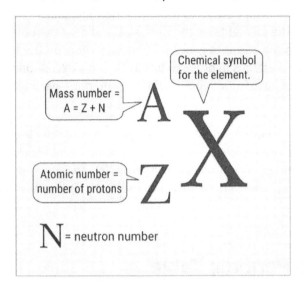

An element's mass number is calculated by adding the number of protons and neutrons of an atom together, while the atomic mass of an element is the weighted average of the naturally occurring atoms of a given element, or the relative abundance of isotopes that might be used in chemistry. For example, the atomic (mass) number of chlorine is 35; however, the atomic mass of chlorine is 35.5 amu (atomic mass unit). This discrepancy exists because there are many isotopes (meaning the nucleus could have 36 instead of 35 protons) occurring in nature. Given the prevalence of the various isotopes, the average of all of the atomic masses turns out to be 35.5 amu, which is slightly higher than chlorine's number on the periodic table. As another example, carbon has an atomic number of 12, but its atomic mass is 12.01 amu because, unlike chlorine, there are few naturally occurring isotopes to raise the average number.

Elements are arranged according to their valence electron configurations, which also contribute to trends in chemical properties. These properties help to further categorize the elements into blocks, including metals, non-metals, transition metals, alkali metals, alkali earth metals, metalloids, lanthanides, actinides, diatomics, post-transition metals, polyatomic nonmetals, and noble gasses. Noble gasses (the far-right column) have a full outer electron valence shell. The elements in this block possess similar characteristics such as being colorless, odorless, and having low chemical reactivity. Another block, the metals, tend to be shiny, highly conductive, and easily form alloys with each other, non-metals, and noble gasses.

The symbols of the elements on the periodic table are a single letter or a two-letter combination that is usually derived from the element's name. Many of the elements have Latin origins for their names, and their atomic symbols do not match their modern names. For example, iron is derived from the word *ferrum*, so its symbol is Fe, even though it is now called iron. The naming of the elements began with those of natural origin and their ancient names, which included the use of the ending "ium." This naming practice has been continued for all elements that have been named since the 1940s. Now, the names of new elements must be approved by the International Union of Pure and Applied Chemistry.

The elements on the periodic table are arranged by number and grouped by trends in their physical properties and electron configurations. Certain trends are easily described by the arrangement of the

periodic table, which includes the increase of the atomic radius as elements go from right to left and from top to bottom on the periodic table. Another trend on the periodic table is the increase in ionization energy (or the tendency of an atom to attract and form bonds with electrons). This tendency increases from left to right and from bottom to top of the periodic table—the opposite directions of the trend for the atomic radius. The elements on the right side and near the bottom of the periodic table tend to attract electrons with the intent to gain, while the elements on the left and near the top usually lose, or give up, one or more electrons in order to bond. The only exceptions to this rule are the noble gasses. Since the noble gasses have full valence shells, they do not have a tendency to lose or gain electrons.

Chemical reactivity is another trend identifiable by the groupings of the elements on the periodic table. The chemical reactivity of metals decreases from left to right and while going higher on the table. Conversely, non-metals increase in chemical reactivity from left to right and while going lower on the table. Again, the noble gasses present an exception to these trends because they have very low chemical reactivity.

Trends in the Periodic Table

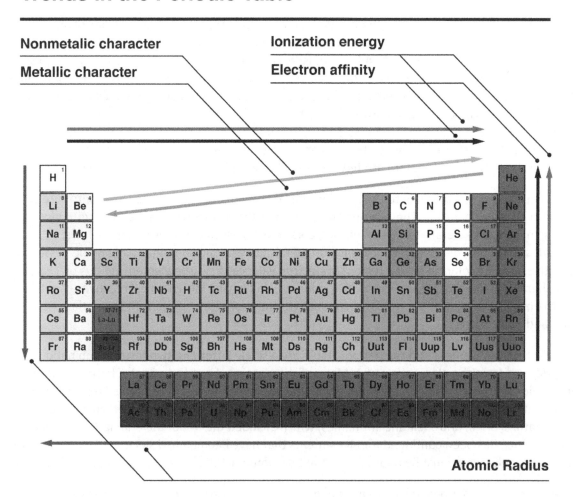

98

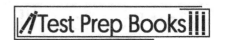

States of Matter and Factors that Affect Phase Changes

Matter is most commonly found in three distinct states: solid, liquid, and gas. A solid has a distinct shape and a defined volume. A liquid has a more loosely defined shape and a definite volume, while a gas has no definite shape or volume. The **Kinetic Theory of Matter** states that matter is composed of a large number of small particles (specifically, atoms and molecules) that are in constant motion. The distance between the separations in these particles determines the state of the matter: solid, liquid, or gas. In gasses, the particles have a large separation and no attractive forces. In liquids, there is moderate separation between particles and some attractive forces to form a loose shape. Solids have almost no separation between their particles, causing a defined and set shape. The constant movement of particles causes them to bump into each other, thus allowing the particles to transfer energy between each other. This bumping and transferring of energy helps explain the transfer of heat and the relationship between pressure, volume, and temperature.

The **Ideal Gas Law** states that pressure, volume, and temperature are all related through the equation: $PV = nRT$, where P is pressure, V is volume, n is the amount of the substance in moles, R is the gas constant, and T is temperature.

Through this relationship, volume and pressure are both proportional to temperature, but pressure is inversely proportional to volume. Therefore, if the equation is balanced, and the volume decreases in the system, pressure needs to proportionally increase to keep both sides of the equation balanced. In contrast, if the equation is unbalanced and the pressure increases, then the temperature would also increase, since pressure and temperature are directly proportional.

When pressure, temperature, or volume change in matter, a change in state can occur. Changes in state include solid to liquid (melting), liquid to gas (evaporation), solid to gas (sublimation), gas to solid (deposition), gas to liquid (condensation), and liquid to solid (freezing). There is one other state of matter called **plasma**, which is seen in lightning, television screens, and neon lights. Plasma is most commonly converted from the gas state at extremely high temperatures.

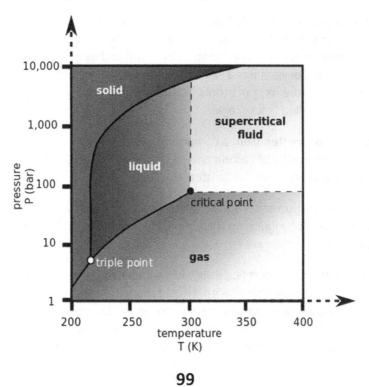

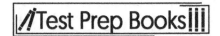

The amount of energy needed to change matter from one state to another is labeled by the terms for phase changes. For example, the temperature needed to supply enough energy for matter to change from a liquid to a gas is called the **heat of vaporization**. When heat is added to matter in order to cause a change in state, there will be an increase in temperature until the matter is about to change its state. During its transition, all of the added heat is used by the matter to change its state, so there is no increase in temperature. Once the transition is complete, then the added heat will again yield an increase in temperature.

Each state of matter is considered to be a phase, and changes between phases are represented by phase diagrams. These diagrams show the effects of changes in pressure and temperature on matter. The states of matter fall into areas on these charts called **heating curves**.

Chemical Nomenclature, Composition, and Bonding

Simple Compounds and Their Chemical Formulas

Chemical formulas represent the proportion of the number of atoms in a chemical compound. Chemical symbols are used for the elements present and numerical values. Parentheses are also sometimes used to show the number of combinations of the elements in relation to their ionic charges. An element's ionic charge can be determined by its location on the periodic table. This information is then used to correctly combine its atoms in a compound.

For example, the chemical formula for sodium chloride (table salt) is the combination of sodium (Na, ionic charge of +1) and chlorine (Cl, ionic charge of -1). From its placement on the periodic table, the electron valence of an outer shell can be determined: sodium has an ionic charge of +1, while chlorine has an ionic charge of -1. Since these two elements have an equal and opposite amount of charge, they combine in a neutral one-to-one ratio: NaCl. The naming of compounds depends mainly on the second element in a chemical compound. If it is a non-metal (such as chlorine), it is written with an "ide" at the end. The compound NaCl is called "sodium chloride."

If the elements forming a compound do not have equal and opposite ionic charges, there will be an unequal number of each element in the compound to balance the ionic charge. This situation happens with many elements, for example, in the combination of nickel and oxygen into nickel oxide (Ni_2O_3). Nickel has a +3 ionic charge and oxygen has a -2 ionic charge, so when forming a compound, there must be two nickel atoms for every three oxygen atoms (a common factor of 6) to balance the charge of the compound. This compound is called "nickel oxide."

A chemical formula can also be written from a compound's name. For instance, the compound carbon dioxide is formed by the combination of carbon and oxygen. The word "dioxide" means there are two oxygen atoms for every carbon atom, so it is written as CO_2.

To better represent the composition of compounds, structural formulas are used. The combination of atoms is more precisely depicted by lining up the electron configuration of the outer electron shell through a Lewis dot diagram.

The Lewis dot diagram, named for Gilbert N. Lewis, shows the arrangement of the electrons in the outer shell and how these electrons can pair/bond with the outer shell electrons of other atoms when forming compounds. The diagram is created by writing the symbol of an element and then drawing dots to represent the outer shell of valence electrons around what would be an invisible square surrounding the symbol. The placement of the first two dots can vary based on the school of teaching. For the given

100

example, the first dot is placed on the top and then the next dot is placed beside it, since it represents the pair of electrons in the 1s valence shell.

The next dots (electrons) are placed one at a time on each side—right, bottom, left, right bottom left, etc.—of the element symbol until all of the valence shell electrons are represented, or the structure has eight dots (electrons), which means it is full. This method gives a more specific picture of compounds, how they are structured, and what electrons are available for bonding, sharing, and forming new compounds. For example, the compound sodium chloride is written separately with sodium having one valence electron and chlorine having seven valence electrons. Then, combined with a total of eight electrons, it is written with two dots being shared between the two elements.

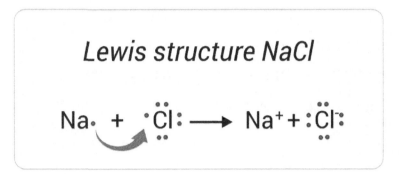

Types of Chemical Bonding

A chemical bond is a strong attractive force that can exist between atoms. The bonding of atoms is separated into two main categories. The first category, **ionic bonding,** primarily describes the bonding that occurs between oppositely charged ions in a regular crystal arrangement. It primarily exists between salts, which are known to be ionic. Ionic bonds are held together by the electrostatic attraction between oppositely charged ions. This type of bonding involves the transfer of electrons from the valence shell of one atom to the valence shell of another atom. If an atom loses an electron from its valence shell, it becomes a positive ion, or **cation**. If an atom gains an electron, it becomes a negative ion, or an **anion**. The Lewis electron-dot symbol is used to more simply express the electron configuration of atoms, especially when forming bonds.

The second type of bonding is covalent bonding. This bonding involves the sharing of a pair of electrons between atoms. There are no ions involved in covalent bonding, but the force holding the atoms together comes from the balance between the attractive and repulsive forces involving the shared electron and the nuclei. Atoms frequently engage this type of bonding when it enables them to fill their outer valence shell.

Mole Concept and Its Applications

The calculation of mole ratios of reactants and products involved in a chemical reaction is called "stoichiometry." To find these ratios, one must first find the proportion of the number of molecules in one mole of a substance. This relates the molar mass of a compound to its mass and this relationship is a constant known as **Avogadro's number** (6.23×10^{23}). Since it is a ratio, there are no dimensions (or units) for Avogadro's number.

Molar Mass and Percent Composition

The molar mass of a substance is the measure of the mass of one mole of the substance. For pure elements, the molar mass is also known as the atomic mass unit (amu) of the substance. For

compounds, it can be calculated by adding the molar masses of each substance in the compound. For example, the molar mass of carbon is 12.01 g/mol, while the molar mass of water (H_2O) requires finding the sum of the molar masses of the constituents:

$$((1.01 \times 2 = 2.02 \text{ g/mol for hydrogen}) + (16.0 \text{ g/mol for oxygen}) = 18.02 \text{ g/mol})$$

The percentage of a compound in a composition can be determined by taking the individual molar masses of each component divided by the total molar mass of the compound, multiplied by 100. Determining the percent composition of carbon dioxide (CO_2) first requires the calculation of the molar mass of CO_2.

$$molar\ mass\ of\ carbon = 12.01 \times 1\ \text{atom} = 12.01 \text{ g/mol}$$

$$molar\ mass\ of\ oxygen = 16.0 \times 2\ \text{atoms} = 32.0 \text{ g/mol}$$

$$molar\ mass\ of\ CO2\ =\ 12.01 \text{ g/mol}\ +\ 32.0 \text{ g/mol}\ =\ 44.01 \text{ g/mol}$$

Next, each individual mass is divided by the total mass and multiplied by 100 to get the percent composition of each component.

$$12.01/44.01 = (0.2729 \times 100) = 27.29\% \text{ carbon}$$

$$32.0/44.01 = (0.7271 \times 100) = 72.71\% \text{ oxygen}$$

(A quick check in the addition of the percentages should always yield 100%.)

Chemical Reactions

Basic Concepts of Chemical Reactions

Chemical reactions rearrange the initial atoms of the reactants into different substances. These types of reactions can be expressed through the use of balanced chemical equations. A **chemical equation** is the symbolic representation of a chemical reaction through the use of chemical terms. The reactants at the beginning (or on the left side) of the equation must equal the products at the end (or on the right side) of the equation.

For example, table salt (NaCl) forms through the chemical reaction between sodium (Na) and chlorine (Cl) and is written as: $Na + Cl_2 \rightarrow NaCl$.

However, this equation is not balanced because there are two sodium atoms for every pair of chlorine atoms involved in this reaction. So, the left side is written as: $2\ Na + Cl_2 \rightarrow NaCl$.

Next, the right side needs to balance the same number of sodium and chlorine atoms. So, the right side is written as: $2\ Na + Cl_2 \rightarrow 2\ NaCl$. Now, this is a balanced chemical equation.

Chemical reactions typically fall into two types of categories: **endothermic** and **exothermic**.

An endothermic reaction absorbs heat, whereas an exothermic reaction releases heat. For example, in an endothermic reaction, heat is drawn from the container holding the chemicals, which cools the container. Conversely, an exothermic reaction emits heat from the reaction and warms the container holding the chemicals.

Factors that can affect the rate of a reaction include temperature, pressure, the physical state of the reactants (e.g., surface area), concentration, and catalysts/enzymes.

The formula $PV = nRT$ shows that an increase in any of the variables (pressure, volume, or temperature) affects the overall reaction. The physical state of two reactants can also determine how much interaction they have with each other. If two reactants are both in a fluid state, they may have the capability of interacting more than if solid. The addition of a catalyst or an enzyme can increase the rate of a chemical reaction, without the catalyst or enzyme undergoing a change itself.

Le Chatelier's principle describes factors that affect a reaction's equilibrium. Essentially, when introducing a "shock" to a system (or chemical reaction), a positive feedback/shift in equilibrium is often the response. In accordance with the second law of thermodynamics, this imbalance will eventually even itself out, but not without counteracting the effects of the reaction.

There are many different types of chemical reactions. A **synthesis reaction** is the combination of two or more elements into a compound. For example, the synthesis reaction of hydrogen and oxygen forms water.

$$2\,H_2(g) + O_2(g) \rightarrow 2\,H_2O(g)$$

A **decomposition reaction** is the breaking down of a compound into its more basic components. For example, the decomposition, or electrolysis, of water results in it breaking down into oxygen and hydrogen gas.

$$2\,H_2O \rightarrow 2\,H_2 + O_2$$

A **combustion reaction** is similar to a decomposition reaction, but it requires oxygen and heat for the reaction to occur. For example, the burning of a candle requires oxygen to ignite and the reaction forms carbon dioxide during the process.

$$CH_4(g) + 2\,O_2(g) \rightarrow CO_2(g) + 2\,H_2O(g)$$

There are also single and double replacement reactions where compounds swap components with each other to form new compounds. In the **single replacement reaction**, a single element will swap into a compound, thus releasing one of the compound's elements to become the new single element. For example, the reaction between iron and copper sulfate will create copper and iron sulfate.

$$1\,Fe(s) + 1\,CuSO_4(aq) \rightarrow 1\,FeSO_4(aq) + 1\,Cu(s)$$

In a **double replacement reaction**, two compounds swap components to form two new compounds. For example, the reaction between sodium sulfide and hydrochloric acid forms sodium chloride and hydrogen sulfide.

$$Na_2S + HCl \rightarrow NaCl + H_2S$$

After balancing the reaction, we get:

$$Na_2S + 2\,HCl \rightarrow 2\,NaCl + H_2S$$

An organic reaction is a chemical reaction involving the components of carbon and hydrogen.

Finally, there are oxidation/reduction (redox or half) reactions. These reactions involve the loss of electrons from one species (oxidation), and the gain of electrons to the other species (reduction). For example, the oxidation of magnesium is as follows:

$$2 \text{ Mg}(\textbf{s}) + O_2(\textbf{g}) \rightarrow 2 \text{ MgO}(\textbf{s})$$

Acid-Base Chemistry

Simple Acid-Base Chemistry

If something has a sour taste, it is acidic, and if something has a bitter taste, it is basic. Unfortunately, it can be extremely dangerous to ingest chemicals in an attempt to classify them as an acid or a base. Therefore, acids and bases are generally identified by the reactions they have when combined with water. An acid will increase the concentration of the hydrogen ion (H^+), while a base will increase the concentration of the hydroxide ion (OH^-).

To better categorize the varying strengths of acids and bases, the pH scale is used. The pH scale provides a logarithmic (base 10) grading to acids and bases based on their strength. The pH scale contains values from 0 through 14, with 7 being neutral. If a solution registers below 7 on the pH scale, it is considered an acid. If it registers higher than 7, it is considered a base. To perform a quick test on a solution, litmus paper can be used. A base will turn red litmus paper blue, whereas an acid will turn blue litmus paper red. To gauge the strength of an acid or base, a test of phenolphthalein can be used. An acid will turn red phenolphthalein colorless, and a base will turn colorless phenolphthalein pink. As demonstrated with these types of tests, acids and bases neutralize each other. When acids and bases react with one another, they produce salts (also called ionic substances).

Acid							Neutral				Alkali			
0	1	2	3	4	5	6	7	8	9	10	11	12	13	14
Battery Acid	Hydrochloric Acid	Gastric Acid	Soda	Acid Rain	Black Coffee	Urine/Saliva	Pure Water	Sea Water	Baking Soda	Milk of Magnesium	Ammonia	Soapy Water	Bleach	Drain Cleaner

Solutions and Solubility

Different Types of Solutions

A **solution** is a homogenous mixture of more than one substance. A **solute** is another substance that can be dissolved into a substance called a **solvent**. If only a small amount of solute is dissolved in a solvent, the solution formed is said to be **diluted**. A solution is considered **concentrated** if a large amount of solute is dissolved into the solvent. For example, water from a typical, unfiltered household tap is diluted because it contains other minerals in very small amounts.

Solution Concentration

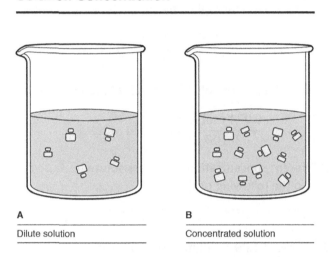

A
Dilute solution

B
Concentrated solution

If more solute is being added to a solvent, but not dissolving, the solution is called **saturated**. For example, when hummingbirds eat sugar-water from feeders, they prefer it as sweet as possible. When trying to dissolve enough sugar (solute) into the water (solvent), there will be a point where the sugar crystals will no longer dissolve into the solution and will remain as whole pieces floating in the water. At this point, the solution is considered saturated and cannot accept more sugar. This level, at which a solvent cannot accept and dissolve any more solute, is called its **saturation point**. In some cases, it is possible to force more solute to be dissolved into a solvent, but this will result in crystallization. The state of a solution on the verge of crystallization, or in the process of crystallization, is called a **supersaturated solution**. This can also occur in a solution that seems stable, but if it is disturbed, the change can begin the crystallization process.

Although the terms *dilute*, *concentrated*, *saturated*, and *supersaturated* give qualitative descriptions of solutions, a more precise quantitative description needs to be established for the use of chemicals. This holds true especially for mixing strong acids or bases. The method for calculating the concentration of a solution is done through finding its molarity. In some instances, such as environmental reporting, molarity is measured in parts per million (ppm). Parts per million, is the number of milligrams of a substance dissolved in one liter of water. To find the **molarity**, or the amount of solute per unit volume of solution, for a solution, the following formula is used:

$$c = \frac{n}{V}$$

In this formula, c is the molarity (or unit moles of solute per volume of solution), n is the amount of solute measured in moles, and V is the volume of the solution, measured in liters.

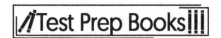

Example:

What is the molarity of a solution made by dissolving 2.0 grams of NaCl into enough water to make 100 mL of solution?

To solve this, the number of moles of NaCl needs to be calculated:

First, to find the mass of NaCl, the mass of each of the molecule's atoms is added together as follows:

$$23.0 \text{ g (Na)} + 35.5 \text{ g (Cl)} = 58.5 \text{ g NaCl}$$

Next, the given mass of the substance is multiplied by one mole per total mass of the substance:

$$2.0 \text{ g NaCl} \times \frac{1 \text{ mol NaCl}}{58.5 \text{ g NaCl}} = 0.034 \text{ mol NaCl}$$

Finally, the moles are divided by the number of liters of the solution to find the molarity:

$$\frac{0.034 \text{ mol NaCl}}{0.100 \text{ L}} = 0.34 \text{ M NaCl}$$

To prepare a solution of a different concentration, the **mass solute** must be calculated from the molarity of the solution. This is done via the following process:

Example:

How would you prepare 600.0 mL of 1.20 M solution of sodium chloride?

To solve this, the given information needs to be set up:

$$1.20 \text{ M NaCl} = \frac{1.20 \text{ mol NaCl}}{1.00 \text{ L of solution}}$$

$$0.600 \text{ L solution} \times \frac{1.20 \text{ mol NaCl}}{1.00 \text{ L of solution}} = 0.72 \text{ moles NaCl}$$

$$0.72 \text{ moles NaCl} \times \frac{58.5 \text{g NaCl}}{1 \text{ mol NaCl}} = 42.12 \text{ g NaCl}$$

This means that one must dissolve 42.12 g NaCl in enough water to make 600.0 L of solution.

Factors Affecting the Solubility of Substances and the Dissolving Process

Certain factors can affect the rate in dissolving processes. These include temperature, pressure, particle size, and agitation (stirring). As mentioned, the *ideal gas law* states that $PV = nRT$, where P equals pressure, V equals volume, and T equals temperature. If the pressure, volume, or temperature are affected in a system, it will affect the entire system. Specifically, if there is an increase in temperature, there will be an increase in the dissolving rate. An increase in the pressure can also increase the dissolving rate. Particle size and agitation can also influence the dissolving rate, since all of these factors contribute to the breaking of intermolecular forces that hold solute particles together. Once these forces are broken, the solute particles can link to particles in the solvent, thus dissolving the solute.

A **solubility curve** shows the relationship between the mass of solute that a solvent holds at a given temperature. If a reading is on the solubility curve, the solvent is **full (saturated)** and cannot hold anymore solute. If a reading is above the curve, the solvent is **unstable (supersaturated)** from holding more solute than it should. If a reading is below the curve, the solvent is **unsaturated** and could hold more solute.

If a solvent has different electronegativities, or partial charges, it is considered to be **polar**. Water is an example of a polar solvent. If a solvent has similar electronegativities, or lacking partial charges, it is considered to be **non-polar**. Benzene is an example of a non-polar solvent. Polarity status is important when attempting to dissolve solutes. The phrase "like dissolves like" is the key to remembering what will happen when attempting to dissolve a solute in a solvent. A polar solute will dissolve in a like, or polar solvent. Similarly, a nonpolar solute will dissolve in a nonpolar solvent. When a reaction produces a solid, the solid is called a **precipitate.** A precipitation reaction can be used for removing a salt (an ionic compound that results from a neutralization reaction) from a solvent, such as water. For water, this process is called ionization. Therefore, the products of a neutralization reaction (when an acid and base react) are a salt and water. Therefore, the products of a neutralization reaction (when an acid and base react) are a salt and water.

When a solute is added to a solvent to lower the freezing point of the solvent, it is called **freezing point depression**. This is a useful process, especially when applied in colder temperatures. For example, the addition of salt to ice in winter allows the ice to melt at a much lower temperature, thus creating safer road conditions for driving. Unfortunately, the freezing point depression from salt can only lower the melting point of ice so far and is ineffectual when temperatures are too low. This same process, with a mix of ethylene glycol and water, is also used to keep the radiator fluid (antifreeze) in an automobile from freezing during the winter.

Physics

Mechanics

Description of Motion in One and Two Dimensions

The description of motion is known as **kinetics**, and the causes of motion are known as **dynamics**. Motion in one dimension is known as a **scalar** quantity. It consists of one measurement such as length (length or distance is also known as displacement), speed, or time. Motion in two dimensions is known as a **vector** quantity. This would be speed with a direction, or velocity.

Velocity is the measure of the change in distance over the change in time. All vector quantities have a direction that can be relayed through the sign of an answer, such as -5.0 m/s or +5.0 m/s. The objects registering these velocities would be in opposite directions, where the change in distance is denoted by Δx and the change in time is denoted by Δt:

$$v = \frac{\Delta x}{\Delta t}$$

Acceleration is the measure of the change in an object's velocity over a change in time, where the change in velocity, $v_2 - v_1$, is denoted by Δv and the change in time, $t_1 - t_2$, is denoted by Δt:

$$a = \frac{\Delta v}{\Delta t}$$

The linear momentum, p, of an object is the result of the object's mass, m, multiplied by its velocity, v, and is described by the equation:

$$p = mv$$

This aspect becomes important when one object hits another object. For example, the linear momentum of a small sports car will be much smaller than the linear momentum of a large semi-truck. Thus, the semi-truck will cause more damage to the car than the car to the truck.

Newton's Three Laws of Motion

Sir Isaac Newton summarized his observations and calculations relating to motion into three concise laws.

First Law of Motion: Inertia

This law states that an object in motion tends to stay in motion or an object at rest tends to stay at rest, unless the object is acted upon by an outside force.

For example, a rock sitting on the ground will remain in the same place, unless it is pushed or lifted from its place.

The First Law also includes the relation of weight to gravity and force between objects relative to the distance separating them.

$$Weight = G\frac{Mm}{r^2}$$

In this equation, G is the gravitational constant, M and m are the masses of the two objects, and r is the distance separating the two objects.

Second Law of Motion: $F = ma$

This law states that the force on a given body is the result of the object's mass multiplied by any acceleration acting upon the object. For objects falling on Earth, an acceleration is caused by gravitational force (9.8 m/s^2).

Third Law of Motion: Action-Reaction

This law states that for every action there is an equal and opposite reaction. For example, if a person punches a wall, the wall exerts a force back on the person's hand equal and opposite to their punching force. Since the wall has more mass, it absorbs the impact of the punch better than the person's hand.

Mass, Weight, and Gravity

Mass is a measure of how much of a substance exists, or how much inertia an object has. The mass of an object does not change based on the object's location, but the weight of an object does vary with its location.

For example, a 15-kg mass has a weight that is determined by acceleration from the force of gravity here on Earth. However, if that same 15-kg mass were to be weighed on the moon, it would weigh much less, since the acceleration force from the moon's gravity is approximately one-sixth of that on Earth.

$$Weight = mass \times acceleration$$

$$W_{Earth} = 15 \text{ kg} \times 9.8 \text{ m/s}^2 \qquad > \qquad W_{Moon} = 15 \text{ kg} \times 1.62 \text{ m/s}^2$$

$$W_{Earth} = 147 \text{ N} \qquad > \qquad 24.3 \text{ N}$$

Analysis of Motion and Forces

Projectile Motion describes the path of an object in the air. Generally, it is described by two-dimensional movement, such as a stone thrown through the air. This activity maps to a parabolic curve. However, the definition of projectile motion also applies to free fall, or the non-arced motion of an object in a path straight up and/or straight down. When an object is thrown horizontally, it is subject to the same influence of gravity as an object that is dropped straight down. The farther the projectile motion, the farther the distance of the object's flight.

Friction is a force that opposes motion. It can be caused by a number of materials; there is even friction caused by air. Whenever two differing materials touch, rub, or pass by each other, it will create friction, or an oppositional force, unless the interaction occurs in a true vacuum. To move an object across a floor, the force exerted on the object must overcome the frictional force keeping the object in place. Friction is also why people can walk on surfaces. Without the oppositional force of friction to a shoe pressing on the floor, a person would not be able to grip the floor to walk—similar to the challenge of walking on ice. Without friction, shoes slip and are unable to help people propel forward and walk.

When calculating the effects of objects hitting (or colliding with) each other, several things are important to remember. One of these is the definition of momentum: the mass of an object multiplied by the object's velocity. As mentioned, it is expressed by the following equation:

$$p = mv$$

Here, p is equal to an object's momentum, m is equal to the object's mass, and v is equal to the object's velocity.

Another important thing to remember is the principle of the conservation of linear momentum. The total momentum for objects in a situation will be the same before and after a collision. There are two primary types of collisions: elastic and inelastic. In an elastic collision, the objects collide and then travel in different directions. During an inelastic collision, the objects collide and then stick together in their final direction of travel. The total momentum in an elastic collision is calculated by using the following formula:

$$m_1 v_1 + m_2 v_2 = m_1 v_1 + m_2 v_2$$

Here, m_1 and m_2 are the masses of two separate objects, and v_1 and v_2 are the velocities, respectively, of the two separate objects.

The total momentum in an inelastic collision is calculated by using the following formula:

$$m_1 v_1 + m_2 v_2 = (m_1 + m_2)v_f$$

Here, v_f is the final velocity of the two masses after they stick together post-collision.

Example:

If two bumper cars are speeding toward each other, head-on, and collide, they are designed to bounce off of each other and head in different directions. This would be an elastic collision.

If real cars are speeding toward each other, head-on, and collide, there is a good chance their bumpers might get caught together and their direction of travel would be together in the same direction.

An **axis** is an invisible line on which an object can rotate. This is most easily observed with a toy top. There is actually a point (or rod) through the center of the top on which the top can be observed to be spinning. This is called the axis.

When objects move in a circle by spinning on their own axis, or because they are tethered around a central point (also an axis), they exhibit circular motion. Circular motion is similar in many ways to linear (straight line) motion; however, there are a few additional points to note. A spinning object is always accelerating because it is always changing direction. The force causing this constant acceleration on or around an axis is called **centripetal force** and is often associated with centripetal acceleration. Centripetal force always pulls toward the axis of rotation. An imaginary reactionary force, called **centrifugal force**, is the outward force felt when an object is undergoing circular motion. This reactionary force is not the real force; it just feels like it is there. For this reason, it has also been referred to as a "frictional force." The true force is the one pulling inward, or the centripetal force.

The terms *centripetal* and *centrifugal* are often mistakenly interchanged. If the centripetal force acting on an object moving with circular motion is removed, the object will continue moving in a straight line tangent to the point on the circle where the object last experienced the centripetal force. For example, when a traditional style washing machine spins a load of clothes to expunge the water from the load, it rapidly spins the machine barrel. A force is pulling in toward the center of the circle (centripetal force). At the same time, the wet clothes, which are attempting to move in a straight line, are colliding with the outer wall of the barrel that is moving in a circle. The interaction between the wet clothes and barrel wall causes a reactionary force to the centripetal force and this expels the water out of the small holes that line the outer wall of the barrel.

Conservation of Angular Momentum

An object moving in a circular motion also has momentum; for circular motion, it is called **angular momentum**. This is determined by rotational inertia, rotational velocity, and the distance of the mass from the axis or center of rotation. When objects exhibit circular motion, they also demonstrate the **conservation of angular momentum**, meaning that the angular momentum of a system is always constant, regardless of the placement of the mass. Rotational inertia can be affected by how far the mass of the object is placed with respect to the axis of rotation. The greater the distance between the mass and the axis of rotation, the slower the rotational velocity. Conversely, if the mass is closer to the axis of rotation, the rotational velocity is faster. A change in one affects the other, thus conserving the angular momentum. This holds true as long as no external forces act upon the system.

For example, ice skaters spinning in on one ice skate extends their arms out for a slower rotational velocity. When skaters bring their arms close to their bodies (which lessens the distance between the mass and the axis of rotation), their rotational velocity increases and they spin much faster. Some skaters extend their arms straight up above their head, which causes an extension of the axis of

rotation, thus removing any distance between the mass and the center of rotation, which maximizes their rotational velocity.

Another example is when a person selects a horse on a merry-go-round: the placement of their horse can affect their ride experience. All of the horses are traveling with the same rotational speed, but in order to travel along the same plane as the merry-go-round turns, a horse on the outside will have a greater linear speed because it is further away from the axis of rotation. Essentially, an outer horse has to cover a lot more ground than a horse on the inside in order to keep up with the rotational speed of the merry-go-round platform. Thrill seekers should always select an outer horse.

The center of mass is the point that provides the average location for the total mass of a system. The word "system" can apply to just one object/particle or to many. The center of mass for a system can be calculated by finding the average of the mass of each object and multiplying by its distance from an origin point using the following formula:

$$x_{center\ of\ mass} = \frac{m_1 x_1 + m_2 x_2}{m_1 + m_2}$$

In this case, x is the distance from the point of origin for the center of mass and each respective object, and m is the mass of each object.

To calculate for more than one object, the pattern can be continued by adding additional masses and their respective distances from the origin point.

Simple Machines

A simple machine is a mechanical device that changes the direction or magnitude of a force. There are six basic types of simple machines: lever, wedge, screw, inclined plane, wheel and axle, and pulley.

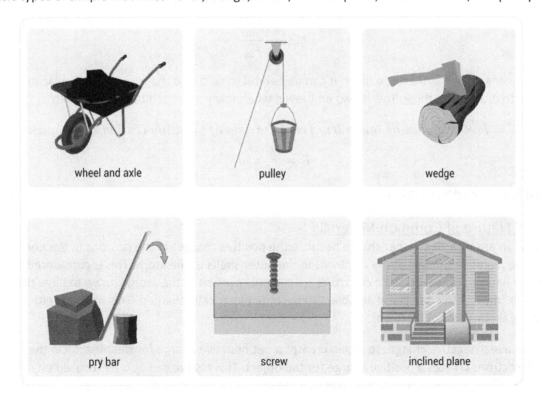

wheel and axle   pulley   wedge

pry bar   screw   inclined plane

Here is how each type works and an example:

- A lever helps lift heavy items higher with less force, such as a crowbar lifting a large cast iron lid.

- A wedge helps apply force to a specific area by focusing the pressure, such as an axe splitting a tree.

- An inclined plane, such as a loading dock ramp, helps move heavy items up vertical distances with less force.

- A screw is an inclined plane wrapped around an axis and allows more force to be applied by extending the distance of the plane. For example, a screw being turned into a piece of wood provides greater securing strength than hitting a nail into the wood.

- A wheel and axle allows the use of rotational force around an axis to assist with applying force. For example, a wheelbarrow makes it easier to haul large loads by employing a wheel and axle at the front.

- A pulley is an application of a wheel and axle with the addition of cords or ropes and it helps move objects vertically. For example, pulling a bucket out of a well is easier with a pulley and ropes.

Using a simple machine employs an advantage to the user. This is referred to as the mechanical advantage. It can be calculated by comparing the force input by the user to the simple machine with the force output from the use of the machine (also displayed as a ratio).

$$Mechanical\ Advantage\ = \frac{output\ force}{input\ force}$$

$$MA\ = \frac{F_{out}}{F_{in}}$$

In the following instance of using a lever, it can be helpful to calculate the torque, or circular force, necessary to move something. This is also employed when using a wrench to loosen a bolt.

$$Torque\ =\ F\ \times\ distance\ of\ lever\ arm\ from\ the\ axis\ of\ rotation\ (called\ the\ moment\ arm)$$

$$T\ =\ F\ \times\ d$$

Electricity and Magnetism

Electrical Nature of Common Materials

Generally, an atom carries no net charge because the positive charges of the protons in the nucleus balance the negative charges of the electrons in the outer shells of the atom. This is considered to be electrically neutral. However, since electrons are the only portion of the atom known to have the freedom to "move," this can cause an object to become electrically charged. This happens either through a gain or a loss of electrons.

Electrons have a negative charge, so a gain creates a net negative charge for the object. On the contrary, a loss of electrons creates a positive charge for the object. This charge can also be focused on specific areas of an object, causing a notable interaction between charged objects. For example, if a person rubs

a balloon on a carpet, the balloon transfers some of its electrons to the carpet. So, if that person were to hold a balloon near their hair, the electrons in the "neutral" hair would make the hair stand on end. This is due to the electrons wanting to fill the deficit of electrons on the balloon. Unless electrically forced into a charged state, most natural objects in nature tend toward reestablishing and maintaining a neutral charge.

When dealing with charges, it is easiest to remember that *like charges repel* each other and *opposite charges attract* each other. Therefore, negatives and positives attract, while two positives or two negatives will repel each other. Similarly, when two charges come near each other, they exert a force on one another. This is described through **Coulomb's Law**:

$$F = k\frac{q_1 q_2}{r^2}$$

In this equation, F is equal to the force exerted by the interaction, k is a constant ($k = 8.99 \times 10^9$ N m^2/C^2), q_1 and q_2 are the measure of the two charges, and r is the distance between the two charges.

When materials readily transfer electricity or electrons, or can easily accept or lose electrons, they are considered to be good conductors. The transferring of electricity is called **conductivity**. If a material does not readily accept the transfer of electrons or readily loses electrons, it is considered to be an **insulator**. For example, plastic is an insulator because it does not transfer electricity. Copper wire, on the other hand, easily transfers electricity; therefore, it is a good conductor.

Basic Electrical Concepts

In an electrical circuit, the flow from a power source, or the voltage, is "drawn" across the components in the circuit from the positive end to the negative end. This flow of charge creates an electric current (I), which is the time (t) rate of flow of net charge (q). It is measured with the formula:

$$I = \frac{q}{t}$$

Current is measured in amperes (amps). There are two main types of currents:

1. **Direct current (DC)**: a unidirectional flow of charges through a circuit

2. **Alternating current (AC)**: a circuit with a changing directional flow of charges or magnitude

Every circuit will show a loss in voltage across its conducting material. This loss of voltage is from resistance within the circuit and can be caused by multiple factors, including resistance from wiring and components such as light bulbs and switches. To measure the resistance in a given circuit, Ohm's law is used:

$$Resistance = \frac{Voltage}{current} = R = \frac{V}{I}$$

Resistance (R) is measured in Ohms (Ω).

Components in a circuit can be wired *in series* or *in parallel*. If the components are wired in series, a single wire connects each component to the next in line. If the components are wired in parallel, two wires connect each component to the next. The main difference is that the voltage across those in series

113

is directly related from one component to the next. Therefore, if the first component in the series becomes inoperable, no voltage can get to the other components. Conversely, the components in parallel share the voltage across each other and are not dependent on the prior component wired to allow the voltage across the wire.

To calculate the resistance of circuit components wired in series or parallel, the following equations are used:

Resistance in series:

$$R_{total} = R_1 + R_2 + R_3 + \ldots$$

Resistance in parallel:

$$R_{total} = \frac{1}{R_1} + \frac{1}{R_2} + \frac{1}{R_3} + \ldots$$

To make electrons move so that they can carry their charge, a change in voltage must be present. On a small scale, this is demonstrated through the electrons traveling from the light switch to a person's finger. This might happen in a situation where a person runs their socks on a carpet, touches a light switch, and receives a small jolt from the electrons that run from the switch to the finger. This minor jolt is due to the deficit of electrons created by rubbing the socks on the carpet, and then the electrons going into the ground. The difference in charge between the switch and the finger caused the electrons to move.

If this situation were to be created on a larger and more sustained scale, the factors would need to be more systematic, predictable, and harnessed. This could be achieved through batteries/cells and generators. Batteries or cells have a chemical reaction that occurs inside, causing energy to be released and charges to be able to move freely. Batteries generally have nodes (one positive and one negative), where items can be hooked up to complete a circuit and allow the charge to travel freely through the item. Generators convert mechanical energy into electric energy using power and movement.

Basic Properties of Magnetic Fields and Forces

Consider two straight rods that are made from magnetic material. They will naturally have a negative end (pole) and a positive end (pole). These charged poles react just like any charged item: opposite charges attract and like charges repel. They will attract each other when arranged from positive pole to negative pole. However, if one rod is turned around, the two rods will now repel each other due to the alignment of negative to negative and positive to positive. These types of forces can also be created and amplified by using an electric current. For example, sending an electric current through a stretch of wire creates an electromagnetic force around the wire from the charge of the current. This force exists as long as the flow of electricity is sustained. This magnetic force can also attract and repel other items with magnetic properties. Depending on the strength of the current in the wire, a greater or smaller magnetic force can be generated around the wire. As soon as the current is stopped, the magnetic force also stops.

Optics and Waves

Electromagnetic Spectrum

The movement of light is described like the movement of waves. Light travels with a wave front, has an amplitude (height from the neutral), a cycle or wavelength, a period, and energy. Light travels at approximately 3.00×10^8 m/s and is faster than anything created by humans thus far.

Light is commonly referred to by its measured wavelengths, or the distance between two successive crests or troughs in a wave. Types of light with the longest wavelengths include radio, TV, and micro, and infrared waves. The next set of wavelengths are detectable by the human eye and create the **visible spectrum**. The visible spectrum has wavelengths of 10^{-7} m, and the colors seen are red, orange, yellow, green, blue, indigo, and violet. Beyond the visible spectrum are shorter wavelengths (also called the **electromagnetic spectrum**) containing ultraviolet light, X-rays, and gamma rays. The wavelengths outside of the visible light range can be harmful to humans if they are directly exposed or are exposed for long periods of time.

Basic Characteristics and Types of Waves

A **mechanical wave** is a type of wave that passes through a medium (solid, liquid, or gas). There are two basic types of mechanical waves: longitudinal and transverse.

A **longitudinal wave** has motion that is parallel to the direction of the wave's travel. This can best be visualized by compressing one side of a tethered spring and then releasing that end. The movement travels in a bunching/un-bunching motion across the length of the spring and back.

A **transverse wave** has motion that is perpendicular to the direction of the wave's travel. The particles on a transverse wave do not move across the length of the wave; instead, they oscillate up and down, creating peaks and troughs.

A wave with a combination of both longitudinal and transverse motion can be seen through the motion of a wave on the ocean—with peaks and troughs, and particles oscillating up and down.

Mechanical waves can carry energy, sound, and light, but they need a medium through which transport can occur. An electromagnetic wave can transmit energy without a medium, or in a vacuum.

A more recent addition in the study of waves is the **gravitational wave**. Its existence has been proven and verified, yet the details surrounding its capabilities are still somewhat under inquiry. Gravitational waves are purported to be ripples that propagate as waves outward from their source and travel in the curvature of space/time. They are thought to carry energy in a form of radiant energy called **gravitational radiation**.

Basic Wave Phenomena

When a wave crosses a boundary or travels from one medium to another, certain things occur. If the wave can travel through one medium into another medium, it experiences **refraction**. This is the bending of the wave from one medium to another due to a change in density of the mediums, and thus, the speed of the wave changes. For example, when a pencil is sitting in half of a glass of water, a side view of the glass makes the pencil appear to be bent at the water level. What the viewer is seeing is the refraction of light waves traveling from the air into the water. Since the wave speed is slowed in water, the change makes the pencil appear bent.

When a wave hits a medium that it cannot penetrate, it is bounced back in an action called **reflection**. For example, when light waves hit a mirror, they are reflected, or bounced, off the mirror. This can cause it to seem like there is more light in the room, since there is a "doubling back" of the initial wave. This same phenomenon also causes people to be able to see their reflection in a mirror.

When a wave travels through a slit or around an obstacle, it is known as **diffraction**. A light wave will bend around an obstacle or through a slit and cause what is called a **diffraction pattern**. When the waves bend around an obstacle, it causes the addition of waves and the spreading of light on the other side of the opening.

Dispersion is used to describe the splitting of a single wave by refracting its components into separate parts. For example, if a wave of white light is sent through a dispersion prism, the light appears as its separate rainbow-colored components, due to each colored wavelength being refracted in the prism.

When wavelengths hit boundaries, different things occur. Objects will absorb certain wavelengths of light and reflect others, depending on the boundaries. This becomes important when an object appears to be a certain color. The color of an object is not actually within that object, but rather, in the wavelengths being transmitted by that object. For example, if a table appears to be red, that means the table is absorbing all other wavelengths of visible light except those of the red wavelength. The table is reflecting, or transmitting, the wavelengths associated with red back to the human eye, and so it appears red.

Interference describes when an object affects the path of a wave, or another wave interacts with a wave. Waves interacting with each other can result in either **constructive interference** or **destructive interference**, based on their positions. With constructive interference, the waves are in sync with each other and combine to reinforce each other. In the case of deconstructive interference, the waves are out of sync and reduce the effect of each other to some degree. In **scattering**, the boundary can change the direction or energy of a wave, thus altering the entire wave. **Polarization** changes the oscillations of a wave and can alter its appearance in light waves. For example, polarized sunglasses remove the "glare" from sunlight by altering the oscillation pattern observed by the wearer.

When a wave hits a boundary and is completely reflected, or if it cannot escape from one medium to another, it is called **total internal reflection**. This effect can be seen in the diamonds with a brilliant cut. The angle cut on the sides of the diamond causes the light hitting the diamond to be completely reflected back inside the gem, making it appear brighter and more colorful than a diamond with different angles cut into its surface.

The **Doppler effect** applies to situations with both light and sound waves. The premise of the Doppler effect is that, based upon the relative position or movement of a source and an observer, waves can seem shorter or longer than they actually are. When the Doppler effect is noted with sound, it warps the noise being heard by the observer. This makes the pitch or frequency seem shorter or higher as the source is approaching, and then longer or lower as the source is getting farther away. The frequency/pitch of the source never actually changes, but the sound in respect to the observer makes it seem like the sound has changed. This can be observed when a siren passes by an observer on the road. The siren sounds much higher in pitch as it approaches the observer and then lower after it passes and is getting farther away.

The Doppler effect also applies to situations involving light waves. An observer in space would see light approaching as being shorter wavelengths than the light actually is, causing it to look blue. When the

light wave gets farther away, the light would appear red because of the apparent elongation of the wavelength. This is called the **red-blue shift**.

Basic Optics

When reflecting light, a mirror can be used to observe a virtual (not real) image. A **plane mirror** is a piece of glass with a coating in the background to create a reflective surface. An image is what the human eye sees when light is reflected off the mirror in an unmagnified manner. If a **curved mirror** is used for reflection, the image seen will not be a true reflection. Instead, the image will either be enlarged or miniaturized compared to its actual size. Curved mirrors can also make the object appear closer or farther away than the actual distance the object is from the mirror.

Lenses can be used to refract or bend light to form images. Examples of lenses are the human eye, microscopes, and telescopes. The human eye interprets the refraction of light into images that humans understand to be actual size. **Microscopes** allow objects that are too small for the unaided human eye to be enlarged enough to be seen. **Telescopes** allow objects to be viewed that are too far away to be seen with the unaided eye. **Prisms** are pieces of glass that can have a wavelength of light enter one side and appear to be divided into its component wavelengths on the other side. This is due to the ability of the prism to slow certain wavelengths more than others.

Sound

Sound travels in waves and is the movement of vibrations through a medium. It can travel through air (gas), land, water, etc. For example, the noise a human hears in the air is the vibration of the waves as they reach the ear. The human brain translates the different frequencies (pitches) and intensities of the vibrations to determine what created the noise.

A tuning fork has a predetermined frequency because of the length and thickness of its tines. When struck, it allows vibrations between the two tines to move the air at a specific rate. This creates a specific tone, or note, for that size of tuning fork. The number of vibrations over time is also steady for that tuning fork and can be matched with a frequency. All pitches heard by the human ear are categorized by using frequency and are measured in Hertz (cycles per second).

The level of sound in the air is measured with sound level meters on a decibel (dB) scale. These meters respond to changes in air pressure caused by sound waves and measure sound intensity. One decibel is 1/10th of a *bel*, named after Alexander Graham Bell, the inventor of the telephone. The decibel scale is logarithmic, so it is measured in factors of 10. This means, for example, that a 10 dB increase on a sound meter equates to a 10-fold increase in sound intensity.

Practice Quiz

1. What information is used to calculate the quantity of solute in a solution?
   a. Molarity of the solution
   b. Equivalence point
   c. Limiting reactant
   d. Theoretical yield

2. Which factor does NOT affect the solubility of a compound?
   a. Mass
   b. Chemical structure of the solute
   c. Temperature
   d. Common ion effects

3. Water that has seeped into rock cracks and freezes will most likely result in what process?
   a. Chemical weathering
   b. Mechanical weathering
   c. Erosion
   d. Deposition

4. What type of chemical reaction produces a salt?
   a. Oxidation reaction
   b. Neutralization reaction
   c. Synthesis reaction
   d. Decomposition reaction

5. Circular motion occurs around what?
   a. The center of mass
   b. The center of matter
   c. An elliptical
   d. An axis

See answers on next page

Answer Explanations

1. A: The quantity of a solute in a solution can be calculated by multiplying the molarity of the solution by the volume. The equivalence point is the point at which an unknown solute has completely reacted with a known solute concentration. The limiting reactant is the reactant completely consumed by a reaction. The theoretical yield is the maximum quantity of product produced by a reaction, according to stoichiometric ratios.

2. A: Mass is the only listed factor that does not affect the solubility of a compound. Chemical structure (*B*) can influence solubility because "like dissolves like" i.e., a polar compound will not dissolve in a nonpolar solvent; temperature (*C*) can increase or decrease solubility; common ion effects (*D*) can decrease solubility if there are similarly charged dissociating agents in the solution; and pressure (*E*) affects the solubility of gases in solution.

3. B: Freezing water expands because ice is less dense than liquid water. This expansion can break up solid rocks, which describes a form of mechanical weathering. Chemical weathering occurs when water dissolves rocks. Erosion is the movement of broken rock, and deposition is the process of laying down rocks from erosion.

4. B: A neutralization reaction produces a salt. A solid produced during a reaction in solution is called a *precipitate*. A precipitation reaction can be used for removing a salt (an ionic compound that results from a neutralization reaction) from a solvent such as water. For water, this process is called ionization. Therefore, the products of a neutralization reaction (when an acid and base react) are a salt and water. Choice *A*, oxidation reaction, involves the transfer of an electron. Choice *C*, synthesis reaction, involves the joining of two molecules to form a single molecule. Choice *D*, decomposition reaction, involves the separation of a molecule into two other molecules.

5. D: Circular motion occurs around an invisible line around which an object can rotate; this invisible line is called an axis. Choice *A*, center of mass, is the average placement of an object's mass. Choice *B* is not a real term. Choice *C*, elliptical, describes an elongated circle and is not a viable selection.

Table Reading

This section of the test measures whether you can read a table accurately. The table below shows X- and Y-values in a grid format. The numbers on the horizontal, or top, part of the table are the X-values, and the numbers on the vertical, or side, part of the table are the Y-values. In other words, the X-values correspond to columns, and the Y-values correspond to rows. Each question will provide you with two coordinates, an X and a Y, and you must quickly interpret the table to determine the correct value. Each question will have five possible answers, and you should choose the correct one.

Using the example table below, here are some practice questions and explanations to better help you understand how to use these tables.

	-3	-2	-1	0	+1	+2	+3
+3	14	15	17	19	20	21	22
+2	15	17	19	21	22	23	24
+1	16	18	20	22	24	25	26
0	18	19	21	23	25	26	28
-1	20	22	23	25	27	28	30
-2	21	23	24	26	28	29	31
-3	22	24	25	27	29	30	32

Example Problem 1

X	Y		A	B	C	D	E
0	+1		22	25	20	19	16

The answer to this example question would be A, 22. To answer this problem, first go to the X-axis and find the 0 column. Then follow the 0 column down to the +1 row on the Y-axis. The number at that point is 22. Some corresponding coordinates for the incorrect answers in this example would be:

B = 25: +1, 0

C = 20: +1, +3

D = 19: 0, +3

E = 16: -3, +1

What are some helpful tips for answering these questions correctly?

- Take your time. The easiest way to make mistakes in this section is assuming that the questions are easy and subsequently making simple mistakes.

- Make sure to correctly read the X and Y headings. It is easy to select the second column when you have an X-value of 2, but that wouldn't be the right column.

- Start with the X coordinate and stay within that selected column. Do not mistakenly travel to another column when you are selecting the Y-value.

- After you have the X column selected, go down to the corresponding Y-value row. Remember, don't change columns!

- Use your fingers or a piece of paper to mark the columns and rows as it helps you keep track of where you are and not jump to a neighboring column or row.

- Practice these types of questions until you are comfortable answering them correctly and within a certain window of time. On test day, take the same amount of time as you had been with the practice questions.

Practice Quiz

	X	Y	A	B	C	D	E
1.	3	13	214	332	-230	497	-49
2.	-8	3	16	263	305	141	371
3.	0	-10	460	111	-285	-451	293
4.	-1	2	381	94	-140	337	113
5.	3	10	50	-1	-59	225	5
6.	-12	9	203	387	-119	-436	-283
7.	-7	6	-78	311	294	100	347
8.	-6	9	254	-163	0	-232	169
9.	-9	6	379	207	316	111	-87
10.	-10	-13	-386	267	414	-80	-432
11.	-16	-6	198	52	326	226	440
12.	-4	-15	401	232	-270	288	-202
13.	16	5	35	-267	-5	-495	-44
14.	11	0	284	361	-203	72	472
15.	7	-11	157	-21	295	340	-367
16.	11	-14	466	190	43	480	155
17.	-1	17	-262	309	342	121	-400
18.	13	3	-474	197	91	108	382
19.	3	-15	295	38	340	320	135
20.	2	15	20	111	266	300	291

122

17	16	15	14	13	12	11	10	9	8	7	6	5	4	3	2	1	0	-1	-2	-3	-4	-5	-6	-7	-8	-9	-10	-11	-12	-13	-14	-15	-16	-17
-264	-286	-494	270	118	-216	-220	96	-214	441	29	146	-396	-381	219	408	362	29	406	-144	295	420	-471	-450	-480	375	-461	72	-498	-172	391	-333	-246	-106	132
302	203	-89	-177	452	345	83	115	491	370	364	-292	-14	73	125	-14	215	-394	328	-364	114	-435	378	210	163	229	461	252	434	316	427	148	-195	-244	-117
382	274	-67	94	-147	-93	-185	-447	-326	177	219	-113	-99	458	25	266	-302	347	101	454	-443	-142	435	-338	-121	-105	62	-410	103	316	-147	-373	454	-489	-66
-257	-270	404	325	-70	53	-422	-254	277	-315	276	-433	417	51	-173	115	-134	-361	479	-203	-51	-65	-454	-370	494	-201	-373	-459	123	224	186	-382	256	-101	256
416	470	-20	432	186	-76	-52	-213	329	-159	136	-290	-16	-292	214	142	-234	-162	-10	-282	407	-282	403	337	-297	177	-488	-321	281	145	186	-3	-312	87	-393
-79	-343	-290	-97	-189	445	188	123	375	483	484	299	-427	-426	-240	161	88	-364	49	-119	-293	-371	-97	292	-273	41	180	-392	-452	293	-189	-79	-30	24	437
473	377	421	-105	-290	-72	456	-469	-112	-429	-458	190	-347	72	20	59	-187	121	-248	18	88	-198	366	49	127	257	-352	126	-179	-401	73	-425	290	-479	423
-490	-430	-320	30	105	148	-313	397	-434	-408	-125	-300	-439	380	50	-43	-338	-59	-196	382	328	93	181	370	-61	420	245	285	-298	-401	-49	-97	23	184	358
-25	4	123	24	148	211	-489	438	368	-478	210	405	214	355	-334	34	-17	191	-185	-98	146	-483	-117	0	471	-185	166	140	-14	-250	174	-96	422	-231	285
491	310	13	-178	278	46	271	500	473	216	428	332	116	-199	236	-172	-470	-17	-133	-486	-382	215	-112	-144	-191	-476	-317	491	462	297	191	293	83	93	-42
94	289	278	-251	174	292	-3	433	-163	191	27	-69	-320	106	-477	229	-338	60	-185	192	430	-244	68	405	88	69	-16	354	-275	-363	186	-3	130	-395	-111
-292	-167	174	16	197	441	237	-216	161	494	174	22	-50	133	-391	32	-51	416	126	13	-111	-410	-167	-416	347	379	-317	-91	462	-308	338	149	-141	-368	-127
139	-410	404	-456	-315	165	-51	-352	136	61	362	-50	431	-8	304	-4	34	482	94	83	363	-483	381	470	-115	153	45	-484	96	-363	-256	-3	-383	-64	-481
-495	-467	-315	438	-292	148	-184	-467	-467	191	-437	106	-322	-330	-228	-325	-86	60	-485	-486	-111	-234	-390	-483	88	124	64	-411	196	-308	338	50	293	-463	434
369	362	-486	455	214	211	-3	-184	-300	494	-380	372	-50	136	-477	499	-12	-193	177	192	430	215	-167	405	347	-103	5	-352	238	-90	191	331	-251	142	-368
-12	-425	-91	258	142	-192	-60	-352	45	61	-349	411	-322	-345	136	-325	-322	335	-346	13	363	189	174	14	-7	109	148	156	-78	-41	197	331	277	-64	434
438	-408	-34	182	-234	-60	34	-184	-203	350	301	-7	-167	261	-153	-141	10	-107	-215	-341	-306	-175	-91	192	330	437	257	-40	183	284	-454	-153	-241	-92	57
353	474	-337	-128	-162	-364	-86	197	28	-21	-82	373	-91	-171	28	232	-322	111	-323	-200	-451	-92	-86	-49	-367	-282	-32	155	442	-172	410	-259	281	-196	-205
-93	335	359	-455	-91	370	191	329	-80	-238	-211	-7	-61	196	189	75	-195	145	-215	-201	-461	-331	-84	-87	171	-230	-315	306	289	-432	410	-417	298	-223	-9
-456	59	-107	8	-34	423	-233	45	28	-75	-387	373	174	261	28	113	10	145	154	-341	-306	92	-41	163	191	190	-341	-138	-404	-172	-490	-259	-417	477	225
219	-117	-257	6	-337	-14	-65	158	-36	-125	342	-497	-91	317	460	232	389	-40	442	35	-393	-205	-172	-19	55	-462	-315	-451	418	-461	-490	-259	-417	-385	-422
316	-361	83	81	359	-41	410	156	-50	153	-7	-405	-475	437	55	-3	-307	156	-59	386	-30	-1	324	478	-395	325	-32	306	289	475	328	182	265	477	-330
172	34	365	-423	-107	-297	238	223	64	124	348	-443	-390	-376	-297	466	-322	309	-32	-200	278	-100	-417	-48	-296	222	307	155	183	250	-259	295	261	-196	-191
293	30	328	0	-257	284	-78	200	-331	-411	-440	-29	-390	-60	-129	319	-290	462	281	-74	226	-460	-479	-93	-313	456	-130	267	463	-92	362	-189	-94	18	274
404	291	453	-287	83	334	170	-451	148	109	433	14	-82	-422	-238	397	-53	362	367	207	242	78	494	140	262	369	11	-137	58	-398	-53	76	469	8	297

Answer Key

1. A: (3, 13) is 214.

2. E: (-8, 3) is 371.

3. B: (0, -10) is 111.

4. B: (-1, 2) is 94.

5. A: (3, 10) is 50.

6. C: (-12, 9) is -119.

7. E: (-7, 6) is 347.

8. C: (-6, 9) is 0.

9. A: (-9, 6) is 379.

10. B: (-10, -13) is 267.

11. B: (-16, -6) is 52.

12. D: (-4, -15) is 288.

13. D: (16, 5) is -495.

14. C: (11, 0) is -203.

15. E: (7, -11) is -367.

16. D: (11, -14) is 480.

17. D: (-1, 17) is 121.

18. B: (13, 3) is 197.

19. B: (3, -15) is 38.

20. C: (2, 15) is 266.

Instrument Comprehension

Purpose of Instrument-Comprehension Questions

The purpose of the instrument-comprehension questions is to ensure that vital instruments are understood. There needs to be a familiarity with the instruments and knowledge of their purposes, as well as how to read them.

Presentation of the Instrument-Comprehension Questions

Depending on the types of instruments covered in the test, the comprehension questions will vary in layout. For example, the practice questions in this section pertain to the artificial horizon and the compass. These two instruments are presented with the readings that you would need to be able to translate in order to determine the orientation of the aircraft, were they presented to you in the cockpit.

Reading the Compass and Artificial-Horizon Instruments

The **compass** on an aircraft is a navigational instrument used to determine the direction of flight, or the "aircraft heading." Compass reading is simple. As most people are aware, the needle reflects the direction being faced. When the aircraft is facing north, the needle will be pointing at the "N." If the aircraft is facing southwest, the needle will point to "SW."

The **artificial horizon**, also known as the **attitude indicator**, is an aircraft instrument that shows the aircraft orientation as compared with the Earth's horizon. This instrument indicates the pitch and bank of the aircraft, which is the tilt of the nose and the wings. The artificial horizon becomes relatively easy to read and interpret once you visualize it from the pilot seat.

The artificial horizon utilizes a small airplane or wings and a horizon bar. The aircraft in the instrument is representative of the host aircraft that is being flown. The **horizon bar** represents the actual horizon of the Earth. Many artificial-horizon instruments are blue in the upper half representing the sky and dark on the lower half, which represents the ground. If the aircraft or wings in the instrument are above the horizon bar, the aircraft is *nose up or climbing*. If the aircraft is shown below the horizon bar in the instrument, then the aircraft is *nose down, or descending in altitude*. When the symbolic aircraft is even with the horizon bar, the plane is in level flight.

125

The artificial-horizon instrument typically will have degree marks that indicate the amount of aircraft banking that occurs during turning maneuvers. The horizon bar will tilt opposite of the direction of the wings, which will show the orientation of the aircraft to the horizon during banking.

The questions in this section will provide compass and artificial-horizon indications instruments (see example below), and you will be required to determine the orientation of the aircraft using these two. Besides looking at the compass for direction, pay close attention to the artificial horizon to determine if the indication is that of a climbing or descending aircraft, or possibly an aircraft in level flight. Also, it is important to verify the direction of banking. Once you have figured out the heading, the pitch, and the banking, you should be able to choose the correct answer from the simulated aircraft images provided.

For the purpose of these questions, the simulated aircraft will appear to be flying away from your view for north, facing you for south, facing with the nose to the left of the page for west and to the right for east.

Example practice question: Looking at the instruments on the left, which choice depicts the orientation of the aircraft?

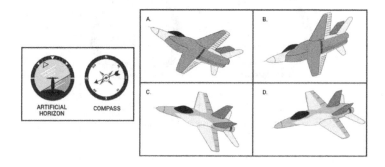

The correct answer to the example question is "A". The compass is showing a west-southwest heading. The artificial horizon shows the wings are above the horizon bar, indicating the aircraft is in a climb. Lastly, the artificial horizon shows the right wing is dipped, as the horizon bar is tilted opposite. This indicates the aircraft is banked to the right. Put it all together and you have an aircraft heading west-southwest (facing away and to the left), while it is in a climb and a right bank. The only choice that corresponds to this orientation is answer A.

Studying for the compass and artificial horizon portion of the test

You may want to practice with a standard compass if you are not familiar with compass reading. Many smartphones have compass capabilities, or you can find one at a sporting-goods store. You probably will not be able to find an artificial horizon to practice with, so it is recommended that you prepare for this portion of the test using the following practice questions.

127

Practice Quiz

1. Looking at the instruments on the left, which choice depicts the orientation of the aircraft?

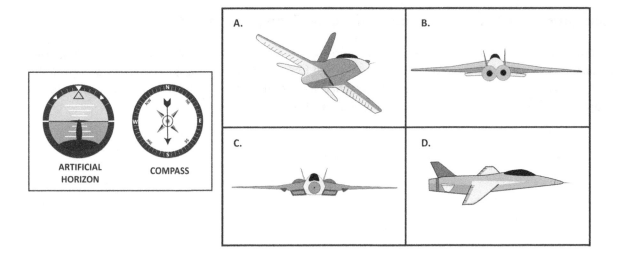

2. Looking at the instruments on the left, which choice depicts the orientation of the aircraft?

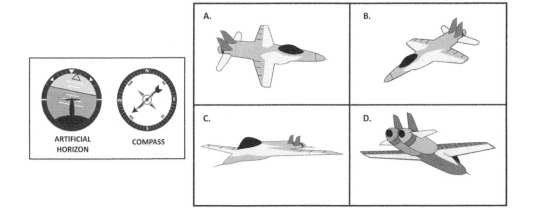

3. Looking at the instruments on the left, which choice depicts the orientation of the aircraft?

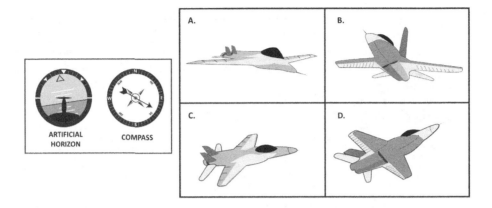

4. Looking at the instruments on the left, which choice depicts the orientation of the aircraft?

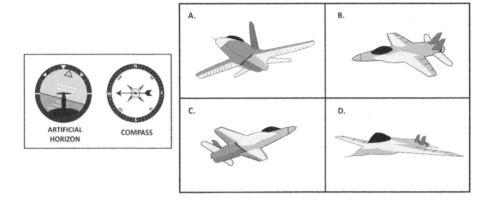

5. Looking at the instruments on the left, which choice depicts the orientation of the aircraft?

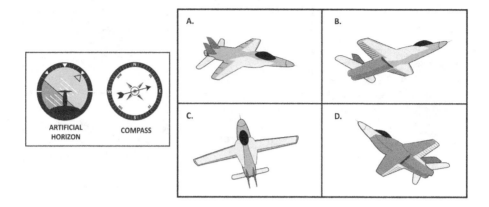

See answers on next page

Answer Explanations

1. C: The aircraft is heading south, in level flight, and without banking.

2. B: The aircraft is heading southwest, descending, and banking left.

3. C: The aircraft is heading east-southeast, ascending, and banking right.

4. B: The aircraft is heading west, ascending, and banking left.

5. B: The aircraft is heading east-northeast, ascending, and banking left.

Block Counting

This section of the test measures your spatial reasoning and logic. You will be shown a three-dimensional (3-D) drawing of blocks. Some of these blocks may be touching, and, if so, you will be asked to determine the number of blocks that one particular block is touching. Keep in mind that some of the blocks may not be visible. There is no prior knowledge of block counting that is needed for this section of the test; just use logic and spatial reasoning.

In order for a block to "touch" another block, their faces must touch. If only two blocks' corners touch and not their faces, then they are not considered to be touching.

See the example problem below.

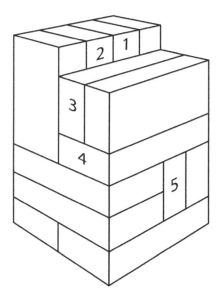

In this example, you know that Block 1 is touching 5 other blocks. Block 1 is touching Block 2 and 3, the block to the right of Block 1, Block 4, and Block 5.

Block 2 is also touching 5 blocks: Block 1, the block to the left of Block 2, Block 3, Block 4, and one of the horizontal blocks beside Block 5.

What about Block 4? Block 4 is touching an astonishing 9 blocks: Block 3, the block to the right of Block 3, Blocks 1 and 2 and the two on either side of them, Block 5 and the top block on the left of it, and the one block on the right of Block 5.

Sometimes you will have to infer how big a block is when only part of the block is shown.

Practice Quiz

For questions 1-5, determine how many blocks the given block is touching.

Use the following block for questions 1-5.

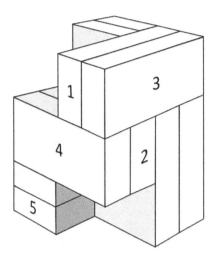

1. Block 1
   a.   4
   b.   5
   c.   6
   d.   7
   e.   8

2. Block 2
   a.   4
   b.   5
   c.   6
   d.   7
   e.   8

3. Block 3
   a.   5
   b.   6
   c.   7
   d.   8
   e.   9

4. Block 4

    a. 3

    b. 4

    c. 4

    d. 6

    e. 7

5. Block 5

    a. 1

    b. 2

    c. 3

    d. 4

    e. 5

See answers on next page

Answer Explanations

1. D: Block 1 is touching seven other blocks. There are four underneath it, two on the back left side, and one on the right side.

2. C: Block 2 is touching six other blocks. There are two on top of it, two to the right of it, one to the left of it, and one underneath it.

3. A: Block 3 is touching five blocks. There are four underneath it and one to the left of it (Block 1).

4. B: Block 4 is touching four blocks. It is touching Blocks 1, 2, and 3, as well as one block underneath it.

5. C: Block 5 is touching 3 blocks. It has one above it and two to the right of it.

Aviation Information

The aviation information contained in this section can help provide some basic knowledge in the following areas:

- Fixed-wing aircraft
- Flight envelope
- Flight concepts and terminology
- Flight maneuvers
- Helicopters
- Airport information

Fixed-wing aircraft

A fixed-wing aircraft is one in which movement of the wings in relation to the aircraft is not used to generate lift, even though technically they flex in flight, as do all wings. In contrast, helicopters generate lift through rotating airfoils.

Fixed-wing aircraft have the following items in common: wings, flight controls, tail assembly, landing gear, fuselage, and an engine or powerplant. Here's an illustration of many of the parts of planes:

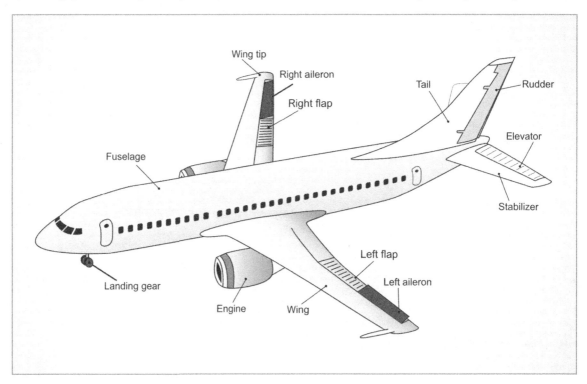

136

Wings

An airfoil is a surface such as a wing, elevator, or aileron that is designed to help create lift and control of an aircraft by using and manipulating air flow. The standard wing, or airfoil, is mounted to the sides of the fuselage. The outline or cross section of the airfoil is referred to as the airfoil profile. The standard wing has an upper surface that is curved while the lower surface is relatively flat. The air moves over the curved surface of the wing at a higher speed than it moves under the flat surface. The difference in airflow on the surfaces of the wing creates lift due to the aircraft's forward airspeed, which enables flight.

Many modern aircraft structures use full cantilever wings, meaning no external bracing is required. The strength in this design is from the internal structural members and the fuselage. Semi-cantilever wings use some form of external bracing, whether it be wires or struts.

Aircraft wing designs vary based on the characteristics and type of performance needed for the aircraft. Changing the wing design changes the amount of lift that can be created and the amount of stability and control the aircraft will have at different speeds. Some aircraft have wings that are designed to tilt, sweep, or fold. So long as they do not generate lift, they are still considered fixed-wing aircraft. Wing geometry is related to the shape of the aircraft wings when viewed from the front of the aircraft, or from above.

Flight Controls

Flight controls, like the name implies, are used to direct the forces on an aircraft in flight for the purpose of directional and attitude control. Flight controls vary from simple mechanical (manually operated) systems, to hydro-mechanical systems, to fly-by-wire systems. Fly-by-wire systems send signals via wire to control the plane.

When discussing flight controls, it's important to understand the terms leading edge and trailing edge. **Leading edge** refers to the front part of the wing that separates air, forcing it to go above or below the wing. **Trailing edge** is the back part of the wing and where the air comes back together.

The flight controls typically are divided into primary and secondary systems.

The primary flight controls are responsible for the movement of the aircraft along its three axes of flight. Primary flight controls on an aircraft are the **elevators**, **ailerons**, and **rudder**. Elevators are mounted on the trailing edges of horizontal stabilizers and are used for controlling aircraft pitch about the lateral axis. The ailerons are mounted on the trailing edges of the wings and are used for controlling aircraft roll about the longitudinal axis. The rudder is mounted on the trailing edge of the vertical fin and is used for controlling rotation (yaw) around the vertical axis.

Here's an illustration of pitch, roll, and yaw along the three axes.

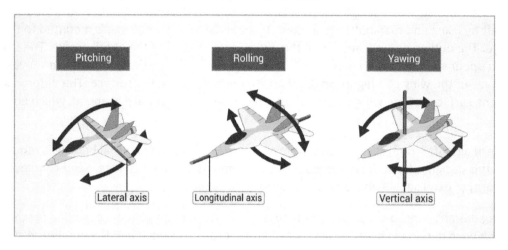

Secondary, or auxiliary, flight controls include (but are not limited to): flaps, slats, spoilers, speed brakes, and the trim system. Flaps are the hinged portion of the wing trailing edge between the ailerons and the fuselage, and sometimes may be located on the leading edge of a wing as well. If used during takeoff, flaps reduce the amount of runway and time needed to takeoff. During landings, flaps increase the drag on the wings slowing the plane down and allowing it to go slower right before it lands, which then reduces the amount of runway needed. Essentially, flaps allow the aircraft to produce more lift at slower airspeeds. Flaps are also utilized on some planes to increase maneuverability. The amount of flap extension and the angle can be adjusted by the flap levers located in the cockpit.

Spoilers are located on the upper, or trailing edge, of the wing and are used to decrease lift. They allow the nose of the aircraft to be pitched down without increasing the airspeed, allowing for a safe landing speed. Slats are located on the middle to outboard portion of the leading edge of the wing. They are used to create additional lift and slower flight by extending the shape of the wing. Flaps and slats are hidden inside the wing and are extended during takeoff and landing.

The trim system is an inexpensive autopilot that eliminates the need for the pilot to constantly maintain pressure on the controls. Most aircraft trim systems contain trim, balance, anti-balance, and servo tabs. These tabs are found on the trailing edge of primary flight control surfaces and are used to counteract hydro-mechanical and aerodynamic forces acting on the aircraft.

Tail Assembly
The tail assembly of an aircraft is commonly referred to as the empennage. The empennage structure typically includes a tail cone, fixed stabilizers (horizontal and vertical), and moveable surfaces to assist in directional control. The moveable surfaces are the rudder, which is attached to the vertical stabilizer, and the elevators attached to the horizontal stabilizers.

Landing Gear
Aircraft require landing gear not only for takeoffs and landings but also to support the aircraft while it is on the ground. The landing gear must be designed to support the entire weight of the aircraft and handle the loads placed on it during landing, as well as be as light as possible. Small aircraft that fly at low-speeds usually have fixed landing gear, which means it is stationary and does not have the ability to retract in flight. Aircraft that fly at higher speeds require retractable landing gear so that the gear is not

damaged in the airstream. Retractable landing gear makes the aircraft more aerodynamic by reducing drag, but usually at the cost of additional weight when compared to the fixed landing gear.

Also, the landing gear should only be operated (extended or retracted) when the airspeed indicator is at or below the aircraft's maximum landing-gear operating speed, or V_{LO}. Airspeeds above V_{LO} can damage the landing gear operating mechanism. When the gear is down and locked, the aircraft should not be operated above the aircraft's maximum landing-gear extended speed, or V_{LE}. Since landing gear is more stable when all the way down than when being moved, V_{LE} will be higher for an aircraft than V_{LO}. A switch or lever that resembles the shape of a wheel is used to raise and lower the landing gear.

Landing gear is made from a variety of materials, such as magnesium, steel, and aluminum. Most landing gear has some type of shock absorbers and braking system. Not all landing gear uses wheels. Depending on what the aircraft is used for, it may have skis, skids, pontoons, or floats instead of tires for landing on snow, ice, or water.

Landing gear is typically found in two configurations: tricycle gear and conventional gear (also known as tail wheel gear).

Tricycle gear is the most common configuration. Tricycle gear has a single wheel in the front (usually under the nose) and two wheels side-by-side at the center of gravity of the aircraft. Large, heavy aircraft may contain extra wheels in this configuration. Small aircraft equipped with nose landing gear can typically be steered with rudder pedals.

Conventional tail wheel aircraft or "taildraggers" were more common in the early days of aviation. The two main wheels supported the heaviest portion of the aircraft, with the third smaller wheel was near the tail. Having the smaller wheel in the tail allowed the aircraft to rest at an incline on the ground, which provided more clearance for the nose propeller. In some conventional gear, the tail wheel could be steered mechanically with the rudder pedals.

Fuselage

The fuselage is the main structure, or airframe, of an aircraft. The fuselage is where the cockpit, or cabin, of the aircraft is, and where passengers or cargo may be located. It provides attachment points for the main components of the aircraft such as the wings, engines, and empennage. If an aircraft is a single-engine, the fuselage houses the powerplant as well. If the powerplant is a reciprocating engine, it is mounted in the front of the aircraft, while a turbine engine would be mounted in the rear of the aircraft. **Cowling** is the term for the covering of an airplane's engine which is streamlined to maximize aerodynamics.

Aircraft contain a battery that is charged by an alternator or generator. Wiring takes the electric current to where it's needed throughout the plane. Some type of warning system will be in place to warn of inadequate current output. This could be a warning light or an ammeter. If the number showing on an ammeter is positive, it means the battery is charging. If the number is negative, it means that the alternator or generator cannot keep up with the amount of current being used. Some aircraft have a loadmeter, which shows the amount of current being drawn from the battery.

Fuselage structures are usually classified as truss, monocoque, and semi-monocoque. The truss fuselage is typically made of steel tubing welded together, which enables the structure to handle tension and compression loads. In lighter aircraft, an aluminum alloy may be used along with cross-bracing. A single shell fuselage is referred to as monocoque, which uses a stronger skin to handle the tension and

compression loads. There is also a semi-monocoque fuselage, which is basically a combination of the truss and monocoque fuselage, and is the most commonly used.

Powerplant

The powerplant of an aircraft is its engine, which is a component of the propulsion system that generates mechanical power and thrust. Most modern aircraft engines are typically either turbine or piston engines.

Flight Envelope

The flight envelope (also known as the performance envelope or service envelope) refers to the capabilities of an aircraft based on its design in terms of altitude, airspeed, loading factors, and maneuverability. When an aircraft is pushed to the point it exceeds design limitations for that specific aircraft, it is considered to be operating outside the envelope, which is considered dangerous.

All aircraft have approved flight manuals that contain the flight limitations or parameters. To ensure an aircraft is being operated properly, a pilot needs to be familiar with the aircraft's flight envelope prior to flight. The flight parameters are based on the engine and wing design and include the following: maximum and minimum speed, stall speed, climb rate, glide ratio, maximum altitude, and the maximum amount of gravity forces (g-forces) the aircraft can withstand.

- The **maximum speed** of an aircraft is based on air resistance getting lower at higher altitudes, to a point where increased altitude no longer increases maximum speed due to lack of oxygen to "feed" the engine.

- The stalling speed is the minimum speed at which an aircraft can maintain level flight. As the aircraft gains altitude, the stall speed increases (since the aircraft's weight can be better supported through speed).

- The **climb rate** is the vertical speed of an aircraft, which is the increase in altitude in respect to time.

- The **climb gradient** is the ratio of the increase in altitude to the horizontal air distance.

- The **glide ratio** is the ratio of horizontal distance traveled per rate of fall.

- The **maximum altitude** of an aircraft is also referred to as the service ceiling. The ceiling is usually determined by the aircraft performance and the wings, and is where an altitude at a given speed can no longer be increased at level flight.

- The **maximum g-forces** each aircraft can withstand varies, but is based on its design and structural strength.

Commercial aircraft are considered to have a small flight envelope, since the range of speed and maneuverability is rather limited, and they are designed to operate efficiently under moderate conditions. The Federal Aviation Administration (FAA) is the controlling body in the United States pertaining to authorized flight envelopes and restrictions for commercial and civilian aircraft. The FAA may reduce a flight envelope for added safety as needed.

Military aircraft, especially fighter jets, have extremely large flight envelopes. By design, these aircraft are very maneuverable and can operate at high speeds as their purpose requires. The term "pushing the envelope" originally referred to military pilots taking an aircraft to the extreme limits of their capabilities, mostly during combat, but also during aircraft flight testing. The term "outside the envelope" is when the aircraft is pushed outside the design specifications and is considered very dangerous. Operating outside the limits of the aircraft can severely degrade the life of components, or even lead to mechanical failure.

Some of the modern fly-by-wire aircraft have built in flight envelope protection. This protection is built into the control system and helps prevent a pilot from forcing an aircraft into a situation that exceeds its structural and aerodynamic operational limits. This system is beneficial in emergency situations because it prevents the pilots from endangering the aircraft while making split-second decisions.

Flight Concepts and Terminology

Aerodynamics is the study of objects in motion through the air, such as when the air interacts with an aircraft wing, and the forces that produce or change such motion. It is important to note that the air affects the aerodynamics of an aircraft in flight. Therefore, it is important that the aircraft's operating environment, the atmosphere, is understood.

Atmospheric pressure differs depending on altitude. The higher the altitude above sea level, the less pressure exists. Air density varies with pressure. The higher the altitude, the less dense the air. Humidity, the amount of water vapor in the air, varies with the temperature.

There are four main forces that act on all aircraft: *gravity*, *lift*, *thrust*, and *drag*. The four main forces are always present during aircraft flight. For flight to occur, thrust and lift always need to be greater than the gravity and drag forces.

Gravity
Gravity is the downward force that pulls everything toward the surface of the Earth at a rate of 9.8 m/s^2. The weight of an object's mass is the result of gravity acting upon the object. The pull is also called the weight force. Aircraft need to provide enough lift force to overcome gravity to fly.

Lift
The **lift** force is created by the motion of the aircraft through the air. The air that travels over the curved surface of a wing has farther to go than the air moving below the wing. The air above must travel faster than the air below to reach the back of the wing at the same time. The air traveling faster over the top of a wing creates lower pressure. The lower pressure above the wing causes it to lift. **Bernoulli's principle** illustrates that an increase in velocity is always accompanied by a decrease in pressure and creates lift on an airfoil.

Thrust
The engine, or powerplant, of the aircraft creates thrust, which is necessary to create forward motion. **Thrust** is the force that propels the aircraft forward to provide airflow beneath the wings for lift. The purpose of thrust is not to lift an aircraft, but to overcome the force of drag. The direction of thrust can be varied by the design of the aircraft propulsion system.

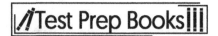
Drag

Drag is the force generated when an aircraft is moving through the air. Drag is air resistance that opposes thrust, basically aerodynamic friction or wind resistance. The amount of drag is dependent on several factors, including the shape of the aircraft, the speed it is traveling, and the density of the air it is passing through. There are two categories of drag: **induced drag** and **parasitic drag**. Induced drag is created through the generation of lift and is caused by wingtip vortices (rotating air coming off wings). Parasitic drag is created by the shape of the aircraft.

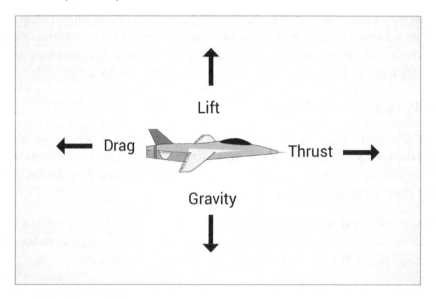

The angular difference measured between an aircraft's axis and the line of the horizon is the flight attitude. Aircraft attitude is based on relative positions of the nose and wings on the natural horizon. There are four types of attitude flying: pitch control, bank control, power control, and trim control. The angle formed by the longitudinal axis of the aircraft is pitch attitude. The angle formed by the lateral axis is bank attitude. Yaw is the rotation of the aircraft around its vertical axis, which is not relative to the horizon, but to the flightpath. Power control is used when there is a need for a change in thrust in the aircraft. Trim is for relieving all possible control pressures held after the desired attitude has been reached. The moveable surfaces on the wings and tail introduced earlier allow for control of an aircraft's attitude and orientation. These airfoils work on the same principle as the lift on the wing.

Here are some examples of pitch control and bank control:

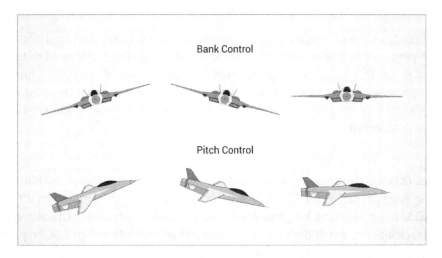

Flight Controls and Forces

The vertical stabilizer, or the tail fin, keeps the aircraft aligned in the desired direction. Air presses on both sides of the tail with equal force when operating in a straight line. When the aircraft yaws left or right, the air pressure increases on one side of the tail and decreases on the other side. The imbalance of the pressure acting upon the tail will push it back in line.

The horizontal stabilizer provides for leveling of an aircraft in flight. If the aircraft tilts up or down, the air pressure increases on one side of the stabilizer and decreases on the other. This imbalance on the stabilizer will push the aircraft back into level flight. The horizontal stabilizer holds the tail down as well, since most aircraft designs induce a tendency for the nose to tilt down due to the center of gravity being forward of the center of lift.

Ailerons are located on the outer, trailing edges of the wings, and control the roll of an aircraft. The ailerons operate opposite each other, up and down, to decrease lift on one wing and increase lift on the other. The change in lift will cause the aircraft to roll either to the left or right; therefore, the pilot will use the ailerons to tilt the aircraft in the direction of a turn.

The elevators are moveable control surfaces attached to the trailing edge of the horizontal stabilizer. The elevators tilt up and down to increase or decrease lift on the tail. The increase or decrease in lift will cause the nose of the aircraft to tilt up or down.

The rudder is a moveable control surface located on the aft end of the aircraft vertical tail fin. The rudder moves from side to side, pushing the tail left or right. The rudder is used in conjunction with the ailerons to turn an aircraft.

Trim Control

In-flight variable trim control along the three axes is used to level an aircraft in pitch and roll while eliminating yaw. The trim system serves to counter the aerodynamic forces that affect the balance of the aircraft in flight. The control pressures on an aircraft change as conditions change during a flight. Trim control systems can compensate for the change in weight and center of gravity that occurs in flight as the aircraft burns fuel, as well as compensating for change in wind and atmospheric pressure. Trim can relieve all possible control pressures held after the desired attitude has been reached. Larger and

more sophisticated aircraft tend to have a more sophisticated trim system in the pitch, roll, and yaw axes. Smaller aircraft tend to have only pitch control.

The primary flight controls are positioned in-line with the aircraft surfaces during straight-and-level flight. When the flight is not balanced, one or more flight control surfaces will need to be adjusted by continuous control input. This input can be performed through the use of trim tabs; therefore, avoiding the need for constant adjustments by the pilot. The trim systems also prevent the pilot from having to exert strong control force for an extended amount of time—essentially easing the physical workload required to control the aircraft.

Angle of Attack

The angle of attack (AOA) is the angle between the relative wind and the chord line (line between the leading and trailing edge of the airfoil). The AOA can be used to affect the amount of lift on an aircraft. The greater the AOA, the greater the lift generated until the AOA reaches the critical angle of attack. The critical angle of attack induces a stall because the induced drag exceeds the lift. During a stall, the wing is no longer able to create sufficient lift to oppose gravity. Stall angle is usually around 20°. Thus, once it's been reached, any subsequent increase in the AOA hurts aerodynamics.

Additional Related Terms

Center of gravity: In flight, the aircraft rotates around its center of gravity.

Ground effect: The reduced drag and increased lift that is experienced by an aircraft flying in close proximity to the ground is called the ground effect. For fixed-wing aircraft it is considered in ground effect when the wing is in close proximity to the ground. A helicopter is considered to be in ground effect when it is within one rotor diameter of the ground. For example, if the rotor diameter of the helicopter is 50 feet, then 50 feet and below is considered to be in ground effect.

Flight Maneuvers

There are four fundamental maneuvers in flight: straight-and-level, turns, climbs, and descents. Every controlled flight usually includes a combination of these four fundamentals.

The duration and the amount of pressure used on the flight controls determine the displacement of the corresponding flight control, which controls the maneuver being made. Since the airspeed differs during maneuvers, the distance the flight controls move is not as important as the appropriate pressure the pilot applies to the control for each maneuver.

Straight-and-Level Flight

Maintaining a heading and altitude, with only minor adjustments to flight controls, is referred to as straight-and-level flight. Straight-and-level flight may require adjustment depending on the atmospheric conditions — just as keeping an automobile going in a straight line can require adjustments. This laterally level flight can be achieved by checking the relationship of the aircraft wingtips with the natural horizon. The distance of both wingtips above or below the horizon should be the same. Any adjustments should be made with the ailerons. To a lesser extent, the wingtips can also be used to determine pitch attitude. During straight-and-level flight, small deviations from lateral flight can be addressed quickly with small corrections. Almost no control pressure is required to maintain straight-and-level if the aircraft is properly trimmed and is in smooth air. Airspeed will usually remain consistent when a constant power setting is used.

Turns

A turn in an aircraft is performed by banking the wings in the direction of the turn. The appropriate amount of control pressures need to be applied by the pilot to achieve and hold the desired banking for the turn. All primary controls are required and should be coordinated during a turn.

Turns are divided into three classes: shallow, medium, and steep. Shallow turns are typically less than 20°, which is so shallow that the aircraft's lateral stability acts to level the wings, unless an aileron is used to maintain banking. Medium turns range from approximately 20° to 45°, and the aircraft holds a constant bank. Steep turns are more than 45°, and the aircraft will have a tendency to overbank without the addition of aileron control.

During constant altitude and airspeed turns, the elevator should be up to increase the angle-of-attack (AOA) of the wing when rolling into a turn. Use of the elevator during a turn is needed because the vertical lift has been changed to a horizontal lift. To stop the turn, the aileron and rudder are used in the opposite direction to return the wings to level flight.

Climbs

An aircraft's climb is restricted by the amount of thrust available, since the thrust needs to be able to overcome the increased drag that occurs during climbing maneuvers. In a climb, the weight is no longer perpendicular to the flightpath; it is directed rearward.

Climbs require the simultaneous increase in throttle and back-pressure on the elevator to lift the nose of the aircraft. Nose-up elevator trim may be used after the climb has been established to make minor adjustments in pitch.

Descents

Descent is when an aircraft changes flight path to a downward inclined plane, normally losing altitude with partial power. The settings recommended by the aircraft manufacturer should be used when setting pitch and power for a descent. The power, pitch, and airspeed should be kept constant.

Helicopters

Helicopters, a type of rotary-wing or rotorcraft, are extremely versatile aircraft that may be used for a wide array of situations where a typical aircraft could not perform. A helicopter differs from other types of aircraft that derive lift from their wings, as it gets its lift and thrust from the rotors. The rotors are basically rotating airfoils; hence the name rotorcraft. The "rotating wing," or main rotor, may have two or more blades whose profiles resemble that of aircraft wings.

Although rotorcraft come in many shapes and sizes, they mostly have the same major components in common. There is a cabin, an airframe, landing gear, a power plant, a transmission, and an anti-torque system. The cabin of the rotorcraft houses the crew and cargo. The airframe is the fuselage where components are mounted and attached. The landing gear may be made up of wheels, skis, skids, or floats.

Due to its operating characteristics, a helicopter is able to:

- Take off and land vertically (in almost any small, clear area)
- Fly forward, backward, and laterally
- Operate at lower speeds

- Hover for extended periods of time

Common uses for the helicopter include military operations, search and rescue, law enforcement, firefighting, medical transport, news reporting, and tourism.

Helicopters are subjected to the same forces as other aircraft: lift, weight, thrust, and drag. In addition, helicopters also have some unique forces they are subjected to: torque, centrifugal and centripetal force, gyroscopic precession, dissymmetry of lift, effective translational lift, transverse flow effect, and Coriolis effect.

Here are some examples of different helicopter designs:

Torque
Torque from the engine turning the main rotor forces the body of the helicopter in the opposite direction. Most helicopters use a tail rotor, which counters this torque force by pushing or pulling against the tail.

Centrifugal and Centripetal Force
Centrifugal force is the apparent force that causes rotating bodies to move away from the center of rotation. Centripetal force is the force that keeps an object a certain distance from the center of rotation.

Gyroscopic Precession
Gyroscopic precession is when the applied force to a rotating object is shown 90º later than where the force was applied.

Dissymmetry of Lift
Dissymmetry of lift is the difference in lift between the advancing and retreating blades of the rotor system. The difference in lift is due to directional flight. The rotor system compensates for dissymmetry of lift with blade flapping, which allows the blades to twist and lift in order to balance the advancing and retreating blades. The pilot also compensates by cyclic feathering. Together, blade flapping and cyclic feathering eliminate dissymmetry of lift.

Effective Translational Lift
Effective translational lift (ETL) is the improved efficiency that results from directional flight. Efficiency is gained when the helicopter moves forward, as opposed to hovering. The incoming airflow essentially

pushes the turbulent air behind the helicopter, which provides a more horizontal airflow for the airfoil to move through. This typically occurs between 16 and 24 knots.

Transverse Flow Effect

Transverse flow effect is the difference in airflow between the forward and aft portions of the rotor disk. During forward flight, there is more downwash in the rear portion of the rotor disk. The downward flow on the rear portion of the disk results in a reduced AOA and produces less lift. The front half of the rotor produces more lift due to an increased AOA. Transverse flow occurs between 10 and 20 knots and can be easily recognized by the increased vibrations during take-off and landing.

Coriolis Effect

The Coriolis Effect is when an object moving in a rotating system experiences an inertial force (Coriolis) acting perpendicular to the direction of motion and the axis of rotation. In a clockwise rotation, the force acts to the left of the motion of an object. If the rotation is counterclockwise, the force acts to the right of the motion of an object.

A typical helicopter is controlled through use of the cyclic control stick, the collective controls lever, and the anti-torque pedals.

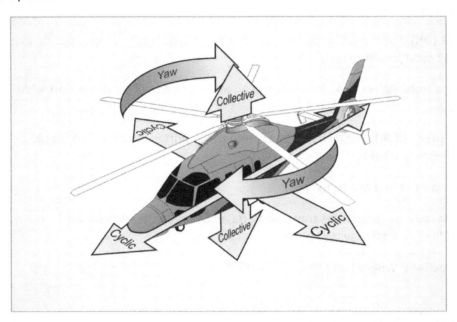

Cyclic Control

The cyclic is the control stick that is used to control the movement of the helicopter forward, backward, or sideways. Simply stated, the cyclic changes the pitch of the rotor blades cyclically in any of 360°. The cyclic stick also contains several buttons that control the trim, intercom, and radio. These will differ slightly depending on each model helicopter.

Collective Controls

The collective control is used to increase the pitch of the main rotor simultaneously at all points of the rotor blade rotation. The collective increases or decreases total rotor thrust; the cyclic changes the direction of rotor thrust. In forward flight, the collective pitch changes the amount of thrust, which in turn can change the speed or altitude based on the use of the cyclic. During hovering, the collective control is used to adjust the altitude of hover.

Anti-Torque Pedals

The anti-torque pedals are used to control yaw on a helicopter. These pedals are located in the same place, and serve a similar purpose, as rudder pedals on an airplane. Application of pressure on a pedal changes the pitch of the tail rotor blade, which will increase or reduce the tail rotor thrust and cause the nose of the helicopter to yaw in the desired direction.

Airport Information

Airports come in all shapes and sizes, from tiny dirt strips to enormous concrete runways. Pilots are required to know the procedures and rules of the specific airports being used, and understand pavement markings, lights, and signs that provide takeoff, landing, and taxiway information.

Procedures have been developed for airport traffic patterns and traffic control. These procedures include specific routes or specific runways for takeoffs and landings. Each airport traffic pattern depends on a number of factors, including obstructions and wind conditions.

Terms

Clearway: A specified area after the runway that is clear of obstacles, at the same or nearly the same altitude as the runway, and specifically for planes to fly over in their initial ascent.

Decision height (DH): The lowest height (in feet) in which if a pilot cannot see specified visual references, they must stop landing

Holding/Flying a Hold: Refers to a plane flying in an oval flight path near the airport while waiting for clearance to land

Runway visual range (RVR): The distance away from the airport in which a pilot should be able to see runway markings and/or lights.

Threshold: The start or end of a runway

Taxiway: The paved area that planes travel on to travel between the terminal and runway. The path a plane should follow on a taxiway is marked by a yellow line

Taxiway intersections: Where two taxiway routes intersect.

Signs

Here are some common taxiway signs:

Name	Sign Color	Letter Color	Function
no entry	red	white	indicates an area planes should not go into
runway location	black	yellow	displays current runway name
taxiway location	black	yellow	displays current taxiway name
direction/runway exit	yellow	black	displays name of upcoming taxiway that airplane is about to intersect with
runway	red	white	displays name of runway that airplane is about to intersect with

Lighting

These lights are visible to about 3 miles in the daytime and up to 20 miles at night.

- **Approach Lighting Systems (ALS)**: A series of light bars leading up to a runway that assist the pilot in lining up with the runway.

- **Runway centerline lights:** these are used to aid aircraft when landing in darkness or other difficult visibility conditions. These lights are embedded into the runway. They begin as white, then alternate between red and white, and then are completely red at the end of the runway.

- **Obstructions/aircraft warning lights**: *Red* or *white* lights used to mark obstructions (like buildings and cell towers) both in airports and outside of them.

- **Runway edge lights**: These are *white* and highlight the boundaries of the runway. These are referred to a high, medium, or low intensity depending on the maximum intensity they can produce.

- **Runway end identifier lights (REIL):** Many airport runways have these two flashing *red* lights. They provide a warning that the runway is ending.

- **Taxiway centerline lights**: *Green* lights indicating the middle of a taxiway.

- **Taxiway edge lights**: *Blue* lights denoting the edge of a taxiway.

- **Threshold lights**: *Green* lights that indicate the start of the runway

Visual Approach Slope Indicators (VASI)

The visual approach slope indicator (VASI) is a light system of two sets of lights designed to provide visual guidance during approach of a runway. The light indicators are visible 3-5 miles away during daylight hours and up to 20 miles away in darkness. The indicators are designed to be used once the aircraft is already visually aligned with the runway. Both sets of lights can appear as white or red. When the front lights appear white and the back lights appear red, it indicates that the plane is at the proper angle. If both lights appear white, it means the pilot is too high, and if both appear red, it means the pilot is too low.

Precision Instrument Runways

Precision instrument runways have operational visual and electronic aids that provide directional guidance. These aides may be the ILS, Precision Approach Radar (PAR), or Microwave Landing System

(MLS). Instrument runways have visual aids with a decision height greater than 200 feet and a runway visual range of 2,600 feet. These runways have *runway end lights*, which consists of eight lights (four on each side of the runway) that can appear as green or red—green to approaching planes and red to planes on the runway.

Non-Precision Instrument Runways

Non-precision instrument runways provide horizontal guidance only when there is an approved procedure for a straight-in non-precision instrument approach. The non-precision runways do not have full Instrument Landing System (ILS) capabilities, but they have approved procedures for localizer, Global Positioning System (GPS), Automatic Direction Finder (ADF), and Very High Frequency Omni-Directional Range (VOR) instrument approaches.

Visual Flight Rules Runways (VFR)

Visual flight rules (VFR) runways, also known as visual runways, operate completely under visual approach procedures. The pilot must be able to see the runway to land safely. There are no instrument approach procedures for this type of runway. They are typically found at small airports. Visual runways have centerline, designators, and threshold markings, as well as hold position markings for taxiway intersections.

Localizer Type Directional Aid (LDA)

Directional runways use a Localizer Type Directional Aid (LDA). The LDA provides a localizer-based instrument approach to an airport where, usually due to terrain, the localizer antenna is not in alignment with the runway. The LDA is more of a directional tool to enable the pilot to get close enough to where the runway can be seen.

Practice Quiz

1. Between which speeds does a helicopter achieve effective translational lift?
   a. 8 and 12 knots
   b. 16 and 24 knots
   c. 10 and 20 knots
   d. 15 and 30 knots
   e. 18 and 26 knots

2. What principle illustrates that an increase in velocity is always accompanied by a decrease in pressure and creates lift on an airfoil?
   a. Bernini's principle
   b. Benetti's principle
   c. Beerli's principle
   d. Bernoulli's principle
   e. Buchman's principle

3. Which of the following is not one of the types of flight attitude?
   a. Pitch control
   b. Bank control
   c. Lift control
   d. Trim control
   e. Power control

4. What is indicated by V_{LO}?
   a. The aircraft's maximum landing-gear operating speed.
   b. The aircraft's minimum landing-gear operating speed.
   c. The aircraft's maximum landing-gear extended speed.
   d. The aircraft's minimum landing-gear extended speed.
   e. The aircraft's maximum landing-gear retraction speed.

5. What colors are on a No Entry runway sign?
   a. White and black
   b. Yellow and white
   c. Red and black
   d. Yellow and black
   e. Red and white

See answers on next page

151

Answer Explanations

1. B: Effective translational lift (ETL) is the improved efficiency that results from directional flight. Efficiency is gained when the helicopter moves forward, as opposed to hovering. The incoming airflow essentially pushes the turbulent air behind the helicopter, which provides a more horizontal airflow for the airfoil to move through. This typically occurs between 16 and 24 knots. Choice C is incorrect because between 10 and 20 knots is the speed at which transverse flow occurs and can be easily recognized by the increased vibrations during take-off and landing. Choices A, D, and E are random speeds that do not correspond to ETL.

2. D: Bernoulli's principle illustrates that an increase in velocity is always accompanied by a decrease in pressure and creates lift on an airfoil. Choices A, B, C, and E are not the names of flight principles.

3. C: Aircraft attitude is based on relative positions of the nose and wings on the natural horizon. There are four types of attitude flying: pitch control, bank control, power control, and trim control. Lift control is not one of these four flight attitudes. Choices A, B, D, and E are incorrect because they are the four types of flight attitude.

4. A: V_{LO} represents the aircraft's maximum landing-gear operating speed. Choice C, the maximum landing-gear extended speed, is represented by V_{LE}. Options B, D, and E are not correct indications for V_{LO}.

5. E: The runway No Entry sign is red with white lettering. Choices A, B, and C are not colors of runway signs. Choice D represents either a runway location or taxiway location sign (both black with yellow letters) or a direction/runway exit (yellow with black letters).

AFOQT Practice Test #1

Verbal Analogies

1. **Cat** is to **paws** as
   a. Giraffe is to neck.
   b. Elephant is to ears.
   c. Horse is to hooves.
   d. Snake is to skin.
   e. Turtle is to shell.

2. **Dancing** is to **rhythm** as **singing** is to
   a. Pitch.
   b. Mouth.
   c. Sound.
   d. Volume.
   e. Words.

3. **Towel** is to **dry** as **hat** is to
   a. Cold.
   b. Warm.
   c. Expose.
   d. Cover.
   e. Top.

4. **Sand** is to **glass** as
   a. Protons are to atoms.
   b. Ice is to snow.
   c. Seeds are to plants.
   d. Water is to steam.
   e. Air is to wind.

5. **Design** is to **create** as **allocate** is to
   a. Finish.
   b. Manage.
   c. Multiply.
   d. Find.
   e. Distribute.

6. **Books** are to **reading** as
   a. Movies are to making.
   b. Shows are to watching.
   c. Poetry is to writing.
   d. Scenes are to performing.
   e. Concerts are to music.

7. **Cool** is to **frigid** as **warm** is to
   a. Toasty.
   b. Summer.
   c. Sweltering.
   d. Hot.
   e. Mild.

8. **Cereal boxes** are to **rectangular prisms** as **globes** are to
   a. Circles.
   b. Maps.
   c. Wheels.
   d. Spheres.
   e. Movement.

9. **Backpacks** are to **textbooks** as
   a. Houses are to people.
   b. Fences are to trees.
   c. Plates are to food.
   d. Chalkboards are to chalk.
   e. Computers are to mice.

10. **Storm** is to **rainbow** as **sunset** is to
    a. Clouds.
    b. Sunrise.
    c. Breakfast.
    d. Bedtime.
    e. Stars.

11. **Falcon** is to **mice** as **giraffe** is to
    a. Leaves.
    b. Rocks.
    c. Antelope.
    d. Grasslands.
    e. Hamsters.

12. **Car** is to **motorcycle** as **speedboat** is to
    a. Raft.
    b. Jet-ski.
    c. Sailboat.
    d. Plane.
    e. Canoe.

13. **Arid** is to **damp** as **anxious** is to
    a. Happy.
    b. Petrified.
    c. Ireful.
    d. Confident.
    e. Sorrowful.

14. **Mechanic** is to **repair** as
   a. Mongoose is to cobra.
   b. Rider is to bicycle.
   c. Tree is to grow.
   d. Food is to eaten.
   e. Doctor is to heal.

15. **Whistle** is to **blow horn** as **painting** is to
   a. View.
   b. Criticize.
   c. Sculpture.
   d. Painter.
   e. Paintbrush.

16. **Paddle** is to **boat** as **keys** are to
   a. Unlock.
   b. Success.
   c. Illuminate.
   d. Piano.
   e. Keychain.

17. **Monotonous** is to **innovative** as
   a. Gorgeous is to beautiful.
   b. Ancient is to archaic.
   c. Loquacious is to silent.
   d. Sturdy is to fortified.
   e. Spectacular is to grandiose.

18. **Mountain** is to **peak** as **wave** is to
   a. Ocean.
   b. Surf.
   c. Fountain.
   d. Wavelength.
   e. Crest.

19. **Ambiguous** is to **indecisive** as **uncertain** is to
   a. Indefinite.
   b. Certain.
   c. Flippant.
   d. Fearful.
   e. Rounded.

20. **Fluent** is to **communication** as
   a. Crater is to catastrophe.
   b. Gourmet is to cooking.
   c. Ink is to pen.
   d. Crow is to raven.
   e. Whistle is to whistler.

155

21. **Validate** is to **truth** as **conquer** is to
    a. Withdraw.
    b. Subjugate.
    c. Expand.
    d. Surrender.
    e. Expose.

22. **Winter** is to **autumn** as **summer** is to
    a. Vacation.
    b. Fall.
    c. Spring.
    d. March.
    e. Weather.

23. **Penguin** is to **lemur** as **eagle** is to
    a. Howler monkey.
    b. Osprey.
    c. Warthog.
    d. Kestrel.
    e. Moose.

24. **Fiberglass** is to **surfboard** as
    a. Bamboo is to panda.
    b. Capital is to D.C.
    c. Copper is to penny.
    d. Flint is to knapping.
    e. Wind is to windmill.

25. **Myth** is to **explain** as **joke** is to
    a. Enlighten.
    b. Inspire.
    c. Collect.
    d. Laughter.
    e. Amuse.

Arithmetic Reasoning

1. If a car can go 300 miles in 4 hours, how far can it go in an hour and a half?
    a. 100 miles
    b. 112.5 miles
    c. 135.5 miles
    d. 150 miles
    e. 165.5 miles

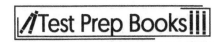

2. At the store, Jan buys $90 of apples and oranges. Apples cost $1 each and oranges cost $2 each. If Jan buys the same number of apples as oranges, how many oranges did she buy?
   a. 20
   b. 25
   c. 30
   d. 35
   e. 40

3. A box with rectangular faces is 5 feet long, 6 feet wide, and 3 feet high. What is its volume?
   a. 60 cubic feet
   b. 75 cubic feet
   c. 90 cubic feet
   d. 100 cubic feet
   e. 115 cubic feet

4. A train traveling 50 miles per hour takes a trip of 3 hours. If a map has a scale of 1 inch per 10 miles, how many inches apart are the train's starting point and ending point on the map?
   a. 10
   b. 12
   c. 13
   d. 14
   e. 15

5. A traveler takes an hour to drive to a museum, spends 3 hours and 30 minutes there, and takes half an hour to drive home. What percentage of this time was spent driving?
   a. 15%
   b. 30%
   c. 40%
   d. 50%
   e. 60%

6. A truck is carrying three cylindrical barrels. Their bases have a diameter of 2 feet, and they have a height of 3 feet. What is the total volume of the three barrels in cubic feet?
   a. 3π
   b. 9π
   c. 12π
   d. 15π
   e. 36π

7. Greg buys a $10 lunch with 5% sales tax. He leaves a $2 tip after his bill. How much money does he spend?
   a. $12
   b. $12.50
   c. $13
   d. $13.25
   e. $16

8. Marty wishes to save $150 over a 4-day period. How much must Marty save each day on average?
    a. $33.50
    b. $35
    c. $37.50
    d. $40
    e. $45.75

9. Bernard can make $80 per day. If he needs to make $300 and only works full days, how many days will this take?
    a. 2
    b. 3
    c. 4
    d. 5
    e. 6

10. A couple buys a house for $150,000. They sell it for $165,000. What percentage did the house's value increase?
    a. 10%
    b. 13%
    c. 15%
    d. 17%
    e. 19%

11. A school's faculty consists of 15 teachers and 20 teaching assistants. They have 200 students. What is the ratio of faculty to students?
    a. 3:20
    b. 4:17
    c. 11:54
    d. 3:2
    e. 7:40

12. A map has a scale of 1 inch per 5 miles. A car can travel 60 miles per hour. If the distance from the start to the destination is 3 inches on the map, how long will it take the car to make the trip?
    a. 12 minutes
    b. 15 minutes
    c. 17 minutes
    d. 20 minutes
    e. 25 minutes

13. Taylor works two jobs. The first pays $20,000 per year. The second pays $10,000 per year. She donates 15% of her income to charity. How much does she donate each year?
    a. $4,500
    b. $5,000
    c. $5,500
    d. $6,000
    e. $6,500

14. A box with rectangular sides is 24 inches wide, 18 inches deep, and 12 inches high. What is the volume of the box in cubic feet?
   a.   2
   b.   3
   c.   4
   d.   5
   e.   6

15. Kristen purchases $100 worth of CDs and DVDs. The CDs cost $10 each and the DVDs cost $15. If she bought four DVDs, how many CDs did she buy?
   a.   One
   b.   Two
   c.   Three
   d.   Four
   e.   Five

16. Alan currently weighs 200 pounds, but he wants to lose weight to get down to 175 pounds. What is this difference in kilograms? (1 pound is approximately equal to 0.45 kilograms.)
   a.   9 kg
   b.   15.5 kg
   c.   78.75 kg
   d.   90 kg
   e.   11.25 kg

17. Johnny earns $2,334.50 from his job each month. He pays $1,437 for monthly expenses. Johnny is planning a vacation in 3 months that he estimates will cost $1,750 total. How much will Johnny have left over from 3 months of saving once he pays for his vacation?
   a. $948.50
   b. $584.50
   c. $852.50
   d. $942.50
   e. $984.50

18. The total perimeter of a rectangle is 36 cm. If the length is 12 cm, what is the width?
   a.   3 cm
   b.   12 cm
   c.   6 cm
   d.   8 cm
   e.   9 cm

19. Dwayne has received the following scores on his math tests: 78, 92, 83, 97. What score must Dwayne get on his next math test to have an overall average of 90?
   a.   89
   b.   98
   c.   95
   d.   100
   e.   105

159

20. In Jim's school, there are a total of 650 boys and girls. There are 3 girls for every 2 boys. How many students are girls?
    a. 260
    b. 130
    c. 65
    d. 390
    e. 90

21. Kimberley earns $10 an hour babysitting, and after 10 p.m., she earns $12 an hour. The time she works is rounded to the nearest hour for pay purposes. On her last job, she worked from 5:30 p.m. to 11 p.m. In total, how much did Kimberley earn on her last job?
    a. $45
    b. $57
    c. $62
    d. $42
    e. $67

22. Keith's bakery had 252 customers go through its doors last week. This week, that number increased to 378. Express this increase as a percentage.
    a. 26%
    b. 50%
    c. 35%
    d. 12%
    e. 42%

23. For a group of 20 men, the median weight is 180 pounds and the range is 30 pounds. If each man gains 10 pounds, which of the following would be true?
    a. The median weight will increase, and the range will remain the same.
    b. The median weight and range will both remain the same.
    c. The median weight will stay the same, and the range will increase.
    d. The median weight and range will both increase.
    e. The median weight will decrease, and the range will remain the same.

24. Apples cost $2 each, while bananas cost $3 each. Maria purchased 10 fruits in total and spent $22. How many apples did she buy?
    a. 5
    b. 6
    c. 7
    d. 8
    e. 9

25. Five students take a test. The scores of the first four students are 80, 85, 75, and 60. If the median score is 80, which of the following could NOT be the score of the fifth student?
    a. 60
    b. 80
    c. 85
    d. 100
    e. 90

Word Knowledge

1. DEDUCE
   a. Explain
   b. Win
   c. Reason
   d. Gamble
   e. Undo

2. ELUCIDATE
   a. Learn
   b. Enlighten
   c. Plan
   d. Corroborate
   e. Conscious

3. VERIFY
   a. Criticize
   b. Change
   c. Teach
   d. Substantiate
   e. Resolve

4. INSPIRE
   a. Motivate
   b. Impale
   c. Exercise
   d. Patronize
   e. Collaborate

5. PERCEIVE
   a. Sustain
   b. Collect
   c. Prove
   d. Lead
   e. Comprehend

6. NOMAD
   a. Munching
   b. Propose
   c. Wanderer
   d. Conscientious
   e. Blissful

161

7. MALEVOLENT
   a. Evil
   b. Concerned
   c. Maximum
   d. Cautious
   e. Crazy

8. PERPLEXED
   a. Annoyed
   b. Vengeful
   c. Injured
   d. Confused
   e. Prepared

9. LYRICAL
   a. Whimsical
   b. Vague
   c. Fruitful
   d. Expressive
   e. Playful

10. BREVITY
   a. Dullness
   b. Dangerous
   c. Brief
   d. Ancient
   e. Calamity

11. IRATE
   a. Anger
   b. Knowledge
   c. Tired
   d. Confused
   e. Taciturn

12. LUXURIOUS
   a. Faded
   b. Bright
   c. Lavish
   d. Inconsiderate
   e. Overwhelming

13. IMMOBILE
   a. Fast
   b. Slow
   c. Eloquent
   d. Vivacious
   e. Sedentary

14. MENDACIOUS
    a. Earnest
    b. Bold
    c. Criminal
    d. Liar
    e. Humorous

15. CHIVALROUS
    a. Fierce
    b. Annoying
    c. Rude
    d. Dangerous
    e. Courteous

16. RETORT
    a. Conversation
    b. Jest
    c. Counter
    d. Flexible
    e. Erudite

17. SUBLIMINAL
    a. Subconscious
    b. Transportation
    c. Underground
    d. Substitute
    e. Penumbral

18. INCITE
    a. Understanding
    b. Illumination
    c. Rally
    d. Judgment
    e. Compose

19. MONIKER
    a. Name
    b. Mockery
    c. Umbrella
    d. Insult
    e. Burden

20. SERENDIPITOUS
    a. Creation
    b. Sympathy
    c. Unfortunate
    d. Calm
    e. Coincidental

163

21. OVERBEARING
    a. Neglect
    b. Overacting
    c. Clandestine
    d. Formidable
    e. Amicable

22. PREVENT
    a. Avert
    b. Rejoice
    c. Endow
    d. Fulfill
    e. Ensure

23. REPLENISH
    a. Falsify
    b. Hindsight
    c. Dwell
    d. Refresh
    e. Nominate

24. REGALE
    a. Remember
    b. Grow
    c. Outnumber
    d. Entertain
    e. Bore

25. ABATE
    a. Anger
    b. Forlorn
    c. Withdraw
    d. Excellent
    e. Crazed

Math Knowledge

1. $\frac{14}{15} + \frac{3}{5} - \frac{1}{30} =$
    a. $\frac{19}{15}$

    b. $\frac{43}{30}$

    c. $\frac{4}{3}$

    d. $\frac{3}{2}$

    e. 3

2. Solve for x and y, given $3x + 2y = 8, -x + 3y = 1$.
   a. $x = 2, y = 1$
   b. $x = 1, y = 2$
   c. $x = -1, y = 6$
   d. $x = 3, y = 1$
   e. $x = 4, y = 4$

3. What is the result of evaluating $\frac{1}{2}\sqrt{16}$?
   a. 0
   b. 1
   c. 2
   d. 4
   e. 8

4. The factors of $2x^2 - 8$ are:
   a. $2(4x^2)$
   b. $2(x^2 + 4)$
   c. $2(x + 2)(x + 2)$
   d. $2(x - 2)(x - 2)$
   e. $2(x + 2)(x - 2)$

5. Two of the interior angles of a triangle are 35° and 70°. What is the measure of the last interior angle?
   a. 60°
   b. 75°
   c. 90°
   d. 100°
   e. 105°

6. A square field has an area of 400 square feet. What is its perimeter?
   a. 100 feet
   b. 80 feet
   c. $40\sqrt{2}$ feet
   d. 40 feet
   e. 2 feet

7. $\frac{5}{3} \times \frac{7}{6} =$
   a. $\frac{3}{5}$

   b. $\frac{18}{3}$

   c. $\frac{45}{31}$

   d. $\frac{17}{6}$

   e. $\frac{35}{18}$

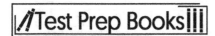

8. One apple costs $2. One papaya costs $3. If Samantha spends $35 and gets 15 pieces of fruit, how many papayas did she buy?
   a. Three
   b. Four
   c. Five
   d. Six
   e. Seven

9. If $x^2 - 6 = 30$, then one possible value for x is:
   a. -6
   b. -4
   c. 3
   d. 5
   e. 8

10. A cube has a side length of 6 inches. What is its volume?
    a. 6 cubic inches
    b. 36 cubic inches
    c. 144 cubic inches
    d. 200 cubic inches
    e. 216 cubic inches

11. A square has a side length of 4 inches. A triangle has a base of 2 inches and a height of 8 inches. What is the total area of the square and triangle?
    a. 24 square inches
    b. 28 square inches
    c. 32 square inches
    d. 36 square inches
    e. 40 square inches

12. $-\frac{1}{3}\sqrt{81} =$
    a. -9
    b. -3
    c. 0
    d. 3
    e. 9

13. Simplify $(2x - 3)(4x + 2)$
    a. $8x^2 - 8x - 6$
    b. $6x^2 + 8x - 5$
    c. $-4x^2 - 8x - 1$
    d. $4x^2 - 4x - 6$
    e. $5x^2 + 4x + 3$

14. $\frac{11}{6} - \frac{3}{8} =$

    a. $\frac{5}{4}$

    b. $\frac{51}{36}$

    c. $\frac{35}{24}$

    d. $\frac{3}{2}$

    e. $\frac{39}{16}$

15. A triangle is to have a base $\frac{1}{3}$ as long as its height. Its area must be 6 square feet. How long will its base be?

    a. 1 foot
    b. 1.5 feet
    c. 2 feet
    d. 2.5 feet
    e. 3 feet

16. Which is closest to 17.8×9.9?

    a. 140
    b. 180
    c. 200
    d. 350
    e. 400

17. 6 is 30% of what number?

    a. 18
    b. 22
    c. 24
    d. 26
    e. 20

18. $3\frac{2}{3} - 1\frac{4}{5} =$

    a. $1\frac{13}{15}$

    b. $\frac{14}{15}$

    c. $2\frac{2}{3}$

    d. $\frac{4}{5}$

    e. $1\frac{2}{3}$

19. What is $\frac{420}{98}$ rounded to the nearest integer?
   a. 7
   b. 3
   c. 5
   d. 6
   e. 4

20. Which of the following is largest?
   a. 0.45
   b. 0.096
   c. 0.3
   d. 0.313
   e. 0.078

21. What is the value of b in this equation?

$$5b - 4 = 2b + 17$$

   a. 13
   b. 24
   c. 7
   d. 21
   e. 32

22. 20 is 40% of what number?
   a. 50
   b. 8
   c. 200
   d. 5000
   e. 80

23. Which of the following expressions is equivalent to this expression?

$$\frac{2xy^2 + 4x - 8y}{16xy}$$

   a. $\frac{y}{8} + \frac{1}{4y} - \frac{1}{2x}$

   b. $8xy + 4y - 2x$

   c. $xy^2 + \frac{x}{4y} - \frac{1}{2x}$

   d. $\frac{y}{8} + 4y - 8y$

   e. $\frac{y}{8} - 4y + 8y$

168

24. Arrange the following numbers from least to greatest value: $0.85, \frac{4}{5}, \frac{2}{3}, \text{ or } \frac{91}{100}$

    a. $0.85, \frac{4}{5}, \frac{2}{3}, \frac{91}{100}$

    b. $\frac{4}{5}, 0.85, \frac{91}{100}, \frac{2}{3}$

    c. $\frac{2}{3}, \frac{4}{5}, 0.85, \frac{91}{100}$

    d. $0.85, \frac{91}{100}, \frac{4}{5}, \frac{2}{3}$

    e. $\frac{2}{3}, 0.85, \frac{4}{5}, \frac{91}{100}$

25. Simplify the following expression:

$$(3x + 5)(x - 8)$$

    a. $3x^2 - 19x - 40$
    b. $4x - 19x - 13$
    c. $3x^2 - 19x + 40$
    d. $3x^2 + 5x - 3$
    e. $4x - 5x + 9$

Reading Comprehension

Aircraft propulsion must achieve two objectives: it has to balance the thrust and drag of a craft in cruising flight, and thrust must exceed drag in order to accelerate movement. Balancing the thrust and drag of a craft in cruising mode follows Sir Isaac Newton's first law of motion. This law states that an object in motion will remain so, in a straight line, with the absence of a net force to affect a change. In other words, if all external forces cancel each other, an object remains at a constant velocity. This is necessary to understand the idea of flight at a constant altitude. However, if a pilot affects a change to a craft's thrust, the balance between that thrust and the drag of a craft is disrupted. The net forces have been changed in a manner that will affect acceleration and propel the aircraft until there is a new balance between thrust and drag in velocity.

1. What is the topic of the paragraph above?
    a.   Aircraft propulsion is a difficult concept to understand.
    b.   External forces must cancel each other out in order for an aircraft to fly.
    c.   An aircraft that remains at a constant velocity will remain at a constant altitude as well.
    d.   Aircraft propulsion involves two objectives involving the laws of motion.
    e.   Thrust must exceed drag in order for an aircraft to accelerate.

2. Choose the option below that does NOT support the topic of this paragraph:

One of the four forces that affects aerodynamics is weight. The total weight of an aircraft must be factored into the mechanics of flight. Lift also affects flight and must be considered. Weight must include the craft itself, accompanying gear, the fuel load, and any personnel. Carefully assessing weight will help a pilot calculate how to oppose the downward force of weight during flight.
   a. The sum weight of an aircraft is important to consider.
   b. Personnel should be calculated in overall weight.
   c. The mechanics of flight also includes lift.
   d. Weight is a downward force in aerodynamics.
   e. Fuel load cannot be eliminated in measuring weight.

3. Read the following paragraph, then select the topic:

Standard weather briefings can be obtained from a variety of sources, including the FAA. Pilots can obtain abbreviated weather information from briefers to supplement available electronic information. Information that a pilot has previously obtained should be provided to the briefer in case conditions have changed. An outlook weather briefing is obtained six or more hours in advance of the flight. Lastly, it's important to obtain in-flight briefings to monitor ongoing weather conditions during the flight course itself.
   a. In-flight briefings monitor ongoing weather conditions during flight.
   b. Briefers are people who provide meteorological information to pilots.
   c. Standard weather briefings are the most comprehensive types.
   d. All briefings should be updated.
   e. There are a variety of weather briefing types.

4. Which of the options can be inferred by the passage below?

Don't attempt to fly through thunderstorms. Try to safely and wisely circumnavigate them. Know your personal skills and limitations regarding weather flight before you gather forecast information. Keep in mind that a variety of conditions in-flight can change quickly. Don't fly into areas of rain where the air temperature is at or close to freezing. Always allow more margin of error for weather at night, and do not attempt to navigate through cloud "holes."
   a. Flying in inclement weather involves using sound judgment.
   b. Thunderstorms are not navigable.
   c. Changing conditions will lead to flight trouble.
   d. Freezing rain can be managed if the pilot knows what he is doing.
   e. Flying at night is tricky.

170

5. Read the following passage and select the best definition for the word in **bold**:

Everyone had said his piloting **acumen** was not to be questioned. He had a knack for feeling the aircraft, as if it was an instinctual part of himself. He had a knowledge base he'd built up over years of study and thousands of flying hours; but moreover, he had the ability to think and act quickly in the most unexpected circumstances.

The word *acumen* means:
   a. Ability to fly
   b. Knowledge
   c. Shrewdness and keen insight
   d. Visual ability
   e. Impressive number of flight hours

6. Read the following passage and select the best conclusion:

Piloting requires consummate skill, but it isn't an impossible goal. A potential pilot must be versed in flight instruction, which consists of many classroom hours and even more flight hours. A potential pilot needs to have a logical mind, be armed with the right information for each flight, and be correctly trained in all piloting procedures. Anyone who lacks a crucial ingredient in training takes a serious risk when flying. With the right education and the right instruction, becoming a pilot is a rewarding venture.
   a. Anyone can become a pilot.
   b. Becoming a pilot is a risky proposition.
   c. Innate ability is key in flight instruction.
   d. Learning to fly, if taught and practiced correctly, is a fulfilling skill.
   e. Piloting can be impossible to learn.

7. Read the following passage and identify the statement that best describes the author's position.

Piloting is a consummate skill to obtain, and for many, it's a skill that remains unattainable. A potential pilot must be so well-versed in flight instruction that studying the requirements can seem overwhelming. In addition, thousands of flight hours must be logged in practice before a pilot can begin a career. The physical and mental demands made on many potential students can be prohibitive. It's a dedicated person who perseveres and becomes successful in the flight industry.
   a. Piloting is a difficult goal requiring serious consideration.
   b. Becoming a pilot is cost-prohibitive.
   c. Piloting careers are few and far between.
   d. The physical and mental demands on piloting students should be the main consideration when deciding on a career in flight.
   e. Piloting involves a lot of luck and practice.

8. Carefully read the following passage, taking note of the letters that precede each sentence. Then select the option that best describes the text's correct sequence:

Aviation's history expands over 2,000 years. A) Eventually, Leonardo da Vinci studied the flight of birds and began noting some basic principles of aerodynamics. B) It is said that kites were the first airborne, man made "vehicles." They existed in China around the fifth century B.C. and were capable of carrying a person into the air. C) The first recorded attempt at flight was made by a Spanish citizen who covered his arms in feathers and jumped. D) The late 18th century saw a major development in ballooning, and the steerable airship, or dirigible, was developed. E) Sir George Cayley significantly impacted aerodynamics in the early 19th century by contributing key ideas to flight physics. F) In 1903, Orville Wright flew 130 feet in twelve seconds.
   a. The sequence is correct
   b. B, D, C, A, F, E
   c. A, C, F, D, E, B
   d. C, B, A, D, E, F
   e. D, F, E, B, C, A

9. Which of the following best states the author's purpose?

While many innovative aircraft have been developed throughout the history of flight, certain aircraft can be referred to as groundbreaking and revolutionary. Their existence has transformed flight and advanced the study of aviation. The Wright Brothers' 1905 plane, The Flyer, was the first to have three-axis control. It had innovative seating for its pilot and attained faster speeds due to increased power. The Monocoque, developed by Deperdussin manufacturers, introduced a new shell structure capable of handling the forces of stress. In 1919, Hugo Junkers introduced all-metal structures with thicker wings. The Douglas DC-1 bears the title of the first American, scientifically-designed structure.
   a. The purpose is to inform by presenting examples of revolutionary aircraft inventions throughout flight history.
   b. The purpose is to entertain the reader with stories about airplanes.
   c. The purpose is to argue that Deperdussin's model, which handled the forces of stress, was the most revolutionary development in flight.
   d. The purpose is to convince the reader that American, scientifically-designed structures were the best.
   e. The purpose is to convince the reader that these examples are the only ones worth considering in the development of innovative flight.

10. Read the following passage, then select the option that best identifies cause and effect:

While it can be dangerous, turbulence during flight is common and manageable. Turbulence is a disruption in air flow. Think of it as a bump on the road while driving to work. It happens all the time and, when managed effectively, it's fairly benign. One type of turbulence is CAT (Clear Air Turbulence). It cannot be seen, and one way to avoid it is to fly at a higher, and likely smoother, altitude. Severe turbulence, a disturbance that results in an altitude deviation of 100 feet, is uncomfortable, but not dangerous.
   a. Turbulence causes plane crashes.
   b. Turbulence is caused by a disruption in air flow.
   c. Turbulence is common and the effects are always dangerous.
   d. Turbulence is uncommon and the effects are usually benign.
   e. Turbulence is manageable by flying at a higher altitude.

172

11. Read the same, expanded passage below, then select the answer that best states the outcome:

While it can be dangerous, turbulence during flight is common and manageable. Turbulence is a disruption in air flow. Think of it as a bump on the road while driving to work. It happens all the time and, when managed effectively, it's fairly benign. One type of turbulence is CAT (Clear Air Turbulence). It cannot be seen, and one way to avoid it is to fly at a higher, and likely smoother altitude. Severe turbulence, a disturbance that results in an altitude deviation of 100 feet, is uncomfortable, but not dangerous. A disruptive air flow that causes turbulence doesn't have to result in difficulty for the pilot. A well-trained pilot and crew can manage turbulence so that it isn't disruptive to passengers in flight.
   a. If not managed, turbulence will result in disaster.
   b. Weather maps predict CAT.
   c. Flying at a higher altitude always solves the problem of turbulence.
   d. A bump in the road is potentially more invasive than air turbulence.
   e. Encountering turbulence is not a significant issue for pilots and will not likely result in air disaster.

12. Read the passage below and select the option that best states the author's purpose:

The mechanics of flight are not difficult to understand, although the concepts often contain difficult terminology. Words such as yaw, pitch, and roll define aircraft axes, or dimensional center lines of gravity that intersect an airplane. Understanding these terms is crucial to understanding the mechanics of flight. Controls such as actuators generate forces that act on an aircraft. Rotational dynamics operate in tandem with translational ones to affect an aircraft's position and trajectory.
   a. The purpose of the passage is to convince the reader that the mechanics of flight are easy to understand.
   b. The purpose of the passage is to confuse the reader by using difficult terminology to explain a simple concept.
   c. The purpose of the passage is to inform the reader about terminology in the mechanics of flight.
   d. The purpose of the passage is to describe how axes and aircraft controls affect the mechanics of flight.
   e. C and D.

13. Read the below paragraph and select the option that likely defines the word in **bold** within context:

A helicopter pilot maneuvers many controls to maintain **equilibrium** in flight. These controls include the cyclic stick, anti-torque pedals, and the collective lever. The cyclic control maintains the pitch angle of the craft's rotating blades. The anti-torque pedals control the nose of the helicopter. The collective lever controls the pitch angle of the rotating blades together or independently as needed. All three controls help the pilot stay stable in flight.
   a. Equilibrium means unsteady.
   b. Equilibrium means pitchy.
   c. Equilibrium means the collective pitch angle of a helicopter's blades.
   d. Equilibrium means flight stability.
   e. Equilibrium means the controls used to fly a helicopter.

173

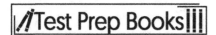
14. Read the paragraph and select the option that best states cause and effect:

The pilot looked to the left, and there it was: a tiny glimmer of white on the left wing. He was on the leading edge of it. He knew the temperature had dropped. He'd checked it repeatedly. He had been cleared at 9,000 feet but needed to go down. He needed to get to warmer air and get there quickly. He checked the terrain clearance and decided it was now or never. He popped out of the clouds and began his descent, chunks of ice flying off the fuselage.

    a. Not checking a weather report ahead of time led to ice on the aircraft.
    b. Flying too high resulted in icing.
    c. The pilot didn't have the right clearance and encountered icing as a result.
    d. A sudden, unexpected drop in temperature resulted in icing that the pilot had to account for.
    e. Icing led to additional weight on the fuselage.

15. Read the paragraph and select the option that best defines the words in **bold**:

Differential pitch control is a factor in helicopter flight. Differential pitch control affects the yaw axis and causes the helicopter to spin in the direction of its rotational, tilted rotors. **Coaxial** mounted helicopters, or crafts with dual rotors mounted above each other concentrically, require interaction between rotors. **Intermeshing** rotors, or helicopter rotors at a set angle to each other and turn in opposite directions, require increasing collective pitch on one blade set.

    a. From the passage, it's impossible to tell what coaxial and intermeshing rotators are.
    b. Coaxial rotors are dual and mounted above each other, while intermeshing rotors are angled apart from each other.
    c. Coaxial means interaction and intermeshing means turning in an opposite direction.
    d. Coaxial and intermeshing mean the same thing.
    e. Coaxial and intermeshing rotors have nothing to do with differential pitch control.

16. Read the passage below and select the option that best identifies the main idea:

The synchropter arrangement was first designed for use in Germany's anti-submarine war craft. Often referred to as intermeshing rotor configuration, this design sets two oppositional rotors at a slight angle from each other in a transverse manner so that they actually intermesh. The configuration allows a helicopter to function without a tail rotor in order to save power.

    a. The development of the synchropter began during World War II.
    b. Synchropter configuration is best understood as an intermeshing rotor configuration, oppositional in nature.
    c. Oppositional rotors always intermesh.
    d. Functioning without a tail rotor saves power for a helicopter.
    e. Transverse rotors always intermesh.

17. Choose the option that best defines the word in **bold** below:

A helicopter pilot's use of control in a hover is critical to success. Correct use of the cyclic, the collective, and the anti-torque pedal controls help maintain balance. The cyclic is used to cut down on **drift** in the craft's horizontal plane. The collective helps maintain altitude, and the anti-torque control is used to direct the craft's nose direction.
   a.   Drift means unwanted movement within the helicopter's horizontal plane.
   b.   Drift refers to stable air around the helicopter.
   c.   Drift refers to the pilot's ability to control the cyclic.
   d.   Drift means hover.
   e.   Drift can be defined as unwanted movement within the helicopter's vertical plane.

18. Read the passage and select the answer that best states the logical conclusion:

A chain of events often defines incidents that lead to an accident. In aviation, this chain of events is often referred to as the "error chain." This term purports that it isn't one single event that leads to an air disaster but a chain of separate events. In other words, an accident is caused by more than one problem and most likely has more than one root cause. These events can be caused by human error or mechanical issues. A recent study indicates that pilot error is more likely to contribute to air disasters than mechanical problems.
   a.   Air disaster is unavoidable.
   b.   The error chain is specific to aviation.
   c.   A pilot's appropriate risk assessment before and during a flight will cut down on negative error chain events.
   d.   Mechanics aren't a consideration in the error chain.
   e.   Mechanics should be the primary consideration during flight.

19. Read the passage and select the correct answer to the question below:

   Proper risk assessment for flight is critical for avoiding air disaster. As most events in the error chain can be addressed and controlled by the pilot, it's essential to consider all risks before and during flight. A pilot must perform all necessary informational checks prior to a scheduled flight. The flight path itself must be registered and approved. During the flight, a pilot must communicate regularly with others in the air and on the ground. Making sudden, unapproved changes during flight can lead to a negative chain of events. Being unprepared, uncommunicative, and unaware are all mistakes a pilot can make while on the job. Constant risk assessment is necessary to a successful and happily uneventful flight.

Which of the following statements provides the most encompassing overview with which the author would most likely agree?
   a.   Risk assessment includes mechanical checks and balances.
   b.   The pilot is the leading force in appropriate risk assessment.
   c.   Risk assessment is best conducted on the ground prior to flight.
   d.   Unapproved changes during a flight will always lead to problems.
   e.   Communication is the key factor in a successful flight.

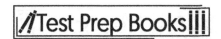

20. Read the passage below and select the best meaning for the word in **bold**:

> The United States attack helicopter came into its own during the 1990s. During Operation Desert Storm, the Apache fired against early warning radar sites to, in part, support ground troops. In addition, Apaches were able to destroy surface-to-air (SAM) sites via their Hellfire missile technology. The missiles **obliterated** many armored cars and tanks as well.

    a. Obliterated can be defined as a type of Apache missile.
    b. Obliterated means thoroughly destroyed.
    c. Obliterated is defined as a military strategy.
    d. Obliterated means flying low over armored cars and tanks.
    e. Obliterated can be defined as an Apache flight technique, specific to Operation Desert Storm.

Use the passage below for questions 21–24:

> Learning how to write a ten-minute play may seem like a monumental task at first; but, if you follow a simple creative writing strategy, similar to writing a narrative story, you will be able to write a successful drama. The first step is to open your story as if it is a puzzle to be solved. This will allow the reader a moment to engage with the story and to mentally solve the story with you, the author. Immediately provide descriptive details that steer the main idea, the tone, and the mood according to the overarching theme you have in mind. For example, if the play is about something ominous, you may open Scene One with a thunderclap. Next, use dialogue to reveal the attitudes and personalities of each of the characters who have a key part in the unfolding story. Keep the characters off balance in some way to create interest and dramatic effect. Maybe what the characters say does not match what they do. Show images on stage to speed up the narrative; remember, one picture speaks a thousand words. As the play progresses, the protagonist must cross the point of no return in some way; this is the climax of the story. Then, as in a written story, you create a resolution to the life-changing event of the protagonist. Let the characters experience some kind of self-discovery that can be understood and appreciated by the patient audience. Finally, make sure all things come together in the end so that every detail in the play makes sense right before the curtain falls.

21. Based on the passage above, which of the following statements is FALSE?
    a. Writing a ten-minute play may seem like an insurmountable task.
    b. Providing descriptive details is not necessary until after the climax of the storyline.
    c. Engaging the audience by jumping into the storyline immediately helps them solve the story's developing ideas with you, the writer.
    d. Descriptive details give clues to the play's intended mood and tone.

22. In the passage above, the writer suggests that writing a ten-minute play is accessible for a novice playwright because of which of the following reasons?
    a. It took the author of the passage only one week to write his first play.
    b. The format follows similar strategies of writing a narrative story.
    c. There are no particular themes or points to unravel; a playwright can use a stream of consciousness style to write a play.
    d. Dialogue that reveals the characters' particularities is uncommonly simple to write.

176

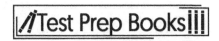

23. Based on the passage above, which basic feature of narrative writing is NOT mentioned with respect to writing a ten-minute play?
   a. Character development
   b. Descriptive details
   c. Style
   d. Mood and tone

24. Based on the passage above, which of the following is true?
   a. The class of eighth graders quickly learned that it is not that difficult to write a ten-minute play.
   b. The playwrights of the twenty-first century all use the narrative writing basic feature guide to outline their initial scripts.
   c. In order to follow a simple structure, a person can write a ten-minute play based on some narrative writing features.
   d. Women find playwriting easier than men because they are used to communicating in writing.

25. After applying for a job multiple times, Bob was finally granted an interview. During the interview, he fumbled several questions, mispronounced his potential supervisor's name, and forgot the name of the company. Soon it was clear he knew he wouldn't be working there. At the end of the interview, he stood up and, with *spurious* confidence, shook the interviewer's hand firmly.

Based on the context of the word *spurious*, a good substitution might be:
   a. Extreme
   b. Mild
   c. Fake
   d. Genuine

Situational Judgment

Situation 1

You have an innovative plan for your unit that, in your opinion, will improve performance. Not everyone in the unit is of the same opinion, and some downright oppose your plan. Even though the plan has not been put in motion, someone has already written a letter of complaint and sent it to your superior.

What would you do?
   a. Don't worry about anyone else's opinion, and implement the plan.
   b. Ignore the letter of complaint, and push forward with the plan.
   c. Have a meeting with the unit, including the person who wrote the complaint to your superior, and explain to everyone again the chain-of-command and how it is to be used.
   d. Discipline the person who wrote the letter of complaint so that no one else in the unit will break the chain-of-command in the future.
   e. Give up your plan in the wake of opposition, and see what the unit would like to do.

1. Select the answer that contains the MOST EFFECTIVE way to respond to the situation.
2. Select the answer that contains the LEAST EFFECTIVE way to respond to the situation.

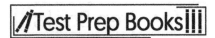
Situation 2

You have had a successful working relationship with an aide assigned to you. On a personal level, you dislike the assignee based on your opinion that they are arrogant and too critical of others. A senior officer is thinking of giving the aide a promotion, which would greatly benefit their future and put the aide on a fast track for future promotions.

What would you do?
   a. Attempt to dissuade the senior officer by sharing your personal feelings about the aide.
   b. You want the aide to just go away, so you give a recommendation for promotion.
   c. You do not want the aide to be rewarded, so you recommend that the senior officer give it to someone else.
   d. Other than expressing your opinion of the aide, you do not interfere with the selection process.
   e. Write a letter of support about the aide in an anonymous letter to the senior officer.

3. Select the answer that contains the MOST EFFECTIVE way to respond to the situation.
4. Select the answer that contains the LEAST EFFECTIVE way to respond to the situation.

Situation 3

A coworker, who is another officer in your division, has to give an important speech in a few days. The officer has spent a great deal of time and effort on the report, but is still nervous about presenting it. After being asked by the officer to look over the report, you find some items that you feel need to be changed. You discuss these items with the other officer, who disagrees with you. You are positive that the changes you identified need to be made.

What would you do?
   a. Mention the conversation to a senior officer prior to the speech as a way to make yourself look better, since you are right and the other officer wouldn't listen to you.
   b. Do everything you can to convince the officer to review the report and supporting information and make the changes you have recommended.
   c. Avoid going to the speech if at all possible.
   d. Attempt to get a senior officer involved to order that the report be changed.
   e. Do not say or do anything. You are not giving the speech.

5. Select the answer that contains the MOST EFFECTIVE way to respond to the situation.
6. Select the answer that contains the LEAST EFFECTIVE way to respond to the situation.

Situation 4

You have been teamed up with another officer on an important one-month assignment to draft a report. Unfortunately, early in the project your coworker has become ill and is required to be on leave. The illness keeps him/her out of the office much longer than expected. At the one-month mark on the

report, your coworker is still ill and remains on leave. There is no way of knowing when your coworker will return to work and their expertise is needed to complete the assignment.

What would you do?
   a. Order a subordinate onto the project in an attempt to complete the report.
   b. To the best of your ability, put in as many hours as it takes to finish it yourself.
   c. Don't give any details; just ask for the deadline to be extended.
   d. Relay the situation to your superior and request help to finish the report.
   e. Wait indefinitely for the coworker to return without regard to the timeline for the report.

7. Select the answer that contains the MOST EFFECTIVE way to respond to the situation.
8. Select the answer that contains the LEAST EFFECTIVE way to respond to the situation.

Situation 5

After a long day at work, you are at home and you realize you forgot to sign documents that need to go on to another unit for completion. The documents cannot move forward without your signature. While the documents are not urgent in nature, your oversight will cause another officer to be delayed and have to stay at work later than usual.

What would you do?
   a. Go back to work and sign the papers.
   b. The documents are not urgent, so you wait until the next day to sign them.
   c. Show up to work early the next day to sign the documents, get them moving first thing in the morning, and hope the other officer won't have to stay late.
   d. Get a subordinate at your office to sign your name on the documents so they can move forward.
   e. Call the officer that this will impact and explain that the documents will be late in arriving.

9. Select the answer that contains the MOST EFFECTIVE way to respond to the situation.
10. Select the answer that contains the LEAST EFFECTIVE way to respond to the situation.

Situation 6

A week before you are about to be transferred to a new unit you receive a message from the officer in charge of that unit. The officer explains you are entering the unit at a critical time, as they are leading training exercises for highly skilled airmen. The message goes on to indicate that you are expected to be

a valuable contributor from the moment you arrive, with minimal assistance. However, your experience in this area is minimal.

What would you do?

    a. Send a courteous thank you message in return and attempt to study for the new position.

    b. Send no response to the email. You should have no problem taking on this new position.

    c. Discreetly ask one of the officers in the new unit if he/she will be able to train you upon arrival.

    d. You think you should remain with your current unit, so you request that your transfer be cancelled.

    e. Respond to the senior officer's message with a request for a meeting, where you can discuss transition into the new position.

11. Select the answer that contains the MOST EFFECTIVE way to respond to the situation.

12. Select the answer that contains the LEAST EFFECTIVE way to respond to the situation.

Situation 7

A coworker, who is another officer, has lied about their time off. The officer had requested leave for a week to visit an ailing family member. The request for leave was granted. Through social media, you learned the officer was at the beach on vacation, hundreds of miles away from the ailing family member he/she was supposedly visiting.

What would you do?

    a. Go see the commanding officer immediately to relay what you just discovered.

    b. Anonymously send the social media evidence of the officer's actions to the commanding officer.

    c. Since you now have a bargaining chip, you tell the officer you will keep this information to yourself in exchange for him taking on part of your weekly workload.

    d. Tell the officer if he/she does anything unethical like that again you will have no choice but to report it.

    e. You mind your own business and do nothing.

13. Select the answer that contains the MOST EFFECTIVE way to respond to the situation.

14. Select the answer that contains the LEAST EFFECTIVE way to respond to the situation.

Situation 8

After being in the same unit and performing the same job for two years, you are beginning to feel burned out. Even though you are successful in your current position, you wonder what other options

may be available. You have been asking around to people in other units to gauge their experiences. Within a month the rumors in your unit have started that you are looking for a transfer.

What would you do?
a. Address the concerns that are brought up and refocus on your current position.
b. Ask for a leave of absence so you can find a way to handle the situation.
c. Send a formal request for transfer to your senior officer, acknowledging the truth of the rumors.
d. Refocus on your position and ignore the rumors, even though they are true.
e. Continue looking for a new unit to transfer to, but deny the rumors that are circulating.

15. Select the answer that contains the MOST EFFECTIVE way to respond to the situation.
16. Select the answer that contains the LEAST EFFECTIVE way to respond to the situation.

Situation 9

Your current workload has you extremely busy, but you are managing to meet your deadlines and are producing quality work. A senior officer has asked if you would perform an additional assignment in conjunction with the work you are performing. While you would like to impress the senior officer and take on the additional work, you are already pushing yourself with your current workload. If you took on the extra work, the quality of work on both assignments would suffer.

What would you do?
a. Tell the senior officer that you would be glad to do the work, and then pass it on to a coworker to complete.
b. Apologize to the senior officer, and say you are too busy and that you cannot do the extra assignment.
c. Ask for a few days to think about it.
d. You can't say no so you take the assignment; you will just have to find a way to complete the work as quickly as possible.
e. Present an offer to pass the assignment to another qualified coworker, and inform the senior officer that unfortunately you are unable to complete the work yourself at this time.

17. Select the answer that contains the MOST EFFECTIVE way to respond to the situation.
18. Select the answer that contains the LEAST EFFECTIVE way to respond to the situation.

Situation 10

While assigned to a field office, you become aware that a coworker is extremely overworked with assignments being sent from other offices. The coworker's senior officers do not seem to notice that this

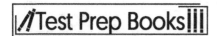

person is overworked because your coworker does an excellent job, but they need to work extra hours to get the tasks completed.

What would you do?
- a. You do nothing. That situation has nothing to do with you.
- b. Sympathize with the coworker about their workload.
- c. Assist the coworker and help with their workload as much as possible.
- d. Request a meeting with the coworker's senior officer to inform the officer of the situation.
- e. Task one of your subordinates to assist this person in the workload.

19. Select the answer that contains the MOST EFFECTIVE way to respond to the situation.
20. Select the answer that contains the LEAST EFFECTIVE way to respond to the situation.

Situation 11

You are in attendance at a meeting where two officers get in a heated dispute over policy changes. It is considered common knowledge around work that these two officers do not like each other on a personal level, but no one is sure why. Unable to come to an agreement on the policy, they ask you to settle the disagreement.

What would you do?
- a. Resolve the dispute on the side of the officer that you favor.
- b. Resolve the dispute on the side of the officer who can benefit your career the most in the future.
- c. Put all personal feelings aside and choose what you believe is the best option.
- d. Point out the officers' blatant issues with each other as the reason they cannot agree, and then remove yourself from the situation.
- e. Disregard the request to settle the dispute on the policy; this is a good time to lecture these two on teamwork and cooperation in the military.

21. Select the answer that contains the MOST EFFECTIVE way to respond to the situation.
22. Select the answer that contains the LEAST EFFECTIVE way to respond to the situation.

Situation 12

You are working on reports for your senior officers with a coworker. The reports are used by the officers to track the training and readiness of airmen for the most hazardous and difficult missions. You noticed your coworker appears to be manipulating these numbers, and they are not being entered correctly. If

the airmen are reported as having a higher amount of training than is required for these missions and then chosen, this could pose a huge risk to the missions and put lives in jeopardy.

What would you do?
- a. Do nothing yet, but monitor the coworker to see what is going on.
- b. Report this issue to your senior officer right away.
- c. Review your coworker's numbers and correct them yourself.
- d. Leave an anonymous note to your coworker to stop changing the numbers in the report and make sure what is turned in is accurate.
- e. Wait for the coworker to finish the assignment, and then you will have proof of what is going on.

23. Select the answer that contains the MOST EFFECTIVE way to respond to the situation.
24. Select the answer that contains the LEAST EFFECTIVE way to respond to the situation.

Situation 13

A senior officer asks you in private how you feel about your supervisor. Your supervisor reports to this senior officer. You feel the officer in question overall does a good job, but could do better in a certain aspect of their job.

What would you do?
- a. Express just that: They do a good job overall, but could use improvement in this one area.
- b. Refuse to answer the question.
- c. Give the supervisor a glowing review, without mentioning their weak area.
- d. Discuss the solutions to improving the area where the officer is weak.
- e. Write a note that explains your thoughts about the officer.

25. Select the answer that contains the MOST EFFECTIVE way to respond to the situation.
26. Select the answer that contains the LEAST EFFECTIVE way to respond to the situation.

Situation 14

You are serving on a board of three officers interviewing three candidates for promotion. Candidate 1 is a known family friend of your commanding officer, but is the most impressive of the three candidates through the interview process. Candidate 2 seems to be another good choice for the position. Candidate 3 did not do well in the interview process and does not seem like a good choice for promotion at this point. The other two officers on the board have voted, one for each of the first two candidates. You have the deciding vote.

What would you do?
- a. You cast your vote for the second candidate, to avoid the appearance of favoritism.
- b. You remove yourself from the board so that you do not have to vote.
- c. You vote for Candidate 3, so you do not have to decide who gets the promotion.
- d. You vote for Candidate 1, because that candidate is most qualified.
- e. You refrain from the vote and ask for a new group of candidates.

27. Select the answer that contains the MOST EFFECTIVE way to respond to the situation.
28. Select the answer that contains the LEAST EFFECTIVE way to respond to the situation.

183

Situation 15

You are given an important assignment that involves working with an officer from a different unit. This officer appears to already have "one foot out the door," as retirement is near. The officer does not put much effort into the assignment, leaving you to do the bulk of the work.

What would you do?
a. Explain your feelings to your new coworker. Point out that the situation is not fair to you and that the work is very important and should be shared equally.
b. Put in a request for a new partner on the assignment.
c. Say nothing and do all the work necessary to successfully complete the assignment.
d. Just do the best you can with the realization the assignment will likely be unsuccessful due to lack of participation of your coworker.
e. Inform your senior officer of the situation.

29. Select the answer that contains the MOST EFFECTIVE way to respond to the situation.
30. Select the answer that contains the LEAST EFFECTIVE way to respond to the situation.

Situation 16

You have had a feeling that one of your subordinates may have an ambitious agenda and be deliberately undermining your work. Other officers have discussed that this subordinate wants to take your job.

What would you do?
a. Publicly attempt to humiliate the subordinate and reprimand him/her.
b. Do nothing and the situation may just go away.
c. Discuss the situation with the subordinate and explain that you expect their cooperation and support.
d. Ask for another officer to step in and discuss the problem with your subordinate.
e. File a report for insubordination to your senior officer.

31. Select the answer that contains the MOST EFFECTIVE way to respond to the situation.
32. Select the answer that contains the LEAST EFFECTIVE way to respond to the situation.

Situation 17

Recently it has come to your attention that office supplies are disappearing from the supply closet at a much faster rate than usual. There is no apparent reason that would account for the change in supply usage. Your gut is telling you that the officer that is last to leave the office may be taking items with him/her after everyone else has left. You do not have any evidence of your suspicion, but it does seem like things disappear on the shifts for which this officer is the last to leave.

What would you do?
a. Report your suspicions to a senior officer.
b. Secretly set up hidden cameras in an attempt to catch the thief.
c. Discuss your suspicions with the officer you suspect and ask for an explanation.
d. Discuss with fellow officers to see what they think is going on.
e. Don't do anything.

33. Select the answer that contains the MOST EFFECTIVE way to respond to the situation.
34. Select the answer that contains the LEAST EFFECTIVE way to respond to the situation.

Situation 18

Rumors have been circulating that your base is going to be shut down due to budgetary restraints. You are in attendance at a meeting between local community leaders and senior officers from your unit. The community leaders are willing to lobby to keep the base open in return for the support of the military leadership in some local initiatives, specifically disaster-relief coordination efforts. A community leader asks your opinion on the matter being discussed.

What would you do?
a. Answer the question honestly to the best of your ability, but explain you are not a senior officer.
b. Tell the leader you are not a senior officer and cannot give your opinion.
c. Defer the question to a senior officer without giving your opinion.
d. Give a thorough answer even though you have little knowledge on this topic.
e. Answer the question, but keep it positive; do not mention any possible negative result of what is being proposed.

35. Select the answer that contains the MOST EFFECTIVE way to respond to the situation.
36. Select the answer that contains the LEAST EFFECTIVE way to respond to the situation.

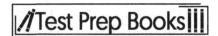

Situation 19

A subordinate in your unit has recently been showing signs of burnout and seems frustrated with their current position over the last month. You notice this coincides with a decline in the quality and quantity of their work. This negative attitude has been affecting the overall work environment with the fellow workers in the unit.

What would you do?
  a. Report the situation to your senior officer.
  b. Do nothing and hope the situation will improve on its own.
  c. Point out this behavior and bad performance in a meeting with the entire unit.
  d. Meet with the subordinate to discuss these issues, along with the effects on the unit, and present possible solutions.
  e. Reassign the subordinate to alleviate the problem in your unit.

37. Select the answer that contains the MOST EFFECTIVE way to respond to the situation.
38. Select the answer that contains the LEAST EFFECTIVE way to respond to the situation.

Situation 20

In your current position, one of your many responsibilities is to brief a small team of some activities that are confidential in nature. You have accidentally sent an email containing some of this confidential information to an officer that is not on this team, and who does not have the security clearance to have access to the information you sent.

What would you do?
  a. Immediately email this person and request they destroy the information you just sent. Then, immediately inform your supervisor of your mistake.
  b. Tell your supervisor what happened and let him/her handle it.
  c. Do nothing. Wait and see what happens.
  d. Ask your senior officer if they can request that the individual be cleared for a higher security level since they have been presented with the material.
  e. Send an email to the same person saying your email was hacked and to disregard any previous messages.

39. Select the answer that contains the MOST EFFECTIVE way to respond to the situation.
40. Select the answer that contains the LEAST EFFECTIVE way to respond to the situation.

Situation 21

Airmen in your unit have been awaiting training at a nearby base. A request was made to be in the next training cycle, but airmen from a different unit were chosen for the next block of training—even though they had not been waiting as long. You have no evidence, but you have a feeling your unit may not have been given the training block requested due to the training director disliking you on a personal level.

What would you do?
  a. Ask the director if your airmen can attend the same training along with the other airmen selected.
  b. Meet with the training director to determine the reason your airmen were passed over and emphasize the importance of this training to your unit.
  c. Do nothing; the decision has been made.
  d. Send a critical letter to the director and your senior officer over this perceived injustice.
  e. Discuss the situation with the other unit's senior officer to see if they would give up their training spots so your airmen could have them.

41. Select the answer that contains the MOST EFFECTIVE way to respond to the situation.
42. Select the answer that contains the LEAST EFFECTIVE way to respond to the situation.

Situation 22

When you joined a new unit a couple of months ago, the leader of the unit was very helpful. You were given a great deal of training to carry out the duties and responsibilities of your new position. You are now feeling pretty confident in your abilities, but still have not been given the freedom to work your position independently.

What would you do?
  a. Tell the unit leader's supervisor that they need to back off and give you the leeway to do your job.
  b. Provide evidence and demonstrate your competence so the leader will leave you alone.
  c. Meet with the leader, thank him for all the assistance and guidance, and discuss that you feel ready to work more independently.
  d. Try to avoid the leader as much as possible and maybe the situation will correct itself.
  e. Request another officer be assigned to your unit so that the leader will need to refocus attention on someone else.

43. Select the answer that contains the MOST EFFECTIVE way to respond to the situation.
44. Select the answer that contains the LEAST EFFECTIVE way to respond to the situation.

Situation 23

Almost two months ago you were assigned to a new unit. In that brief amount of time you have identified numerous deficiencies in existing operations and have developed solutions for these problems. The majority of the people you have discussed these issues with agree with your proposed solutions. However, the senior officer believes the solutions are too risky and may cause more harm than good.

What would you do?
   a.   Implement your proposed solutions, believing the senior officer will come around once he/she witnesses their success.
   b.   Accept the senior officer's decision and work within the current structure without making your changes.
   c.   Using the majority support of the unit, again confront the senior officer with your solutions.
   d.   In detail, create a comprehensive report on the benefits of implementing your proposed solutions. Deliver your report and subsequently accept your senior officer's decision either way.
   e.   Accept the senior officer's decision, then keep a log of the ways your solutions could have improved performance.

45. Select the answer that contains the MOST EFFECTIVE way to respond to the situation.
46. Select the answer that contains the LEAST EFFECTIVE way to respond to the situation.

Situation 24

You have always excelled in your work, and you received a promotion six months ago. Recent budget cuts have affected the quality of your work over the last few weeks. The budget cuts prevented you from having what you needed to perform your job efficiently and in the proper way. Your senior officer, however, is unaware of the budget effects and has expressed that you are the problem, your work is not up to par, and the performance drop is a result of poor management on your part.

What would you do?
   a.   Ask for advice or ideas from other officers who are dealing with the same issues resulting from budget problems.
   b.   Tell your senior officer the problem lies with your subordinates.
   c.   Get a list of complaints from your senior officer.
   d.   Ask for time off to get some perspective.
   e.   Defend your position and remind the senior officer of the budget cuts.

47. Select the answer that contains the MOST EFFECTIVE way to respond to the situation.
48. Select the answer that contains the LEAST EFFECTIVE way to respond to the situation.

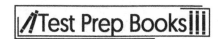

Situation 25

Supply and delivery logistics are maintained in a base computer program. While you are coordinating a long line of deliveries, the computer system crashes. You are advised by computer support that the problem may take an hour or more to fix. The delivery drivers are already getting impatient.

What would you do?
- a. Request guidance from a senior officer.
- b. Ask the drivers if they have any other deliveries they could make in the meantime and return later.
- c. Try to avoid the drivers by going on a break.
- d. Ask for assistance in advising all drivers of the issue and the possible wait time, and accommodate them in whatever way you can.
- e. Receive the deliveries anyway.

49. Select the answer that contains the MOST EFFECTIVE way to respond to the situation.
50. Select the answer that contains the LEAST EFFECTIVE way to respond to the situation.

Physical Science

1. What is the total mechanical energy of a system?
- a. The total potential energy
- b. The total kinetic energy
- c. Kinetic energy plus potential energy
- d. Kinetic energy minus potential energy
- e. Potential energy divided by kinetic energy

2. What does the Lewis dot structure of an element represent?
- a. The outer proton valence shell population
- b. The inner electron valence shell population
- c. The positioning of the element's protons
- d. The positioning of the element's neutrons
- e. The outer electron valence shell population

3. What is the name of the scale used in sound level meters to measure the intensity of sound waves?
- a. Doppler
- b. Electron
- c. Watt
- d. Decibel
- e. Seismograph

4. Which statement is true regarding electrostatic charges?
- a. Like charges attract.
- b. Like charges repel.
- c. Like charges are neutral.
- d. Like charges neither attract nor repel.
- e. Like charges attack each other.

5. What is the name of this compound: CO?
    a. Carbonite oxide
    b. Carbonic dioxide
    c. Carbonic monoxide
    d. Carbon monoxide
    e. Carbonite dioxide

6. What is the molarity of a solution made by dissolving 4.0 grams of NaCl into enough water to make 120 mL of solution? The atomic mass of Na is 23.0 g/mol and Cl is 35.5 g/mol.
    a. 0.34 M
    b. 0.57 M
    c. 0.034 M
    d. 0.057 M
    e. 0.094 M

7. Considering a gas in a closed system, at a constant volume, what will happen to the temperature if the pressure is increased?
    a. The temperature will stay the same.
    b. The temperature will decrease.
    c. The temperature will increase.
    d. It cannot be determined with the information given.
    e. The temperature will increase and then slowly decrease.

8. What is the current when a 3.0 V battery is wired across a lightbulb that has a resistance of 6.0 ohms?
    a. 0.5 A
    b. 18.0 A
    c. 0.5 J
    d. 18.0 J
    e. 9.0 J

9. According to Newton's Three Laws of Motion, which of the following is true?
    a. Two objects cannot exert a force on each other without touching.
    b. An object at rest has no inertia.
    c. The weight of an object is the same as the mass of the object.
    d. Volume is equal to the change in momentum per change in time.
    e. The weight of an object is equal to the mass of an object multiplied by gravity.

10. The chemical reaction when a compound is broken down into its basic components is called:
    a. A synthesis reaction
    b. A decomposition reaction
    c. An organic reaction
    d. An oxidation reaction
    e. A composition reaction

11. Explain the law of conservation of mass as it applies to this reaction: $2\,H_2 + O_2 \rightarrow 2\,H_2O$
    a. Electrons are lost.
    b. The hydrogen loses mass.
    c. New oxygen atoms are formed.
    d. There is no decrease or increase of matter.
    e. The hydrogen gains mass.

12. Which of the following depicts a form of potential energy?
    a. The light given off by a lamp
    b. The gravitational pull of a black hole
    c. The heat from a microwaved burrito
    d. The motion of a pendulum
    e. The motion of a carousel

13. What is the electrical charge of the nucleus?
    a. A nucleus always has a positive charge.
    b. A stable nucleus has a positive charge, but a radioactive nucleus may have no charge and instead be neutral.
    c. A nucleus always has no charge and is instead neutral.
    d. A stable nucleus has no charge and is instead neutral, but a radioactive nucleus may have a charge.
    e. A nucleus always has a negative charge.

14. Which statement is true about the pH of a solution?
    a. The more hydroxide ions in the solution, the higher the pH.
    b. The more hydrogen ions in the solution, the higher the pH.
    c. A solution cannot have a pH less than 1.
    d. If an acid has a pH of greater than 2, it is considered a weak base.
    e. A solution with a pH of 2 has ten times more hydrogen ions than a solution with a pH of 1.

15. Salts like sodium iodide (NaI) and potassium chloride (KCl) use what type of bond?
    a. Ionic bonds
    b. Disulfide bridges
    c. Covalent bonds
    d. London dispersion forces
    e. Combustion

16. What is the term for when a wave bends?
    a. Refraction
    b. Diffraction
    c. Reflection
    d. Convection
    e. Radiation

191

17. Which of the following reside in the nucleus of an atom?
    a. Protons and neutrons
    b. Neutrons and electrons
    c. Electrons and ions
    d. Ions and protons
    e. Protons and electrons

18. For circular motion, what is the name of the actual force pulling toward the axis of rotation?
    a. Centrifugal force
    b. Gravity
    c. Centripetal force
    d. Friction
    e. No force is acting

19. What coefficients are needed to balance the following combustion equation?

$$\_\,C_2H_{10} + \_\,O_2 \rightarrow \_\,H_2O + \_\,CO_2$$

    a. 1:5:5:2
    b. 1:9:5:2
    c. 2:9:10:4
    d. 2:5:10:4
    e. 4:10:20:8

20. Which of the following is unique to covalent bonds?
    a. Most covalent bonds are formed between the elements H, F, N, and O.
    b. Covalent bonds are dependent on forming dipoles.
    c. Bonding electrons are shared between two or more atoms.
    d. Molecules with covalent bonds tend to have a crystalline solid structure.
    e. The valence electrons move freely between multiple atoms in a lattice.

Table Reading

	X	Y	A	B	C	D	E
1.	11	-11	481	339	216	350	-46
2.	-5	7	25	482	256	421	-106
3.	-5	15	19	32	248	173	-196
4.	2	13	-14	-60	458	50	-155
5.	15	17	-39	459	166	460	-275
6.	3	7	-273	385	-424	-86	274
7.	-14	-10	454	251	225	417	-220
8.	-17	15	25	103	-67	-262	101
9.	10	-17	355	270	374	-296	-83
10.	-14	-11	430	119	312	-201	391
11.	15	4	-314	-439	-30	-391	331
12.	17	-11	123	84	224	177	290
13.	-14	-6	-246	381	346	-329	-66
14.	6	-12	95	141	-256	358	350
15.	13	-9	16	251	6	-405	134
16.	-1	13	-438	-12	184	490	463
17.	-12	4	298	-154	-416	270	122
18.	-14	7	-337	96	-175	-484	87
19.	-12	5	72	-11	478	267	485
20.	-1	-15	148	-167	192	-51	-294

	X	Y	A	B	C	D	E
21.	-1	6	264	436	-432	-317	-355
22.	14	2	309	-8	-306	259	494
23.	13	-5	-347	-92	-303	-267	189
24.	16	-8	165	-374	-235	39	357
25.	15	15	327	402	-78	-167	296
26.	-10	-5	166	-239	366	-127	-168
27.	3	17	-71	-243	-138	-159	90
28.	13	-11	-249	104	277	262	-84
29.	8	11	423	-339	33	195	68
30.	-7	11	-287	486	460	-359	105
31.	1	-13	423	140	-346	260	83
32.	3	-15	131	340	-27	-318	-366
33.	13	0	265	-168	-191	389	-238
34.	2	-12	-222	491	142	-234	-57
35.	-7	-12	-283	-103	-120	-434	110
36.	-8	-13	332	110	322	-433	452
37.	14	8	179	372	59	-131	-29
38.	0	-15	-425	-197	-121	29	97
39.	9	-8	-370	210	277	-323	268
40.	-3	-14	-203	-109	-69	34	310

	17	16	15	14	13	12	11	10	9	8	7	6	5	4	3	2	1	0	-1	-2	-3	-4	-5	-6	-7	-8	-9	-10	-11	-12	-13	-14	-15	-16	-17
17	-37	214	459	212	-350	-296	379	0	-13	-479	408	50	-141	449	90	-310	483	84	-88	359	295	197	224	-126	423	-82	-349	112	84	382	301	57	249	-156	-157
16	-267	-406	389	-40	-210	-117	-301	27	-53	-453	-500	125	371	5	-89	-9	-46	-417	9	130	350	399	158	208	368	-160	357	56	233	-429	-10	300	-169	144	448
15	-288	17	-78	-315	134	-125	-460	480	-441	488	-396	370	428	-191	-30	9	81	-201	-59	359	306	275	32	-260	433	-214	172	-76	323	258	294	-30	144	-48	101
14	372	134	166	-122	-112	350	455	233	234	-14	80	-238	-64	392	-444	358	-6	493	-74	-414	346	375	-144	-118	-437	357	47	270	-20	-174	-143	141	-102	-254	218
13	148	303	292	-128	29	307	-158	-276	208	313	-93	-286	-16	-436	-318	-155	306	485	490	237	31	-137	426	-280	240	199	190	-297	363	-242	-43	86	-498	281	167
12	215	150	-107	-430	226	-389	-415	299	-161	-257	-350	310	-420	305	-303	142	-330	80	286	-193	-181	380	-477	-170	-43	-64	-130	76	-323	249	90	438	-310	-213	-178
11	151	-180	310	290	-65	-111	133	213	222	-339	-483	405	-62	-29	-57	490	240	-268	151	85	207	-29	146	34	460	3	-47	242	-339	-131	261	288	-347	364	463
10	-169	-169	-494	-361	-169	99	221	275	-40	-193	159	-487	321	-160	-287	228	422	-349	-73	-402	-316	-329	-214	-231	-74	-342	274	-461	149	385	-194	-41	-130	423	-201
9	140	34	415	-411	300	-375	294	25	190	-261	-403	140	-473	-247	74	18	-20	-276	-133	-121	192	481	261	-401	294	362	-34	434	-159	166	-267	68	432	167	207
8	-181	-74	-365	372	149	-286	-41	-331	191	297	174	-226	52	4	312	421	196	398	251	129	90	-110	52	-115	477	455	163	147	332	-138	-473	163	-7	475	-388
7	-175	439	343	19	-431	-8	332	226	236	160	297	-5	411	180	-424	401	-261	358	29	-52	8	397	-106	427	-484	-130	-187	-56	-329	-126	21	-175	-350	500	-171
6	-218	267	18	487	-83	181	-18	415	337	411	-481	-368	405	249	-394	232	-481	240	264	494	202	-475	-30	-346	194	-303	232	-316	-407	-401	-315	-428	310	62	130
5	-455	-361	-288	45	-259	69	343	127	487	-182	-75	-116	-283	-254	-334	323	112	353	17	266	-76	500	62	250	99	118	473	-267	-415	485	-34	-129	-285	-110	-481
4	-108	232	-391	-423	181	-124	-480	466	51	-442	-327	-112	-149	-394	-415	311	448	-137	445	-382	-467	464	49	281	-18	145	-110	5	-361	270	92	189	264	420	251
3	-85	-362	-64	-196	-418	489	-309	-492	-74	-28	-186	-223	453	6	-97	122	-235	301	-305	-358	41	10	38	246	108	-411	-120	-447	300	320	-25	-53	335	-26	-237
2	2	-403	79	309	268	-194	475	-94	396	127	-450	225	-217	-51	-350	-380	203	275	102	383	463	170	105	-396	-422	-450	-247	243	-334	377	347	352	484	-33	110
1	-72	457	-170	484	333	-75	476	-194	-188	-147	336	201	241	133	-228	-14	-183	245	-293	230	-72	-212	490	480	-132	-192	-128	197	70	-399	498	-358	475	-224	-247
0	-381	127	-108	330	265	-240	-404	-449	-475	323	-462	-316	-172	-200	438	-363	472	415	-408	134	-136	107	-54	385	-368	-288	383	-429	355	-9	129	242	201	498	-79
-1	-151	-16	-364	-452	247	-171	-50	-213	496	-304	-451	-86	351	-346	-173	211	154	-134	-22	39	-303	341	-11	466	50	251	-55	-33	-252	-45	82	442	-119	370	-447
-2	-210	-169	-23	-90	-87	272	-230	-28	-188	-339	-317	-353	-201	-34	-259	189	-42	-167	330	7	-40	199	-472	-223	228	49	48	-33	176	222	65	-185	-162	-20	-324
-3	-174	-383	-23	400	-179	-223	95	337	-356	343	-289	-110	-194	-274	-153	-161	-160	193	184	-208	-398	228	310	-188	79	-413	48	400	305	286	-327	21	-317	50	-166
-4	321	40	-86	400	465	-411	492	148	160	-224	-43	-224	-459	130	224	429	280	423	70	221	451	158	51	-119	212	-259	286	-127	102	368	137	-462	-191	-433	42
-5	-328	-100	-113	57	-267	-213	213	164	-6	195	125	22	484	239	160	-264	61	434	-389	99	-250	-101	222	365	470	-240	405	384	-444	157	449	381	-328	54	119
-6	131	-408	-407	131	-33	-411	102	109	-282	255	358	-55	-201	-326	29	-420	223	469	-426	-76	105	-200	280	38	416	-189	224	-67	106	-302	379	255	-123	-98	123
-7	-328	42	107	131	209	213	213	164	-467	255	125	358	222	49	-363	-264	415	-130	264	-462	91	-200	320	365	229	-205	224	-423	213	-361	-225	297	295	-255	226
-8	40	-374	-119	255	178	452	106	-225	-151	468	150	13	145	73	188	285	415	97	-80	218	84	133	145	-333	127	49	493	426	452	201	97	-82	201	75	249
-9	-487	443	-162	297	131	16	125	426	-14	287	125	-12	127	-28	167	500	373	-461	-167	-285	-188	287	-297	-182	-219	-205	473	-475	-175	-217	-431	310	15	-409	377
-10	-375	-113	-64	479	144	402	213	-225	493	479	150	423	485	459	-27	-16	440	-468	180	-462	84	287	-297	62	-324	479	-409	483	51	496	234	-125	275	-169	-99
-11	177	298	-119	119	56	201	-395	-225	-151	49	489	423	127	-28	-474	-16	221	97	-80	218	-188	73	9	411	16	-260	-151	426	452	16	97	310	164	251	223
-12	156	174	275	295	-58	157	106	-427	-5	255	334	-12	451	421	-22	-239	440	428	-497	221	-271	287	451	62	-324	479	-386	483	-175	85	246	-125	164	251	223
-13	-72	312	-162	258	234	496	452	426	-386	468	-219	423	-297	459	167	500	440	-461	180	-285	-188	287	-297	62	-324	287	-386	475	-175	496	246	310	275	251	377
-14	-37	-448	310	-125	246	85	51	-475	-409	479	-171	62	451	287	-271	-16	440	428	-497	221	-271	287	428	62	-324	226	-409	483	51	85	246	-125	164	251	223
-15	271	470	-38	258	-130	426	334	63	454	-92	334	423	-297	459	-474	500	440	-461	180	-285	-188	287	-297	62	-219	287	-386	475	-175	496	234	310	275	-169	377
-16	118	312	-444	-439	-229	-107	229	374	-161	-245	-171	423	428	287	-22	-16	440	428	-497	221	-271	287	451	62	-324	479	-409	483	51	85	246	-125	275	251	223
-17	1	322	96	289	-229	463	175	374	-161	-245	-171	130	428	421	-22	-239	440	428	-497	221	-271	287	428	62	-324	226	-409	483	51	85	246	-125	223	251	223

Instrument Comprehension

1. Looking at the instruments on the left, which choice depicts the orientation of the aircraft?

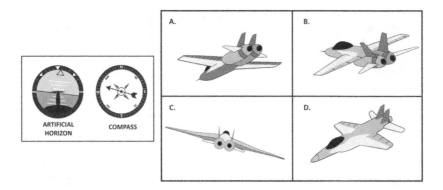

2. Looking at the instruments on the left, which choice depicts the orientation of the aircraft?

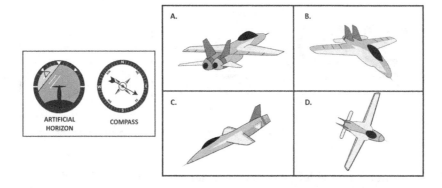

3. Looking at the instruments on the left, which choice depicts the orientation of the aircraft?

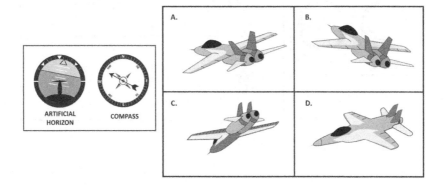

195

4. Looking at the instruments on the left, which choice depicts the orientation of the aircraft?

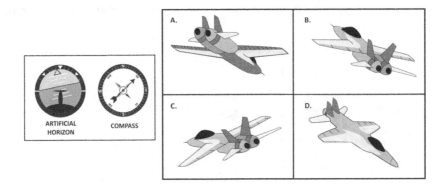

5. Looking at the instruments on the left, which choice depicts the orientation of the aircraft?

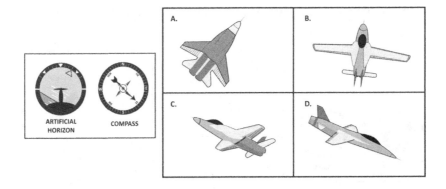

6. Looking at the instruments on the left, which choice depicts the orientation of the aircraft?

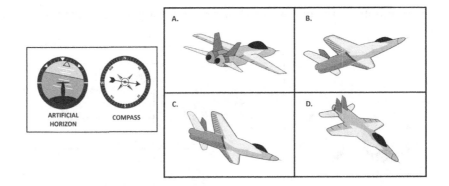

7. Looking at the instruments on the left, which choice depicts the orientation of the aircraft?

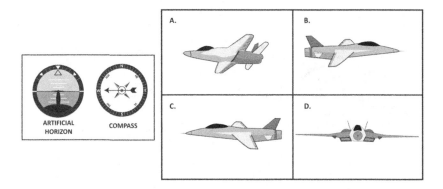

8. Looking at the instruments on the left, which choice depicts the orientation of the aircraft?

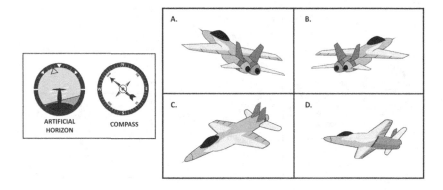

9. Looking at the instruments on the left, which choice depicts the orientation of the aircraft?

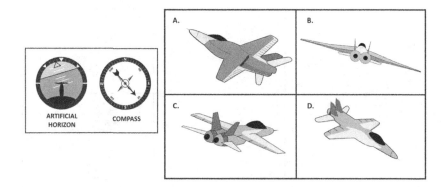

197

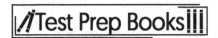
10. Looking at the instruments on the left, which choice depicts the orientation of the aircraft?

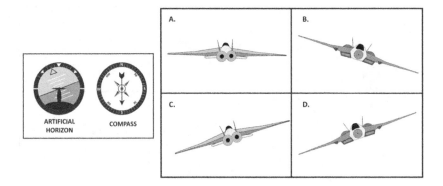

11. Looking at the instruments on the left, which choice depicts the orientation of the aircraft?

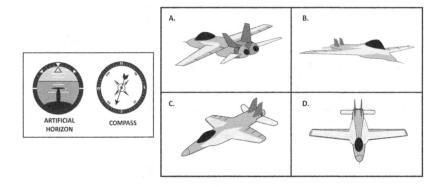

12. Looking at the instruments on the left, which choice depicts the orientation of the aircraft?

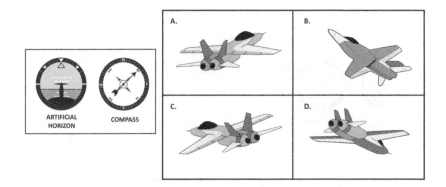

13. Looking at the instruments on the left, which choice depicts the orientation of the aircraft?

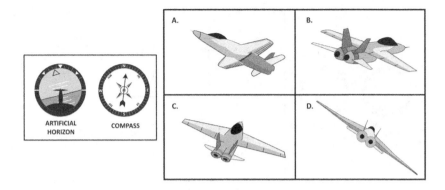

14. Looking at the instruments on the left, which choice depicts the orientation of the aircraft?

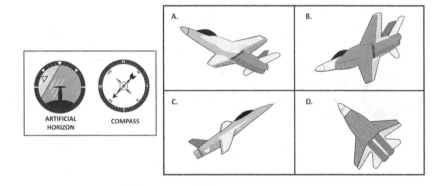

15. Looking at the instruments on the left, which choice depicts the orientation of the aircraft?

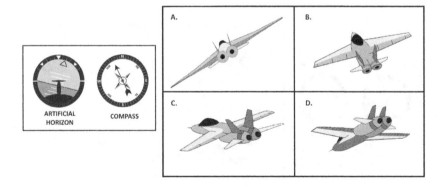

16. Looking at the instruments on the left, which choice depicts the orientation of the aircraft?

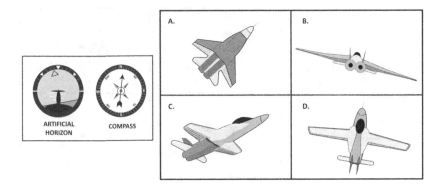

17. Looking at the instruments on the left, which choice depicts the orientation of the aircraft?

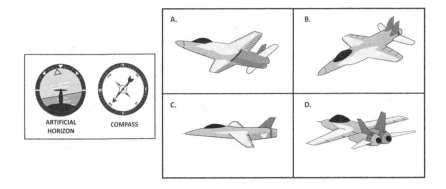

18. Looking at the instruments on the left, which choice depicts the orientation of the aircraft?

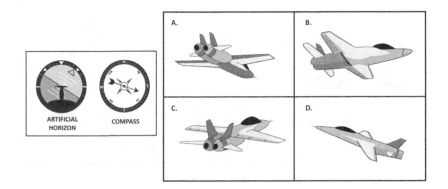

19. Looking at the instruments on the left, which choice depicts the orientation of the aircraft?

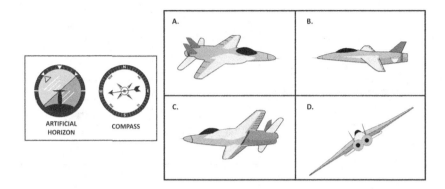

20. Looking at the instruments on the left, which choice depicts the orientation of the aircraft?

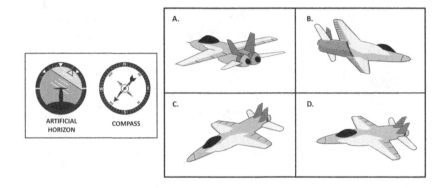

21. Looking at the instruments on the left, which choice depicts the orientation of the aircraft?

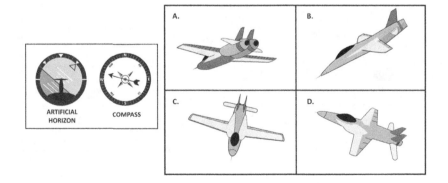

201

22. Looking at the instruments on the left, which choice depicts the orientation of the aircraft?

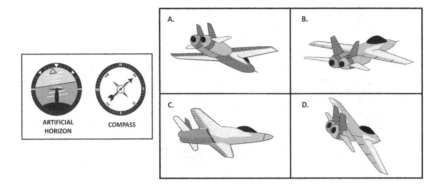

23. Looking at the instruments on the left, which choice depicts the orientation of the aircraft?

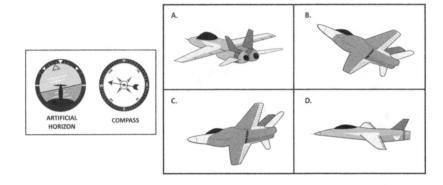

24. Looking at the instruments on the left, which choice depicts the orientation of the aircraft?

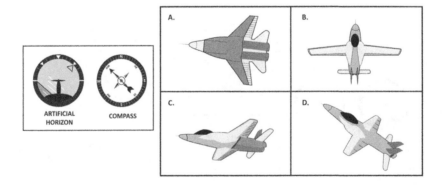

25. Looking at the instruments on the left, which choice depicts the orientation of the aircraft?

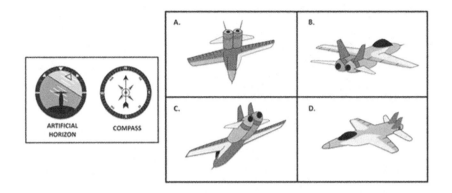

Block Counting

For questions 1–30, determine how many blocks the given block is touching.

Use the figure below for questions 1–5.

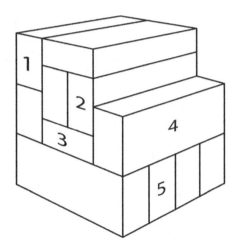

1. Block 1
   a. 1
   b. 2
   c. 3
   d. 4
   e. 5

2. Block 2
   a. 4
   b. 5
   c. 6
   d. 7
   e. 8

3. Block 3
   a. 5
   b. 6
   c. 7
   d. 8
   e. 9

4. Block 4
   a. 4
   b. 5
   c. 6
   d. 7
   e. 8

5. Block 5
   a. 2
   b. 3
   c. 4
   d. 5
   e. 6

Use the figure below for questions 6–10.

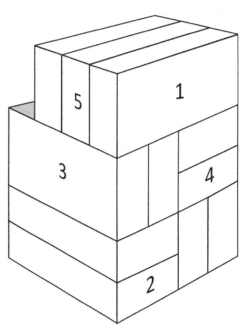

6. Block 1
   a. 1
   b. 2
   c. 3
   d. 4
   e. 5

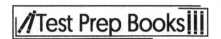

7. Block 2
   a. 2
   b. 3
   c. 4
   d. 5
   e. 6

8. Block 3
   a. 2
   b. 3
   c. 4
   d. 5
   e. 6

9. Block 4
   a. 4
   b. 5
   c. 6
   d. 7
   e. 8

10. Block 5
   a. 3
   b. 4
   c. 5
   d. 6
   e. 7

Use the figure below for questions 11–15.

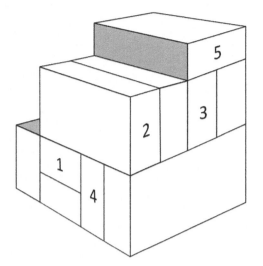

11. Block 1
   a. 3
   b. 4
   c. 5
   d. 6
   e. 7

12. Block 2
   a. 4
   b. 5
   c. 6
   d. 7
   e. 8

13. Block 3
   a. 5
   b. 6
   c. 7
   d. 8
   e. 9

14. Block 4
   a. 4
   b. 5
   c. 6
   d. 7
   e. 8

15. Block 5
   a. 1
   b. 2
   c. 3
   d. 4
   e. 5

Use the figure below for questions 16–20.

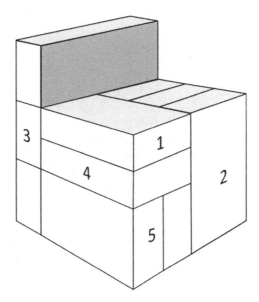

16. Block 1
   a. 1
   b. 2
   c. 3
   d. 4
   e. 5

17. Block 2
   a. 2
   b. 3
   c. 4
   d. 5
   e. 6

18. Block 3
   a. 1
   b. 2
   c. 3
   d. 4
   e. 5

19. Block 4
   a. 4
   b. 5
   c. 6
   d. 7
   e. 8

20. Block 5
   a. 2
   b. 3
   c. 4
   d. 5
   e. 6

Use the figure below for questions 21–25.

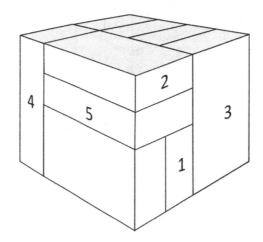

21. Block 1
   a. 3
   b. 4
   c. 5
   d. 6
   e. 7

22. Block 2
   a. 5
   b. 6
   c. 7
   d. 8
   e. 9

23. Block 3
   a. 2
   b. 3
   c. 4
   d. 5
   e. 6

24. Block 4
    a. 2
    b. 3
    c. 4
    d. 5
    e. 6

25. Block 5
    a. 3
    b. 4
    c. 5
    d. 6
    e. 7

Use the figure below for questions 26–30.

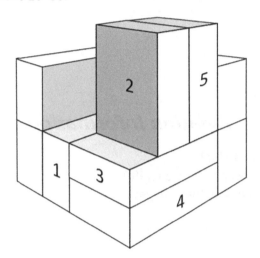

26. Block 1
    a. 2
    b. 3
    c. 4
    d. 5
    e. 6

27. Block 2
    a. 1
    b. 2
    c. 3
    d. 4
    e. 5

28. Block 3
   a. 2
   b. 3
   c. 4
   d. 5
   e. 6

29. Block 4
   a. 3
   b. 4
   c. 5
   d. 6
   e. 7

30. Block 5
   a. 2
   b. 3
   c. 4
   d. 5
   e. 6

Aviation Information

1. Which of the following will create lift?
   a. Airflow against the tail section of the aircraft
   b. Faster flow of air over the wing than beneath it
   c. Raised ailerons
   d. Helium in the wings
   e. Thrust from the engine

2. Which of the following axes is controlled by ailerons?
   a. Lateral
   b. Longitudinal
   c. Vertical
   d. Equatorial
   e. Felling axes

3. Which of the following axes is controlled by elevators?
   a. Lateral
   b. Longitudinal
   c. Vertical
   d. Equatorial
   e. All of the above

4. Which of the following axes is controlled by a rudder?
   a. Lateral
   b. Longitudinal
   c. Vertical
   d. Equatorial
   e. None of the above

5. Which of the following is not a secondary or auxiliary flight control?
   a. Flap
   b. Spoiler
   c. Aileron
   d. Slat
   e. All of the above

6. What component is not part of an empennage?
   a. Stabilizer
   b. Rudder
   c. Elevator
   d. Truss
   e. Slats

7. Which of the following is not a type of landing gear?
   a. Ski
   b. Skate
   c. Skid
   d. Float
   e. Pontoon

8. Which is not a type of fuselage?
   a. Monocoque
   b. Semicoque
   c. Semi-Monocoque
   d. Truss
   e. None of the above

9. Who should be the most concerned about an aircraft's flight envelope?
   a. The pilot
   b. Air traffic controller
   c. Passengers
   d. Aircraft mechanic
   e. People on the ground

10. What is the minimum speed at which an aircraft can maintain level flight?
    a. Ceiling speed
    b. Cruising speed
    c. Stalling speed
    d. Mach 1
    e. Gliding speed

11. What is the maximum operating altitude for a design of an aircraft?
    a. Stratosphere roof
    b. Service ceiling
    c. Stratosphere ceiling
    d. Overhead ceiling
    e. Upper limit

12. Which of the following is another word for aerodynamic friction or wind resistance?
    a. Lift
    b. Gravity
    c. Thrust
    d. Drag
    e. Stall

13. What is the purpose of the horizontal stabilizer?
    a. Pushes the tail left or right in line with the aircraft
    b. Levels the aircraft in flight
    c. Controls the roll of an aircraft
    d. Decreases speed for landing
    e. Decreases speed in a turn

14. Where are ailerons located?
    a. The trailing edge of a rudder
    b. The outer leading edge of a wing
    c. The outer trailing edge of a wing
    d. The inner trailing edge of a wing
    e. The empennage

15. What occurs when the induced drag on an aircraft exceeds its lift?
    a. Roll
    b. Yaw
    c. Pitch
    d. Stall
    e. Gravity

16. Which is not considered to be one of the four fundamental flight maneuvers?
    a. Landing
    b. Straight and level
    c. Turns
    d. Descent
    e. Climbing

17. What force acting upon a helicopter attempts to turn the body of the helicopter in the opposite direction of the main rotor travel?
    a. Gyroscopic precession
    b. Centrifugal force
    c. Torque
    d. Coriolis effect
    e. Centripetal force

18. What is used to increase the pitch of the main rotor at the same time at all points of the rotor blade rotation?
    a. Cyclic control
    b. Collective control
    c. Coriolis control
    d. Symmetry control
    e. Anti-torque control

19. Visual approach slope indicators are visible from what distance during clear, daylight hours?
    a. 1-2 miles away
    b. 3-5 miles away
    c. 5-10 miles away
    d. 10-20 miles away
    e. 20-25 miles away

20. Non-precision instrument runways provide what kind of guidance?
    a. Horizontal
    b. Vertical
    c. Locational
    d. Directional
    e. Multi-directional

Answer Explanations #1

Verbal Analogies

1. C: This is a part/whole analogy. The common thread is what animals walk on. Choices *A*, *B*, and *E* all describe signature parts of animals, but paws are not the defining feature of cats. While snakes travel on their skins, they do not walk.

2. A: This is a characteristic analogy. The connection lies in what observers will judge a performance on. While the other choices are also important, an off-key singer is as unpleasant as a dancer with no rhythm.

3. D: This is a use/tool analogy. The analogy focuses on an item's use. While hats are worn when it's cold with the goal of making the top of your head warm, this is not always guaranteed—their primary use is to provide cover. There is also the fact that not all hats are used to keep warm, but all hats cover the head.

4. D: This is a source/comprised of analogy. The common thread is addition of fire. Protons contribute to atoms and seeds grow into plants, but these are simple matters of building and growing without necessarily involving fire. B and E relate objects that already have similar properties.

5. E: This is a synonym analogy. The determining factor is synonymous definition. Design and create are synonyms, as are allocate and distribute. Typically, items are found and allocated as part of management to finish a project, but these qualities are not innate in the word. Allocation generally refers to the division of commodities instead of multiplication.

6. B: This is a tool/use analogy. The common thread is audience response to an art form. *A*, *C*, and *D* deal with the creation of artwork instead of its consumption. Choice *E* describes a form of art instead of the audience engagement with such.

7. C: This is an intensity analogy. The common thread is degree of severity. While *A*, *D*, and *E* can all describe warmth, they don't convey the harshness of sweltering. *B* simply describes a time when people may be more likely to think of warmth.

8. D: This is a characteristic analogy and is based on matching objects to their geometric shapes. Choice *A* is not correct because globes are three-dimensional, whereas circles exist in two dimensions. While wheels are three-dimensional, they are not always solid or perfectly round.

9. A: This is a tool/use analogy. The key detail of this analogy is the idea of enclosing or sealing items/people. When plates are filled with food, there is no way to enclose the item. While trees can be inside a fence, they can also be specifically outside of one.

10. E: This is a sequence of events analogy. The common thread is celestial cause-and-effect. Not everyone has breakfast or goes to bed after sunset. Sunrise is not typically thought of as the next interesting celestial event after sunsets. While clouds can develop after sunsets, they are also present before and during this activity. Stars, however, can be seen after dark.

11. A: This is a provider/provision analogy. The theme of this analogy is pairing a specific animal to their food source. Falcons prey on mice. Giraffes are herbivores and only eat one of the choices: leaves. Grasslands describe a type of landscape, not a food source for animals.

12. B: This is a category analogy. The common thread is motorized vehicles. While Choices *A*, *C*, and *E* also describe vehicles that move on water, they are not motorized. Although relying on engines, planes are not a form of water transportation.

13. D: This is an antonym analogy. The prevailing connection is opposite meanings. While happy can be an opposite of anxious, it's also possible for someone to experience both emotions at once. *B*, *C*, and *E* are also concurrent with anxious, not opposite.

14. E: This is a provider/provision analogy. This analogy looks at professionals and what their job is. Just as a mechanic's job is to repair machinery, a doctor works to heal patients.

15. C: This is a category analogy. Both whistles and blow horns are devices used to project/produce sound. Therefore, the analogy is based on finding something of a categorical nature. While *A*, *B*, *D*, and *E* involve or describe painting, they do not pertain to a distinct discipline alongside painting. Sculpture, however, is another form of art and expression, just like painting.

16. D: This is a part/whole analogy. This analogy examines the relationship between two objects. Specifically, this analogy examines how one object connects to another object, with the first object(s) being the means by which people use the corresponding object to produce a result directly. People use a paddle to steer a boat, just as pressing keys on a piano produces music. *B* and *C* can be metaphorically linked to keys but are unrelated. *A* is related to keys but is a verb, not another object. Choice *E* is the trickiest alternative, but what's important to remember is that while keys are connected to key chains, there is no result just by having the key on a key chain.

17. C: This is an antonym analogy. The common thread is opposite meanings. Monotonous refers to being dull or being repetitive, while innovative means new and bringing in changes. All of the other choices reflect synonymous word pairs. However, loquacious, which means talkative, is the opposite of silent.

18. E: This is a part/whole analogy. This analogy focuses on natural formations and their highest points. The peak of a mountain is its highest point just as the crest is the highest rise in a wave.

19. A: This is a negative connotations analogy. Essentially all of the given words in the example express the same idea of uncertainty or not taking a definitive stance. Ambiguous means open to possibilities, which parallels to not being able to make a decision, which describes indecisive as well as uncertain. Uncertain also means not definite, which not only relates to the given words but also directly to indefinite.

20. B: This is an intensity analogy. Fluent refers to how well one can communicate, while gourmet describes a standard of cooking. The analogy draws on degrees of a concept.

21. B: This is a synonym analogy, which relies on matching terms that are most closely connected. Validate refers to finding truth. Therefore, finding the term that best fits conquer is a good strategy. While nations have conquered others to expand their territory, they are ultimately subjugating those lands and people to their will. Therefore, subjugate is the best-fitting answer.

22. C: This is a sequence of events analogy. This analogy pairs one season with the season that precedes it. Winter is paired with autumn because autumn actually comes before winter. Out of all the answers, only *B* and *C* are actual seasons. Fall is another name for autumn, which comes after summer, not before. Spring, of course, is the season that comes before summer, making it the right answer.

23. A: This is a pairs analogy. None of the given terms are really related. To find the analogy, the way that each term is paired should be analyzed. Penguin, a bird, is paired with lemur, which is a primate. When given eagle, the only logical analogy to be made is to find another primate to pair with a bird, which is howler monkey.

24. C: This is a source/comprised of analogy. This analogy focuses on pairing a raw material with an object that it's used to create. Fiberglass is used to build surfboards just as copper is used in the creation of pennies. While wind powers a windmill, there is no physical object produced, like with the fiberglass/surfboard pair.

25. E: This is an object/function analogy. The common thread between these words is that one word describes a kind of story and it is paired with the purpose of the story. Myth is/was told in order to explain fundamental beliefs and natural phenomena. While laughter can result from a joke, the purpose of telling a joke is to amuse the audience, thus making *E* the right choice.

Arithmetic Reasoning

1. B: 300 miles in 4 hours is $\frac{300}{4} = 75$ miles per hour. In 1.5 hours, the car will go 1.5×75 miles, or 112.5 miles.

2. C: One apple/orange pair costs $3 total. Jan therefore bought $\frac{90}{3} = 30$ total pairs, and hence 30 oranges.

3. C: The volume of a box with rectangular sides is the length times width times height, so:

$$5 \times 6 \times 3 = 90 \text{ cubic feet}$$

4. E: First, the train's journey in the real world is:

$$3 \text{ h} \times 50 \frac{\text{mi}}{\text{h}} = 150 \text{ mi}$$

On the map, 1 inch corresponds to 10 miles, so that is equivalent to:

$$150 \text{ mi} \times \frac{1 \text{ in}}{10 \text{ mi}} = 15 \text{ in}$$

Therefore, the start and end points are 15 inches apart on the map.

5. B: The total trip time is:

$$1 + 3.5 + 0.5 = 5 \text{ hours}$$

The total time driving is:

$$1 + 0.5 = 1.5 \text{ hours}$$

216

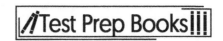

So, the fraction of time spent driving is $\frac{1.5}{5}$, or $\frac{3}{10}$. To get the percentage, convert this to a fraction out of 100. The numerator and denominator are multiplied by 10, with a result of $\frac{30}{100}$. The percentage is the numerator in a fraction out of 100, so 30%.

6. B: The formula for the volume of a cylinder is $\pi r^2 h$, where r is the radius and h is the height. The diameter is twice the radius, so these barrels have a radius of 1 foot. That means each barrel has a volume of:

$$\pi \times 1^2 \times 3 = 3\pi \text{ ft}^3$$

Since there are three of them, the total is:

$$3 \times 3\pi = 9\pi \text{ ft}^3$$

7. B: The tip is not taxed, so he pays 5% tax only on the $10. 5% of $10 is:

$$0.05 \times 10 = \$0.50$$

Add up $10 + $2 + $0.50 to get $12.50.

8. C: Divide the total amount by the number of days:

$$\frac{\$150}{4} = \$37.5$$

She needs to save an average of $37.50 per day.

9. C: The number of days can be found by taking the total amount Bernard needs to make and dividing it by the amount he earns per day:

$$\frac{300}{80} = \frac{30}{8} = \frac{15}{4} = 3.75$$

But Bernard is only working full days, so he will need to work 4 days since 3 days is not a sufficient amount of time.

10. A: The value went up by:

$$\$165,000 - \$150,000 = \$15,000$$

Out of $150,000, this is:

$$\frac{15,000}{150,000} = \frac{1}{10}$$

Convert this to having a denominator of 100, the result is $\frac{10}{100}$, or 10%.

11. E: The total faculty is:

$$15 + 20 = 35$$

217

So, the ratio is 35:200. Then, divide both of these numbers by 5, since 5 is a common factor to both, with a result of 7:40.

12. B: The journey will be:

$$5 \times 3 = 15 \text{ miles}$$

A car traveling at 60 miles per hour is traveling at 1 mile per minute. The resulting equation would be:

$$\frac{15 \text{ mi}}{1 \text{ mi/min}} = 15 \text{ min}$$

Therefore, it will take 15 minutes to make the journey.

13. A: Taylor's total income is $20,000 + $10,000 = $30,000. Fifteen percent of this is $\frac{15}{100} = \frac{3}{20}$. So:

$$\frac{3}{20} \times \$30,000 = \frac{\$90,000}{20} = \frac{\$9,000}{2}$$

$$\frac{\$9,000}{2} = \$4,500$$

14. B: Since the answer will be in cubic feet rather than inches, start by converting from inches to feet for the dimensions of the box. There are 12 inches per foot, so the box is $\frac{24}{12} = 2$ ft wide, $\frac{18}{12} = 1.5$ ft deep, and $\frac{12}{12} = 1$ ft high. The volume is the product of these three together:

$$2 \times 1.5 \times 1 = 3 \text{ cubic feet}$$

15. D: Kristen bought four DVDs, which would total a cost of:

$$4 \times 15 = \$60$$

She spent a total of $100, so she spent $100 − $60 = $40 on CDs. Since they cost $10 each, she must have purchased $\frac{40}{10} = 4$ CDs.

16. E: Using the conversion rate, multiply the projected weight loss of 25 lb by $0.45 \frac{\text{kg}}{\text{lb}}$ to get the amount in kilograms (11.25 kg).

17. D: First, subtract $1,437 from $2,334.50 to find Johnny's monthly savings; this equals $897.50. Then, multiply this amount by 3 to find out how much he will have in three months before he pays for his vacation; this equals $2,692.50. Finally, subtract the cost of the vacation ($1,750) from this amount to find how much Johnny will have left: $942.50.

18. C: The formula for the perimeter of a rectangle is $P = 2l + 2w$, where P is the perimeter, l is the length, and w is the width. The first step is to substitute all of the data into the formula:

$$36 = 2(12) + 2W$$

Simplify by multiplying 2×12:

$$36 = 24 + 2W$$

218

Simplifying this further by subtracting 24 on each side, which gives:

$$36 - 24 = 24 - 24 + 2W$$

$$12 = 2W$$

Divide by 2:

$$6 = W$$

The width is 6 cm. Remember to test this answer by substituting this value into the original formula:

$$36 = 2(12) + 2(6)$$

19. D: To find the average of a set of values, add the values together and then divide by the total number of values. In this case, include the unknown value, x, of what Dwayne needs to score on his next test. The average must equal 90. Set up the equation and solve:

$$\frac{78 + 92 + 83 + 97 + x}{5} = 90$$

$$\frac{350 + x}{5} = 90$$

$$350 + x = 450$$

$$x = 100$$

Dwayne would need to get a perfect score of 100 in order to get an average of at least 90.

Test this answer by substituting back into the original formula.

$$\frac{78 + 92 + 83 + 97 + 100}{5} = 90$$

20. D: Three girls for every two boys can be expressed as a ratio: 3: 2. This can be visualized as splitting the school into 5 groups: 3 girl groups and 2 boy groups. The number of students that are in each group can be found by dividing the total number of students by 5:

$$\frac{650 \text{ students}}{5 \text{ groups}} = \frac{130 \text{ students}}{\text{group}}$$

To find the total number of girls, multiply the number of students per group (130) by the number of girl groups in the school (3). This equals 390, Choice *D*.

21. C: Kimberley worked 4.5 hours at the rate of \$10/h and 1 hour at the rate of \$12/h. The problem states that her time is rounded to the nearest hour, so the 4.5 hours would round up to 5 hours at the rate of \$10/h.

$$(5h)(\$10/h) + (1h)(\$12/h) = \$50 + \$12 = \$62$$

22. B: First, calculate the difference between the larger value and the smaller value.

$$378 - 252 = 126$$

To calculate this difference as a percentage of the original value, and thus calculate the percentage *increase*, divide 126 by 252 to get 0.5, then multiply by 100 to reach the percentage 50%, Choice *B*.

23. A: If each man gains 10 pounds, every original data point will increase by 10 pounds. Therefore, the man with the original median will still have the median value, but that value will increase by 10. The smallest value and largest value will also increase by 10, so the difference between the two (the range) will remain the same.

24. D: Let a be the number of apples and b be the number of bananas.

Then, the total cost is $2a + 3b = 22$, while it also known that:

$$a + b = 10$$

Using the knowledge of systems of equations, cancel the b variables by multiplying the second equation by -3. This makes the equation:

$$-3a - 3b = -30$$

Adding this to the first equation, the b values cancel to get $-a = -8$, which simplifies to $a = 8$.

25. A: Putting the scores in order from least to greatest, we have 60, 75, 80, and 85, as well as one unknown. The median is 80, so 80 must be the middle data point out of these five. Therefore, the unknown data point must be the fourth or fifth data point, meaning it must be greater than or equal to 80. The only answer that fails to meet this condition is 60.

Word Knowledge

1. C: To deduce something is to figure it out using reason. Although this might cause a win and prompt an explanation to further understanding, the art of deduction is logical reasoning.

2. B: To elucidate, a light is figuratively shined on a previously unknown or confusing subject. This Latin root, *lux* meaning *light*, prominently figures into the solution. Enlighten means to educate, or bring into the light.

3. D: Looking at the Latin word *veritas*, meaning *truth*, will yield a clue as to the meaning of verify. To verify is the act of finding or assessing the truthfulness of something. This usually means amassing evidence to substantiate a claim. Substantiate, of course, means to provide evidence to prove a point.

4. A: If someone is inspired, they are motivated to do something. Someone who is an inspiration motivates others to follow their example.

5. E: All the connotations of perceive involve the concept of seeing. Whether figuratively or literally, perceiving implies the act of understanding what is presented. Comprehending is synonymous with this understanding.

6. C: Nomadic tribes are those who, throughout history and even today, prefer to wander their lands instead of settling in any specific place. Wanderer best describes these people.

7. A: Malevolent literally means bad or evil-minded. The clue is also in the Latin root *mal-* that translates to bad.

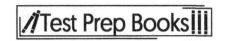

8. D: Perplexed means baffled or puzzled, which are synonymous with confused.

9. D: Lyrical is used to refer to something being poetic or song-like, characterized by showing enormous imagination and description. While the context of lyrical can be playful or even whimsical, the best choice is expressive, since whatever emotion lyrical may be used to convey in context will be expressive in nature.

10. C: Brevity literally means brief or concise. Note the similar beginnings of brevity and brief—from the Latin *brevis*, meaning brief.

11. A: Irate means being in a state of anger. Clearly this is a negative word that can be paired with another word in kind. The closest word to match this is obviously anger. Research would also reveal that irate comes from the Latin *ira*, which means anger.

12. C: Lavish is a synonym for luxurious—both describe elaborate and/or elegant lifestyles and/or settings.

13. E: Immobile means *not able to move*. The two best selections are *B* and *E*—but slow still implies some form of motion, whereas sedentary has the connotation of being seated and/or inactive for a significant portion of time and/or as a natural tendency.

14. D: Mendacious describes dishonesty or lying in several ways. This is another word of classical lineage. *Mendacio* in Latin means *liar*. While liar lacks the Latin root, the meanings fit.

15. E: Chivalrous reflects showing respect and courtesy toward others, particularly women.

16. C: Retort is a verb that means *to answer back*, usually in a sharp manner. This term embodies the idea of a response, emphasized by the *re-* prefix meaning *back*, *again*. While a retort is used in conversations and even as a jest, neither term embodies the idea of addressing someone again. Counter, however, means to respond in opposition when used as a verb.

17. A: Subliminal and subconscious share the Latin prefix *sub-*, meaning under or below, or more commonly used when talking about messages the sender doesn't want the receiver to consciously take note of. The word subliminal means beneath the consciousness. Thus, subconscious is the perfect match.

18. C: Although incite usually has negative connotations, leaders can incite their followers to benevolent actions as well. In both cases, people rally to support a cause.

19. A: While a moniker commonly refers to a title, this is technically a designated name. Monikers can be mockeries, insults, and/or burdens, but none of these are direct forms of a title or identification.

20. E: Events that occur through serendipity happen purely by chance. Serendipitous conveys the idea of something unplanned yet potentially desirable. Coincidental is defined as happening by chance.

21. B: Overbearing refers to domineering or being oppressive. This is emphasized in the *over* prefix, which emphasizes an excess in definitions. This prefix is also seen in overacting. Similar to overbearing, overacting reflects an excess of action.

22. A: The *pre* prefix describes something that occurs before an event. Prevent means to stop something before it happens. This leads to a word that relates to something occurring beforehand and, in a way, is

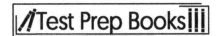

preventive—wanting to stop something. Avert literally means to turn away or ward off an impending circumstance, making it the best fit.

23. D: Refresh is synonymous with replenish. Both words mean to restore or refill. Additionally, these terms do share the *re-* prefix as well.

24. D: Regale literally means to amuse someone with a story. This is a very positive word; the best way to eliminate choices is to look for a term that matches regale in both positive context/sound and definition. Entertain is both a positive word and a synonym of regale.

25. C: Abate is defined as something becoming less intense and fading. The only word that matches abate is withdraw, which means to go back or draw away from a particular position.

Math Knowledge

1. D: Start by taking a common denominator of 30.

$$\frac{14}{15} = \frac{28}{30}, \frac{3}{5} = \frac{18}{30}, \frac{1}{30} = \frac{1}{30}$$

Add and subtract the numerators for the next step.

$$\frac{28}{30} + \frac{18}{30} - \frac{1}{30}$$

$$\frac{28 + 18 - 1}{30} = \frac{45}{30} = \frac{3}{2}$$

Where in the last step the 15 is factored out from the numerator and denominator.

2. A: From the second equation, add x to both sides and subtract 1 from both sides:

$$-x + 3y + x - 1 = 1 + x - 1$$

With the result of $3y - 1 = x$, substitute this into the first equation and get:

$$3(3y - 1) + 2y = 8 \text{ or } 9y - 3 + 2y = 8$$

$$11y = 11$$

$$y = 1$$

Putting this into $3y - 1 = x$ gives $3(1) - 1 = x$ or $x = 2$, $y = 1$.

3. C: The square root of 16 is 4, so this expression simplifies to:

$$\frac{1}{2}\sqrt{16} = \frac{1}{2}(4) = 2$$

Therefore, Choice *C* is correct.

4. E: The easiest way to approach this problem is to factor out a 2 from each term.

$$2x^2 - 8 = 2(x^2 - 4)$$

Use the formula $x^2 - y^2 = (x + y)(x - y)$ to factor:

$$x^2 - 4 = x^2 - 2^2 = (x + 2)(x - 2)$$

So,

$$2(x^2 - 4) = 2(x + 2)(x - 2)$$

5. B: The total of the interior angles of a triangle must be 180°. The sum of the first two is 105°, so the remaining is:

$$180° - 105° = 75°$$

6. B: The length of the side will be $\sqrt{400}$. The calculation is performed a bit more easily by breaking this into the product of two square roots:

$$\sqrt{400} = \sqrt{4 \times 100}$$

$$\sqrt{4} \times \sqrt{100} = 2 \times 10 = 20 \text{ feet}$$

However, there are 4 sides, so the total is $20 \times 4 = 80$ feet.

7. E: To take the product of two fractions, just multiply the numerators and denominators

$$\frac{5}{3} \times \frac{7}{6} = \frac{5 \times 7}{3 \times 6} = \frac{35}{18}$$

The numerator and denominator have no common factors, so this is simplified completely.

8. C: Let a be the number of apples purchased, and let p be the number of papayas purchased. There is a total of 15 pieces of fruit, so one equation is:

$$a + p = 15$$

The total cost is $35, and in terms of the total apples and papayas purchased as:

$$2a + 3p = 35$$

If we multiply the first equation by 2 on both sides, it becomes:

$$2a + 2p = 30$$

We then subtract this equation from the second equation:

$$2a + 3p - (2a + 2p) = 35 - 30$$

$$p = 5$$

So, five papayas were purchased.

9. A: This equation can be solved as follows: $x^2 = 36$, so:

$$x = \pm\sqrt{36} = \pm 6$$

Only -6 shows up in the list.

10. E: The volume of a cube is given by cubing the length of its side.

$$6^3 = 6 \times 6 \times 6$$

$$216$$

11. A: The area of the square is the square of its side length, so $4^2 = 16$ square inches. The area of a triangle is half the base times the height. So,

$$\frac{1}{2} \times 2 \times 8 = 8 \text{ square inches}$$

The total is $16 + 8 = 24$ square inches

12. B: $-\frac{1}{3}\sqrt{81} = -\frac{1}{3}(9) = -3$

13. A: Multiply each of the terms in the first parentheses and then multiply each of the terms in the second parentheses.

$$(2x - 3)(4x + 2)$$

$$2x(4x) + 2x(2) - 3(4x) - 3(2)$$

$$8x^2 + 4x - 12x - 6$$

$$8x^2 - 8x - 6$$

14. C: Use a common denominator of 24.

$$\frac{11}{6} - \frac{3}{8}$$

$$\frac{44}{24} - \frac{9}{24}$$

$$\frac{44 - 9}{24} = \frac{35}{24}$$

15. C: The formula for the area of a triangle with base b and height h is $\frac{1}{2}bh$, where the base is one-third the height, or $b = \frac{1}{3}h$ or equivalently $h = 3b$. Using the formula for a triangle, this becomes:

$$\frac{1}{2}b(3b) = \frac{3}{2}b^2$$

Now, this has to be equal to 6. So,

$$\frac{3}{2}b^2 = 6$$

224

$$b^2 = 4$$

$$b = \pm 2$$

However, lengths are positive, so the base must be 2 feet long.

16. B: Instead of multiplying these out, we can estimate the product by using $18 \times 10 = 180$.

17. E: This can be set up an equation:

$$0.30x = 6$$

That equation is asking, "30% of what number equals 6?" Working out the problem gives us:

$$x = \frac{6}{0.3}$$

$$x = 20$$

18. A: First, these numbers need to be converted to improper fractions: $\frac{11}{3} - \frac{9}{5}$. Take 15 as a common denominator:

$$\frac{11}{3} - \frac{9}{5} = \frac{55}{15} - \frac{27}{15} = \frac{28}{15} = 1\frac{13}{15}$$

19. E: Dividing by 98 can be approximated by dividing by 100, which would mean shifting the decimal point of the numerator to the left by 2. The result is 4.2 and rounds to 4.

20. A: To figure out which is largest, look at the first nonzero digits. Answer *B* and *E*'s first nonzero digit is in the hundredths place. The other three all have nonzero digits in the tenths place, so it must be *A*, *C*, or *D*. Of these, *A*'s first nonzero digit is the largest.

21. C: To solve for the value of b, it needs to be isolated on one side of the equation. Do this by performing inverse operations to both sides of the equation.

Start by canceling out the lower value of -4 by adding 4 to both sides:

$$5b - 4 = 2b + 17$$

$$5b - 4 + 4 = 2b + 17 + 4$$

$$5b = 2b + 21$$

The variable b is the same on each side, so subtract the lower $2b$ from each side:

$$5b = 2b + 21$$

$$5b - 2b = 2b + 21 - 2b$$

$$3b = 21$$

Then divide both sides by 3 to get the value of b:

225

$$3b = 21$$

$$\frac{3b}{3} = \frac{21}{3}$$

$$b = 7$$

22. A: Setting up a proportion is the easiest way to represent this situation. The proportion is $\frac{20}{x} = \frac{40}{100}$, and cross-multiplication can be used to solve for x. Here, $40x = 2{,}000$, so $x = 50$.

23. A: First, separate each element of the numerator with the denominator as follows:

$$\frac{2xy^2}{16xy} + \frac{4x}{16xy} - \frac{8y}{16xy}$$

Simplify each expression accordingly, reaching Choice A:

$$\frac{y}{8} + \frac{1}{4y} - \frac{1}{2x}$$

24. C: There are multiple ways to tackle this problem. One way is to make each a decimal. 0.85 is already a decimal. You may know that $\frac{4}{5}$ is 0.80. Otherwise, you can work it out:

$$\frac{4}{5} \times \frac{20}{20} = \frac{80}{100}$$

Any numerator over 100 can be converted to a decimal: 0.80

$\frac{2}{3}$ can be estimated to be 0.67, or worked out roughly to be:

$$\frac{2}{3} \times \frac{33}{33} = \frac{66}{99} = 0.66$$

$\frac{91}{100}$ then becomes 0.91. Rearrange each expression in ascending (increasing) order, as found in Choice C.

25. A: When parentheses are around two expressions, they need to be *multiplied*. In this case, separate each expression into its parts (separated by addition and subtraction) and multiply by each of the parts in the other expression. Then, add the products together:

$$(3x)(x) + (3x)(-8) + (+5)(x) + (+5)(-8)$$

$$3x^2 - 24x + 5x - 40$$

Remember that when multiplying a positive integer by a negative integer, it will remain negative. Then add $-24x + 5x$ to get the simplified expression, Choice A.

Reading Comprehension

1. D: Choice A can be eliminated, as this idea isn't stated in the selection. Choice B only represents a portion of the subject. Choice C is stated in the passage, but the paragraph isn't solely about constant velocity. Choice E is a supporting concept, not the main topic. Only Choice D answers the question.

2. C: Choices *A*, *B*, and *E* are stated in the passage. The sum weight of an aircraft is important to calculate, as are personnel and fuel load. Notice that Choice *E* states fuel load *cannot* be eliminated in measuring weight. Careful comprehension is important when reading Choice *E*. Choice *D* also supports the idea that weight affects aerodynamics. In Choice *C*, while it's true that the mechanics of flight includes lift, that detail doesn't support the overall topic of weight.

3. E: Choices *A*, *B*, and *D* are true, but they don't encompass all of the ideas presented in the passage. Choice *C* isn't stated and is incorrect. Choice *E* encapsulates all of the ideas presented in the passage.

4. A: From the provided paragraph, a reader may infer that a pilot should use sound judgment when flying. Choice *B* is not stated. Choice *C* is stated as fact but isn't true. Choices *D* and *E* are false as stated.

5. C: All of the options indicate some aspect of the pilot's acumen, but each is a contextual clue that, when put together, indicate the pilot has an overall shrewdness and keen insight when it comes to his flight talent. Choice *A* is incorrect as *acumen* isn't specific to flight. Choice *B* is insufficient, for knowledge alone doesn't encompass the other passage descriptors. The same can be said for Choice *D*; and, while Choice *E* is directly mentioned in the paragraph, an impressive number of flight hours is just one accomplishment of the pilot and too specific to encompass the pilot's other skills.

6. D: Choice *A* is incorrect; the passage doesn't state that anyone can become a pilot. The text implies that becoming a pilot carries some risk, but Choice *B* is not the correct answer, as the rest of the paragraph doesn't support that statement. Choices *C* and *E* are incorrect because they aren't stated. Only Choice *D* encompasses all of the text as the logical conclusion.

7. A: While the reader may disagree with the author's position, all of the statements in the passage indicate the author's position is that piloting is a difficult goal that requires serious consideration on the part of a potential flight student. Choices *B*, *C*, and *E* aren't stated. Choice *D* can be ruled out because the physical and mental toll on piloting students isn't the main position of the paragraph.

8. D: The text indicates a sequence throughout time. Sentence C relates the very first recorded attempt at flight. Sentence B indicates the first manmade vehicles in fifth century China. Sentence A addresses Leonardo da Vinci's famous work in flight during the Renaissance. Then, Sentences D, E, and F occur in the correct historical order.

9. A: The purpose is to inform the reader of certain facts by presenting examples of revolutionary aircraft throughout flight history. Choice *B* is incorrect. While the passage may be fun to read, its primary purpose is not entertainment. It doesn't tell a story. Choice *C* is incorrect. The main focus of the passage is not Deperdussin's model. Choice *D* is incorrect. The passage doesn't indicate that American structures were better than any other. Choice *E* is also incorrect. The reader would have to assume that the author intended to argue that these examples of aircraft development are the only ones worth considering. The first paragraph of the passage indicates they aren't.

10. B: Turbulence is caused by a disruption in air flow. Choices *A*, *C*, and *D* are incorrect as stated. Choice *E* is true, but it doesn't indicate a cause and effect relationship.

11. E: Choices *A*, *B*, and *D* are incorrect as stated. Choice *C* is likely correct but it isn't always correct as stated, and it doesn't encompass a conclusion or outcome. Only Choice *E* summarizes the best potential outcome to encountering turbulence.

12. E: The answer is Choice *E*, which encompasses the idea that the author's purposes are both to inform and describe. Choice *A* doesn't address the entire purpose. Yes, the author states the mechanics of flight are not difficult to understand, but that's not all the author does in the passage. Choice *B* is incorrect as stated.

13. D: Notice that the main idea of the passage—maintaining equilibrium in flight—is stated in the first sentence and re-stated in the last. The word *equilibrium* is re-defined for the reader as staying stable in flight. All other options are incorrect as stated.

14. D: The reader isn't given enough information to determine if Choice *A* is correct. Nowhere in the passage does the author indicate that 9,000 feet is too high, so Choice *B* is incorrect. The pilot had the correct clearance, so Choice *C* is incorrect as stated. Although icing led to additional weight on the fuselage, Choice *E* doesn't best address the cause and effect relationship depicted in the passage.

15. B: All other four options are incorrect as stated. Notice that after each bolded word, the author actually defines the words *coaxial* and *intermeshing*, as both are used to describe types of rotor configurations in helicopter design.

16. B: The main idea of the paragraph is best stated in Choice *B*. Choices *A* and *D* are true, but they don't reflect the entire main idea. Choices *C* and *E* are incorrect as stated. Notice that both options use the word *always*. Be wary of test options that use absolutes; rarely are such options correct.

17. A: Although the passage doesn't directly define drift, the reader can use previous knowledge in answering the question correctly. In addition, the reader can eliminate all other options as incorrect because none of them are true.

18. C: Choice *A* is untrue. Choice *B* doesn't state a conclusion applicable to the entire passage. Choice *D* is untrue as stated. Although mechanics should be considered during flight, Choice *E*, as it's written, doesn't state a conclusion applicable to the information in the passage.

19. B: Choice *A* is correct but doesn't encompass all of the main ideas in the passage. Choice *C* is untrue. Choice *D* is partially true but again, note the use of the word "always." In this case, making unapproved changes during flight (while highly inadvisable) doesn't always lead to problems. Choice *E* isn't true as stated. While communication is important to successful flight, it's not the key factor. As the author stated that most events in the error chain can be addressed and controlled by the pilot, Choice *B* is the best answer.

20. B: In this case, all other choices are incorrect. By using context around the word *obliterated*, the reader can infer that the meaning is "thoroughly destroyed."

21. B: Readers should carefully focus their attention on the beginning of the passage to answer this series of questions. Even though the sentences may be worded a bit differently, all but one statement is true. It presents a false idea that descriptive details are not necessary until the climax of the story. Even if one does not read the passage, he or she probably knows that all good writing begins with descriptive details to develop the main theme the writer intends for the narrative.

22. B: To suggest that a ten-minute play is accessible does not imply any timeline, nor does the passage mention how long a playwright spends with revisions and rewrites. So, Choice *A* is incorrect. Choice *B* is correct because of the opening statement that reads, "Learning how to write a ten-minute play may seem like a monumental task at first; but, if you follow a simple creative writing strategy, similar to

writing a narrative story, you will be able to write a successful drama." None of the remaining choices are supported by points in the passage.

23. C: Note that the only element not mentioned in the passage is the style feature that is part of a narrative writer's tool kit. It is not to say that ten-minute plays do not have style. The correct answer denotes only that the element of style was not illustrated in this particular passage.

24. C: This choice allows room for the fact that not all people who attempt to write a play will find it easy. If the writer follows the basic principles of narrative writing described in the passage, however, writing a play does not have to be an excruciating experience. None of the other options can be supported by points from the passage.

25. C: To arrive at the correct answer, find the best synonym for *spurious*. *Fake* makes the most sense because Bob is trying to hide his true emotions. Based on his horrible performance, he understands that he didn't get the job, so the reader can infer that his confidence is not at an all-time high. Therefore, *fake* would make just as much sense in this case as *spurious*. *Extreme* would indicate that Bob is euphoric and the interview went well. *Mild* would indicate that Bob thought he had a slight chance at getting hired. In this instance, *genuine* would be an antonym (i.e., the exact opposite of what Bob is feeling).

Situational Judgment

1. C: (Most effective) Having an open meeting with everyone would reemphasize the importance of the chain-of-command and resolve problems at the lowest possible level.

2. E: (Least effective) Giving up your position because of opposition would demonstrate weakness as a leader and lead to similar actions in future decisions.

3. D: (Most effective) This is a case of "integrity first." It is fine to voice your opinion to the aid, but better to refrain from interfering with the selection process based on personal feelings.

4. B: (Least effective) Giving a recommendation to make the aide go away would not uphold the core value of integrity. An honest opinion should always be given. Officers should always be forthright and honest when giving recommendations.

5. B: (Most effective) Part of being a good officer is to help peers. Try and point out what you would change in the speech and include why you would do it.

6. A: (Least effective) Never go to a superior with the intention of trying to make yourself look better by slandering a coworker. This is an integrity violation and will erode your credibility as an officer.

7. D: (Most effective) Situations come up in every unit that can impact the mission. In this situation, notify your supervisor immediately so they can get someone to replace the ill coworker and accomplish the mission.

8. E: (Least effective) Waiting indefinitely for the coworker to return is the least effective way to handle this situation. You should notify your supervisor immediately and request help to finish the project.

9. A: (Most effective) Be a professional and return to work. Sign the documents so that you are not causing another officer to work late due to your honest mistake.

10. D: (Least effective) Having a subordinate forge the documents puts your integrity and that of the subordinate at risk. Do not let a minor mistake like forgetting to sign a piece of paper ruin your credibility.

11. E: (Most effective) A response to the new commander's email would be the best solution to this scenario. Let him know that you are excited to take the new position and that you would like to set up a date and time to discuss the new role. This will help ensure a smooth transition.

12. B: (Least effective) Always take the opportunity to respond to an email from your new commander. It is the professional thing to do and will allow time to discuss what is expected of the new position, answer any questions, and learn how to excel.

13. D: (Most effective) This is an opportunity to teach, coach, and mentor a fellow officer by discussing the Air Force core values. By talking to the coworker and not telling their superior officer, you offer this person a chance to grow from the mistake without hurting their career.

14. C: (Least effective) Resorting to blackmail would make you just as guilty as your peer and would put your integrity on the line.

15. C: (Most effective) It is normal to reach a plateau in assignments. Let your senior officer know, and express that you are looking for a more challenging assignment to further your career and benefit the Air Force.

16. E: (Least effective) Remember, integrity first. Be honest in everything you do and no one can question your integrity.

17. E: (Most effective) Be honest with the officer and let him/her know that you are already dealing with a maximum workload. In addition, you have offered a solution to the problem by offering to distribute the work to another qualified coworker.

18. D: (Least effective) Taking on additional work without sufficient time will cause the quality of both projects to diminish.

19. D: (Most effective) Inform the senior officer of the situation and see if the projects can be redistributed to help alleviate stress for coworkers that are overwhelmed.

20. A: (Least effective) You were attentive to notice the situation; this is a good time to put service before self and offer a solution to the problem.

21. C: (Most effective) They asked you to resolve the dispute, so be professional and make a decision.

22. E: (Least effective) Giving a lecture to both officers that asked you to settle the dispute would probably turn both of them against you. They must value your opinion, or they would not have asked for your assistance.

23. B: (Most effective) Safety issues need to be addressed immediately. It is your duty as an officer to notify the senior officer in charge if a coworker is manipulating numbers that could lead to an accident or incident.

24. A: (Least effective) It is your responsibility to speak up in this scenario. Again, integrity first. Anyone can prevent an accident.

25. A: (Most effective) If the senior officer asks the question, they want an answer. Be honest, and offer a candid assessment in the area in which he/she could improve.

26. B: (Least effective) Again, if a senior officer asks the question, he/she is looking for an answer. Refusing makes you and your supervisor look bad.

27. D: (Most effective) Make the correct decision and vote for the most qualified candidate.

28. C: (Least effective) By voting for Candidate 3, you are not being honest. Remember the honest decision is not always going to be the easiest. If you are always honest, no one will ever question your integrity.

29. A: (Most effective) Let your new coworker know that you want to do your best on this project, you value their help, and you think the work should be shared equally. In addition, offer congratulations on the coworker's upcoming retirement and encourage him/her to finish strong.

30. D: (Least effective) Do not have the frame of mind that the project is going to be mediocre or it will. Talk to your new coworker and come up with a plan to share the workload and develop a quality product.

31. C: (Most effective) Talk with the subordinate and let him/her know what you have heard and that you need their support in accomplishing the unit's mission.

32. B: (Least effective) Something has to be done in this scenario. If not, the situation is going to get worse.

33. C: (Most effective) The best action to take in this scenario would be to question the last officer to leave the supply room. This would allow him/her to explain the situation without directly accusing him/her of stealing, and it would be an initial step in the investigative process.

34. E: (Least effective) If no action is taken, supplies are going to keep disappearing, and the situation is not going to get any better.

35. A: (Most effective) Give an honest opinion on the subject, and explain you are not a subject-matter expert. In addition, refer to media and to the base public affairs office for further information.

36. B: (Least effective) Not answering the question could portray a negative opinion of the officer.

37. D: (Most effective) Meet with the unit and discuss the issue that has been presented. Offer a solution to the problem, stay positive, and make sure there is an opportunity for subordinates to take a break.

38. B: (Least effective) Always try and solve the problem before going to senior leadership. However, worse than going to senior leadership is to just ignore the problem altogether. If you notice a subordinate (or any coworker) is burned out or struggling, you should always make attempts to get them the help they need. A person's mental health is very important in this line of work.

39. A: (Most effective) Be honest and admit your mistake. The person receiving the email will be more than willing to delete the material. Your supervisor will appreciate the honesty and inform the chain-of-command.

40. E: (Least effective) Do not lie about the situation. All classified email chains are monitored, and covering up this mistake could lead to revocation of a security clearance.

41. B: (Most effective) Meeting with the training director may open up an opportunity for training in the near future. It also shows the commanding officer cares about the unit and people.

42. D: (Least effective) Sending out letters would be perceived as a false accusation, damage your reputation, and could have an effect on future requests for training.

43. C: (Most effective) The leader may not have realized they were creating this environment. Meeting with the superior will clear the air, and it should afford an opportunity to work more independently.

44. A: (Least effective) Telling the supervisor to back off would create animosity and make the situation worse.

45. D: (Most effective) Ultimately, the boss has the final decision. A well thought out plan with actions and contingencies may sway their decision.

46. A: (Least effective) This would be insubordination no matter how the plan worked out. Either way, the boss would feel disrespected.

47. A: (Most effective) Budget cuts will affect everyone in the unit. Talking to peers can offer solutions that may not have been previously discovered.

48. B: (Least effective) Do not blame subordinates. This will erode trust in the unit.

49. D: (Most effective) Keeping the drivers informed of the delay will help with them understand the situation. Accommodating them will help build rapport for future deliveries.

50. C: (Least effective) This would frustrate the drivers even more and may have an effect on future deliveries.

Physical Science

1. C: In any system, the total mechanical energy is the sum of the potential energy and the kinetic energy. Either value could be zero but it still must be included in the total. Choices *A* and *B* only give the total potential or kinetic energy, respectively. Choice *D* gives the difference in the kinetic and potential energy. Choice *E* gives the quotient of potential energy divided by kinetic energy, which is incorrect.

2. E: A Lewis dot diagram shows the alignment of the valence (outer) shell electrons and how readily they can pair or bond with the valence shell electrons of other atoms to form a compound. Choice *B* is incorrect because the inner shell does not help us understand how likely an atom is to bond with another atom. The positioning of protons and neutrons concerns the nucleus of the atom, which again would not relate to the likelihood of bonding.

3. D: The decibel scale is a ratio of a particular sound's intensity to a standard value. It is a logarithmic scale; in other words, as decibels increase linearly, sound intensity goes up by factors of 10. Choice *A* is an effect experienced by an observer who is moving relative to the source of a wave; Choice *B* is a particle in an atom; Choice *C* is a unit for measuring power; and Choice *E* is a device used to measure an earthquake.

4. B: For charges, like charges repel each other and opposite charges attract each other. Negatives and positives will attract, while two positive charges or two negative charges will repel each other. Charges have an effect on each other, so Choices *C* and *D* are incorrect.

5. D: The naming of compounds focuses on the second element in a chemical compound. Elements from the nonmetal category are written with an "ide" at the end. The compound CO has one carbon and one oxygen, so it is called carbon monoxide. Choices *B* and *E* represent that there are two oxygen atoms, and Choices *A, B, C,* and *E* incorrectly alter the name of the first element, which should remain as carbon.

6. B: To solve this, the number of moles of NaCl needs to be calculated:

First, to find the mass of NaCl, the mass of each of the molecule's atoms is added together as follows:

$$23.0 \text{ g Na} + 35.5 \text{ g Cl} = 58.5 \text{ g NaCl}$$

Next, the given mass of the substance is multiplied by one mole per total mass of the substance:

$$4.0 \text{ g NaCl} \times \frac{1 \text{ mol NaCl}}{58.5 \text{ g NaCl}} = 0.068 \text{ mol NaCl}$$

Finally, the moles are divided by the number of liters of the solution to find the molarity:

$$\frac{0.068 \text{ mol NaCl}}{0.120 \text{ L}} = 0.57 \text{ M NaCl}$$

7. C: According to the *ideal gas law* ($PV = nRT$), if volume is constant, the temperature is directly related to the pressure in a system. Therefore, if the pressure increases, the temperature will increase in direct proportion. Choice *A* would not be possible, since the system is closed and a change is occurring, so the temperature will change. Choice *B* incorrectly exhibits an inverse relationship between pressure and temperature, or $P = \frac{1}{T}$. Choice *D* is incorrect because even without actual values for the variables, the relationship and proportions can be determined. Choice *E* is incorrect; the temperature will slowly increase as the pressure increases.

8. A: According to Ohm's Law: $V = IR$, so using the given variables:

$$3.0 \text{ V} = I \times 6.0 \text{ }\Omega$$

Solving for I:

$$I = \frac{3.0 \text{ V}}{6.0 \text{ }\Omega}$$

$$I = 0.5 \text{ A}$$

Choice *B* shows a miscalculation in the equation by multiplying 3.0 V by 6.0 Ω, rather than dividing. Choices *C* and *D* are labeled with the wrong units; Joules measure energy, not current.

9. E: According to Newton's second law of motion,

$$F = m \times a$$

233

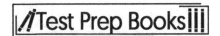

Weight is the force resulting from a given situation, so the mass of the object needs to be multiplied by the acceleration of gravity on Earth:

$$W = m \times g$$

Choice *A* is incorrect because, according to Newton's first law, all objects exert some force on each other, based on their distance from each other and their masses. This is seen in planets, which affect each other's paths and those of their moons. Choice *B* is incorrect because an object in motion or at rest can have inertia; inertia is the resistance of a physical object to change its state of motion. Choice *C* is incorrect because the mass of an object is a measurement of how much substance of there is to the object, while the weight is gravity's effect of the mass. Choice *D* is incorrect; force is equal to the change in momentum per change in time, not volume.

10. B: A decomposition reaction breaks down a compound into its constituent elemental components. Choice *A* is incorrect because a synthesis reaction joins two or more elements into a single compound. Choice *C*, an organic reaction, is a type of reaction involving organic compounds, primarily those containing carbon and hydrogen. Choice *D*, an oxidation/reduction (redox or half) reaction, is incorrect because it involves the loss of electrons from one species (oxidation) and the gain of electrons to the other species (reduction). There is no mention of this occurring within the given reaction, so it is not correct. Choice *E* is incorrect; A composition reaction produces a single substance from multiple reactants, opposed to producing multiple products from a single reactant.

11. D: The law states that matter cannot be created or destroyed in a closed system. In this equation, there are the same number of molecules of each element on either side of the equation. Matter is not gained or lost, although a new compound is formed. As there are no ions on either side of the equation, no electrons are lost. The law prevents the hydrogen from losing or gaining mass and prevents oxygen atoms from being spontaneously spawned.

12. B: In broad terms, energy is divided into kinetic and potential energy. Kinetic energy refers to an object in motion. It is the product of mass and velocity:

$$KE = \frac{1}{2}mv^2$$

Potential energy refers to the capacity for doing work. Its gravitational configuration is the product of mass, acceleration due to gravity, and height ($PE = mgh$). Examples of kinetic energy include heat (which is the thermal energy from atoms and molecules moving around), waves like light, and physical motion. Potential energy examples include gravitational energy and chemical energy stored in bonds.

13. A: The neutrons and protons make up the nucleus of the atom. The nucleus is positively charged due to the presence of the protons. The negatively charged electrons are attracted to the positively charged nucleus by the electrostatic or Coulomb force; however, the electrons are not contained in the nucleus. The positively charged protons create the positive charge in the nucleus, and the neutrons are electrically neutral, so they have no effect. Radioactivity does not directly have a bearing on the charge of the nucleus.

14. A: Substances with higher amounts of hydroxide ions will have higher pHs, while substances with higher amounts of hydrogen ions will have lower pHs. It is possible to have an extremely strong acid with a pH less than 1, as long as its molarity of hydrogen ions is greater than 1. A weak base is determined by having a pH lower than some value, not higher. Substances with pHs greater than 2

include anything from neutral water to extremely caustic lye. A solution with a pH of 2 has ten times fewer hydrogen ions than a solution of pH 1.

15. A: Salts are formed from compounds that use ionic bonds. Disulfide bridges are special bonds in protein synthesis which hold the protein in their secondary and tertiary structures. Covalent bonds are strong bonds formed through the sharing of electrons between atoms and are typically found in organic molecules like carbohydrates and lipids. London dispersion forces are fleeting, momentary bonds which occur between atoms that have instantaneous dipoles but quickly disintegrate. Combustion is not a type of bond; it is a reaction that requires oxygen and heat for the reaction to occur.

16. A: The definition of refraction is when a wave bends (such as when the medium it is traveling through changes). Diffraction is when a wave bends around an object (such as when the medium it is traveling through runs into a barrier), so is too specific an answer for the question. Reflection is when a wave bounces off a surface without losing energy or becoming distorted, and convection is the thermal energy transferred through gases and liquids by convection currents. Radiation occurs when the nucleus of an atom is unstable and constantly emits particles due to this instability.

17. A: Protons and neutrons are both found in the atomic nucleus, while electrons move freely in the electron cloud of an atom. Ions are a different name for entire atoms with unequal numbers of protons and electrons; since this includes electrons, it cannot describe things solely found in the nucleus (unless you were visualizing a hydrogen ion, which is a particular case and is arguably not general enough for the question).

18. C: This is the actual force recognized in a rotational situation. The reactive force acting opposite of the centripetal force is named the centrifugal force, but it is not an actual force on its own. A common mistake is to interchange the two terms. The real force acting in a rotational situation is pulling in toward the axis of rotation and is called the centripetal force. Gravity and friction technically act on all masses, so Choices *B* and *D* are not specific enough for the question.

19. C: These are the coefficients that follow the law of conservation of matter. The coefficient times the subscript of each element should be the same on both sides of the equation.

20. C: Covalent bonds are special because they share electrons between multiple atoms. Most covalent bonds are formed between the elements H, F, N, O, S, and C, while hydrogen bonds are formed nearly exclusively between H and either O, N, or F of other molecules. Covalent bonds may inadvertently form dipoles, but this does not necessarily happen. With similarly electronegative atoms like carbon and hydrogen, dipoles do not form, for example. Crystal solids are typically formed by substances with ionic bonds like the salts sodium iodide and potassium chloride. Metallic bonding allows electrons to move freely between atoms, whereas covalently bound electrons stay within the electron clouds of the covalently bound atoms.

Table Reading

1. A: (11, -11) is 481.

2. E: (-5, 7) is -106.

3. B: (-5, 15) is 32.

4. E: (2, 13) is -155.

5. B: (15, 17) is 459.

6. C: (3, 7) is -424.

7. C: (-14, -10) is 225.

8. E: (-17, 15) is 101.

9. C: (10, -17) is 374.

10. B: (-14, -11) is 119.

11. D: (15, 4) is -391.

12. D: (17, -11) is 177.

13. B: (-14, -6) is 381.

14. D: (6, -12) is 358.

15. C: (13, -9) is 6.

16. D: (-1, 13) is 490.

17. D: (-12, 4) is 270.

18. C: (-14, 7) is -175.

19. E: (-12, 5) is 485.

20. B: (-1, -15) is -167.

21. A: (-1, 6) is 264.

22. A: (14, 2) is 309.

23. D: (13, -5) is -267.

24. B: (16, -8) is -374.

25. C: (15, 15) is -78.

26. D: (-10, -5) is -127.

27. E: (3, 17) is 90.

28. A: (13, -11) is -249.

29. B: (8, 11) is -339.

30. C: (-7, 11) is 460.

31. B: (1, -13) is 140.

32. C: (3, -15) is -27.

33. A: (13, 0) is 265.

34. D: (2, -12) is -234.

35. E: (-7, -12) is 110.

36. D: (-8, -13) is -433.

37. B: (14, 8) is 372.

38. E: (0, -15) is 97.

39. C: (9, -8) is 277.

40. B: (-3, -14) is -109.

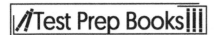
Instrument Comprehension

1. B: The aircraft is heading west-northwest, in level flight, and banking left.

2. D: The aircraft is heading east-southeast, descending, and banking right.

3. C: The aircraft is heading west-northwest, descending, and banking left.

4. A: The aircraft is heading northeast, descending, and banking right.

5. A: The aircraft is heading southeast, ascending, and banking left.

6. C: The aircraft is heading east-southeast, descending, and banking left.

7. C: The aircraft is heading west, in level fight, and without banking.

8. A: The aircraft is heading northwest, ascending, and banking right.

9. D: The aircraft is heading southeast, descending, and banking right.

10. D: The aircraft is heading south, in level flight, and banking right.

11. C: The aircraft is heading south-southwest, descending, and without banking.

12. A: The aircraft is heading northeast, ascending, and without banking.

13. C: The aircraft is heading north-northeast, ascending, and banking right.

14. B: The aircraft is heading southwest, descending, and banking right.

15. B: The aircraft is heading north-northwest, ascending, and banking left.

16. D: The aircraft is heading north-northeast, ascending, and banking right.

17. A: The aircraft is heading southwest, ascending, and banking right.

18. B: The aircraft is heading east-southeast, in level flight, and banking left.

19. C: The aircraft is heading west, in level flight, and banking right.

20. C: The aircraft is heading southwest, descending, and banking left.

21. D: The aircraft is heading west-northwest, ascending, and banking left.

22. D: The aircraft is heading northeast, descending, and banking right.

23. B: The aircraft is heading west-northwest, ascending, and banking right.

24. D: The aircraft is heading northwest, ascending, and banking left.

25. A: The aircraft is heading north, descending, and banking left.

Block Counting

1. C: Block 1 touches 3 blocks: block below Block 1 and 2 blocks on the right side.

2. A: Block 2 touches 4 blocks: block above Block 2, block on the left of Block 2, Block 3, and Block 4.

3. D: Block 3 touches 8 blocks: 4 blocks on the bottom (including Block 5), Block 4, Block 2, block on the left of Block 2, and block below Block 1.

4. C: Block 4 touches 6 blocks: 4 blocks below (including Block 5), Block 2, and Block 3.

5. D: Block 5 touches 5 blocks: block on the left of Block 5, block on the right of Block 5, Block 4, Block 3, and block below Block 1.

6. D: Block 1 touches 4 blocks: three blocks below, one block on the left

7. A: Block 2 touches 2 blocks: one above and one to the right of it

8. D: Block 3 touches 5 blocks: three above, one to the right, and one below

9. A: Block 4 touches 4 blocks: two below, one to the left, and one above

10. C: Block 5 touches 5 blocks: three below, one to the left, and one to the right

11. E: Block 1 touches 7 blocks: four above, one below, one to the left, and one to the right

12. A: Block 2 touches 4 blocks: three below, and one to the right

13. B: Block 3 touches 6 blocks: three below, one above, one to the left, and one to the right

14. D: Block 4 touches 7 blocks: four above, two to the left, and one to the right

15. B: Block 5 touches 2 blocks: two below

16. E: Block 1 touches 5 blocks: three to the right, one below, and one behind it on the left

17. C: Block 2 touches 4 blocks: three to the left, and one behind it

18. E: Block 3 touches 5 blocks: one below, one above, and three to the right

19. D: Block 4 touches 7 blocks: Block 3, one above, two below, and three on the back right

20. B: Block 5 touches 3 blocks: on above, one to the right, and one behind and under Block 3

21. D: Block 1 touches 6 blocks: one above, one to the left, Block 4, and three to the right

22. A: Block 2 touches 5 blocks: Block 4, one below, and three to the right

23. C: Block 3 touches 4 blocks: Block 1, Block 2, Block 5, and one behind it

24. D: Block 4 touches 5 blocks: Block 1, Block 2, Block 5, and one to the right

25. E: Block 5 touches 7 blocks: Block 4, two below, one above, and three to the right

26. C: Block 1 touches 3 blocks: one to the left, and two to the right

27. B: Block 2 touches 2 blocks: Block 3 and Block 5

28. D: Block 3 touches 5 blocks: Block 1, Block 2, Block 4, Block 5, and one behind

29. A: Block 4 touches 3 blocks: Block 1, Block 2, and one behind on the right

30. B: Block 5 touches 3 blocks: Block 2, Block 3, and one behind on the right

Aviation Information

1. B: Faster flow of air over the wing than beneath it. The air moves over the curved surface of the wing at a higher rate of speed than the air moves under the lower flat surface, which creates lift due to the aircraft's forward airspeed and enables flight.

2. B: Longitudinal. The ailerons are mounted on the trailing edges of the wings, and they are used for controlling aircraft roll about the longitudinal axis.

3. A: Lateral. Elevators are mounted on the trailing edges of horizontal stabilizers and are used for controlling aircraft pitch about the lateral axis.

4. C: Vertical. The rudder is mounted on the trailing edge of the vertical fin and is used for controlling rotation (yaw) around the vertical axis.

5. C: Aileron. The aileron is a primary flight control.

6. E: Slats. Slats are part of the wing. The tail assembly of an aircraft is commonly referred to as the empennage. The empennage structure usually includes a tail cone, fixed stabilizers (horizontal and vertical), and moveable surfaces to assist in directional control. The moveable surfaces are the rudder, which is attached to the vertical stabilizer, and the elevators attached to the horizontal stabilizers.

7. B: Skate. Depending on what the aircraft is used for, it may have skis, skids, pontoons, or floats, instead of tires, for landing on ice or water.

8. B: Semicoque. There are two types of fuselage structures: truss and monocoque. The truss fuselage is typically made of steel tubing welded together, which enables the structure to handle tension and compression loads. In lighter aircraft, an aluminum alloy may be used along with cross-bracing. A single-shell fuselage is referred to as monocoque, which uses a stronger skin to handle the tension and compression loads. There is also a semi-monocoque fuselage, which is basically a combination of the truss and monocoque fuselage and is the most commonly used. The semi-monocoque structure includes the use of frame assemblies, bulkheads, formers, longerons, and stringers.

9. A: The pilot. To ensure an aircraft is being operated properly, a pilot needs to be familiar with the aircraft's flight envelope before flying.

10. C: Stalling speed. The stalling speed is the minimum speed at which an aircraft can maintain level flight. As the aircraft gains altitude, the stall speed increases, since the aircraft's weight can be better supported through speed.

11. B: Service ceiling. The maximum altitude of an aircraft is also referred to as the service ceiling. The ceiling is usually decided by the aircraft performance and the wings and is where an altitude at a given speed can no longer be increased at level flight.

12. D: Drag. Drag is the force generated when aircraft is moving through the air. Drag is air resistance that opposes thrust, basically aerodynamic friction or wind resistance. The amount of drag is dependent upon several factors, including the shape of the aircraft, the speed it is traveling, and the density of the air it is passing through.

13. B: Levels the aircraft in flight. The horizontal stabilizer provides for leveling of aircraft in flight. If the aircraft tilts up or down, air pressure increases on one side of the stabilizer and decreases on the other. This imbalance on the stabilizer will push the aircraft back into level flight. The horizontal stabilizer holds the tail down as well, since most aircraft designs induce the tendency of the nose to tilt downward because the center of gravity is forward of the center of lift in the wings.

14. C: The outer trailing edge of the wing. Ailerons are located on the outer trailing edges of the wings and control the roll of an aircraft.

15. D: Stall. An aircraft stall occurs at the critical angle of attack (AOA), where the induced drag exceeds the lift. During a stall, the wing is no longer able to create sufficient lift to oppose gravity. Stall angle is usually around 20°.

16. A: Landing. There are four fundamental maneuvers in flight: straight-and-level, turns, climbs, and descents. Every controlled flight usually includes a combination of these four fundamentals.

17. C: Torque. Torque from the engine turning the main rotor forces the body of the helicopter in the opposite direction. Most helicopters use a tail rotor, which counters this torque force by pushing or pulling against the tail.

18. B: Collective control. The collective control is used to increase the pitch of the main rotor simultaneously at all points of the rotor blade rotation. The collective increases or decreases total rotor thrust; the cyclic changes the direction of rotor thrust. In forward flight, the collective pitch changes the amount of thrust, which in turn can change the speed or altitude based on the use of the cyclic. During hovering, the collective pitch will alter the hover height.

19. B: 3-5 miles away. Visual approach slope indicator (VASI) is a light system designed to provide visual guidance during approach of a runway. The light indicators are visible 3-5 miles away during daylight hours and up to 20 miles away in darkness. The indicators are designed to be used once the aircraft is already visually aligned with the runway.

20. A: Horizontal. Non-precision instrument runways provide horizontal guidance only when there is an approved procedure for a straight-in non-precision instrument approach.

Verbal Analogies

1. **Clock** is to **time** as:
   a. Ruler is to length.
   b. Jet is to speed.
   c. Alarm is to sleep.
   d. Drum is to beat.
   e. Watch is to wrist.

2. **Wire** is to **electricity** as:
   a. Power is to lamp.
   b. Pipe is to water.
   c. Fire is to heat.
   d. Heat is to fire.
   e. Water is to pipe.

3. **Executive Branch** is to **President** as **Judicial Branch** is to:
   a. Supreme Court Justice
   b. Judge
   c. Senator
   d. Lawyer
   e. Congressmen

4. **Begonia** is to **flower** as:
   a. Daisy is to pollen.
   b. Cat is to catnip.
   c. Cardiologist is to doctor.
   d. Radiology is to disease.
   e. Nutrition is to reproduction.

5. **Malleable** is to **pliable** as:
   a. Corroborate is to invalidate.
   b. Avenue is to city.
   c. Blacksmith is to anvil.
   d. Hostile is to hospitable.
   e. Disparage is to criticize.

6. **Cerebellum** is to **brain** as:
   a. Nurse is to medication.
   b. Nucleus is to cell.
   c. Bacteria is to spores.
   d. Refraction is to light.
   e. Painting is to sculpting.

7. **Whisk** is to **baking** as:
   a. Glove is to boxing.
   b. Swimming is to water.
   c. Love is to romance.
   d. Azalea is to flower.
   e. Bench is to park.

8. **Umpire** is to **officiate** as:
   a. Coaching is to coach.
   b. Baseball is to pastime.
   c. Counselor is to guide.
   d. Notary is to paper.
   e. Messenger is to letter.

9. **Chuckle** is to **guffaw** as:
   a. Snicker is to lament.
   b. Affection is to nurturing.
   c. Sensitivity is to brevity.
   d. Whisper is to bellow.
   e. Serenity is to tranquility.

10. **Fire** is to **passion** as:
    a. Sultry is to ferment.
    b. Emotion is to stagnant.
    c. Heat is to happiness.
    d. Ice is to rigidity.
    e. Comfort is to travel.

11. **Geriatric** is to **youth** as:
    a. Transparent is to opaque.
    b. Soldier is to war.
    c. Subtle is to sophisticated.
    d. Yellow is to happiness.
    e. Surly is to scandalous.

12. **Lying** is to **distrust** as:
    a. Prohibit is to outlaw.
    b. Petulant is to children.
    c. Exploit is to gain.
    d. Imprudent is to money.
    e. Hurricane is to devastation.

13. **Desolate** is to **barren** as:
    a. Defend is to prosecute.
    b. Contend is to maintain.
    c. Avid is to cheerleader.
    d. Bittersweet is to happiness.
    e. King is to ambition.

243

14. **Chapter** is to **novel** as:
    a. Whisper is to silence.
    b. Tangle is to lengthening.
    c. Poem is to poet.
    d. Feeling is to past.
    e. Stroke is to painting.

15. **Carpenter** is to **construction** as:
    a. Adaptation is to insect.
    b. Acquisition is to possession.
    c. Wizard is to magic.
    d. Baker is to bread.
    e. Microsoft is to programming.

16. **Tepid** is to **boiling** as:
    a. Moon is to femininity.
    b. Cornered is to immunity.
    c. Greedy is to rapacious.
    d. Sword is to dagger.
    e. Burning is to smoke.

17. **Read** is to **learn** as:
    a. Ball is to soccer.
    b. Brand is to marketing.
    c. Exercise is to health.
    d. Disease is to energy.
    e. Party is to birthday.

18. **Competent** is to **impotent** as:
    a. Demur is to accept.
    b. Dispute is to argument.
    c. Brandish is to gold.
    d. Honorary is to metal.
    e. Reach is to grab.

19. **Merengue** is to **music** as:
    a. Cluster is to assemblage.
    b. Tension is to headache.
    c. Fiscal is to government.
    d. Hunger is to starving.
    e. Nomadic is to tribe.

20. **Car** is to **transport** as:
    a. Radio is to sound.
    b. Volume is to voice.
    c. Triangles are to circles.
    d. Fireplace is to heat.
    e. Mangos are to fruit.

21. **Flower** is to **femininity** as:
    a. Sunflower is to bees.
    b. Technology is to cell phones.
    c. Envy is to relationships.
    d. Plant is to carbon dioxide.
    e. Light is to transcendence.

22. **Principle** is to **truth** as:
    a. Squalid is to shabby.
    b. Frame is to picture.
    c. Static is to movement.
    d. Format is to index.
    e. Sour is to sweet.

23. **Careful** is to **fastidious** as:
    a. Indulge is to deprive.
    b. Fluctuate is to trapeze.
    c. Majesty is to a lion.
    d. Endow is to bestow.
    e. Grieve is to lament.

24. **Mantle** is to **earth** as:
    a. Volcano is to lava.
    b. Bundle is to uniform.
    c. Bun is to hamburger.
    d. Letter is to mailman.
    e. Spider is to spiderweb.

25. **Maestro** is to **conducting** as:
    a. Barista is to coffee.
    b. Acupuncturist is to healing.
    c. Professor is to essay.
    d. President is to executive branch.
    e. Agent is to housing.

Arithmetic Reasoning

1. What is the sum of $\frac{1}{3}$ and $\frac{2}{5}$?

    a. $\frac{3}{8}$

    b. $\frac{2}{3}$

    c. $\frac{11}{30}$

    d. $\frac{4}{5}$

    e. $\frac{11}{15}$

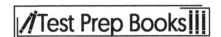

2. A construction company is building a new housing development with the property of each house measuring 30 feet wide. If the length of the street is zoned off at 345 feet, how many houses can be built on the street?
    a. 11
    b. 115
    c. 11.5
    d. 12
    e. 10

3. It costs Chad $12 to produce 3 necklaces. If he can sell each necklace for $20, how much profit would he make if he sold 60 necklaces?
    a. $240
    b. $360
    c. $960
    d. $1200
    e. $720

4. The value of 6×12 is the same as:
    a. $2 \times 4 \times 4 \times 2$
    b. $7 \times 4 \times 3$
    c. $6 \times 6 \times 3$
    d. $3 \times 3 \times 4 \times 2$
    e. 9×9

5. If Sarah reads at an average rate of 21 pages in four nights, how long will it take her to read 140 pages?
    a. 6 nights
    b. 26 nights
    c. 8 nights
    d. 14 nights
    e. 27 nights

6. Mom's car drove 72 miles in 90 minutes. There are 5,280 feet per mile. How fast did she drive in feet per second?
    a. 0.8 feet per second
    b. 48.9 feet per second
    c. 0.009 feet per second
    d. 1.25 feet per second
    e. 70.4 feet per second

7. This chart indicates how many sales of CDs, vinyl records, and MP3 downloads occurred over the last year. Approximately what percentage of the total sales was from CDs?

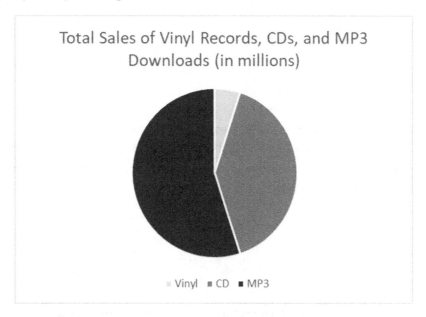

Total Sales of Vinyl Records, CDs, and MP3 Downloads (in millions)

▪ Vinyl ▪ CD ▪ MP3

a. 55%
b. 25%
c. 40%
d. 5%
e. 75%

8. After a 20% sale discount, Frank purchased a new refrigerator for $850. How much did he save compared to the original price?
a. $170
b. $212.50
c. $105.75
d. $200
e. $1,062.50

9. A student gets an 85% on a test with 20 questions. How many questions did the student solve correctly?
a. 15
b. 16
c. 12
d. 18
e. 17

10. A family purchases a vehicle in 2005 for $20,000. In 2010, they decide to sell it for a newer model. They are able to sell the car for $8,000. By what percentage did the value of the family's car drop?
a. 40%
b. 68%
c. 60%
d. 33%
e. 67%

11. On May 1, 2010, a couple purchased a house for $100,000. On September 1, 2016, the couple sold the house for $93,000 so they could purchase a bigger one to start a family. How many months did they own the house?
   a. 76
   b. 54
   c. 85
   d. 93
   e. 72

12. At the beginning of the day, Xavier has 20 apples. At lunch, he meets his sister Emma and gives her half of his apples. After lunch, he stops by his neighbor Jim's house and gives him 6 of his apples. He then uses $\frac{3}{4}$ of his remaining apples to make an apple pie for dessert at dinner. At the end of the day, how many apples does Xavier have left?
   a. 4
   b. 6
   c. 2
   d. 1
   e. 7

13. Four people split a bill. The first person pays for $\frac{1}{5}$, the second person pays for $\frac{1}{4}$, and the third person pays for $\frac{1}{3}$. What fraction of the bill does the fourth person pay?
   a. $\frac{13}{60}$

   b. $\frac{47}{60}$

   c. $\frac{1}{4}$

   d. $\frac{4}{15}$

   e. $\frac{1}{2}$

14. Five of six numbers have a sum of 25. The average of all six numbers is 6. What is the sixth number?
   a. 8
   b. 10
   c. 11
   d. 12
   e. 13

15. If $\frac{5}{2} \div \frac{1}{3} = n$, then n is between:
   a. 5 and 7
   b. 1 and 3
   c. 9 and 11
   d. 3 and 5
   e. 7 and 9

16. A closet is filled with red, blue, and green shirts. If $\frac{1}{3}$ of the shirts are green and $\frac{2}{5}$ are red, what fraction of the shirts are blue?

    a. $\frac{4}{15}$

    b. $\frac{1}{5}$

    c. $\frac{7}{15}$

    d. $\frac{1}{2}$

    e. $\frac{1}{3}$

17. In an office, there are 50 workers. A total of 60% of the workers are women. 50% of the women (and none of the other workers) are wearing skirts. How many workers are wearing skirts?

    a. 12
    b. 15
    c. 16
    d. 20
    e. 21

18. 32 is 25% of what number?

    a. 64
    b. 128
    c. 12.65
    d. 8
    e. 155

19. Which of the following numbers has the greatest value?

    a. 1.43785
    b. 1.07548
    c. 1.43592
    d. 0.89409
    e. 0.94739

20. A piggy bank contains 12 dollars' worth of nickels. A nickel weighs 5 grams, and the empty piggy bank weighs 1050 grams. What is the total weight of the full piggy bank?

    a. 1,110 grams
    b. 1,200 grams
    c. 2,150 grams
    d. 2,250 grams
    e. 2,500 grams

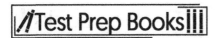

21. Last year, the New York City area received approximately $27\frac{3}{4}$ inches of snow. The Denver area received approximately 3 times as much snow as New York City. How much snow fell in Denver?

    a. $71\frac{3}{4}$ inches

    b. $27\frac{1}{4}$ inches

    c. $89\frac{1}{4}$ inches

    d. $83\frac{1}{4}$ inches

    e. $64\frac{3}{4}$ inches

22. Subtract and express in reduced form: $\frac{23}{24} - \frac{1}{6}$

    a. $\frac{22}{18}$

    b. $\frac{11}{9}$

    c. $\frac{19}{24}$

    d. $\frac{4}{5}$

    e. $\frac{1}{2}$

23. Store-brand coffee beans cost $1.23 per pound. A local coffee bean roaster charges $1.98 per $1\frac{1}{2}$ pounds. How much more would 5 pounds from the local roaster cost than 5 pounds of the store brand?

    a. $0.55

    b. $1.55

    c. $1.45

    d. $0.45

    e. $0.35

24. What is the solution to the following problem in decimal form?

$$\frac{3}{5} \times \frac{7}{10} \div \frac{1}{2}$$

    a. 0.042

    b. 84%

    c. 0.84

    d. 0.42

    e. 42%

25. On Monday, Robert mopped the floor in 4 hours. On Tuesday, he did it in 3 hours. If on Monday, his average rate of mopping was p sq. ft. per hour, what was his average rate on Tuesday?

    a. $\frac{4}{3}p$ sq. ft. per hour

    b. $\frac{3}{4}p$ sq. ft. per hour

    c. $\frac{5}{4}p$ sq. ft. per hour

    d. $p + 1$ sq. ft. per hour

    e. $\frac{1}{3}p$ sq. ft. per hour

Word Knowledge

1. OFFSPRING
    a. Bounce
    b. Parent
    c. Music
    d. Child
    e. Skip

2. PERMIT
    a. Law
    b. Parking
    c. Crab
    d. Jail
    e. Allow

3. WOMAN
    a. Man
    b. Lady
    c. Women
    d. Girl
    e. Mother

4. ROTATION
    a. Wheel
    b. Year
    c. Spin
    d. Flip
    e. Orbit

5. CONSISTENT
    a. Stubborn
    b. Contains
    c. Sticky
    d. Texture
    e. Steady

6. PRINCIPLE
    a. Principal
    b. Leader
    c. President
    d. Foundation
    e. Royal

7. PERIMETER
    a. Outline
    b. Area
    c. Side
    d. Volume
    e. Inside

8. SYMBOL
    a. Drum
    b. Music
    c. Clang
    d. Emblem
    e. Text

9. GERMINATE
    a. Doctor
    b. Sick
    c. Infect
    d. Plants
    e. Grow

10. GARISH
    a. Drab
    b. Flashy
    c. Gait
    d. Hardy
    e. Lithe

11. INANE
    a. Ratify
    b. Illicit
    c. Uncouth
    d. Senseless
    e. Wry

12. SOLACE
    a. Marred
    b. Induce
    c. Depose
    d. Inherent
    e. Comfort

13. COPIOUS
    a. Dire
    b. Adept
    c. Indignant
    d. Ample
    e. Nuance

14. SUPERCILIOUS
    a. Tenuous
    b. Waning
    c. Arrogant
    d. Placate
    e. Extol

15. LURID
    a. Gruesome
    b. Placid
    c. Irate
    d. Quell
    e. Torpor

16. VANQUISH
    a. Saturate
    b. Conquer
    c. Reproach
    d. Parch
    e. Surrender

17. TRITE
    a. Scanty
    b. Banal
    c. Polemical
    d. Indulgent
    e. Eclectic

18. DIVULGE
    a. Dupe
    b. Flummox
    c. Indulgent
    d. Germinate
    e. Admit

19. INDOLENT
    a. Adamant
    b. Dour
    c. Noisome
    d. Lackadaisical
    e. Remiss

20. BOLSTER
    a. Bequeath
    b. Abate
    c. Support
    d. Palliate
    e. Tractable

21. UNWITTING
    a. Undermine
    b. Unintentional
    c. Rife
    d. Pernicious
    e. Stolid

22. UNGAINLY
    a. Clumsy
    b. Absurd
    c. Unruly
    d. Tenuous
    e. Petulant

23. PRATTLE
    a. Babble
    b. Prosaic
    c. Deluded
    d. Meddle
    e. Folly

24. PROLIFIC
    a. Devoid
    b. Elusive
    c. Laconic
    d. Productive
    e. Judicious

25. FORTITUDE
    a. Aura
    b. Disparage
    c. Finesse
    d. Cowardice
    e. Courage

Math Knowledge

1. An equilateral triangle has a perimeter of 18 feet. The sides of a square have the same length as the triangle's sides. What is the area of the square?
   a. 6 square feet
   b. 36 square feet
   c. 256 square feet
   d. 1,000 square feet
   e. 24 square feet

2. What is the measure of angle 2 be in the diagram below?

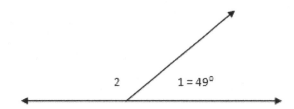

   a. 131°
   b. 41°
   c. 311°
   d. 49°
   e. 90°

3. A rectangle was formed out of pipe cleaner. Its length was 3 in, and its width was 8 inches. What is its area in square inches?
   a. 22 in^2
   b. 11 in^2
   c. 32 in^2
   d. 16 in^2
   e. 24 in^2

4. What is the simplified quotient of $\frac{5x^3}{3x^2y} \div \frac{25}{3y^9}$?

   a. $\frac{125x}{9y^{10}}$

   b. $\frac{x}{5y^8}$

   c. $\frac{5}{xy^8}$

   d. $\frac{xy^8}{5}$

   e. $\frac{3xy^8}{15}$

255

5. What is the solution for the following equation?

$$\frac{x^2 + x - 30}{x - 5} = 11$$

    a. $x = -6$
    b. $x = -5$
    c. $x = 16$
    d. $x = 5$
    e. There is no solution.

6. Which equation is NOT a function?
    a. $y = |x|$

    b. $y = \frac{1}{x}$

    c. $x = 3$

    d. $y = 4$

    e. $y = x^2$

7. For the following similar triangles, what are the values of x and y (rounded to one decimal place)?

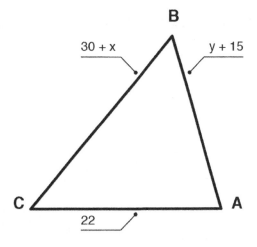
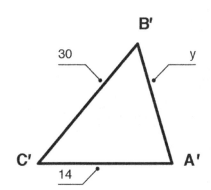

    a. $x = 16.5, y = 25.1$
    b. $x = 19.5, y = 24.1$
    c. $x = 17.1, y = 26.3$
    d. $x = 26.3, y = 17.1$
    e. $x = 18.5, y = 23.3$

8. Which of the following is NOT a way to write 40 percent of N?

    a. $(0.4)N$

    b. $\frac{2}{5}N$

    c. $40N$

    d. $\frac{4N}{10}$

    e. $\frac{8N}{20}$

9. If $6t + 4 = 16$, what is t?

    a. 1
    b. 2
    c. 3
    d. 4
    e. 5

10. There are $4x + 1$ treats in each party favor bag. If a total of $60x + 15$ treats is distributed, how many bags are given out?

    a. 15
    b. 16
    c. 20
    d. 22
    e. 24

11. Suppose $\frac{x+2}{x} = 2$. What is x?

    a. -1
    b. 0
    c. 2
    d. 4
    e. -2

12. A rectangle has a length that is 5 feet longer than three times its width. If the perimeter is 90 feet, what is the length in feet?

    a. 10
    b. 20
    c. 25
    d. 35
    e. 40

13. A clock reads 5:00 am. What is the measure of the angle formed by the two hands of that clock?

    a. 300 degrees
    b. 150 degrees
    c. 75 degrees
    d. 210 degrees
    e. 285 degrees

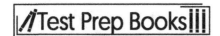

14. Jessica buys 10 cans of paint. Red paint costs $1 per can and blue paint costs $2 per can. In total, she spends $16. How many red cans did she buy?
    a. 2
    b. 3
    c. 4
    d. 5
    e. 6

15. The perimeter of a 6-sided polygon is 56 cm. The length of three of the sides are 9 cm each. The lengths of the two other sides are 8 cm each. What is the length of the missing side?
    a. 11 cm
    b. 12 cm
    c. 13 cm
    d. 10 cm
    e. 9 cm

16. Which of the following formulas would correctly calculate the perimeter of a legal-sized piece of paper that is 14 inches long and $8\frac{1}{2}$ inches wide?
    a. $P = 14 + 8\frac{1}{2}$
    b. $P = 14 + 8\frac{1}{2} + 14 + 8\frac{1}{2}$
    c. $P = 14 \times 8\frac{1}{2}$
    d. $P = 14 \times \frac{17}{2}$
    e. $P = 14 - \frac{17}{2}$

17. What is the solution to the following system of equations?

$$x^2 - 2x + y = 8$$

$$x - y = -2$$

    a. $(-2, 3)$
    b. There is no solution.
    c. $(-2, 0)\ (1, 3)$
    d. $(-2, 0)\ (3, 5)$
    e. $(2, 0)\ (-1, 3)$

18. What is the y-intercept for $y = x^2 + 3x - 4$?
    a. $y = 1$
    b. $y = -4$
    c. $y = 3$
    d. $y = 4$
    e. $y = -3$

19. How could the following function be rewritten to identify the zeros?

$$y = 3x^3 + 3x^2 - 18x$$

a. $y = 3x(x + 3)(x - 2)$
b. $y = x(x - 2)(x + 3)$
c. $y = 3x(x - 3)(x + 2)$
d. $y = (x + 3)(x - 2)$
e. $y = 3x(x + 3)(x + 2)$

20. A line passes through the origin and through the point $(-3, 4)$. What is the slope of the line?
a. $-\dfrac{4}{3}$

b. $-\dfrac{3}{4}$

c. $\dfrac{4}{3}$

d. $\dfrac{3}{4}$

e. $\dfrac{1}{3}$

21. Which of the following inequalities is equivalent to $3 - \dfrac{1}{2}x \geq 2$?
a. $x \geq 2$
b. $x \leq 2$
c. $x \geq 1$
d. $x \leq 1$
e. $x \leq -2$

22. For which of the following are $x = 4$ and $x = -4$ solutions?
a. $x^2 + 16 = 0$
b. $x^2 + 4x - 4 = 0$
c. $x^2 - 2x - 2 = 0$
d. $x^2 - x - 16 = 0$
e. $x^2 - 16 = 0$

23. $(4x^2y^4)^{\frac{3}{2}}$ can be simplified to which of the following?

a. $8x^3y^6$

b. $4x^{\frac{5}{2}}y$

c. $4xy$

d. $32x^{\frac{7}{2}}y^{\frac{11}{2}}$

e. x^3y^6

24. $(2x - 4y)^2 =$
    a. $4x^2 - 16xy + 16y^2$
    b. $4x^2 - 8xy + 16y^2$
    c. $4x^2 - 16xy - 16y^2$
    d. $2x^2 - 8xy + 8y^2$
    e. $4x^2 + 16xy - 16y^2$

25. If the sides of a cube are 3 inches long, what is its volume?
    a. 6 in^3
    b. 18 in^3
    c. 9 in^3
    d. 3 in^3
    e. 27 in^3

Reading Comprehension

1. The Brookside area is an older part of Kansas City, developed mainly in the 1920s and '30s, and is considered one of the nation's first "planned" communities with shops, restaurants, parks, and churches all within a quick walk. A stroll down any street reveals charming two-story Tudor and Colonial homes with smaller bungalows sprinkled throughout the beautiful tree-lined streets. It is common to see lemonade stands on the corners and baseball games in the numerous "pocket" parks tucked neatly behind rows of well-manicured houses. The Brookside shops on 63rd street between Wornall Road and Oak Street are a hub of commerce and entertainment where residents freely shop and dine with their pets (and children) in town. This is also a common "hangout" spot for younger teenagers because it is easily accessible by bike for most. In short, it is an idyllic neighborhood just minutes from downtown Kansas City.

Which of the following states the main idea of this paragraph?
    a. The Brookside shops are a popular hangout for teenagers.
    b. There are a number of pocket parks in the Brookside neighborhood.
    c. Brookside is a great place to live.
    d. Brookside has a high crime rate.
    e. Brookside is close to downtown.

2. At its easternmost part, Long Island opens like the upper and under jaws of some prodigious alligator; the upper and larger one terminating in Montauk Point. The bay that lies in here, and part of which forms the splendid harbor of Greenport, where the Long Island Railroad ends, is called Peconic Bay; and a beautiful and varied water is it, fertile in fish and feathered game. I, who am by no means a skillful fisherman, go down for an hour of a morning on one of the docks, or almost anywhere along shore, and catch a mess of black-fish, which you couldn't buy in New York for a dollar—large fat fellows, with meat on their bones that it takes a pretty long fork to stick through. They have a way here of splitting these fat black-fish and poggies, and broiling them on the coals, beef-steak-fashion, which I recommend your Broadway cooks to copy.

Which of the following is the best summary of this passage?
  a. Walt Whitman was impressed with the quantity and quality of fish he found in Peconic Bay.
  b. Walt Whitman preferred the fish found in restaurants in New York.
  c. Walt Whitman was a Broadway chef.
  d. Walt Whitman was frustrated because he was not a very skilled fisherman.
  e. Long Island reminded Walt Whitman of an alligator.

3. Evidently, our country has overlooked both the importance of learning history and the appreciation of it. But why is this a huge problem? Other than historians, who really cares how the War of 1812 began, or who Alexander the Great's tutor was? Well, not many, as it turns out. So, is history really that important? Yes! History is critical to help us understand the underlying forces that shape decisive events, to prevent us from making the same mistakes twice, and to give us context for current events.

The above is an example of which type of writing?
  a. Expository
  b. Persuasive
  c. Narrative
  d. Poetry
  e. Drama

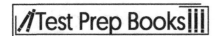

4. Although many Missourians know that Harry S. Truman and Walt Disney hailed from their great state, probably far fewer know that it was also home to the remarkable George Washington Carver. At the end of the Civil War, Moses Carver, the slave owner who owned George's parents, decided to keep George and his brother and raise them on his farm. As a child, George was driven to learn and he loved painting. He even went on to study art while in college but was encouraged to pursue botany instead. He spent much of his life helping others by showing them better ways to farm; his ideas improved agricultural productivity in many countries. One of his most notable contributions to the newly emerging class of Black farmers was to teach them the negative effects of agricultural monoculture (i.e., growing the same crops in the same fields year after year, depleting the soil of much needed nutrients and resulting in a lesser crop yield). Carver was an innovator, always thinking of new and better ways to do things, and is most famous for his over three hundred uses for the peanut. Toward the end of his career, Carver returned to his first love of art. Through his artwork, he hoped to inspire people to see the beauty around them and to do great things themselves. When Carver died, he left his money to help fund ongoing agricultural research. Today, people still visit and study at the George Washington Carver Foundation at Tuskegee Institute.

According to the passage, what was George Washington Carver's first love?
- a. Plants
- b. Art
- c. Animals
- d. Soil
- e. Education

5. Annabelle Rice started having trouble sleeping. Her biological clock was suddenly amiss, and she began to lead a nocturnal schedule. She thought her insomnia was due to spending nights writing a horror story, but then she realized that even the idea of going outside into the bright world scared her to bits. She concluded she was now suffering from heliophobia.

Which of the following most accurately describes the meaning of the underlined word in the sentence above?
- a. Fear of dreams
- b. Fear of sunlight
- c. Fear of strangers
- d. Generalized anxiety disorder
- e. Fear of the outdoors

6. A famous children's author recently published a historical fiction novel under a pseudonym; however, it did not sell as many copies as her children's books. In her earlier years, she had majored in history and earned a graduate degree in Antebellum American History, which is the timeframe of her new novel. Critics praised this newest work far more than the children's series that made her famous. In fact, her new novel was nominated for the prestigious Albert J. Beveridge Award but still isn't selling like her children's books, which fly off the shelves because of her name alone.

Which one of the following statements might be accurately inferred based on the above passage?
a. The famous children's author produced an inferior book under her pseudonym.
b. The famous children's author is the foremost expert on Antebellum America.
c. The famous children's author did not receive the bump in publicity for her historical novel that it would have received if it were written under her given name.
d. People generally prefer to read children's series rather than historical fiction.
e. The famous author's new book is selling better than her children's books because she is an expert in Antebellum America.

7. In 2015, 28 countries, including Estonia, Portugal, Slovenia, and Latvia, scored significantly higher than the United States on standardized high school math tests. In the 1960s, the United States consistently ranked first in the world. Today, the United States spends more than $800 billion on education, which exceeds the next highest country by more than $600 billion. The United States also leads the world in spending per school-aged child by an enormous margin.

If the statements above are true, which of the following statements must be correct?
a. Outspending other countries on education has benefits beyond standardized math tests.
b. The United States' education system is corrupt and broken.
c. The standardized math tests are not representative of American academic prowess.
d. Spending more money does not guarantee success on standardized math tests.
e. The United States' remains a top competitor in education across the globe.

Questions 8–12 are based on the following passage:

Christopher Columbus is often credited with discovering America. This is incorrect. First, it is impossible to "discover" something where people already live; however, Christopher Columbus did explore places in the New World that were previously untouched by Europe, so the term "explorer" would be more accurate. Another correction must be made, as well: Christopher Columbus was not the first European explorer to reach the Americas! Rather, it was Leif Erikson who first came to the New World and contacted the natives, nearly five hundred years before Christopher Columbus.

Leif Erikson, the son of Erik the Red (a famous Viking outlaw and explorer in his own right), was born in either 970 or 980, depending on which historian you read. His own family, though, did not raise Leif, which was a Viking tradition. Instead, one of Erik's prisoners taught Leif reading and writing, languages, sailing, and weaponry. At age 12, Leif was considered a man and returned to his family. He killed a man during a dispute shortly after his return, and the council banished the Erikson clan to Greenland.

In 999, Leif left Greenland and traveled to Norway, where he would serve as a guard to King Olaf Tryggvason. It was there that he became a convert to Christianity. Leif later

263

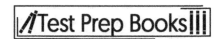

tried to return home with the intention of taking supplies and spreading Christianity to Greenland, but his ship was blown off course and he arrived in a strange new land: present-day Newfoundland, Canada.

When he finally returned to his adopted homeland, Greenland, Leif consulted with a merchant who had also seen the shores of this previously unknown land we now know as Canada. The son of the legendary Viking explorer then gathered a crew of 35 men and set sail. Leif became the first European to set foot in the New World as he explored present-day Baffin Island and Labrador, Canada. His crew called the land Vinland since it was plentiful with grapes.

During their time in present-day Newfoundland, Leif's expedition made contact with the natives, whom they referred to as Skraelings (which translates to "wretched ones" in Norse). There are several secondhand accounts of their meetings. Some contemporaries described trade between the peoples. Other accounts describe clashes where the Skraelings defeated the Viking explorers with long spears, while still others claim the Vikings dominated the natives. Regardless of the circumstances, it seems that the Vikings made contact of some kind. This happened around 1000, nearly five hundred years before Columbus famously sailed the ocean blue.

Eventually, in 1003, Leif set sail for home and arrived at Greenland with a ship full of timber.

In 1020, seventeen years later, the legendary Viking died. Many believe that Leif Erikson should receive more credit for his contributions in exploring the New World.

8. Which of the following best describes how the author generally presents the information?
   a. Chronological order
   b. Comparison-contrast
   c. Cause-effect
   d. Conclusion-premises
   e. Spatial order

9. Which of the following is an opinion, rather than a historical fact, expressed by the author?
   a. Leif Erikson was definitely the son of Erik the Red; however, historians debate the year of his birth.
   b. Leif Erikson's crew called the land Vinland since it was plentiful with grapes.
   c. Leif Erikson deserves more credit for his contributions in exploring the New World.
   d. Leif Erikson explored the Americas nearly five hundred years before Christopher Columbus.
   e. Leif's expedition made contact with the natives whom they referred to as Skraelings.

10. Which of the following most accurately describes the author's main conclusion?
    a. Leif Erikson is a legendary Viking explorer.
    b. Leif Erikson deserves more credit for exploring America hundreds of years before Columbus.
    c. Spreading Christianity motivated Leif Erikson's expeditions more than any other factor.
    d. Leif Erikson contacted the natives nearly five hundred years before Columbus.
    e. Leif Erikson discovered the Americas.

11. Which of the following best describes the author's intent in the passage?
    a. To entertain
    b. To inform
    c. To alert
    d. To suggest
    e. To share

12. Which of the following can be logically inferred from the passage?
    a. The Vikings disliked exploring the New World.
    b. Leif Erikson's banishment from Iceland led to his exploration of present-day Canada.
    c. Leif Erikson never shared his stories of exploration with the King of Norway.
    d. Historians have difficulty definitively pinpointing events in the Vikings' history.
    e. Christopher Columbus knew of Leif Erikson's explorations.

Questions 13–17 are based on the following passage:

Smoking is Terrible

Smoking tobacco products is terribly destructive. A single cigarette contains over 4,000 chemicals, including 43 known carcinogens and 400 deadly toxins. Some of the most dangerous ingredients include tar, carbon monoxide, formaldehyde, ammonia, arsenic, and DDT. Smoking can cause numerous types of cancer, including throat, mouth, nasal cavity, esophageal, gastric, pancreatic, renal, bladder, and cervical cancer.

Cigarettes contain a drug called nicotine, one of the most addictive substances known. Addiction is defined as a compulsion to seek the substance despite negative consequences. According to the National Institute on Drug Abuse, nearly 35 million smokers expressed a desire to quit smoking in 2015; however, more than 85 percent of those who struggle with addiction will not achieve their goal. Almost all smokers regret picking up that first cigarette. You would be wise to learn from their mistake if you have not yet started smoking.

According to the US Department of Health and Human Services, 16 million people in the United States presently suffer from a smoking-related condition, and nearly nine million suffer from a serious smoking-related illness. According to the Centers for Disease Control and Prevention (CDC), tobacco products cause nearly six million deaths per year. This number is projected to rise to over eight million deaths by 2030. Smokers, on average, die ten years earlier than their nonsmoking peers.

In the United States, local, state, and federal governments typically tax tobacco products, which leads to high prices. Nicotine users who struggle with addiction sometimes pay more for a pack of cigarettes than for a few gallons of gas. Additionally, smokers tend to stink. The smell of smoke is all-consuming and creates a pervasive nastiness. Smokers also risk staining their teeth and fingers with yellow residue from the tar.

Smoking is deadly, expensive, and socially unappealing. Clearly, smoking is not worth the risks.

265

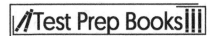

13. Which of the following statements most accurately summarizes the passage?
    a. Almost all smokers regret picking up that first cigarette.
    b. Tobacco is deadly, expensive, and socially unappealing, and smokers would be much better off kicking the addiction.
    c. In the United States, local, state, and federal governments typically tax tobacco products, which leads to high prices.
    d. Tobacco products shorten smokers' lives by ten years and kill more than six million people per year.
    e. Tobacco is less healthy than many alternatives.

14. The author would be most likely to agree with which of the following statements?
    a. Smokers should only quit cold turkey and should avoid all nicotine cessation devices.
    b. Other substances are more addictive than tobacco.
    c. Smokers should quit for whatever reason gets them to stop smoking.
    d. People who want to continue smoking should advocate for a reduction in tobacco product taxes.
    e. Smokers don't have the desire to quit and often don't see their smoking as a bad habit.

15. Which of the following is the author's opinion?
    a. According to the Centers for Disease Control and Prevention (CDC), tobacco products cause nearly six million deaths per year.
    b. Nicotine users who struggle with addiction sometimes pay more for a pack of cigarettes than for a few gallons of gas.
    c. Smokers also risk staining their teeth and fingers with yellow residue from the tar.
    d. Additionally, smokers tend to stink. The smell of smoke is all-consuming and creates a pervasive nastiness.
    e. Smokers, on average, die ten years earlier than their nonsmoking peers.

16. What is the tone of this passage?
    a. Objective
    b. Cautionary
    c. Indifferent
    d. Admiring
    e. Philosophical

17. What does the word *pervasive* mean in paragraph 4?
    a. Pleasantly appealing
    b. A floral scent
    c. To convince someone
    d. Difficult to sense
    e. All over the place

18. *Please read the following two passages and then answer the question that follows.*

    Passage 1

    In the modern classroom, cell phones have become indispensable. Cell phones, which are essentially handheld computers, allow students to take notes, connect to the web, perform complex computations, teleconference, and participate in surveys. Most importantly, though, due to their mobility and excellent reception, cell phones are

necessary in emergencies. Unlike tablets, laptops, or computers, cell phones are a readily available and free resource—most school district budgets are already strained to begin with—and since today's student is already strongly rooted in technology, when teachers incorporate cell phones, they're "speaking" the student's language, which increases the chance of higher engagement.

Passage 2

As with most forms of technology, there is an appropriate time and place for the use of cell phones. Students are comfortable with cell phones, so it makes sense when teachers allow cell phone use at their discretion. Allowing cell phone use can prove advantageous if done correctly. Unfortunately, if that's not the case—and often it isn't—then a sizable percentage of students pretend to pay attention while surreptitiously playing on their phones. This type of disrespectful behavior is often justified by the argument that cell phones are not only a privilege but also a right. Under this logic, confiscating phones is akin to rummaging through students' backpacks. This is in stark contrast to several decades ago when teachers regulated where and when students accessed information.

With which of the following statements would both the authors of Passages 1 and 2 agree?
- a. Teachers should incorporate cell phones into the curriculum whenever possible.
- b. Cell phones are useful only when an experienced teacher uses them properly.
- c. Cell phones and, moreover, technology are a strong part of today's culture.
- d. Despite a good lesson plan, cell phone disruptions are impossible to avoid.
- e. Cell phone disruptions are easily avoidable.

19. The following exchange occurred after the baseball coach's team suffered a heartbreaking loss in the final inning.

Reporter: The team clearly did not rise to the challenge. I'm sure that getting zero hits in twenty at-bats with runners in scoring position hurt the team's chances at winning the game. What are your thoughts on this devastating loss?

Baseball Coach: Hitting with runners in scoring position was not the reason we lost this game. We made numerous errors in the field, and our pitchers gave out too many free passes. Also, we did not even need a hit with runners in scoring position. Many of those at-bats could have driven in the run by simply making contact. Our team did not deserve to win the game.

Which of the following best describes the main point of dispute between the reporter and baseball coach?
- a. The loss was heartbreaking.
- b. Getting zero hits in twenty at-bats with runners in scoring position caused the loss.
- c. Numerous errors in the field and pitchers giving too many free passes caused the loss.
- d. The team deserved to win the game.
- e. There was no dispute between the reporter and the coach.

20. Last week, we adopted a dog from the local animal shelter, after looking for our perfect pet for several months. We wanted a dog that was not too old, but also past the puppy stage, so that training would be less time-intensive and so that we would give an older animal a home. Robin, as she's called, was a perfect match, and we filled out our application and, upon approval, were permitted to bring her home. Her physical exam and lab work all confirmed she was healthy. We went to the pet store and bought all sorts of bedding, food, toys, and treats to outfit our house as a dog-friendly and fun place. The shelter told us she liked dry food only, which is a relief because wet food is expensive and pretty off-putting. We even got fencing and installed a dog run in the backyard for Robin to roam unattended. Then we took her to the vet to make sure she was healthy. Next week, she starts the dog obedience class that we enrolled her in with a discount coupon from the shelter. It will be a good opportunity to bond with her and establish commands and dominance. When we took her to the park the afternoon after we adopted her, it was clear that she is a sociable and friendly dog, easily playing cohesively with dogs of all sizes and dispositions.

Which of the following is out of sequence in the story?
   a. Last week, we adopted a dog from the local animal shelter, after looking for our perfect pet for several months.
   b. Robin, as she's called, was a perfect match, and we filled out our application and, upon approval, were permitted to bring her home.
   c. Her physical exam and lab work all confirmed she was healthy.
   d. Next week, she starts the dog obedience class that we enrolled her in with a discount coupon from the shelter.
   e. It will be a good opportunity to bond with her and establish commands and dominance.

Questions 21–25 are based on the following passage.

The Myth of Head Heat Loss

It has recently been brought to my attention that most people believe that 75% of your body heat is lost through your head. I had certainly heard this before, and I'm not going to attempt to say I didn't believe it when I first heard it. It is natural to be gullible to anything said with enough authority. But the "fact" that the majority of your body heat is lost through your head is a lie.

Let me explain. Heat loss is proportional to surface area exposed. An elephant loses a great deal more heat than an anteater because it has a much greater surface area than an anteater. Each cell has mitochondria that produce energy in the form of heat, and it takes a lot more energy to run an elephant than an anteater.

So, each part of your body loses its proportional amount of heat in accordance with its surface area. The human torso probably loses the most heat, though the legs lose a significant amount as well. Some people have asked, "Why does it feel so much warmer when you cover your head than when you don't?" Well, that's because your head, because it is not clothed, is losing a lot of heat while the clothing on the rest of your body provides insulation. If you went outside with a hat and pants but no shirt, not only would you look silly, but your heat loss would be significantly greater because so much more of you would be exposed. So, if given the choice to cover your chest or your head in the cold, choose the chest. It could save your life.

21. Why does the author compare elephants and anteaters?
    a. To express an opinion
    b. To give an example that helps clarify the main point
    c. To show the differences between them
    d. To persuade why one is better than the other
    e. To educate about animals

22. Which of the following best describes the tone of the passage?
    a. Harsh
    b. Angry
    c. Casual
    d. Indifferent
    e. Comical

23. The author appeals to which branch of rhetoric to prove their case?
    a. Expert testimony
    b. Emotion
    c. Ethics and morals
    d. Author qualification
    e. Factual evidence

24. What does the word *gullible* mean in paragraph 1?
    a. To be angry toward
    b. To distrust something
    c. To believe something easily
    d. To be happy toward
    e. To be frightened

25. What is the main idea of the passage?
    a. To illustrate how people can easily believe anything they are told
    b. To prove that you have to have a hat to survive in the cold
    c. To persuade the audience that anteaters are better than elephants
    d. To convince the audience that heat loss comes mostly from the head
    e. To debunk the myth that heat loss comes mostly from the head

269

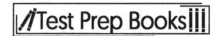
Situational Judgment

Situation 1

You are tasked with training five new recruits. Only one recruit displays the desired level of competency. The other four recruits seem unprepared for training.

What would you do?
   a. Dismiss the unprepared recruits. Their inadequacies are not your problem.
   b. Prioritize the training of the competent recruit. Their development is most important because they show the most potential.
   c. Delegate all responsibilities to the competent recruit.
   d. Emphasize the good work done by the exceptional recruit and help the other recruits attain core competencies in their fields of duty.
   e. Refer the unprepared recruits to other professions more suited to their individual talents and skills.

1. Select the MOST EFFECTIVE action (A-E) in response to the situation.
2. Select the LEAST EFFECTIVE action (A-E) in response to the situation.

Situation 2

A ranking officer assigned you a routine vehicle maintenance task. You are trying to finish several other tasks before the end of the day. You believe your other tasks are more important than the vehicle maintenance task.

What would you do?
   a. Quickly finish the vehicle maintenance task and get back to your other tasks as soon as possible.
   b. Confront the ranking officer about the unfairness of being assigned so many tasks.
   c. Thoroughly complete the vehicle maintenance task, and then spend the rest of the day working on the most crucial elements of your remaining tasks.
   d. Neglect the vehicle maintenance task and dedicate all your time and attention to the other tasks.
   e. Delegate the vehicle maintenance task to a subordinate who shows exceptional skill in mechanics.

3. Select the MOST EFFECTIVE action (A-E) in response to the situation.
4. Select the LEAST EFFECTIVE action (A-E) in response to the situation.

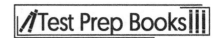

Situation 3

An officer of equal rank lets you know that when you are not around, your team members have been behaving unprofessionally. When the officer confronted them about their behavior, your team members told them that you had granted them license to "let their hair down."

What would you do?
a. Confirm your subordinates' response, whether true or false, and let them off the hook.
b. Dismiss the officer's concern. Your subordinates are your responsibility, and the officer is getting too involved.
c. Acknowledge the officer's concern and thank them for bringing the matter to your attention.
d. Discipline the accused members of your team.
e. Bring the officer's concern to the attention of your team members and prompt them to take responsibility for their behavior.

5. Select the MOST EFFECTIVE action (A-E) in response to the situation.
6. Select the LEAST EFFECTIVE action (A-E) in response to the situation.

Situation 4

During a team-building exercise, an officer of equal rank observes that you have been aloof from the members of your team. The officer reports that your subordinates have been complaining about your disaffected manner throughout the exercise.

What would you do?
a. Take an active role in the exercise to show your team members you are committed to the team-building training.
b. Distance yourself further from your team members. It is your job to stand apart from your team; it is their job to trust each other.
c. Discipline the members of your squad for insubordination.
d. Ask one of your subordinates to act as team leader on your behalf.
e. Wait until the exercise is complete to address the concerns of your team members.

7. Select the MOST EFFECTIVE action (A-E) in response to the situation.
8. Select the LEAST EFFECTIVE action (A-E) in response to the situation.

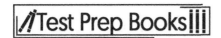

Situation 5

A member of your squad shows leadership potential. She often takes initiative during training exercises, and other members of your squad look to her for guidance in uncertain situations.

What would you do?
   a. Acknowledge the squad member's leadership abilities, but keep her in check, when possible, to avoid losing the respect of your squad.
   b. During training exercises, focus on her and ask her to prove herself by performing more rigorous tasks than the other members of your team.
   c. Encourage other team members to take the lead during exercises, especially if they prefer to follow. It is crucial that all your team members know how to lead.
   d. Work with the team member to unlock her full potential as a leader. Encourage her to make a positive impact on the rest of your team.
   e. Recommend her to another squad. She may benefit from learning from a different officer.

9. Select the MOST EFFECTIVE action (A-E) in response to the situation.
10. Select the LEAST EFFECTIVE action (A-E) in response to the situation.

Situation 6

A squad member informs you that other members of your squad plan to play a prank on another squad. She tells you what they plan to do and when they plan to do it. She says that she doubted whether telling you about the plot was the right thing to do.

What would you do?
   a. Alert the plotters that you have discovered their plan and tell them which one of their peers gave them away.
   b. Address the information with the members of your team, review moral and ethical standards for service, and remind them of the possible consequences of their planned actions.
   c. Tell the informant that you are uninterested in this news and remind her of her place on the team.
   d. Work with the plotted-against squad to devise a counterplot against the mischievous members of your team.
   e. Do nothing. You are happy to see that your team is working together.

11. Select the MOST EFFECTIVE action (A-E) in response to the situation.
12. Select the LEAST EFFECTIVE action (A-E) in response to the situation.

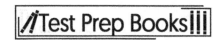

Situation 7

An officer of equal rank shares their observations about the sudden change in behavior of a member of your team. The officer reports that your team member has become withdrawn, spending large amounts of his free time away from the team. The officer believes your team member might be the subject of bullying.

What would you do?
   a. Speak with the withdrawn team member about the officer's concerns and address any issues you discover with the rest of your team.
   b. Acknowledge the issue but do nothing about it. You want your team members to be strong enough to stand on their own.
   c. Excuse the withdrawn team member from team-building assignments and assign him tasks that he can complete on his own.
   d. Work with the withdrawn team member to explore other career options. The Armed Forces are not for everyone.
   e. Talk with your ranking officer about moving the withdrawn team member to another team.

13. Select the MOST EFFECTIVE action (A-E) in response to the situation.
14. Select the LEAST EFFECTIVE action (A-E) in response to the situation.

Situation 8

A ranking officer assigns you an unfinished document that you must complete by the end of the day. You are unfamiliar with the content, but the ranking officer expressed his confidence in your ability to figure it out.

What would you do?
   a. Do your best to complete the document even though you do not fully understand the task.
   b. Tell the ranking officer that you are not able to complete the task, and then focus your attention on your other work.
   c. Take more time than allowed to research the task and complete the document to the highest standard possible.
   d. Assign the document to one of your subordinates. They know as much as you do about how to complete it.
   e. Seek guidance from the ranking officer or another mentor about how to properly complete the document.

15. Select the MOST EFFECTIVE action (A-E) in response to the situation.
16. Select the LEAST EFFECTIVE action (A-E) in response to the situation.

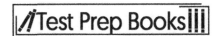

Situation 9

While preparing your squad for an important drill, you receive word that your spouse called the base to request that you return home immediately. Something important is happening at home, and you must be there. However, the drill is also important, and your squad is counting on you.

What would you do?
   a. Begin the drill and complete all the crucial parts. Then turn over the drill to one of your best squad members to finish without you.
   b. Complete the drill as planned and return home after you fulfill your obligations to your squad.
   c. Complete the drill quickly so you can get home to your spouse.
   d. Request that you and your squad complete the drill later.
   e. Return home immediately, even though you will not finish the drill with your squad. Family comes first in the Air Force.

17. Select the MOST EFFECTIVE action (A-E) in response to the situation.
18. Select the LEAST EFFECTIVE action (A-E) in response to the situation.

Situation 10

One of the members of your squad is pregnant. You did not become aware of her pregnancy until she started to show. She is determined to continue her training, despite the risks to her health.

What would you do?
   a. Rally your squad around your pregnant squad member. She is an example to everyone for putting the Air Force above her own health and safety.
   b. Allow her to remain in your squad but exclude her from all physical exercises.
   c. Advise your squad member that her health is most important, and work with her to attain appropriate resources and support for pursuing her career while pregnant.
   d. Assign her a buddy — another member of your squad — to complete difficult tasks for her and monitor her safety.
   e. Dismiss her from training. It was her responsibility to notify the Air Force when she became pregnant, and her negligence may put everyone at risk.

19. Select the MOST EFFECTIVE action (A-E) in response to the situation.
20. Select the LEAST EFFECTIVE action (A-E) in response to the situation.

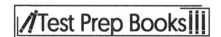

Situation 11

A member of your team informs you that during a leave of absence, several other team members went to a bar and got into a fight with each other. The informant expressed that he was unsure whether he should tell you or not, but he decided it was the right thing to do.

What would you do?
    a. Organize a series of team-building exercises. There are obviously issues among the members of your team.
    b. Ask the informant to consider the situation from the perspective of his team members, and then consider the matter closed since no one was seriously hurt.
    c. Organize more physical exercises. Your team members obviously crave physical activity.
    d. Thank the informant for coming to you with this news and take steps to investigate the situation and discipline your team members, if necessary.
    e. Take a leave of absence. You have lost control of your team, and someone new should have an opportunity to put things right.

21. Select the MOST EFFECTIVE action (A-E) in response to the situation.
22. Select the LEAST EFFECTIVE action (A-E) in response to the situation.

Situation 12

A member of your squad is applying for officer training. She requests that you write a letter of recommendation on her behalf. She attended a top school in the United States, graduated with a high GPA, and has already received several glowing civilian recommendations. However, her performance under your tutelage has been subpar.

What would you do?
    a. Request that you both sit down to discuss her application. You want to share your impressions of her performance so far and offer advice about how she may improve.
    b. Request correspondence with anyone who wrote a letter of recommendation on her behalf. You want to give them a chance to change your mind.
    c. Decline to write a letter of recommendation on her behalf. While she has performed well in civilian life, she has not displayed the skills required to succeed in the military.
    d. Write a letter of recommendation on her behalf. Her proven track record in civilian life ensures her success in the military.
    e. Do not disclose to her whether you will write a letter of recommendation on her behalf. She will have to prove herself over time.

23. Select the MOST EFFECTIVE action (A-E) in response to the situation.
24. Select the LEAST EFFECTIVE action (A-E) in response to the situation.

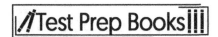

Situation 13

While visiting family during a leave of absence, you are the victim of a burglary. You wake up in the middle of the night to the sound of forced entry. Your presence in the house compels the burglar to flee. You reach the front door in time to see their car speeding away.

What would you do?
a. Provide an accurate description of the burglar's vehicle to members of your squad who are on leave in your area. They can look out for the burglar's car.
b. Alert local law enforcement about the attempted crime and work with them to bring the criminal to justice.
c. Alert local law enforcement about the attempted crime and secure your home and family. Local law enforcement is responsible for maintaining peace in society.
d. Pursue the burglar. Your status as an active member of the military outranks local and state law enforcement agents. Failure to pursue the burglar is failure to complete your duty to serve.
e. Notify local law enforcement only after you attempt to pursue the burglar. Local law enforcement has the resources to begin a prolonged investigation.

25. Select the MOST EFFECTIVE action (A-E) in response to the situation.
26. Select the LEAST EFFECTIVE action (A-E) in response to the situation.

Situation 14

A new officer begins duty at your service site, and a high-ranking officer asks you to show them the ropes. You have a lot of other work to do, and you can tell that the new officer is a natural.

What would you do?
a. Provide on-the-job training by enlisting the new officer's help completing all the work you need to finish by the end of the day.
b. Expedite the training of the new officer so you can invest your time in your own workload.
c. Talk with the high-ranking officer about the increased workload. You are not responsible for anyone except yourself and your team, and no one should get in the way of that priority.
d. Prioritize the training of the new officer, and then complete the most crucial elements of your pre-existing tasks when you can. New situations may arise, and you are responsible for the new officer.
e. Prioritize your own tasks. The new officer has not been assigned any important tasks yet, so you must ensure that you complete everything you need to do.

27. Select the MOST EFFECTIVE action (A-E) in response to the situation.
28. Select the LEAST EFFECTIVE action (A-E) in response to the situation.

Situation 15

While you are in the middle of a field safety drill, you receive a call from a relative. They inform you of a family emergency. Your relative explains that the situation is dire, and you must come immediately. However, if you abandon the drill, you risk the safety of members of your squad.

What would you do?
   a. Leave immediately to tend to the well-being of your family members, regardless of how your absence may affect the outcome of the drill.
   b. Inform your family member that you are unavailable to immediately assist. Complete the safety drill and attend to your family after.
   c. Ignore the call from your family member. You cannot be responsible for the well-being of your family members while fulfilling your job duties.
   d. Delegate authority to a trusted member of your squad. They will complete the safety drill in your place while you attend to your family.
   e. Postpone the safety drill. You and your squad will complete the requirements later.

29. Select the MOST EFFECTIVE action (A-E) in response to the situation.
30. Select the LEAST EFFECTIVE action (A-E) in response to the situation.

Situation 16

A member of your team — one of the best airmen you have ever seen — has developed a bad reputation when given time off to participate in civilian life. You have coached him after each negative report. However, according to a new complaint, his negative behavior has escalated and become intolerable.

What would you do?
   a. Confront whoever submitted the complaint and evaluate whether their testimony was exaggerated.
   b. Recommend the airman for disciplinary action, and, if deemed necessary, dismissal from the Air Force.
   c. Dismiss the report as outlandish and offer your own testimony on the airman's character.
   d. Renew your one-on-one coaching program with the airman. You must bring out the best in him.
   e. Revoke the airman's recreation privileges. He behaves well on-base, so you will keep him there.

31. Select the MOST EFFECTIVE action (A-E) in response to the situation.
32. Select the LEAST EFFECTIVE action (A-E) in response to the situation.

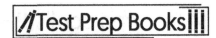

Situation 17

While working on an assigned task, you encounter an obstacle that prevents you from completing it. Your supervising officer encouraged you to reach out to them with any questions, but they are unavailable until your deadline.

What would you do?
    a. Wait to complete the task until you have consulted with your supervising officer.
    b. Inform your supervising officer that you completed the task, even though you were unable to finish it.
    c. Consult an officer of equivalent rank to that of your supervising officer. They may guide you through the rest of the task.
    d. Do your best to complete the task on your own and overcome the present obstacle. You know enough about the task to make progress.
    e. Work even harder on other tasks since you are unable to complete the task assigned to you.

33. Select the MOST EFFECTIVE action (A-E) in response to the situation.
34. Select the LEAST EFFECTIVE action (A-E) in response to the situation.

Situation 18

Your supervising officer recommends you for an award because of the work your team has accomplished in the last six months. You lead an outstanding group of individuals who contributed to your success. Unfortunately, you are the only one being recognized.

What would you do?
    a. Acknowledge your mentors, who helped you learn how to be a great officer.
    b. Celebrate the reward with your friends and family. You earned it.
    c. Make special mention of your team's role in your success.
    d. Refuse the reward. Your team deserves an award, not you.
    e. Thank your supervising officer for picking the right candidate.

35. Select the MOST EFFECTIVE action (A-E) in response to the situation.
36. Select the LEAST EFFECTIVE action (A-E) in response to the situation.

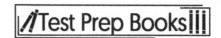

Situation 19

A fellow officer is ill and unable to complete the functions assigned to them. You notice that the officer's tasks have not been re-assigned to any active officers, and this is causing problems for you and your squad.

What would you do?
a. Ignore the issue and focus instead on the work you need to complete.
b. Encourage your squad to add the officer's tasks to their workload.
c. Complain to your supervising officer about the work that has gone undone since your fellow officer fell ill.
d. Prioritize the workload assigned to the absent officer.
e. Add the responsibilities of your fellow officer to your own list of tasks.

37. Select the MOST EFFECTIVE action (A-E) in response to the situation.
38. Select the LEAST EFFECTIVE action (A-E) in response to the situation.

Situation 20

Due to unforeseen circumstances, you are finding it difficult to manage the budget assigned to your unit. Expenses are piling up, and your treasury is running low. You think you can remain within the budget if you cut costs around the edges.

What would you do?
a. Cut costs where you can, even if you upset members of your unit.
b. Exceed your budget, when necessary, to ensure the loyalty of your team members.
c. Request a temporary increase of funds to avoid running out of money.
d. Allocate funds from next quarter's budget to meet your present funding needs.
e. Spend what you must to ensure the loyalty, safety, and comfort of the members of your unit.

39. Select the MOST EFFECTIVE action (A-E) in response to the situation.
40. Select the LEAST EFFECTIVE action (A-E) in response to the situation.

Situation 21

A member of your squad was singled out for disciplinary action after he failed to complete a maneuver that you ordered. Although he did not follow your orders exactly, you can see how he might have misinterpreted your commands.

What would you do?
a. Insist that disciplinary action be avoided.
b. Discipline your subordinate for failing to complete orders.
c. Deny any suggestion that your orders could be misinterpreted.
d. Take responsibility for the orders you gave.
e. Resign from your position for allowing this to happen.

41. Select the MOST EFFECTIVE action (A-E) in response to the situation.
42. Select the LEAST EFFECTIVE action (A-E) in response to the situation.

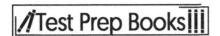

Situation 22

You've thought of a more efficient way to complete a task. However, there is a slight chance your new plan will fail, and you will have to spend more money and time on fixing your mistake.

What would you do?
   a. Dismiss your new plan without trying it. The old ways always work better than new ideas.
   b. Do not undertake either method until you decide which one will work best.
   c. Do not complete the task. Neither method is efficient and it is better off unfinished.
   d. Remember your plan, write it down, and keep it in mind the next time a similar situation presents itself.
   e. Use your innovative new plan to complete the task and try not to make any mistakes.

43. Select the MOST EFFECTIVE action (A-E) in response to the situation.
44. Select the LEAST EFFECTIVE action (A-E) in response to the situation.

Situation 23

A family circumstance compels you to take a brief leave of absence. This is not the first time this family issue has interfered with your responsibilities. When asked about the reason for your absence this time, you are afraid to cite the same family issue.

What would you do?
   a. Report the reason for your absence only to those who must know why you will be absent.
   b. Share the reason for your absence and explain why this issue recurs.
   c. Report that a new circumstance has presented itself, and you must attend to it.
   d. Do not take another leave of absence.
   e. Ask a colleague to vouch for you without disclosing the details of your absence.

45. Select the MOST EFFECTIVE action (A-E) in response to the situation.
46. Select the LEAST EFFECTIVE action (A-E) in response to the situation.

Situation 24

Two of the best members of your squad are not getting along. Although neither squad member wants to bring the problem to your attention, both are struggling to manage the stress caused by their interpersonal conflict.

What would you do?
   a. Directly address the issue by using conflict resolution strategies.
   b. Assign both squad members to separate tasks so they will not have to interact.
   c. Prompt other members of your team to try to resolve the dispute.
   d. Discipline both squad members equally for failing to put the interest of the squad above all else.
   e. Request assistance from a trained Human Resources representative.

47. Select the MOST EFFECTIVE action (A-E) in response to the situation.
48. Select the LEAST EFFECTIVE action (A-E) in response to the situation.

Situation 25

After a weekly team meeting, you receive constructive feedback from one of your team members about your presentation style. They express that the team is having trouble understanding the technical jargon you use, and this is negatively impacting their ability to efficiently complete their assigned tasks.

What would you do?
a. Refer your team members to various resources they may use to interpret your technical jargon.
b. Recommend that the confused members of your team seek help from fellow team members who understand the material.
c. Adjust your verbiage so it is more easily understood by your team members.
d. Prompt your team members to lead team meetings for a while so they can learn from each other in a style that suits them.
e. Listen to the complaints of your subordinates but make no changes to your presentation style. They must learn how to interpret technical jargon.

49. Select the MOST EFFECTIVE action (A-E) in response to the situation.
50. Select the LEAST EFFECTIVE action (A-E) in response to the situation.

Physical Science

1. At what point in its swing does a pendulum have the most mechanical energy?
   a. At the top of its swing, just before going into motion
   b. At the bottom of its swing, in full motion
   c. Halfway between the top of its swing and the bottom of its swing
   d. The same amount of mechanical energy throughout its path
   e. At the very end of its swing, at a stop

2. The energy of motion is also referred to as what?
   a. Potential energy
   b. Kinetic energy
   c. Solar energy
   d. Heat energy
   e. Ionization energy

3. The water cycle involves phase changes. Which example below is evaporation?
   a. Clouds forming in the sky
   b. Rain, snow, or ice storms
   c. River water flowing to the ocean
   d. Sunlight's effect on morning dew
   e. Water soaking into the soil

4. Which of the following is most electronegative?
   a. Hydrogen
   b. Lithium
   c. Fluorine
   d. Cesium
   e. Lead

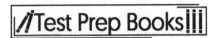
5. Where is most of the Earth's weather generated?
    a. The troposphere
    b. The ionosphere
    c. The thermosphere
    d. The stratosphere
    e. The exosphere

6. To find the moles of a liquid substance from a known volume, what conversion factors or values are necessary?
    a. Density of liquid, molar mass
    b. Viscosity of liquid, relative molecular mass
    c. Chemical formula of liquid, mass of liquid
    d. Temperature of liquid, molecular weight
    e. Mass of liquid, molecular mass

7. From which acid-base combination would you expect the most violent exothermic reaction?
    a. Water added to a weak acid
    b. A weak base added to a weak acid
    c. A strong acid added to water
    d. Water added to a strong base
    e. A weak base added to water

8. Which of the following is considered a force?
    a. Weight
    b. Mass
    c. Acceleration
    d. Gravity
    e. Impulse

9. The Sun transferring heat to the Earth through space is an example of which of the following?
    a. Convection
    b. Conduction
    c. Induction
    d. Radiation
    e. Advection

10. Which pair of atoms has the most polar bond?
    a. CN
    b. OH
    c. NaCl
    d. O_2
    e. HF

11. Which of the following is true of an object at rest on earth?
    a. It has no forces acting upon it.
    b. It has no gravity acting upon it.
    c. It is in transition.
    d. It has constant acceleration.
    e. It is in equilibrium.

282

12. Which of the following is a vector quantity?
    a. Mass
    b. Length
    c. Velocity
    d. Speed
    e. Frequency

13. The following is an example of what type of formula?

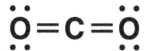

    a. Molecular formula
    b. Lewis dot formula
    c. Structural formula
    d. Empirical formula
    e. Skeletal formula

14. What is the property of all physical matter that resists change in motion?
    a. Velocity
    b. Mass
    c. Momentum
    d. Inertia
    e. Impulse

15. What is the mechanical advantage of the pictured pulley system, assuming there are no losses due to friction?
    a. 1
    b. 2
    c. 3
    d. 4
    e. 5

16. Which is NOT a form of energy?
    a. Light
    b. Sound
    c. Heat
    d. Mass
    e. Microwaves

17. Which of the following liquids is classified as a solution?
    a. Hot cocoa
    b. Salt water
    c. Whole milk
    d. Grape juice
    e. Muddy water

18. For any given element, an isotope is an atom with which of the following?
    a. A different atomic number
    b. A different number of protons
    c. A different number of electrons
    d. A different mass number
    e. A different formal charge

19. Which statement is true regarding atomic structure?
    a. Protons orbit around a nucleus.
    b. Neutrons have a positive charge.
    c. Electrons are in the nucleus.
    d. Protons have a positive charge.
    e. Neutrons pull on electrons.

20. For circular motion, what is the name of the reactionary outward force felt when an object is undergoing circular motion?
    a. Centrifugal force
    b. Gravity
    c. Centripetal force
    d. Coriolis effect
    e. Tension

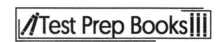

Table Reading

	X	Y	A	B	C	D	E
1.	-3	17	377	484	257	441	173
2.	0	-15	275	-450	137	87	377
3.	0	6	-141	347	-386	123	-171
4.	4	-14	-8	414	-364	65	11
5.	13	-4	-235	120	-473	9	-124
6.	-14	12	19	191	-40	-345	286
7.	11	-4	326	-283	285	-210	-436
8.	13	-13	21	-475	420	-397	-60
9.	-17	16	-124	18	131	491	355
10.	-5	-6	-415	415	341	234	260
11.	-15	3	-445	94	174	-85	-439
12.	-16	9	194	78	282	208	47
13.	-7	11	-237	196	29	442	277
14.	-4	0	431	-258	102	35	-265
15.	15	6	230	-64	-261	307	-160
16.	14	-3	265	-77	-254	-493	-156
17.	3	-17	140	482	-405	295	-499
18.	5	-17	-445	-471	316	255	-128
19.	8	-13	-376	-361	184	144	370
20.	-7	-1	-127	-221	409	315	289

	X	Y	A	B	C	D	E
21.	12	-1	184	86	139	-128	-113
22.	-5	-9	-54	334	416	-224	99
23.	2	-12	197	-68	-153	184	-408
24.	-1	3	-366	-246	331	-154	354
25.	0	2	156	201	44	129	-191
26.	1	-16	-19	472	-79	-170	-204
27.	9	-15	-279	-109	-387	283	-169
28.	1	-15	-297	118	25	-181	381
29.	-11	15	193	74	333	-22	-207
30.	12	0	213	471	322	353	340
31.	17	-6	-367	-482	208	160	205
32.	11	6	200	423	-93	192	-194
33.	14	-7	-91	-479	486	211	-276
34.	-15	11	-23	18	-323	-93	-119
35.	-10	17	-338	-50	-89	89	71
36.	2	-14	26	-54	-247	20	323
37.	2	-12	-41	-4	197	90	-53
38.	7	-1	9	-39	-108	271	320
39.	-5	14	-22	218	164	-38	-80
40.	-5	-5	-127	467	-320	11	179

286

	17	16	15	14	13	12	11	10	9	8	7	6	5	4	3	2	1	0	-1	-2	-3	-4	-5	-6	-7	-8	-9	-10	-11	-12	-13	-14	-15	-16	-17	
17	-76	492	-414	-485	-336	-314	203	282	125	382	-483	-397	-113	-362	-210	351	-282	331	254	120	173	-359	76	-3	330	-88	13	71	285	-230	304	191	-257	-211	-110	17
16	295	217	175	286	371	243	384	73	59	-434	331	491	-69	87	-122	-423	-295	-241	298	-137	404	355	66	-171	269	80	-380	423	239	-352	-414	244	-351	-258	-124	16
15	-98	-382	129	-146	234	-490	416	-408	-245	450	217	-322	207	387	132	-12	-406	-366	112	-130	483	-147	80	498	-13	-291	-380	423	-207	-322	400	91	-380	309	8	15
14	-72	109	157	287	11	358	266	-183	-87	-185	-333	-403	-378	-471	-180	429	142	318	65	-192	-482	-226	-22	157	55	-419	270	-112	10	-114	-70	-236	-10	-18	-356	14
13	136	360	-33	415	-427	162	-247	344	-132	-424	-432	273	117	213	27	191	291	485	-183	-65	-482	399	357	-271	-168	-123	117	16	82	6	490	168	374	218	125	13
12	232	-186	-419	307	197	361	-82	-248	-222	-18	-228	259	274	-381	132	267	-249	314	247	105	34	-276	-451	24	-272	-244	-239	-473	-455	97	341	-345	491	383	102	12
11	-36	-401	337	-129	280	-39	-294	-418	175	-210	222	182	-347	-35	376	309	-258	-356	-33	-93	234	72	-432	59	277	-99	-25	117	485	308	405	-240	-23	-193	15	11
10	-388	-323	141	-151	194	56	343	484	-149	458	119	442	-185	161	414	-141	219	-256	-230	-255	487	481	-309	59	-377	134	-474	-158	-371	-404	324	-89	-266	306	-383	10
9	-200	145	185	-277	-466	314	412	500	336	481	309	-434	404	483	396	-47	387	-32	-384	-113	-107	247	-422	70	150	-163	309	500	378	468	-83	-140	92	483	112	9
8	392	443	196	-243	190	-28	355	452	-106	-319	-354	-381	199	-326	259	-54	-279	-338	-94	250	-413	-227	5	144	227	-197	284	244	371	-260	34	176	-71	-51	-356	8
7	81	331	99	-171	-57	440	-76	249	252	-427	427	442	182	-273	-92	-375	57	493	97	158	252	225	-494	-381	-176	244	302	97	366	10	-21	-128	68	-169	495	7
6	-486	-161	230	-277	169	-267	200	-243	-378	448	-67	-83	129	446	63	133	101	-386	151	481	-403	-227	-18	-381	302	-479	-62	-456	-414	-266	-427	-183	442	394	131	6
5	-479	407	110	465	-2	351	119	-376	249	435	-2	84	159	-67	10	404	28	-140	395	245	322	-156	-238	182	227	-138	160	-490	393	-121	272	362	56	-372	420	5
4	-63	-50	-442	297	-355	-299	-282	333	-268	352	201	-139	-491	-221	287	-191	-173	-445	254	91	-448	-79	441	33	-79	47	-62	96	137	319	-327	-126	385	358	-487	4
3	-80	154	-465	310	213	-378	-380	211	-446	-41	192	364	345	253	278	-79	433	358	331	285	214	-491	-390	87	-343	-212	-79	234	-60	-476	130	425	94	-51	186	3
2	-201	-356	38	319	-182	430	243	-208	40	427	-11	355	69	256	-295	19	155	129	477	413	-74	213	122	-450	135	-180	327	97	371	10	-31	-232	-474	251	-286	2
1	340	40	394	-176	460	-246	-298	348	-374	-56	-175	-342	422	95	-153	-420	404	-142	-278	-145	-389	-255	76	-483	72	-105	-45	-456	-78	-266	-427	215	-157	-3	-237	1
0	-47	-60	81	-214	269	353	467	411	72	-11	417	36	-414	82	247	286	310	-168	157	413	-285	96	436	192	172	-263	23	158	1	-482	328	-459	-201	89	397	0
-1	107	258	78	-299	-73	-113	-7	-364	-401	363	9	-2	113	85	47	495	-23	234	175	271	404	-233	368	87	-221	-423	-407	445	-315	-13	130	460	394	37	397	-1
-2	-63	75	-203	-254	-95	-188	-11	430	-234	-170	374	-287	-439	-170	-336	0	58	337	-354	-426	-284	-330	226	255	127	-152	-183	10	53	-467	-280	55	-249	-82	-149	-2
-3	118	307	415	196	0	-281	-23	212	-238	137	-219	313	-388	-144	415	210	-13	129	-7	-56	90	316	136	391	327	433	-365	-477	291	-195	61	-355	-16	-493	-249	-3
-4	-350	446	105	-332	120	425	326	-208	-341	152	-266	-27	199	-424	47	-488	-106	234	45	470	153	-336	-44	445	-179	3	187	-400	-485	392	-298	104	422	324	132	-4
-5	356	-5	-302	-276	-224	-219	306	-96	189	151	379	143	258	-70	-336	-298	438	337	-461	-320	241	-193	11	192	-45	-124	-356	172	-157	-362	-19	378	-326	102	395	-5
-6	-482	-259	70	33	-459	83	-95	-74	-36	-13	-107	-72	-195	-239	-31	-256	-448	-84	315	-56	-204	-330	-415	391	286	410	-460	10	64	-51	-14	-420	136	-217	462	-6
-7	-236	225	-214	244	250	458	302	-135	-269	-483	-221	-169	-230	-205	50	-388	356	443	-384	-257	-112	-311	-1	192	363	256	275	-130	-217	-128	-373	180	-187	470	-479	-7
-8	-277	-25	-94	33	244	-372	-28	-47	-349	-207	278	99	-465	85	148	-256	252	403	256	385	-262	288	433	-199	181	-266	106	293	-292	324	-253	-182	-154	-386	217	-8
-9	117	153	-263	-429	103	289	420	-125	-188	3	497	-283	-292	-427	-175	-388	-221	-229	-231	404	-264	338	-54	-394	457	60	147	-229	149	-133	103	375	35	141	88	-9
-10	-350	164	130	5	53	452	-300	-320	-384	432	476	-499	260	-210	182	158	-43	0	369	84	90	-137	165	318	-345	-407	-147	493	387	-120	-40	376	-477	96	298	-10
-11	-196	-138	186	-286	-96	-219	-181	280	121	170	-498	-354	449	-73	332	171	-349	-424	-281	179	123	-137	-393	-225	294	14	-178	377	-444	319	-446	400	-448	-69	-443	-11
-12	369	139	-492	6	-44	-241	-14	-458	-112	-77	-376	321	-113	202	-258	197	-34	-293	467	-206	103	-354	452	-29	-111	410	481	-88	-157	-28	-231	-66	276	301	-184	-12
-13	460	-148	-328	204	21	43	301	288	185	-376	410	80	246	311	-148	180	396	-49	167	215	-365	294	-406	-452	-163	288	-291	-461	64	376	47	-36	-456	146	486	-13
-14	50	-274	52	432	445	-71	92	-126	115	191	-366	493	-163	134	140	-247	118	332	140	-378	-454	-315	279	402	0	-430	242	182	-217	382	-262	-116	-31	-261	-500	-14
-15	-387	271	408	-220	284	251	125	-206	283	82	374	217	-6	-170	418	65	-170	332	381	-474	424	463	-406	-77	467	-457	-460	-101	217	88	259	344	95	139	-28	-15
-16	202	20	322	-24	-391	-429	367	157	-7	64	-330	146	-364	311	315	96	-210	49	403	-309	-148	-315	300	-42	487	-359	-291	-101	116	88	33	62	95	146	-28	-16
-17	-373	-34	416	-98	442	-466	-433	322	467	22	448	146	-128	134	140	96	-210	332	39	-474	327	-315	300	402	-42	229	-97	-101	116	88	33	62	95	-261	-28	-17
	17	16	15	14	13	12	11	10	9	8	7	6	5	4	3	2	1	0	-1	-2	-3	-4	-5	-6	-7	-8	-9	-10	-11	-12	-13	-14	-15	-16	-17	

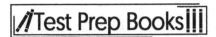
Instrument Comprehension

1. Looking at the instruments on the left, which choice depicts the orientation of the aircraft?

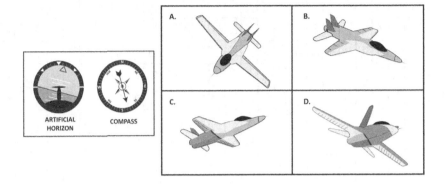

2. Looking at the instruments on the left, which choice depicts the orientation of the aircraft?

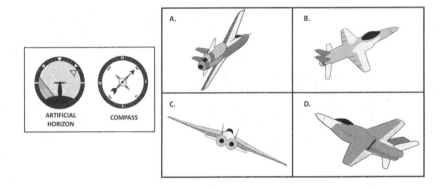

3. Looking at the instruments on the left, which choice depicts the orientation of the aircraft?

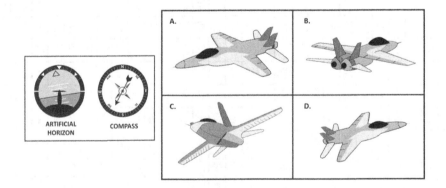

288

4. Looking at the instruments on the left, which choice depicts the orientation of the aircraft?

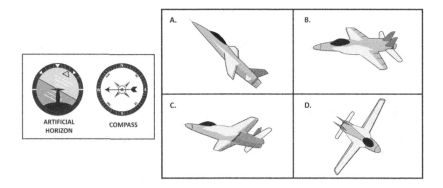

5. Looking at the instruments on the left, which choice depicts the orientation of the aircraft?

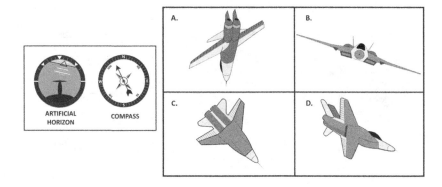

6. Looking at the instruments on the left, which choice depicts the orientation of the aircraft?

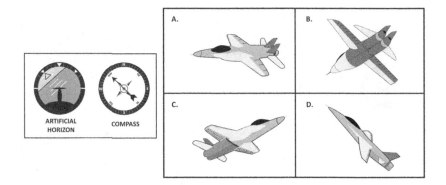

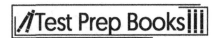
7. Looking at the instruments on the left, which choice depicts the orientation of the aircraft?

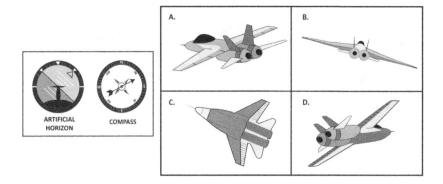

8. Looking at the instruments on the left, which choice depicts the orientation of the aircraft?

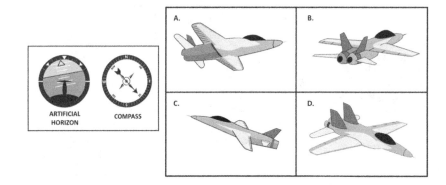

9. Looking at the instruments on the left, which choice depicts the orientation of the aircraft?

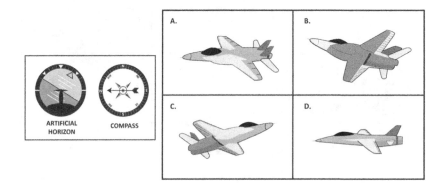

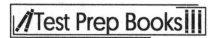

10. Looking at the instruments on the left, which choice depicts the orientation of the aircraft?

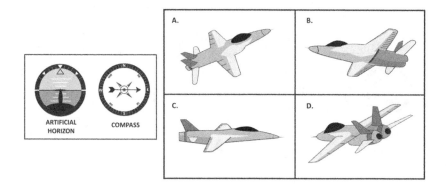

11. Looking at the instruments on the left, which choice depicts the orientation of the aircraft?

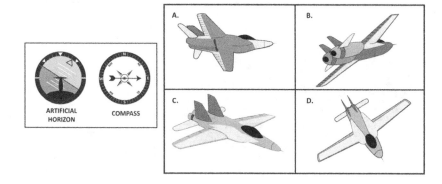

12. Looking at the instruments on the left, which choice depicts the orientation of the aircraft?

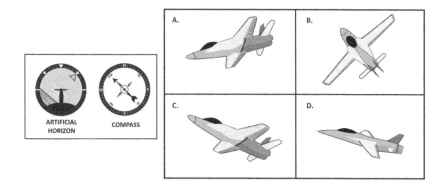

13. Looking at the instruments on the left, which choice depicts the orientation of the aircraft?

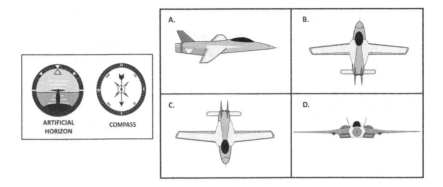

14. Looking at the instruments on the left, which choice depicts the orientation of the aircraft?

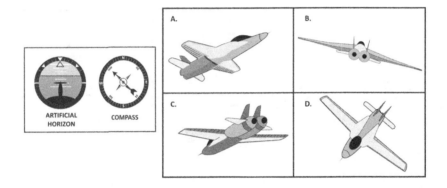

15. Looking at the instruments on the left, which choice depicts the orientation of the aircraft?

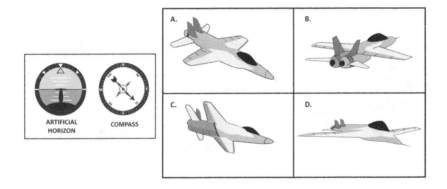

16. Looking at the instruments on the left, which choice depicts the orientation of the aircraft?

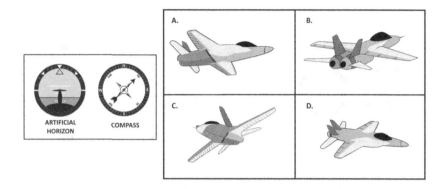

17. Looking at the instruments on the left, which choice depicts the orientation of the aircraft?

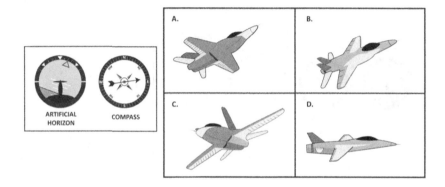

18. Looking at the instruments on the left, which choice depicts the orientation of the aircraft?

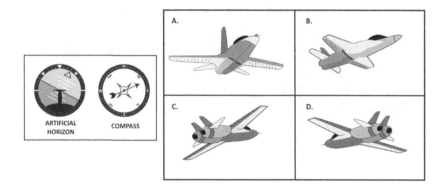

19. Looking at the instruments on the left, which choice depicts the orientation of the aircraft?

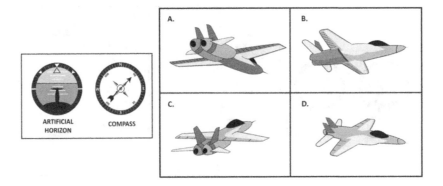

20. Looking at the instruments on the left, which choice depicts the orientation of the aircraft?

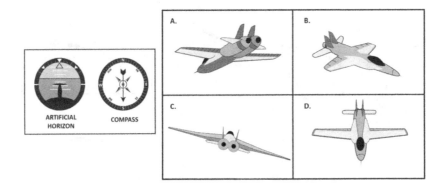

21. Looking at the instruments on the left, which choice depicts the orientation of the aircraft?

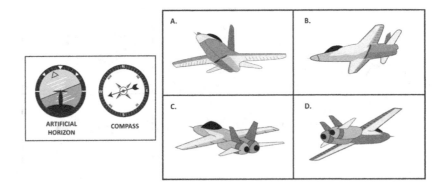

294

22. Looking at the instruments on the left, which choice depicts the orientation of the aircraft?

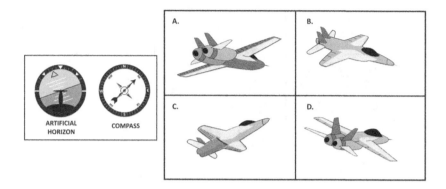

23. Looking at the instruments on the left, which choice depicts the orientation of the aircraft?

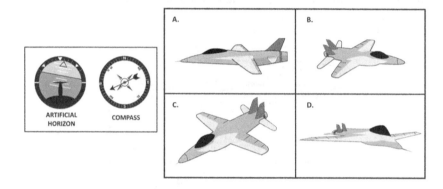

24. Looking at the instruments on the left, which choice depicts the orientation of the aircraft?

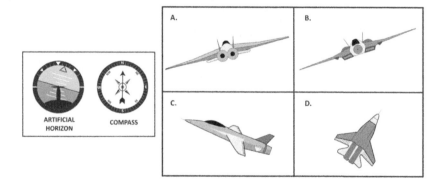

25. Looking at the instruments on the left, which choice depicts the orientation of the aircraft?

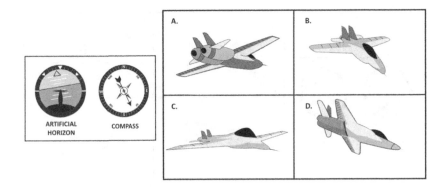

Block Counting

For questions 1–30, determine how many blocks the given block is touching.

Use the following block for questions 1–5.

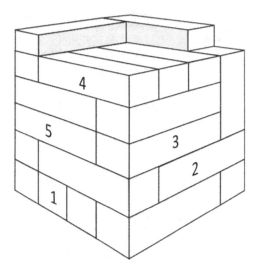

1. Block 1
   a.   1
   b.   2
   c.   3
   d.   4
   e.   5

2. Block 2
   a.   3
   b.   4
   c.   5
   d.   6
   e.   7

3. Block 3
    a. 5
    b. 6
    c. 7
    d. 8
    e. 9

4. Block 4
    a. 3
    b. 4
    c. 5
    d. 6
    e. 7

5. Block 5
    a. 1
    b. 2
    c. 3
    d. 4
    e. 5

Use the following block for questions 6–10.

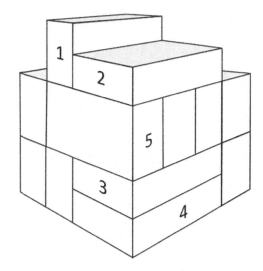

6. Block 1
    a. 2
    b. 3
    c. 4
    d. 5
    e. 6

7. Block 2
   a. 2
   b. 3
   c. 4
   d. 5
   e. 6

8. Block 3
   a. 3
   b. 4
   c. 5
   d. 6
   e. 7

9. Block 4
   a. 3
   b. 4
   c. 5
   d. 6
   e. 7

10. Block 5
   a. 3
   b. 4
   c. 5
   d. 6
   e. 7

Use the following block for questions 11–15.

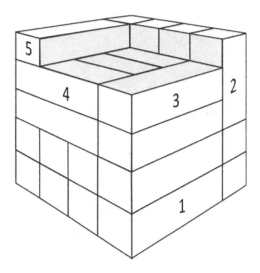

11. Block 1
    a. 2
    b. 3
    c. 4
    d. 5
    e. 6

12. Block 2
    a. 2
    b. 3
    c. 4
    d. 5
    e. 6

13. Block 3
    a. 2
    b. 3
    c. 4
    d. 5
    e. 6

14. Block 4
    a. 2
    b. 3
    c. 4
    d. 5
    e. 6

15. Block 5
  a. 2
  b. 3
  c. 4
  d. 5
  e. 6

Use the following block for questions 16–20.

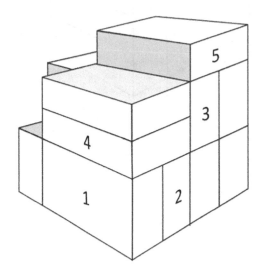

16. Block 1
  a. 2
  b. 3
  c. 4
  d. 5
  e. 6

17. Block 2
  a. 2
  b. 3
  c. 4
  d. 5
  e. 6

18. Block 3
  a. 2
  b. 3
  c. 4
  d. 5
  e. 6

19. Block 4
   a. 2
   b. 3
   c. 4
   d. 5
   e. 6

20. Block 5
   a. 2
   b. 3
   c. 4
   d. 5
   e. 6

Use the following block for questions 21–25.

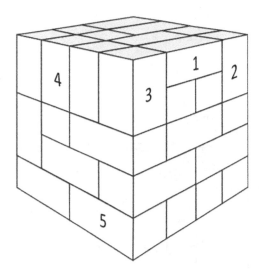

21. Block 1
   a. 2
   b. 3
   c. 4
   d. 5
   e. 6

22. Block 2
   a. 2
   b. 3
   c. 4
   d. 5
   e. 6

301

23. Block 3
   a. 2
   b. 3
   c. 4
   d. 5
   e. 6

24. Block 4
   a. 2
   b. 3
   c. 4
   d. 5
   e. 6

25. Block 5
   a. 2
   b. 3
   c. 4
   d. 5
   e. 6

Use the following block for questions 26–30.

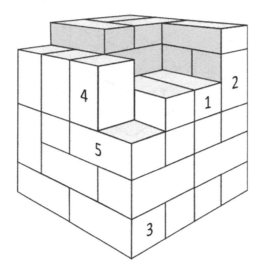

26. Block 1
   a. 2
   b. 3
   c. 4
   d. 5
   e. 6

27. Block 2
    a. 2
    b. 3
    c. 4
    d. 5
    e. 6

28. Block 3
    a. 2
    b. 3
    c. 4
    d. 5
    e. 6

29. Block 4
    a. 2
    b. 3
    c. 4
    d. 5
    e. 6

30. Block 5
    a. 2
    b. 3
    c. 4
    d. 5
    e. 6

Aviation Information

1. Which of the following forces is a helicopter subjected to, but not a fixed-wing aircraft?
    a. Lift
    b. Torque
    c. Weight
    d. Drag
    e. Thrust

2. Which term describes a reduced drag coupled with an increased lift experienced by an aircraft due to extremely close proximity to land?
    a. Center of gravity
    b. Coriolis effect
    c. Effective translational lift
    d. Ground effect
    e. Centrifugal force

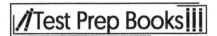

3. Which of the following lights are green lights that indicate the beginning of a runway?
   a. Taxiway centerline lights
   b. Runway edge lights
   c. Approach lighting systems
   d. Threshold lights
   e. Runway centerline lights

4. Which parts of fixed-wing aircrafts are utilized to create a rolling motion?
   a. Stabilizers
   b. Ailerons
   c. Wing tips
   d. Elevators
   e. Rudders

5. Which of the following is NOT considered an airfoil?
   a. Wing
   b. Spoiler
   c. Elevator
   d. Aileron
   e. Fuselage

6. Which term describes the ratio of an increase in altitude to the horizontal air distance?
   a. Climb gradient
   b. Altitude ratio
   c. Climb rate
   d. Glide ratio
   e. Angle of attack

7. Which term describes the difference in airflow between the forward and aft portions of the rotor disk of a helicopter?
   a. Dissymmetry of lift
   b. Torque
   c. Gyroscopic precession
   d. Coriolis effect
   e. Transverse flow effect

8. What is the color of a taxiway location sign?
   a. Red
   b. Yellow
   c. Black
   d. Green
   e. White

9. What is the term for the covering of a plane's engine?
   a. Fuselage
   b. Flight envelope
   c. Cowling
   d. Leading edge
   e. Stabilizer

10. Which of the following is movement about an aircraft's vertical axis?
    a. Pitching
    b. Yawing
    c. Turning
    d. Rolling
    e. Falling

11. Which statement is true when an airplane increases its lift?
    a. Atmospheric pressure decreases.
    b. Airplane temperature increases.
    c. Air pressure below the wing increases.
    d. The airplane loses altitude.
    e. Thrust is decreased.

12. What turning angle is considered a medium turn?
    a. 30°
    b. 75°
    c. 15°
    d. 10°
    e. 50°

13. A vertical stabilizer controls which of the following motions?
    a. Roll
    b. Thrust
    c. Pitch
    d. Drag
    e. Yaw

14. What force is opposed by parasitic drag?
    a. Lift
    b. Weight
    c. Gravity
    d. Thrust
    e. Induced drag

15. Which instrument functions by measuring the differential between static and ram pressure?
    a. Altimeter
    b. Heading indicator
    c. Vertical speed indicator
    d. Turn coordinator
    e. Airspeed indicator

16. A plane does not have external bracing on its wings. What type of wing is this?
    a. Semi-cantilever wing
    b. Cantilever wing
    c. Low wing
    d. Mid wing
    e. Gull wing

17. When landing a small plane, which step occurs first?
    a. Position is announced.
    b. Reduce speed to 100 knots.
    c. Plane descends to traffic pattern altitude.
    d. Bring power to an idle.
    e. Reduce RPM to 1700.

18. A pilot utilizes an instrument to adjust the yaw on a helicopter. What instrument is used?
    a. Cyclic control stick
    b. Anti-torque pedal
    c. Collective control lever
    d. Throttle control
    e. Pitch control

19. A pilot utilizes a radio frequency band of 118-137 MHz. What is the name of this radio frequency band?
    a. VHF Air/Ground
    b. Satellite-based (from aircraft)
    c. Microwave landing system
    d. Unmanned aircraft control link
    e. Airport surveillance and weather radar

20. In what weather conditions do aircraft operate most efficiently in?
    a. Hot air
    b. Rain
    c. Dry air
    d. Humid air
    e. Cold air

Answer Explanations #2

Verbal Analogies

1. A: The relationship in the first half of the analogy is that clocks are used to measure time, so the second half of the analogy should have a tool that is used to measure something followed by what it measures. Rulers can be used to measure length, so that is the best choice. Remember that the key to solving analogies is to be a good detective. Some of the other answer choices are related to clocks and time but not to the relationship between clocks and time.

2. B: Wires are the medium that carry electricity, allowing the current to flow in a circuit. Pipes carry water in a similar fashion, so the best choice is Choice *B*. Test takers must be careful to not select Choice *E*, which reverses the relationship between the components. Choices *A, C,* and *D* contain words that are related to one another but not in the same manner as wires and electricity.

3. A: This question pulls from knowledge in social studies class, understanding the basic roles and positions of the three branches of the government. The president serves in the Executive Branch and the Supreme Court Justices serve in the Judicial Branch.

4. C: This is a category analogy. Remember that we have to figure out the relationship between the first two words so that we can determine the relationship of the answer. Begonia is related to flower by type. Begonia is a type of flower, just as cardiologist is a type of doctor.

5. E: This is a synonym analogy. Notice that the word *malleable* is synonymous to the word *pliable*. Thus, in our answer, we should look for two words that have the same meaning. *Disparage* and *criticize* in Choice *E* have the same meaning, so this is the correct answer.

6. B: This is a part to whole analogy. The relationship between *cerebellum* and *brain* is that the cerebellum makes up part of the brain, while a *nucleus* makes up part of a *cell*.

7. A: This is an object to function analogy. Usually, a *whisk* is a cooking utensil used in the process of *baking*. As such, a *glove* is used in the sport of *boxing*. Both are objects used within a particular process.

8. C: This analogy relies on the logic of performer to related action. The original analogy says *umpires* (performer) *officiate* (action), which means to act as an official in a sporting event. In the same manner, a *counselor* (performer) *guides* (action) their clients toward well-being.

9. D: The analogy used here is degree/intensity. A *chuckle* is a giggle, while a *guffaw* is a burst of laughter. One is more intense than the other. *Whisper* is to talk softly, while *bellow* is to talk loudly. One is more intense than the other.

10. D: This analogy denotes a symbol and its representation. *Fire* can be representative of *passion*, while *ice* represents someone who is cold or *rigid*.

11. A: This is considered an antonym analogy. *Geriatric* means old age, and *youth* is the opposite of old age. Likewise, *transparent* means to see through something, while *opaque* means cloudy or muddy.

12. E: This is a cause and effect analogy. *Lying* causes *distrust,* while *hurricanes* cause *devastation.*

307

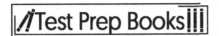

13. B: This is a synonym analogy. *Desolate* and *barren* both mean deserted. Likewise, *contend* and *maintain* are synonyms.

14. E: This is a part to whole analogy. Many *chapters* make up a *novel*, in the same way that many *strokes* make up a *painting*.

15. C: This is a performer to related action analogy. We know that *carpenters* perform *construction*, just as *wizards* perform *magic*.

16. C: This analogy relies on degree of intensity. *Tepid* means lukewarm, while *boiling* means extremely hot. In the same way, *rapacious* is an extreme form of *greed*.

17. C: This is a cause and effect analogy. To *read* is the cause or action, and a direct result that comes from reading is to *learn*. Likewise, when one *exercises* (cause), a direct result becomes better *health*.

18. A: This is an antonym analogy. *Competent* means capable of something, while *impotent* means incapable of something. In the same way, *demur* means to object, which is the opposite of *accept*.

19. B: This is a category/type analogy. *Merengue* is a type of *music*, just as *tension* is a type of *headache*.

20. D: This is an object/function analogy. The *car* (object) has the function of *transporting* people from one place to the other. Likewise, the function of a *fireplace* is to *heat* up a room.

21. E: This is a symbol/representation analogy. In artistic images or literature, *flowers* usually represent *femininity*. Likewise, traditionally in art and religion, the image or presence of *light* represents *transcendence*.

22. A: This is a synonym analogy. *Principle* means assumption or *truth*, while *shabby* means *squalid*.

23. E: This is a degree of intensity analogy. *Fastidious* means to be very *careful*, while *lament* means to *grieve* deeply. The second word in each of these is more intense than the first.

24. C: This is a part to whole analogy. *Mantle* is part of the four layers that make up *earth*. Likewise, a *bun* is one of the things that makes up a *hamburger*.

25. B: This is a performer to related action analogy. A *maestro* is one who is an expert musician and who *conducts* a musical performance. Likewise, an *acupuncturist* deals with natural *healing* within the body.

Arithmetic Reasoning

1. E: Fractions must have like denominators to be added. We are trying to add a fraction with a denominator of 3 to a fraction with a denominator of 5, so we have to convert both fractions to equivalent fractions that have a common denominator. The common denominator is the least common multiple (LCM) of the two original denominators. In this case, the LCM is 15, so both fractions should be changed to equivalent fractions with a denominator of 15.

To determine the numerator of the new fraction, the old numerator is multiplied by the same number by which the old denominator is multiplied to obtain the new denominator.

For the fraction $\frac{1}{3}$, 3 multiplied by 5 will produce 15.

Therefore, the numerator is multiplied by 5 to produce the new numerator:

$$\frac{1 \times 5}{3 \times 5} = \frac{5}{15}$$

For the fraction $\frac{2}{5}$, multiplying both the numerator and denominator by 3 produces $\frac{6}{15}$. When fractions have like denominators, they are added by adding the numerators and keeping the denominator the same:

$$\frac{5}{15} + \frac{6}{15} = \frac{11}{15}$$

2. A: To determine the number of houses that can fit on the street, the length of the street is divided by the width of each house:

$$345 \div 30 = 11.5$$

Although the mathematical calculation of 11.5 is correct, this answer is not reasonable. Half of a house cannot be built, so the company will need to either build 11 or 12 houses. Since the width of 12 houses (360 feet) will extend past the length of the street, only 11 houses can be built.

3. C: In order to calculate the profit, we need to create an equation that models the total income minus the cost of the materials.

$$\$60 \times 20 = \$1,200 \text{ total income}$$

$$60 \div 3 = 20 \text{ sets of materials}$$

$$20 \times \$12 = \$240 \text{ cost of materials}$$

$$\$1,200 - \$240 = \$960 \text{ profit}$$

Choice *A* is not correct, as it is only the cost of materials. Choice *B* is not correct, as it is a miscalculation. Choice *D* is not correct, as it is the total income from the sale of the necklaces. Choice *E* is incorrect as it does not represent the amount of profit made.

4. D: $6 \times 12 = 72$, so we can calculate the values of all four choices and find that only Choice *D* equals 72. That makes sense, because we can rearrange and group these four numbers to make the factors of the original two numbers: $(3 \times 2) \times (4 \times 3) = 6 \times 12$.

Alternatively, each of the answer choices could be prime-factored or multiplied out and compared to the original value. 6×12 has a value of 72 and a prime factorization of $2^3 \times 3^2$. The answer choices respectively have values of 64, 84, 108, 72, and 81 and prime factorizations of:

$$2^6$$

$$2^2 \times 3 \times 7$$

$$2^2 \times 3^3$$

309

Number 4 continued:

$$2^3 \times 3^2$$

$$3^2 \times 3^2$$

So, Choice *D* is correct.

5. E: This problem can be solved by setting up a proportion involving the given information and the unknown value. The proportion is:

$$\frac{21 \text{ pages}}{4 \text{ nights}} = \frac{140 \text{ pages}}{x \text{ nights}}$$

We can cross-multiply to get $21x = 4 \times 140$. Solving this, we find $x \approx 26.67$. Since this is not an integer, we round up to 27 nights. 26 nights would not give Sarah enough time.

6. E: This problem can be solved by using unit conversion. The initial units are miles per minute. The final units need to be feet per second. Converting miles to feet uses the equivalence statement 1 mile equals 5,280 feet. Converting minutes to seconds uses the equivalence statement 1 minute equals 60 seconds. Setting up the ratios to convert the units is shown in the following equation:

$$\frac{72 \text{ mi}}{90 \text{ min}} \times \frac{1 \text{ min}}{60 \text{ s}} \times \frac{5280 \text{ ft}}{1 \text{ mi}} = 70.4 \frac{\text{ft}}{\text{s}}$$

The initial units cancel out, and the new units are left.

7. C: The total percentage of a pie chart equals 100%. We can see that CD sales make up less than half of the chart (50%) and more than a quarter (25%), and the only answer choice that meets these criteria is Choice *C*, 40%.

8. B: Since $850 is the price after a 20% discount, $850 represents 80% (or 0.8) of the original price. In other words, $850 = 0.8x$ (where x is the original price). Solving this, we find $x = \frac{850}{0.8} = 1,062.5$. Now, to find the savings, calculate the original price minus the sale price: $1,062.50 - $850 = 212.50.

9. E: 85% of a number means that number should be multiplied by 0.85: $0.85 \times 20 = \frac{85}{100} \times \frac{20}{1}$, which can be simplified to $\frac{17}{20} \times \frac{20}{1} = 17$. The answer is *E*.

10. C: To find the drop in value, subtract the new value from the old value. To see what percentage of the initial value this is, divide the drop in value by the initial value, then multiply by 100.

$$\frac{20,000 - 8,000}{20,000} = 0.6$$

$$(.60) \times 100 = 60\%$$

11. A: The question only asks how long they owned the house, so ignore the extra details about prices. From May 2010 to May 2016 would be 6 years.

From May 2016 to September 2016 is another 4 months. They owned the house for a total of 6 years and 4 months. Each year has 12 months, so the total number of months is $(6 \times 12) + 4 = 72 + 4 = 76$.

310

12. D: This problem can be solved using basic arithmetic. Xavier starts with 20 apples, then gives his sister half, so 20 is divided by 2.

$$\frac{20}{2} = 10$$

He then gives his neighbor 6, so 6 is subtracted from 10.

$$10 - 6 = 4$$

Finally, he uses $\frac{3}{4}$ of his remaining apples to make a pie. Since $\frac{3}{4}$ of 4 is 3, he uses 3 apples, so 3 is subtracted from 4.

$$4 - 3 = 1$$

13. A: To find the fraction of the bill that the first three people pay, the fractions need to be added, which means finding the common denominator. The common denominator will be 60.

$$\frac{1}{5} + \frac{1}{4} + \frac{1}{3} = \frac{12}{60} + \frac{15}{60} + \frac{20}{60} = \frac{47}{60}$$

The remainder of the bill is:

$$1 - \frac{47}{60} = \frac{60}{60} - \frac{47}{60} = \frac{13}{60}$$

14. C: The average is calculated by adding all six numbers, then dividing by 6. The first five numbers have a sum of 25. This means $\frac{25+n}{6} = 6$, where n is the unknown number. Multiplying both sides by 6, we get $25 + n = 36$, which means $n = 11$.

15. E: $\frac{5}{2} \div \frac{1}{3} = \frac{5}{2} \times \frac{3}{1} = \frac{15}{2} = 7.5$.

16. A: The total fraction taken up by green and red shirts will be:

$$\frac{1}{3} + \frac{2}{5} = \frac{5}{15} + \frac{6}{15} = \frac{11}{15}$$

The remaining fraction is:

$$1 - \frac{11}{15} = \frac{15}{15} - \frac{11}{15} = \frac{4}{15}$$

17. B: If 60% of 50 workers are women, then there are 30 women working in the office. If half of them are wearing skirts, then that means 15 women wear skirts. Since nobody else wears skirts, this means there are 15 people wearing skirts.

18. B: This question involves the percent formula:

$$\frac{32}{x} = \frac{25}{100}$$

311

We multiply the diagonal numbers, 32 and 100, to get 3,200. Dividing by the remaining number, 25, gives us 128.

The percent formula does not have to be used for a question like this. Since 25% is $\frac{1}{4}$ of 100, you know that 32 needs to be multiplied by 4, which yields 128.

19. A: Compare each numeral after the decimal point to figure out which overall number is greatest. In Choices *A* (1.43785) and *C* (1.43592), both have the same value in the tenths (4) and hundredths (3). However, the thousandths is greater in Choice *A* (7), so A has the greatest value overall.

20. D: A dollar contains 20 nickels. Therefore, if there are 12 dollars' worth of nickels, there are:

$$12 \times 20 = 240 \text{ nickels}$$

Each nickel weighs 5 grams. Therefore, the weight of the nickels is $240 \times 5 = 1,200$ grams.

Adding in the weight of the empty piggy bank, the filled bank weighs 2,250 grams.

21. D: To find Denver's total snowfall, 3 must be multiplied by $27\frac{3}{4}$. In order to easily do this, the mixed number should be converted into an improper fraction.

$$27\frac{3}{4} = \frac{27 \times 4 + 3}{4} = \frac{111}{4}$$

Therefore, Denver had approximately $\frac{3 \times 111}{4} = \frac{333}{4}$ inches of snow. The improper fraction can be converted back into a mixed number through division.

$$\frac{333}{4} = 83\frac{1}{4} \text{ inches}$$

22. C: To find a common denominator, look for a number that has both denominators (24 and 6) as factors. 24 works. Multiply the top and bottom of each fraction by whatever number will make the denominator 24:

$$\frac{23}{24} \times \frac{1}{1} = \frac{23}{24} \text{ and } \frac{1}{6} \times \frac{4}{4} = \frac{4}{24}$$

Now that we have a common denominator, subtract the numerators:

$$\frac{23}{24} - \frac{4}{24} = \frac{23 - 4}{24} = \frac{19}{24}$$

Since 19 and 24 have no common factors except 1, this fraction can't be reduced.

23. D: List the givens.

$$\text{Store coffee} = \frac{\$1.23}{\text{lb}}$$

$$\text{Local roaster coffee} = \frac{\$1.98}{1.5 \text{ lb}}$$

Calculate the cost for 5 pounds of store brand.

$$\frac{\$1.23}{1 \text{ lb}} \times 5 \text{ lb} = \$6.15$$

Calculate the cost for 5 pounds of the local roaster.

$$\frac{\$1.98}{1.5 \text{ lb}} \times 5 \text{ lb} = \$6.60$$

Subtract to find the difference in price for 5 pounds.

$$\begin{array}{r} \$6.60 \\ -\$6.15 \\ \hline \$0.45 \end{array}$$

24. C: The first step in solving this problem is expressing the result in fraction form. Multiplication and division are typically performed in order from left to right, but they can be performed in any order. For this problem, let's start with the division operation between the last two fractions. When dividing one fraction by another, invert or flip the second fraction and then multiply the numerators and denominators.

$$\frac{7}{10} \times \frac{2}{1} = \frac{14}{10}$$

Next, multiply the first fraction by this value:

$$\frac{3}{5} \times \frac{14}{10} = \frac{42}{50}$$

In this instance, to find the decimal form, we can multiply the numerator and denominator by 2 to get 100 in the denominator.

$$\frac{42}{50} \times \frac{2}{2} = \frac{84}{100}$$

In decimal form, this would be expressed as 0.84.

25. A: If s is the size of the floor in square feet and r is the rate on Tuesday, then, based on the information given, $p = \frac{s}{4}$ and $r = \frac{s}{3}$. Solve the Monday rate for s, $s = 4p$, and then substitute that in the expression for Tuesday.

Word Knowledge

1. D: *Offspring* are the children of parents. This word is especially common when talking about the animal kingdom, although it can be used with humans as well. *Offspring* does have the word *spring* in it, although it has nothing to do with bouncing or jumping. The other answer choice, *parent*, may be somewhat tricky because parents have offspring, but for this reason, they are not synonyms.

313

2. E: *Permit* can be a verb or a noun. As a verb, it means to allow or give authorization for something. As a noun, it generally refers to a document or something that has been authorized like a parking permit or driving permit, allowing the authorized individual to park or drive under the rules of the document.

3. B: A *woman* is a lady. Test takers must read carefully and remember the difference between *woman* and *women*. *Woman* refers to an individual lady or one person who is female, while *women* is the plural form and refers to more than one, or a group, of ladies. A woman may be a mother but not necessarily, and these words are not synonyms. A girl is a child and not yet a woman.

4. C: *Rotation* means to spin or turn, such as a *wheel* rotating on a car, although *wheel* does not mean rotation.

5. E: Something that is consistent is steady, predictable, reliable, or constant. The tricky one here is that the word *consistency* comes from the word *consistent*, and may describe something that is sticky. *Consistent* also comes from the word *consist,* which means to contain, Choice *B*. Test takers must be discerning readers and knowledgeable about vocabulary to recognize the difference in these words and look for the true synonym of *consistent.*

6. D: A *principle* is a foundation or a guiding idea or belief. Someone with good moral character is described as having strong principles. Test takers must be careful not to get confused with the homonyms *principle* and *principal*, because these words have very different meanings. A *principal* is the leader of a school and the word *principal* also refers to the main or most important idea or thing.

7. A: *Perimeter* refers to the outline or borders of an object. Test takers may recognize that word from math class, where perimeter refers to the edges or distance around an enclosed shape. Some of the other answer choices refer to other math vocabulary encountered in geometry lessons, but do not have the same meaning as *perimeter.*

8. D: A *symbol* is an object, picture, or sign that is used to represent something. For example, a pink ribbon is a symbol for breast-cancer awareness and a flag can be a symbol for a country. The tricky part of this question was also knowing the meaning of *emblem,* which typically describes a design that represents a group or concept, much like a symbol. Emblems often appear on flags or a coat of arms.

9. E: *Germinate* means to develop or grow and most often refers to sprouting seeds as a new plant first breaks through the seed coat. It can also refer to the development of an idea. Choice *D* may be an attractive choice since plants germinate but *germinate* does not mean plant.

10. B: The word *garish* means excessively ornate or elaborate, which is most closely related to the word *flashy*. The word *drab* is the opposite of *garish*. The word *gait* means a particular manner of walking, *hardy* means robust or sturdy, and *lithe* means graceful and supple.

11. D: The word *inane* means senseless or absurd. The word *ratify* means to approve, *illicit* means illegal, *uncouth* means crude, and *wry* means clever.

12. E: The word *solace* most closely resembles the word *comfort. Marred* means scarred, *induce* means to cause something, *depose* means to dethrone, and *inherent* means natural.

13. D: *Copious* is synonymous with the word *ample. Dire* means urgent or dreadful, *adept* means skillful, *indignant* means angered by injustice, and *nuance* means subtle difference.

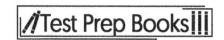

14. C: *Supercilious* means arrogant. *Tenuous* means weak or thin, *waning* means decreasing, *placate* means to appease, and *extol* means to praise or celebrate.

15. A: *Lurid* most closely resembles the word *gruesome*. *Placid* means calm or mild, *irate* means angry, *quell* means defeat or suppress, and *torpor* means lethargy.

16. B: *Vanquish* means to *conquer*. *Saturate* means to soak, *reproach* means to scold, *parch* means to make dry, and *surrender* is the opposite of *vanquish*.

17. B: *Trite* is closest to the word *banal*, which means common. *Scanty* means barely sufficient, *polemical* means controversial, *indulgent* means lenient, and *eclectic* means from diverse sources.

18. E: *Divulge* means to admit or confess something. *Dupe* means to deceive, *flummox* means to confuse, *indulgent* means lenient, and *germinate* means to grow.

19. D: *Indolent* and *lackadaisical* both mean lazy or indifferent. *Adamant* means unyielding, *dour* means gloomy or grim, *noisome* means bad or offensive, and *remiss* means careless or thoughtless.

20. C: *Bolster* and *support* are both synonyms. *Bequeath* means to hand down through a will, *abate* means to lessen, *palliate* means to remove pain, and *tractable* means easily managed.

21. B: *Unwitting* and *unintentional* are synonyms. *Undermine* means weaken, *rife* means excessively abundant, *pernicious* means harmful, and *stolid* means apathetic or impassive.

22. A: *Ungainly* means awkward or clumsy. *Absurd* means ridiculous or senseless, *unruly* means boisterous, *tenuous* means flimsy, and *petulant* means irritable.

23. A: *Prattle* and *babble* are synonyms; they both mean to talk incessantly. *Prosaic* means lacking imagination, *deluded* means tricked or betrayed, *meddle* means to intervene, and *folly* means silliness.

24. D: *Prolific* is most closely related to the word *productive*. *Devoid* means lacking, *elusive* means difficult to define, *laconic* means concise, and *judicious* means fair.

25. E: *Fortitude* means courage. *Aura* means air or character, *disparage* means to criticize or belittle, *finesse* means tact or know-how, and *cowardice* is the opposite of fortitude.

Math Knowledge

1. B: An equilateral triangle has three sides of equal length, so if the total perimeter is 18 feet, each side must be 6 feet long. A square with sides of 6 feet will have an area of $6^2 = 36$ square feet.

2. A: The way to calculate the measure of angle 2 is to subtract angle 1 from the measure of a straight line (180°):

$$180° - 49° = 131°$$

Choice *B* subtracts the value of angle 1 from 90°, Choice *C* subtracts the value of angle 1 from 360°, Choice *D* mistakenly labels angle 2 as equal to angle 1, and Choice *E* incorrectly assumes that angle 2 is a right angle.

3. E: $Area = length \times width$. Therefore, the area of the rectangle is equal to 3 in $\times$ 8 in $= 24$ in^2.

315

4. D: Dividing rational expressions follows the same rule as dividing fractions. The division is changed to multiplication by the reciprocal of the second fraction. This turns the expression into:

$$\frac{5x^3}{3x^2y} \times \frac{3y^9}{25}$$

This can be simplified by finding common factors in the numerators and denominators of the two fractions.

$$\frac{x^3}{x^2y} \times \frac{y^9}{5}$$

Multiplying across creates:

$$\frac{x^3y^9}{5x^2y}$$

Simplifying leads to the final expression is $\frac{xy^8}{5}$.

5. E: We can try to solve the equation by factoring the numerator into:

$$(x+6)(x-5)$$

Since the factor $(x-5)$ is on the top and bottom, it cancels out. This leaves the equation $x+6=11$. Solving the equation gives the answer $x=5$. When this value is plugged into the equation, it yields a zero in the denominator of the fraction. Since this is undefined, there is no solution.

6. C: The equation $x=3$ is not a function of x because it does not pass the vertical-line test: if any vertical line can intersect the equation's graph at more than one point, the equation is not a function. This test comes from the definition of a function, in which each x value in the domain must be mapped to no more than one y value. This equation is a vertical line, so the x value of 3 is mapped to an infinite number of y values.

7. C: Because the triangles are similar, the lengths of the corresponding sides are proportional. Therefore:

$$\frac{30+x}{30} = \frac{22}{14} = \frac{y+15}{y}$$

Using cross multiplication on the first two terms results in the equation:

$$14(30+x) = 22 \times 30$$

which, when solved, gives $x=17.1$. Using cross multiplication on the last two terms results in the equation:

$$14(y+15) = 22y$$

which, when solved, gives $y=26.3$.

8. C: $40N$ would be 4000% of N. The other three choices have coefficients that are equivalent to 40%.

9. B: First, subtract 4 from each side. This yields $6t = 12$. Now, divide both sides by 6 to obtain $t = 2$.

10. A: The total number of treats distributed will be the number of treats per bag $(4x + 1)$ times the number of bags given out, which can be represented by the variable n. This expression is $n(4x + 1)$. Since this is the amount of treats distributed, set it equal to $60x + 15$.

$$n(4x + 1) = 60x + 15.$$

In order to figure out what n is, determine what number times 4 results in 60 $(4n = 60)$ and what number times 1 results in 15 $(1n = 15)$. In both cases, $n = 15$. Therefore, 15 bags are given out.

11. C: Multiply both sides by x to get $x + 2 = 2x$, which simplifies to $-x = -2$, or $x = 2$.

12. D: Denote the width as w and the length as l. Then, $l = 3w + 5$. The perimeter is $2w + 2l = 90$. Substituting the first expression for l into the second equation yields:

$$2(3w + 5) + 2w = 90$$

$$6w + 10 + 2w = 90$$

$$8w = 80$$

$$w = 10$$

Putting this into the first equation, it yields:

$$l = 3(10) + 5 = 35$$

13. B: Each hour on the clock represents 30 degrees. For example, 3:00 represents a right angle. Therefore, 5:00 represents 150 degrees. We know that each hour does not represent 90 degrees, because there are 12 angles on a clock face. The 360 degrees in a circle, divided by the 12 angles, gives us 30 degrees for each hour.

14. C: We are trying to find x, the number of red cans. The equation can be set up like this:

$$x + 2(10 - x) = 16$$

The left x is actually multiplied by \$1, the price per red can. Since we know Jessica bought 10 total cans, $10 - x$ is the number of blue cans that she bought. We multiply the number of blue cans by \$2, the price per blue can.

That should all equal \$16, the total amount of money that Jessica spent. Working that out gives us:

$$x + 20 - 2x = 16$$

$$20 - x = 16$$

$$x = 4$$

15. C: Perimeter is found by calculating the sum of all sides of the polygon.

$9 + 9 + 9 + 8 + 8 + s = 56$, where s is the missing side length. Therefore, 43 plus the missing side length is equal to 56. The missing side length is 13 cm.

317

16. B: The perimeter of a rectangle is the sum of all four sides.

Therefore, the answer is:

$$P = 14 + 8\frac{1}{2} + 14 + 8\frac{1}{2}$$

$$14 + 14 + 8 + \frac{1}{2} + 8 + \frac{1}{2} = 45 \text{ square inches}$$

17. D: This system of equations involves one quadratic equation and one linear equation. One way to solve this is through substitution. Solving for y in the second equation yields $y = x + 2$. Plugging this equation in for the y of the quadratic equation yields:

$$x^2 - 2x + x + 2 = 8$$

Simplify the equation:

$$x^2 - x + 2 = 8$$

Set this equal to zero and factor:

$$x^2 - x - 6 = 0 = (x - 3)(x + 2)$$

Solving these two factors for x gives the zeros:

$$x = 3, -2$$

To find the y-value for the point, plug in each number to either original equation. Solving each one for y yields the points $(3, 5)$ and $(-2, 0)$.

18. B: The y-intercept of an equation is found where the x-value is 0. Plugging 0 into the equation for x allows the first two terms to cancel out, leaving -4.

19. A: The function can be factored to identify the zeros. First, the term $3x$ is factored out to the front because each term contains $3x$. Then, the quadratic is factored into $(x + 3)(x - 2)$.

20. A: The slope is given by:

$$m = \frac{y_2 - y_1}{x_2 - x_1} = \frac{0 - 4}{0 - (-3)} = -\frac{4}{3}$$

21. B: To simplify this inequality, subtract 3 from both sides to get $-\frac{1}{2}x \geq -1$. Then, multiply both sides by -2 (remembering this flips the direction of the inequality) to get $x \leq 2$.

22. E: There are two ways to approach this problem. Each value can be substituted into each equation. Choice A can be eliminated, since $4^2 + 16 = 32$. Choice B can be eliminated, since:

$$4^2 + 4 \times 4 - 4 = 28$$

Choice *C* can be eliminated, since:

$$4^2 - 2 \times 4 - 2 = 6$$

But, plugging either value into $x^2 - 16$ gives the following:

$$(\pm 4)^2 - 16 = 16 - 16 = 0$$

23. A: Simplify this to:

$$(4x^2 y^4)^{\frac{3}{2}} = 4^{\frac{3}{2}}(x^2)^{\frac{3}{2}}(y^4)^{\frac{3}{2}}$$

Now:

$$4^{\frac{3}{2}} = (\sqrt{4})^3 = 2^3 = 8$$

For the rest, recall that the exponents must be multiplied, so this yields:

$$8x^{2 \times \frac{3}{2}} y^{4 \times \frac{3}{2}} = 8x^3 y^6$$

24. A: To expand a squared binomial, it's necessary to use the First, Outer, Inner, Last (FOIL) method.

$$(3x - 7y)^2$$

$$(3x)(3x) + (3x)(-7y) + (-7y)(3x) + (-7y)(-7y)$$

$$9x^2 - 21xy - 21xy + 49y^2$$

$$9x^2 - 42xy + 49y^2$$

25. E: The volume of a cube with sides of length s is $V = s^3$. Here, $s = 3$, so $V = 3^3 = 27$.

Reading Comprehension

1. C: All the details in this paragraph suggest that Brookside is a great place to live, plus the last sentence states that it is an *idyllic neighborhood*, meaning it is perfect, happy, and blissful. Choices *A* and *B* are incorrect, because although they do contain specific details from the paragraph that support the main idea, they are not the main idea. Choice *D* is incorrect because there is no reference in the paragraph of the crime rate in Brookside.

2. A: Choice *A* is correct because there is evidence in the passage to support it, specifically when he mentions catching "a mess of black-fish, which you couldn't buy in New York for a dollar—large fat fellows, with meat on their bones that it takes a pretty long fork to stick through." There is no evidence to support the other answer choices.

3. B: Persuasive is the correct answer because the author is clearly trying to convey the point that history education is very important. Choice *A* is incorrect because expository writing is more informative and less emotional. Choices *C* and *E* are incorrect because narrative and drama writing involve storytelling. Choice *D* is incorrect because this is a piece of prose, not poetry.

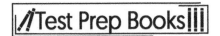

4. B: The passage begins by describing Carver's childhood fascination with painting and later returns to this point when it states that at the end of his career, "Carver returned to his first love of art." For this reason, all the other answer choices are incorrect.

5. B: The passage indicates that Annabelle has a fear of going outside into the daylight. Thus *heliophobia* must refer to a fear of bright lights or sunlight.

6. C: We are looking for an inference—a conclusion that is reached on the basis of evidence and reasoning—from the passage that will likely explain why the famous children's author did not achieve her usual success with the new genre (despite the book's acclaim). Choice *A* is wrong because the statement is false according to the passage. Choice *B* is wrong because, although the passage says the author has a graduate degree on the subject, it would be an unrealistic leap to infer that she is the foremost expert on Antebellum America. Choice *D* is wrong because there is nothing in the passage to lead us to infer that people generally prefer a children's series to historical fiction. In contrast, Choice *C* can be logically inferred since the passage speaks of the great success of the children's series and the declaration that the fame of the author's name causes the children's books to "fly off the shelves." Thus, we can infer that she did not receive any bump from her name since she published the historical novel under a pseudonym, which makes Choice *C* correct.

7. D: Outspending other countries on education could have other benefits, but there is no reference to this in the passage, so Choice *A* is incorrect. Choice *B* is incorrect because the author does not mention corruption. Choice *C* is incorrect because there is nothing in the passage stating that the tests are not genuinely representative. Choice *D* is accurate because spending more money has not brought success. The United States already spends the most money, and the country is not excelling on these tests. Choice *D* is the correct answer.

8. D: The passage does not proceed in chronological order since it begins by pointing out Christopher Columbus's explorations in America, so Choice *A* does not work. Although the author compares and contrasts Erikson with Christopher Columbus, this is not the main way the information is presented; therefore, Choice *B* does not work. Neither does Choice *C*, because there is no mention of or reference to cause and effect in the passage. However, the passage does offer a conclusion (Leif Erikson deserves more credit) and premises (first European to set foot in the New World and first to contact the natives) to substantiate Erikson's historical importance. Thus, Choice *D* is correct. Choice *E* is incorrect because spatial order refers to the space and location of something or where things are located in relation to each other.

9. C: Choice *A* is incorrect because it describes facts: Leif Erikson was the son of Erik the Red and historians debate Leif's date of birth. These are not opinions. Choice *B* is incorrect; Erikson calling the land Vinland is a verifiable fact, as is Choice *D*, because he did contact the natives almost 500 years before Columbus. Choice *E* is also a fact and the passage mentions that there are several secondhand accounts (evidence) of their meetings. Choice *C* is the correct answer because it is the author's opinion that Erikson deserves more credit. That, in fact, is the author's conclusion in the piece, but another person could argue that Columbus or another explorer deserves more credit for opening up the New World to exploration. Rather than being an incontrovertible fact, it is a subjective value claim.

10. B: Choice *A* is incorrect because the author aims to go beyond describing Erikson as merely a legendary Viking. Choice *C* is incorrect because the author does not focus on Erikson's motivations, let alone name the spreading of Christianity as his primary objective. Choice *D* is incorrect because it is a premise that Erikson contacted the natives 500 years before Columbus, which is simply a part of

supporting the author's conclusion. Choice *E* is incorrect because the author states at the beginning that he or she believes it can't be considered "discovering" if people already lived there. Choice *B* is correct because, as stated in the previous answer, it accurately identifies the author's statement that Erikson deserves more credit than he has received for being the first European to explore the New World.

11. B: Choice *B* is correct because the author wants the reader to be informed about Leif Erikson's contribution to exploring the new world. While several other answers are possible options, Choice *B* is the strongest. Choice *A* is incorrect because the author is not in any way trying to entertain the reader. Choice *C* is incorrect because the nature of the writing does not indicate the author would be satisfied with the reader merely being alerted to Erikson's exploration; instead, the author is making an argument about the credit he should receive. Choice *D* is incorrect because the author goes beyond merely a suggestion; *suggest* is too vague.

12. D: Choice *A* is incorrect because the author never addresses the Vikings' state of mind or emotions. Choice *B* is incorrect because the author does not elaborate on Erikson's exile and whether he would have become an explorer if not for his banishment. Choice *C* is incorrect because there is not enough information to support this premise. It is unclear whether Erikson informed the King of Norway of his finding. Although it is true that the king did not send a follow-up expedition, he could have simply chosen not to expend the resources after receiving Erikson's news. It is not possible to logically infer whether Erikson told him. Choice *E* is incorrect because the passage does not mention anything about Columbus' awareness of Erikson's travels. Choice *D* is correct because the uncertainty about Leif Erikson's birth year is an example of historians having trouble pinning down important details in Viking history.

13. B: The author is opposed to tobacco. The author cites disease and deaths associated with smoking, and points to the monetary expense and aesthetic costs. Choices *A* and *C* are incorrect because they do not summarize the passage but rather are just premises. Choice *D* is incorrect because, while these statistics are a premise in the argument, they do not represent a summary of the piece. Choice *E* is incorrect because alternatives to smoking are not addressed in the passage. Choice *B* is the correct answer because it states the three critiques offered against tobacco and expresses the author's conclusion.

14. C: We are looking for something the author would agree with, so it should be anti-smoking or an argument in favor of quitting smoking. Choice *A* is incorrect because the author does not speak against means of cessation. Choice *B* is incorrect because the author does not reference other substances but does speak of how addictive nicotine, a drug in tobacco, is. Choice *D* is incorrect because the author would not encourage reducing taxes to encourage a reduction of smoking costs, thereby helping smokers to continue the habit. Choice *E* is incorrect because the author states that according to the National Institute on Drug Abuse, nearly 35 million smokers expressed a desire to quit smoking in 2015. If the author had used the word "only" instead of "nearly" (and perhaps if the number was a lot lower) that would have changed the argument. Choice *C* is correct because the author is attempting to persuade smokers to quit smoking.

15. D: Here, we are looking for an opinion of the author rather than a fact or statistic. Choice *A* is incorrect because quoting statistics from the CDC is stating facts, not opinions. Choice *B* is incorrect because it expresses the fact that cigarettes sometimes cost more than a few gallons of gas. It would be an opinion if the author said that cigarettes were not affordable. Choice *C* is incorrect because yellow stains are a known possible adverse effect of smoking. Choice *E* is incorrect because decreased life expectancy for smokers is a known fact because of the health problems it can create. Choice *D* is correct as an opinion because smell is subjective. Some people might like the smell of smoke rather than considering it "a pervasive nastiness," so this is the expression of an opinion.

16. B: The passage is cautionary, because the author warns about the hazards of smoking and uses the second-person *you* to offer suggestions, like "You would be wise to learn from their mistake." Choice *A*, objective, means that the passage would be totally without persuasion or suggestions, so this answer choice is incorrect. Choice *C*, indifferent, is incorrect because the author expresses an opinion and makes it clear they dislike smoking. Choice *D* is also incorrect; the passage is the opposite of admiring towards the subject of smoking. Choice *D* is also incorrect; the passage is the opposite of admiring towards the subject of smoking. Finally, Choice *E*, philosophical, is incorrect, because this is a down-to-earth passage that presents facts and gives suggestions based on those facts, and there are no philosophical underpinnings here.

17. E: The word *pervasive* means "all over the place." The passage says that "The smell of smoke is all-consuming and creates a *pervasive* nastiness," which means a smell that is everywhere or all over. Choices *A* and *B*, pleasantly appealing and a floral scent, are too pleasant for the context of the passage. Choice *C* doesn't make sense in the sentence, as "to convince someone" wouldn't really describe the word *nastiness* like pervasive does. Choice *D* is also incorrect because that's the opposite of what the author is describing.

18. C: Despite the opposite stances in Passages 1 and 2, both authors establish that cell phones are a strong part of culture. In Passage 1 the author states, "Today's student is already strongly rooted in technology." In Passage 2 the author states, "Students are comfortable with cell phones." The author of Passage 2 states that cell phones have a "time and place." The author of Passage 2 would disagree with the statement that "teachers should incorporate cell phones into curriculum whenever possible." While passage 2 implies that "cell phones are useful only when an experienced teacher uses them properly," the author in Passage 1 says cell phones are "indispensable." In other words, no teacher can do without them. The statement that "despite a good lesson plan, cell phone disruptions are impossible to avoid" is not supported by either passage. Even though the author in the second passage is more cautionary, the author states, "This can prove advantageous if done correctly." Therefore, there is a possibility that a classroom can run properly with cell phones.

19. B: Choice *A* uses similar language, but it is not the main point of disagreement. The reporter calls the loss devastating, and there's no reason to believe that the coach would disagree with this assessment. Eliminate this choice. Choice *B* is strong since both passages mention the at-bats with runners in scoring position. The reporter asserts that the team lost due to the team failing to get such a hit. In contrast, the coach identifies several other reasons for the loss, including fielding and pitching errors. Additionally, the coach disagrees that the team even needed a hit in those situations.

Choice *C* is mentioned by the coach, but not by the reporter. It is unclear whether the reporter would agree with this assessment. Eliminate this choice.

Choice D is mentioned by the coach but not by the reporter. It is not stated whether the reporter believes that the team deserved to win. Eliminate this choice.

As shown in the reasoning for Choice B, there is a dispute shown between the coach and the reporter, so Choice E is incorrect. Therefore, Choice B is the correct answer.

20. C: The passage is told in chronological order; it details the steps the family took to adopt their dog. The narrator mentions that Robin's physical exam and lab work confirmed she was healthy before discussing that they brought her to the vet to evaluate her health. It is illogical that lab work would confirm good health prior to an appointment with the vet, when, presumably, the lab work would be collected.

21. B: Choice B is correct because the author is trying to demonstrate the main idea, which is that heat loss is proportional to surface area, and so they compare two animals with different surface areas to clarify the main point. Choice A is incorrect because the author uses elephants and anteaters to prove a point, that heat loss is proportional to surface area, not to express an opinion. Choice C is incorrect because though the author does use them to show differences, they do so in order to give examples that prove the above points. Choice D is incorrect because there is no language to indicate favoritism between the two animals. Choice E is incorrect because the passage is not about animals and only uses the elephant and the anteater to make a point.

22. C: Because of the way the author addresses the reader and the colloquial language the author uses (e.g., "let me explain," "so," "well," "didn't," "you would look stupid"), Choice C is the best answer because it has a much more casual tone than the usual informative article. Choice A may be a tempting choice because the author says the "fact" that most of one's heat is lost through their head is a "lie" and that someone who does not wear a shirt in the cold looks stupid. However, this only happens twice within the passage, and the passage does not give an overall tone of harshness. Choice B is incorrect because again, while not necessarily nice, the language does not carry an angry charge. The author is clearly not indifferent to the subject because of the passionate language that they use, so Choice D is incorrect. Choice E is incorrect because the author is not trying to show or use humor in the passage.

23. E: The author gives logical examples and reasons in order to prove that most of one's heat is not lost through their head; therefore, Choice E is correct. Choice A is incorrect because the author never mentions any specific experts as references. Choice B is incorrect because there is not much emotionally charged language in this selection, and even the small amount present is greatly outnumbered by the facts and evidence. Choice C is incorrect because there is no mention of ethics or morals in this selection. Choice D is incorrect because the author never qualifies himself as someone who has the authority to be writing on this topic.

24. C: *Gullible* means to believe something easily. The other answer choices could fit easily within the context of the passage: you can be angry toward, distrustful toward, frightened by, or happy toward authority. For this answer choice and the surrounding context, however, the author talks about a myth that people believe easily, so *gullible* would be the word that fits best in this context.

25. E: The whole passage is dedicated to debunking the head heat loss myth. The passage says that "each part of your body loses its proportional amount of heat in accordance with its surface area," which means an area such as the chest would lose more heat than the head because it's bigger. The other answer choices are incorrect.

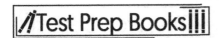

Situational Judgment

1. D: (Most effective) Emphasizing the good work and progress of the exceptional recruit is a way to help motivate the other recruits to work harder.

2. A: (Least effective) There is no reason to completely dismiss the unprepared recruits. They just need more focus in their corresponding training areas. If you dismiss them altogether, you will not get to see what they are actually capable of.

3. C: (Most effective) It is best to complete the assignments given by ranking officers before finishing your other tasks.

4. D: (Least effective) Neglecting the task altogether would not be an appropriate way to approach the situation.

5. E: (Most effective) Bringing the officer's concern to the attention of your team members and prompting them to take responsibility for their actions is the most responsible way to handle this incident.

6. B: (Least effective) Completely dismissing the officer's concerns is not an appropriate way to handle the incident.

7. A: (Most effective) Taking an active role in the activities shows your subordinates that you hold yourself to the same standards to which you are holding them.

8. C: (Least effective) Disciplining your subordinates for your lack of involvement would not be very effective as a leader trying to set an example.

9. D: (Most effective) After noticing someone's potential to move up, it is important to help cultivate that potential and encourage them to make the best impact they can.

10. A: (Least effective) The job of a leader is to train up other leaders. If you were to dismiss her leadership potential, you would not be living up to the full expectations of your own role within leadership.

11. B: (Most effective) Addressing this planned action with the team in order to prevent it is the best course of action. It is important to remind them of the consequences they face for such actions.

12. C: (Least effective) Dismissing the informant would show a lack of responsibility and leadership.

13. A: (Most effective) It is important to speak with any team members that may be showing signs of withdrawal and signs of being bullied. This lets them know that you see what is going on and that you are willing to take initiative to help fix it.

14. B: (Least effective) Not doing anything to help solve the bullying problem has the potential to escalate matters for the victim. Additionally, this sort of neglect of the problem shows that you don't care for your team members.

15. E: (Most effective) When you don't understand something, it is always best to seek out help to come to a better understanding of the task.

16. D: (Least effective) It is never a good idea to deflect responsibility in this way. You want to show that even if you are not necessarily capable, you are more than willing to get the necessary information to complete the task.

17. B: (Most effective) It is important to finish your immediate responsibilities before returning home.

18. E: (Least effective) In the Air Force, or any military branch, family cannot necessarily come first due to the nature of the work.

19. C: (Most effective) In this situation, it would be best to encourage your pregnant squad member to take care of herself and to seek out the necessary resources to guide her through continuing her work while pregnant.

20. E: (Least effective) It is clear that the squad member is dedicated to her career. It would not be right to dismiss her just because she is pregnant when there are resources designed for specific situations such as this.

21. D: (Most effective) In this type of situation, it is important for the leader to make their team members feel like they can come and talk to them should problems arise. Thanking them for the information and taking follow-up action would be the correct steps in this scenario.

22. B: (Least effective) It would be irresponsible to dismiss the information received from the team member. Also, dismissing this information teaches the team member that they should not come to you when there are problems or misbehavior within the team.

23. A: (Most effective) In this situation, it would be best to sit down with the member of your squad and discuss her qualifications and ways she can improve. Moving up may not be the best thing for her right now, but with your guidance and suggestions, she can work her way up to it.

24. C: (Least effective) If you were to just outright decline to write a letter of recommendation and never have a conversation about how she could improve, the team member never would improve. Part of being a good leader is training others to be good leaders.

25. C: (Most effective) In civilian life, it is the responsibility of local law enforcement to handle matters such as burglaries or other civilian crimes.

26. D: (Least effective) A decision to personally pursue the burglar and failure to notify the authorities within the appropriate timing could lead to severe consequences for you. There is a time and a place for exercising your military skills.

27. D: (Most effective) It is your responsibility to train the new officer. Failure to do so properly may put your team at risk. Additionally, once you get the new officer trained, you'll be able to share your workload with them.

28. E: (Least effective) Again, failure to train the new officer may put the entire team at risk. While your other tasks may be important, it is more important to follow the orders of the higher-ranked official and train the new officer.

29. B: (Most effective) The best thing you can do in this scenario is to inform your family that you cannot be immediately available but that you will get there as soon as you have tied up your remaining responsibilities. The safety of the squad has to come first.

30. A: (Least effective) It would be least responsible to leave the training of your squad in order to tend to your family. When you join the military, you first have an obligation to your squad before outside relationships like family and friends.

31. B: (Most effective) Recommending the airman for disciplinary action and even potential dismissal is appropriate in this scenario because you have already had multiple conversations about their behavior.

32. C: (Least effective) It would be dishonest to dismiss the report of the airman, especially since you know that you have had to confront him about this kind of behavior in the past.

33. D: (Most effective) In this situation, it is best to complete as much of the task as is possible based on your current knowledge.

34. B: (Least effective) It would not be wise to lie to the supervising officer and say that you completed a task when in fact you did not. Depending on the task, this could throw off all of the operations or even put your team in danger.

35. C: (Most effective) It is important to acknowledge the successes of you and your team.

36. B: (Least effective) It would be wrong to celebrate the reward as if you were the only one deserving of it.

37. E: (Most effective) If you notice that their tasks aren't being completed and it's affecting your work, then you should volunteer to take on the tasks. After all, you are an officer, and you should take the lead for making sure unfinished work gets completed.

38. A: (Least effective) If you ignore the issue, eventually this unfinished work is going to impact your work to the point that you won't be able to complete your own tasks.

39. A: (Most effective) In this situation, it would be best to cut out unnecessary costs in order to meet the requirements of your assigned budget.

40. E: (Least effective) Disregarding the budget altogether does not keep the team loyal, safe, or comfortable. This type of behavior only causes problems for the team and should be avoided.

41. D: (Most effective) If you recognize that your orders led a team member to not be able to perform their responsibilities, or perform them incorrectly, you should be willing to take responsibility for that.

42. C: (Least effective) It would be dishonest of you, especially as a leader, to not take responsibility for your misleading commands. A good leader is able to take responsibility for their shortcomings.

43. E: (Most effective) If you have a new idea, it is worth it to try so long as it does not put anyone in immediate danger. You'll never know if it's actually more efficient unless you try it.

44. B: (Least effective) The least effective thing you could do in this situation is to avoid doing the work at all.

45. B: (Most effective) It is always best to be honest about your absences, especially if this is going to be a recurring situation that needs constant attention.

46. C: (Least effective) Lying about the reason for your absence can only lead to consequences for you. For one, someone will find out the real reason you are gone. Additionally, if there is a scenario at home

that requires constant attention, it is better to let your superiors know that ahead of time so they can support you in whatever ways you may need.

47. A: (Most effective) In this situation, it would be important to step in, act as a mediator, and guide the two members toward resolving their conflict.

48. D: (Least effective) There is no reason to discipline the squad members as this will only put them under more stress and will not resolve any of the conflict. Additionally, rather than seeing you as someone they go to when seeking help for resolving their conflict, they're going to think that they can't rely on you for such measures.

49. C: (Most effective) In this situation, it would be best to adjust the language you use when giving presentations since it is affecting the entire team. If the technical jargon is something they needed to learn, you could try introducing it more slowly and little by little.

50. E: (Least effective) If you were to listen to your team's complaints and not change anything, you would be failing as a leader. You would not be teaching your team anything, and you could risk putting your team in some sort of danger.

Physical Science

1. D: The pendulum has the same amount of mechanical energy throughout its path. Mechanical Energy is the total amount of energy in the situation; the sum of the potential energy and the kinetic energy. The amount of potential and kinetic energy both vary by the position of an object, but the mechanical energy remains constant.

2. B: Kinetic energy is energy an object has while moving. Potential energy is energy an object has based on its position or height. Solar energy is energy that comes from the sun. Heat energy is the energy produced from moving atoms, molecules, or ions, and can transfer between substances. Ionization energy is the energy required to remove a valence electron of a neutral atom.

3. D: Sunlight evaporates dew from plants. Choice *A* is incorrect because cloud formation is condensation. Choice *B* is incorrect because rain, snow, and ice storms are different forms of precipitation. Choice *C* is incorrect because rivers flowing into the oceans are examples of run-off. Choice *E* is incorrect because water entering the soil is infiltrated.

4. C: Following the electronegativity trend on the periodic table, elements up and to the right tend to be more electronegative. Choices *A*, *B*, and *D* are incorrect as all those elements are in the first group (column) and accordingly have lower electronegativities. Choice *E* can be deduced as incorrect because although lead is on the right side of the periodic table, it is a much heavier element than fluorine, and is thus located lower on the table.

5. A: Technically, the troposphere is a layer of the atmosphere where the majority of the activity that creates weather conditions experienced on Earth occurs. The ozone layer is in the stratosphere; this is also where airplanes fly. The exosphere is the outermost layer of the atmosphere, containing primarily a low density of hydrogen.

6. A: The density and molar mass of the liquid are necessary to solve for the number of moles, given the initial volume. Density gives the ratio of mass to volume, and molar mass gives mass per mole. Shown using units of moles and variables for mass and volume, the correct conversion would look like:

327

$$V \times \frac{m}{V} \times \frac{mol}{m}$$

7. D: Adding water to a strong base would give the most violent reaction. When adding a drop of water to a container of a strong acid or base, the result is an extremely concentrated acid or base solution, which heats up rapidly and can boil and splash liquid. For safety, more reactive or less neutral substances should be added to less reactive or more neutral ones, to reduce the possibility of spluttering.

8. A: Using Newton's equation for motion, $F = ma$, and substituting gravity in for acceleration (a), the weight, or force, could be calculated for an object having mass (m). Weight is a force, mass is the amount of a substance, and acceleration and gravity are rates of speed over time.

9. D: Radiation can be transmitted through electromagnetic waves and needs no medium to travel; it can travel in a vacuum. This is how the Sun warms the Earth and it typically applies to large objects with great amounts of heat, or objects that have a large difference in their heat measurements. Choice *A*, convection, involves atoms or molecules traveling from areas of high concentration to those of low concentration and transferring energy or heat with them. Choice *B*, conduction, involves the touching or bumping of atoms or molecules to transfer energy or heat. Choice *C*, induction, deals with charges and does not apply to the transfer of energy or heat. Choices *A*, *B*, *C*, and *E* need a medium in which to travel, while radiation requires no medium.

10. C: The most polar bond is found in the NaCl pair, which has a high enough difference in electronegativity to completely ionize. This means rather than forming a covalent bond where a pair of electrons are shared between two atoms, the valence electron from sodium (Na) will be strongly attracted to chlorine (Cl). This can be determined by remembering that electronegativity of elements increases trending up and to the right on the periodic table, so the largest gap in both directions is likely to possess the largest difference in electronegativities.

11. E: An object at rest has forces acting upon it, including gravitational, normal, and frictional forces. All of these forces are in balance with each other and cause no movement in the object's position. This is equilibrium. An object in constant motion is also considered to be in equilibrium or a state of balanced forces.

12. C: Motion with one dimension or measurement is known as a *scalar quantity,* and includes things such as length, speed, or time. Motion with two dimensions is known as a *vector quantity*. This would be speed with a direction, or velocity. Choices *A*, *B*, *D,* and *E* (mass, length, speed, and frequency) are all measurements of magnitudes—one-dimensional scalar quantities.

13. B: The illustration shows a Lewis dot formula for carbon dioxide, which explicitly shows valence electrons around element symbols in the model. This is helpful in understanding interactions of some chemicals due to lone pairs and the structure of less complex molecules. Choice *A* is incorrect, because the molecular formula would be the written-out elements in a molecule—CO_2 in the case of carbon dioxide—but not the structure. Choice *C* is incorrect because the typical structural formula shows bonds and three-dimensional structure but not valence electrons like the Lewis model. Choice *D* is incorrect as it is also a written formula, but specifically the most reduced form. While the molecular formula of glucose is $C_6H_{12}O_6$, its empirical formula is instead CH_2O. Choice *E* is also incorrect, as the skeletal formula is one where carbons, and often hydrogens, are implied by bonds without other elements

328

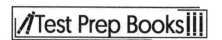

drawn. A skeletal formula is also used to show the three-dimensional structure of many substances in organic chemistry.

14. D: Inertia is the property of matter that resists change in motion. Choice *A* is incorrect since it is simply the rate of change in position. Although related to inertia, mass is the measure of an object's resistance to acceleration, which means it quantifies an object's inertia. Therefore, Choice *B* is incorrect. Choice *C*, momentum, is the product of an object's mass times its velocity. Choice *E*, impulse, refers to the integral of a force for a given duration, which changes the momentum of an object according to the magnitude and direction of the impulse.

15. C: The series of pulleys in the tackle provide a mechanical advantage of 3. This is because three times the length of cord is displaced to produce the same displacement in the weight as before, at the benefit of a third of the force required (in an ideal, frictionless system). This obeys the conservation of energy because the total work (force times distance) remains unchanged.

16. D: Mass refers to the amount or quantity there is of an object. Light, sound, heat, and microwaves are all forms of energy that can travel in waves.

17. B: Salt completely dissolves in water, making salt water the only liquid listed to be an actual solution. The other choices represent emulsions and mixtures, which contain undissolved substances dispersed in the liquid.

18. D: An isotope of an element has an atomic number equal to its number of protons, but a different mass number because of the additional neutrons. Even though there are differences in the nucleus, the behavior and properties of isotopes of a given element are identical. Atoms with different atomic numbers also have different numbers of protons and are different elements, so they cannot be isotopes. A different charge number indicates the net charge of an ion.

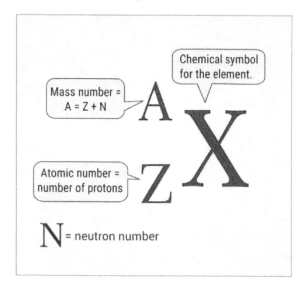

19. D: An atom is structured with a nucleus in the center that contains neutral neutrons and positive protons. Surrounding the nucleus are orbiting electrons that are negatively charged. Choice *D* is the only correct answer.

20. A: Although it is not an actual force on its own, the reactive force acting opposite of the centripetal force is named the centrifugal force. The real force acting in a rotational situation is pulling in toward

the axis of rotation and is called the centripetal force. A common mistake is to interchange the two terms. Gravity and tension are both examples of centripetal forces. Coriolis effect is when an object moving in a rotating system experiences an inertial force (Coriolis) acting perpendicular to the direction of motion and the axis of rotation. In a clockwise rotation, the force acts to the left of the motion of an object. If the rotation is counterclockwise, the force acts to the right of the motion of an object.

Table Reading

1. **E:** (-3, 17) is 173.

2. **B:** (0, -15) is -450.

3. **C:** (0, 6) is -386.

4. **A:** (4, -14) is -8.

5. **B:** (13, -4) is 120.

6. **D:** (-14, 12) is -345.

7. **A:** (11, -4) is 326.

8. **A:** (13, -13) is 21.

9. **A:** (-17, 16) is -124.

10. **A:** (-5, -6) is -415.

11. **B:** (-15, 3) is 94.

12. **D:** (-16, 9) is 208.

13. **E:** (-7, 11) is 277.

14. **B:** (-4, 0) is -258.

15. **A:** (15, 6) is 230.

16. **C:** (14, -3) is -254.

17. **A:** (3, -17) is 140.

18. **E:** (5, -17) is -128.

19. **A:** (8, -13) is -376.

20. **B:** (-7, -1) is -221.

21. **E:** (12, -1) is -113.

22. **A:** (-5, -9) is -54.

23. **A:** (2, -12) is 197.

24. **C:** (-1, 3) is 331.

25. **D:** (0, 2) is 129.

26. **D:** (1, -16) is -170.

27. **D:** (9, -15) is 283.

28. **B:** (1, -15) is 118.

29. **E:** (-11, 15) is -207.

30. **D:** (12, 0) is 353.

31. **B:** (17, -6) is -482.

32. **A:** (11, 6) is 200.

33. **E:** (14, -7) is -276.

34. **A:** (-15, 11) is -23.

35. **E:** (-10, 17) is 71.

36. **C:** (2, -14) is -247.

37. **C:** (2, -12) is 197.

38. **A:** (7, -1) is 9.

39. **A:** (-5, 14) is -22.

40. **D:** (-5, -5) is 11.

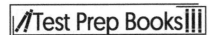

Instrument Comprehension

1. D: The aircraft is heading south-southeast, ascending, and banking left.

2. A: The aircraft is heading northeast, ascending, and banking left.

3. C: The aircraft is heading south-southwest, ascending, and banking right.

4. B: The aircraft is heading west, in level flight, and banking left.

5. A: The aircraft is heading north-northwest, descending, and banking left.

6. B: The aircraft is heading northwest, descending, and banking right.

7. D: The aircraft is heading east-northeast, in level flight, and banking left.

8. D: The aircraft is heading southeast, descending, and banking right.

9. A: The aircraft is heading west, in level flight, and banking left.

10. C: The aircraft is heading east, in level flight, and without banking.

11. A: The aircraft is heading east, in level flight, and banking left.

12. B: The aircraft is heading northwest, ascending, and banking left.

13. D: The aircraft is heading south, ascending, and without banking.

14. C: The aircraft is heading northwest, descending, and without banking.

15. D: The aircraft is heading southeast, in level flight, and without banking.

16. B: The aircraft is heading northeast, ascending, and without banking.

17. A: The aircraft is heading east-northeast, ascending, and banking left.

18. C: The aircraft is heading east-northeast, in level flight, and banking left.

19. A: The aircraft is heading northeast, descending, and without banking.

20. D: The aircraft is heading south, descending, and without banking.

21. B: The aircraft is heading west-southwest, in level flight, and banking right.

22. D: The aircraft is heading northeast, in level flight, and banking right.

23. C: The aircraft is heading west-southwest, descending, and banking left.

24. A: The aircraft is heading north, in level flight, and banking left.

25. B: The aircraft is heading south-southeast, descending, and banking right.

332

Block Counting

1. D: Block 1 touches four blocks; one on either side and two on top.

2. D: Block 2 touches six blocks. There are five blocks on the outside touching it, and there is one on the inside.

3. C: Block 3 touches seven blocks. There are five blocks on the outside touching it, and there are two on the inside.

4. B: Block 4 touches four blocks; two underneath, one to the left of its shorter side, and one to the right of its longer side.

5. E: Block 5 touches five blocks; there are four blocks visibly touching it from the outside and one block on the inside.

6. C: Block 1 touches four blocks; block 2 next to it and the three underneath, including block 5.

7. C: Block 2 touches four blocks; block 1 next to it and the three underneath, including block 5.

8. D: Block 3 touches six blocks; there are three blocks on top of it, one behind it, one underneath, and one to the left side.

9. A: Block 4 touches three blocks; block 3 on top, the block behind it, and the block to the left side of it.

10. D: Block 5 touches six blocks; there are six blocks surrounding the outsides of block 5.

11. B: Block 1 touches three blocks; one above it, one behind it, and one of the left backside.

12. C: Block 2 touches four blocks; one behind it, one below, and two on the left side.

13. D: Block 3 touches five blocks; three on its left side, one underneath, and one behind it on the right side.

14. C: Block 4 touches four blocks; one above it, one behind it, block 3, and one underneath it.

15. C: Block 5 touches four blocks; three below it, and one behind it in the back corner.

16. B: Block 1 touches three blocks; block 2, block 4, and the block behind it on the left.

17. C: Block 2 touches four blocks; block 1, block 4, the block on its right side, and the block behind it.

18. E: Block 3 touches six blocks; two blocks on its left, one underneath, one on its right, one above it, and one behind it in the back.

19. C: Block 4 touches four blocks; one above it, block 3, block 1, and block 2.

20. A: Block 5 touches two blocks; the two underneath it.

21. D: Block 1 touches five blocks; one on each side, two below it, and one behind it.

22. C: Block 2 touches four blocks; one underneath, two on the left side of it, and one behind it.

23. C: Block 3 touches four blocks; one underneath, one on the left side, and two on the right side.

24. C: Block 4 touches four blocks; one below it, one on either side of it, and one behind it.

25. C: Block 5 touches four blocks; two above it, one to the left of it, and one to the right.

26. D: Block 1 touches five blocks; one below, one to the left of it, two to the right of it, and one behind it on the back side.

27. C: Block 2 touches four blocks; one below, one to the left of it, one behind it, and one above it.

28. C: Block 3 touches four blocks; there are four blocks surrounding block 3.

29. B: Block 4 touches three blocks; one below it, one to the left of it, and one behind it on the right side.

30. D: Block 5 touches five blocks; one on the left side, two underneath, one behind it, and one above it.

Aviation Information

1. B: Torque is the correct answer because it is one of the forces subjected to a helicopter, but not an aircraft. Choice *A*, lift, is incorrect because it is an upward force on an airplane's wing. Choice *C*, weight, is incorrect because it is a force on any object created by gravitational pull towards earth. Therefore, weight is a force relevant to both airplanes and helicopters. Choice *D*, drag, is incorrect because it affects both airplanes and helicopters. Drag is a force that resists an object's movement through air. Choice *E*, thrust, is incorrect because it is necessary for the flight of helicopters and airplanes. Thrust is the force which moves an aircraft in the direction it is traveling.

2. D: Ground effect is the correct answer because it refers to increased lift and reduced drag when an aircraft is within close proximity to the ground. Choice *A*, center of gravity, is incorrect because it is the average location of the weight of an aircraft. Choice *B*, Coriolis effect, is incorrect because it is an inertial force that is perpendicular to the direction of motion in a rotating system. Choice *C*, effective translational lift, is incorrect because it is an improved efficiency in flight that results in directional flight. Choice *E*, centrifugal force, is incorrect because it is a force causing objects to move away from a center of rotation.

3. D: Threshold lights is correct because they are green lights that show the start of a runway. Choice *A*, taxiway centerline lights, is incorrect because they are green lights that show the edges of a taxiway. Choice *B*, runway edge lights, is incorrect because they are white lights that indicate the borders of a runway. Choice *C*, approach lighting systems, is incorrect because it is a series of lights that lead towards a runway to allow a pilot to line up with the runway. Choice *E*, runway centerline lights, is incorrect because they indicate the center of a runway.

4. B: Ailerons is the correct answer because when they are positioned in opposite directions on an airplane, they initiate a roll. Choice *A*, stabilizers, is incorrect because their purpose is to maintain straight and steady flight of an airplane. Choice *C*, wing tips, is incorrect because their purpose is to reduce drag. Choice *D*, elevators, is incorrect because they control the pitch of an airplane. Choice *E*, rudders, is incorrect because they control the yaw of an airplane.

334

5. E: Fuselage is the correct answer because an airfoil is a surface that controls an aircraft by manipulating the air around it. A fuselage is the main body of an aircraft and does not affect movement of the aircraft. Choice *A*, wing, is incorrect because wings create lift for an airplane when air travels at different speeds across the top and bottom of them. Choice *B*, spoiler, is incorrect because a spoiler eliminates lift when landing. Choice *C*, elevator, is incorrect because they adjust the lift of an aircraft to control pitch. Choice *D*, aileron, is incorrect because it manipulates air to enable rotational movement.

6. A: Climb gradient is the correct answer because it is the ratio of an increase in altitude to distance traveled through the air. Choice *B*, altitude ratio, is incorrect because it is not a term used to describe the movement of an aircraft. Choice *C*, climb rate, is incorrect because it is the vertical speed of an aircraft over time. Choice *D*, glide ratio, is incorrect because it indicates the distance traveled compared to rate of descent. Choice *E*, angle of attack, is incorrect because it is the angle that wind meets an airfoil.

7. E: Transverse flow effect is the correct answer because it is a difference in airflow between the aft and forward positions of a rotor disk. Transverse flow occurs between 10 and 20 knots. Choice *A*, dissymmetry of lift, is incorrect because it is a difference in lift between blades of a rotor system. Choice *B*, torque, is incorrect because it is the rotating force created by a motor. Choice *C*, gyroscopic precession, is incorrect because it is a force that is shown 90° later than where the force was applied on a rotating object. Choice *D*, Coriolis effect, is incorrect because it is an inertial force perpendicular to a rotating motion.

8. C: Black is correct because the taxiway location sign, which displays the name of a taxiway, is black with yellow letters. Choice *A*, red, is incorrect because it is the color of the no entry signs. Choice *B*, yellow, is incorrect because it is the color of the direction and runway exit signs. Choice *D*, green, is incorrect because it is not the color of any taxiway signs. Choice *E*, white, is incorrect because it is the color of the letters on the no entry and runway signs, but not the sign color of any common taxiway signs.

9. C: Cowling is the correct answer because it is the casing on a fuselage that covers the engine of an airplane. Choice *A*, fuselage, is incorrect because it is the body of an airplane. Choice *B*, flight envelope, is incorrect because it describes the capabilities of a specific aircraft. Choice *D*, leading edge, is incorrect because it refers to the front edge of an airplane's wing. Choice *E*, stabilizer, is incorrect because it is on the tail of an airplane and enables straight flight.

10. B: Yawing is correct because it is movement about an airplane's vertical axis that is controlled by the rudder of an airplane. Choice *A*, pitching, is incorrect because it is movement along the lateral axis of a plane. Choice *C*, turning, is incorrect because it is not specific. Turns may involve changes in pitch, yaw, and roll movements. Choice *D*, rolling, is incorrect because it is movement around the longitudinal axis of an aircraft. Choice *E*, falling, is incorrect because it is not a movement around an axis of an aircraft.

11. C: "Air pressure below the wing increases" is the correct answer because for lift to occur, air pressure below the wing gets higher and air pressure above the wing decreases. Choice *A*, atmospheric pressure decreases, is incorrect because it is changed by variations in air density. Choice *B*, airplane temperature increases, is incorrect because the temperature of the aircraft is irrelevant to lift. Choice *D*, the airplane loses altitude, is incorrect because when lift increases, an airplane will increase in altitude. Choice *E*, thrust is decreased, is incorrect because lift is not dictated by thrust alone.

335

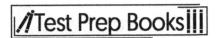

12. A: 30° is the correct answer because a medium turn is defined as a turn between 20° and 45°. All other answer choices are incorrect because they do not fall within this range. Turns that are less than 20° are considered shallow, and turns that are greater than 45° are considered steep.

13. E: Yaw is the correct answer because the purpose of a vertical stabilizer is to control the yaw of a flying plane. Choices *A* and *C,* roll and pitch, are incorrect because various other stabilizers prevent unwanted changes in pitch and roll. Choices *B* and *D,* thrust and drag, are incorrect because they are not movements of an airplane.

14. D: Thrust is the correct answer because parasitic drag is a rearward slowing force caused by an aircraft's shape or material. Thrust is a force in the opposite direction of drag that causes acceleration. Choice *A,* lift, is incorrect because it is an upward force that is opposed by weight and gravity. Choices *B* and *C,* weight and gravity, are incorrect because they are downward forces that are opposed by lift. Choice *E,* induced drag, which is caused by lift, is incorrect because it does not oppose parasitic drag.

15. E: Airspeed indicator is the correct answer because it works by utilizing the differential between static and ram pressure to measure the forward speed of an aircraft. Choice *A,* altimeter, is incorrect because it works by measuring static air pressure to give an altitude of the aircraft. Choice *B,* heading indicator, is incorrect because it gives the direction of an aircraft and works like a compass. Choice *C,* vertical speed indicator, is incorrect because it measures changes in static pressure to measure the rate of change of altitude. Choice *D,* turn coordinator, is incorrect because it is a gyro-driven instrument that measures the rate of a turn.

16. B: Cantilever wing is the correct answer because it is a type of wing that is supported internally and has no external braces or struts. Choice *A,* semi-cantilever wing, is incorrect because they have one or two supportive struts or wires. Choices *C, D,* and *E* are incorrect because they are all wing shapes and have nothing to do with the way wings are supported.

17. C: "Plane descends to traffic pattern altitude" is the correct answer because it is the first step when beginning to land an aircraft. Choice *A,* position is announced, is incorrect because it is the second step for landing a plane when a field is uncontrolled. Choice *B,* reduce speed to 100 knots, is incorrect because it is done along with adding 50% flaps after announcing position. Choice *D,* bring power to an idle, is incorrect because it is done just before touching down. Choice *E,* reduce rpm to 1700, is incorrect because it occurs just before the descent to the runway.

18. B: Anti-torque pedal is the correct answer because it is utilized to adjust yaw. Choice *A,* cyclic control stick, is incorrect because it controls the tilt of the main rotor to adjust the direction of flight. Choice *C,* collective control lever, is incorrect because it changes the pitch of rotors to adjust the lift. Choice *D,* throttle control, is incorrect because it controls the output of the engine. Choice *E,* pitch control, is incorrect because it is the same thing as the collective control lever.

19. A: VHF Air/Ground is the correct answer because it uses the 118-137 MHz frequency range. Choice *B,* satellite-based (from aircraft), is incorrect because it uses the 1646.5-1660.5 MHz frequency range. Choice *C,* microwave landing system, is incorrect because it uses the 5000-5250 MHz range. Choice *D,* unmanned aircraft control link, is incorrect because it uses the 5030-5091 MHz range. Choice *E,* airport surveillance and weather radar, is incorrect because it uses the 2700-3000 MHz range.

20. E: Cold air is the correct answer because cooler air allows an engine to use more mass of air and fuel mixture with the same intake volume. This allows the engine to generate more power. All other choices are incorrect because they do not allow the engine to cool down and operate as efficiently.

AFOQT Practice Test #3

To keep the size of this book manageable, save paper, and provide a digital test-taking experience, the 3rd practice test can be found online. Scan the QR code or go to this link to access it:

testprepbooks.com/bonus/afoqt

The first time you access the tests, you will need to register as a "new user" and verify your email address.

If you have any issues, please email support@testprepbooks.com.

Dear AFOQT Test Taker,

Thank you again for purchasing this study guide for your AFOQT exam. We hope that we exceeded your expectations.

Our goal in creating this study guide was to cover all of the topics that you will see on the test. We also strove to make our practice questions as similar as possible to what you will encounter on test day. With that being said, if you found something that you feel was not up to your standards, please send us an email and let us know.

We would also like to let you know about other books in our catalog that may interest you.

ASVAB

amazon.com/dp/1637753241

ASTB

amazon.com/dp/1637750277

OAR

amazon.com/dp/1637751087

SIFT

amazon.com/dp/1628458585

We have study guides in a wide variety of fields. If the one you are looking for isn't listed above, then try searching for it on Amazon or send us an email.

Thanks Again and Happy Testing!
Product Development Team
info@studyguideteam.com

FREE Test Taking Tips Video/DVD Offer

To better serve you, we created videos covering test taking tips that we want to give you for FREE. **These videos cover world-class tips that will help you succeed on your test.**

We just ask that you send us feedback about this product. Please let us know what you thought about it—whether good, bad, or indifferent.

To get your **FREE videos**, you can use the QR code below or email freevideos@studyguideteam.com with "Free Videos" in the subject line and the following information in the body of the email:

      a. The title of your product

      b. Your product rating on a scale of 1-5, with 5 being the highest

      c. Your feedback about the product

If you have any questions or concerns, please don't hesitate to contact us at info@studyguideteam.com.

Thank you!

Made in United States
Orlando, FL
16 October 2023